Walkable Westchester

Jane and Walt Daniels

2009

NEW YORK-NEW JERSEY TRAIL CONFERENCE

Library of Congress Cataloging-in-Publication Data

Daniels, Jane.
Walkable Westchester / Jane Daniels, Walt Daniels.
p. cm.
Includes bibliographical references and index.
ISBN 978-1-880775-57-8 (alk. paper)
1. Walking--New York (State)--Westchester County--Guidebooks. 2. Hiking--New York
(State)--Westchester County--Guidebooks. 3. Westchester County (N.Y.)--Description
and travel. I. Daniels, Walt. II. Title.
GV199.42.N652W4733 2009
917.47'27704--dc22
2008053090

Published by
New York-New Jersey Trail Conference
156 Ramapo Valley Road
Mahwah, NJ 07430-1199

Cartography: Allison Werberg
Photographs: Jane Daniels unless credited otherwise
Cover and back photos: Herb Chong
Book and cover design: Nora Porter

Front cover: Boardwalk at Teatown Lake as seen from the Lakeside Trail at Teatown Lake Reservation

Welcome to *Walkable Westchester*, an encyclopedic volume about where to walk in Westchester County. It is published by the New York-New Jersey Trail Conference as part of its mission to educate people on where and how to hike.

I know that you will find this carefully researched book a useful tool as you set out on your route. Walking and hiking are fun, low-cost ways to get fit, and this book will guide you to some of the most spectacular walks and hikes on hundreds of miles of trails in every part of the county. I am especially proud of the network of recreational trails within our county parks; our parks and planning departments have done outstanding work over the years in developing these trails. I use them often and I hope that you will, too. But don't forget to try out some of the state and local parks and the smaller walks the authors also recommend: along a country lane, an interesting stretch of a downtown sidewalk or even just the perimeter of a small neighborhood park. Long hikes or short strolls—they're great ways to discover Westchester County and learn about its history and geography at your own pace.

This comprehensive guide surveys approximately 600 miles of trails and provides opportunities to experience different parks and terrain throughout the county. As you go through the pages, you will find many shining examples of how local, county, state governments, and not-for-profit partners work together to preserve open space for everyone to treasure now and in the future.

Andrew J. Spano
Westchester County Executive

TABLE OF CONTENTS

FROM THE AUTHORS

A ragged shoreline with the smell of salt in the air, rolling hills, open fields with horses, rock outcroppings, and mixed hardwood forests all describe Westchester County. Not usually thought of as a hiking destination, it has more than 600 miles of trails, a surprise considering its small size and proximity to New York City.

As avid hikers, we had noticed that there was not one book devoted entirely to the hiking opportunities in the county. Information about where to walk or hike is scattered in newspaper articles, booklets, publications, and on the Web. The same few hikes appear in hiking books covering the metro New York region. When we started the project in 2001, we thought that there were about 80 places to walk and quickly discovered we had grossly underestimated. Over the course of the project, we visited 62 places we had never heard of; by the time we were finalizing the contents of this book, we had added 22 new parks to our final list of 187 places.

Since moving to Westchester in 1968, we have noticed many changes. Former summer bungalow colonies have become year-round residences. The parkways became commuting routes. Unregulated growth with the resulting sprawl has appeared in far too many places. But during that same time, land was being set aside as open space and for public use. In the late 1990s and early 2000s, the county, local municipalities, and land trusts working together and separately have secured donations or purchased former estates and critical wildlife habitat. Towns in the northeastern corner of the county have been working to preserve their rural character. Suburban towns are now watching to ensure that their community is not overbuilt. South of I-287, work is underway to preserve what tiny open spaces are left. Even though the population has grown and Westchester has become more developed, places to walk continue to increase.

While doing the on-the-ground work, we discovered a wide range of walking opportunities, and in the process saw vistas, scenic spots, and wildlife. We have returned to many places for the joy of hiking there again. It is our wish that you enjoy the walking opportunities in Westchester County as much as we did.

But our work is not done. Because trails and parks are in a state of flux, please let us know of new walking opportunities by visiting www.westchester.nynjtc.org or e-mailing us at info@nynjtc.org.

Jane and Walt Daniels
Mohegan Lake, New York

Acknowledgments

Walkable Westchester would not have been possible without the help of many people. The number of hours spent were enormous. Aside from the cartographer, Allison Werberg, and book designer, Nora Porter, all others involved in the project are volunteers. Special thanks go to Don Derr, Herb Hochberg, Erik and Carol Jensen, Mark Linehan, and Ruth Rosenthal for the many hours they spent.

Project Manager: Ruth Rosenthal

Providers of information, advice, and general assistance:

Bobbie Buske	David DeLucia (Westchester Parks)
Christian Lenz Cesar	Don Derr
Daniel Chazin	Paul Gisando (Westchester Planning)
Linsay Cochran	Carol Jensen
Bob DelTorto (Westchester Parks)	Dietrich Schmidt

Manager of trail checkers: TJ Mancini

Editors:

Ruth Rosenthal	Barry Fingerhut
Daniel Chazin	TJ Mancini

Indexer: Suse Bell

Trail checkers, who like astronauts, went out on missions in poorly charted areas under the guidance from mission control (the authors):

Rochelle Griffithskig Auslander	TJ Mancini
Michael Bennett	Barry R. Mark
Daniel Chazin	Naomi K. Mark
Nora Cheng	MA Massey
Don Derr	Mary Mallonee
Margaret Douglas	Chip Meakem
Ann Gruhn	Paul Meck
Peter Hibbard	Catharine Raffaele
Herb Hochberg	Will Raffaele
Carol Jensen	Kate Ray
Erik Jensen	Bob Ross
Irwin Levine	Dietrich Schmidt
Paula Levine	Jim Stirbis
Mark H. Linehan	Carol Stix
Bruce Lucas	Tom Sullivan
Priscilla Lucas	Robert Willimann

USING THIS BOOK

Walkable Westchester is about parks and trails. In addition to trail descriptions, there are maps, photographs, and sidebars with local history or ecology. Those readers wishing to learn more, should check Additional Resources.

Frequently, town parks are only for residents, but by omitting parks with such restrictions, readers might not learn of these nearby walking opportunities. Enforcing a residents-only policy is possible when there is a means of checking park permits. Parks requiring a permit are so noted.

Layout

Because most of the parks are north of I-287, there is no convenient way to group them geographically. Thus, parks are organized into sections based on the number of miles of trails, making it easier to plan a walk based on the amount of time available.

A park is a chapter within a section, only if it has more than 1.1 miles of trails. When parks are adjacent and can be on the same map, they are considered a chapter. Parks with under 1.2 miles of trails are in one section. The small parks along the Hudson River and on Long Island Sound are described in their respective chapters.

Location

The star on the locator map on the masthead identifies the general location of a park. A name of a hamlet is used to clarify its location. If the park is town-owned, the name used is not necessarily the name of the town. For example, the location of Sunny Ridge Preserve is listed as Ossining, but it is owned by the Town of New Castle whose offices are in Chappaqua. For Along the River and Along the Sound, there are large locator maps, showing all the parks in each chapter.

Miles

The miles listed are the physical miles on the ground and take into account co-aligned trails, but not the duplicate miles or steps retraced. For example, at Ward Pound Ridge Reservation the only miles of the Green Trail that are counted are those miles not co-aligned with the Red Trail. An access trail to a loop such as the Shadow Lake Trail at Teatown Lake Reservation is counted only once.

Allowable Users and Uses

Icons for mountain bikes, horses, and dogs indicate whether they are permitted or not. Only when a park is handicapped accessible or suitable for cross-country skiing is that icon shown.

Maps

A park map with trails, nearby roads, parking, train stations, and bus stops is included for all but the smallest parks. A few parks have more than one map. If a small park is adjacent to a larger park, both are included on one map. Marked and named trails are bold dashed lines. Unmarked trails are light dashed lines. Roads are light double lines. In areas with predominantly wide trails, dotted lines indicate narrow trails.

Nearby or connecting parks and trails

To help plan longer excursions, connecting and nearby parks and trails are listed.

Driving

Directions are given from highways, parkways, and major roads such as routes 1, 9, 9A, or 100. The uni-directional instructions use north, east, south, west, or "toward the river," rather than right or left. When necessary, directions from northbound and southbound exits are given.

Public transportation

When applicable, train stations and Beeline Bus numbers are listed. For information, see www.beelinebus.com and www.mta.info/mta/schedule.html. If public transportation is not available, it is so noted.

For more information

The contact information for all parks is arranged alphabetically, regardless of whether the owner is the state, county, town, or a not-for-profit. Additional information about the parks as well as suggested hikes and photographs are online at www.westchester.nynjtc.org.

Use of the information in *Walkable Westchester* is at the sole discretion and risk of the hiker. The New York-New Jersey Trail Conference and its authors make every effort to keep their publications up-to-date, however, trail conditions do change.

If you notice discrepancies or inaccuracies in this book, let us know. E-mail your comments to info@nynjtc.org; please include name of the park, the trail, the relevant page number(s), and the date of your observations.

HIKER'S ETIQUETTE

To make sure you are in the category of courteous and polite people on the trail:

- Obey posted regulations including when the park is open and what is permitted.
- Keep to the right on wide or paved paths.
- Greet people you meet and let others know you are passing them. After all, everyone is enjoying the outdoors.
- Bikers yield to hikers and horses; hikers yield to horses.
- Hike quietly. There is such a thing as noise pollution.
- When meeting a group of hikers, move to the side of the trail to let them pass.
- When meeting a horse:
  - Move to the downhill side of the trail.
  - Ask the rider if you are okay to stay where you are.
  - Stand quietly until the horse passes.
- Leave only footprints; take only pictures.
- Pack it in, pack it out; even better, pick up any litter you find.
- Keep your dog on a six-foot leash.
  - Dogs running loose threaten wildlife.
  - Other dogs might not be friendly.
  - Some people are intimidated by dogs they don't know.

When I Went Walking

In the spring, when I went walking
I took a co-worker who had never been on a hike
 to an old quarry with rusty cable.
We saw pink lady slippers and smelled the skunk cabbage.
She wants to go hiking again.

In the summer, when I went walking
I showed three ten-year-old boys a pond
 with frogs singing and slime around the edges.
We picked blueberries and ate them all.
They want to go hiking again.

In the fall, when I went walking
I pointed out to my friend the hawks flying by
 as we sat overlooking the Hudson River.
We enjoyed the colorful foliage along the trail.
We want to go hiking again.

In the winter, when I went walking
I heard the crisp snow crunch under my husband's boots
 and felt the cold air.
He shared hot chocolate from a thermos with me.
We will go hiking again.

When you went walking
Did you feel rain on your face, hear the birds sing, or find a spider?
You shared them with someone, I hope.
Will you go hiking again?

         —Jane Daniels

PAUL MECK

Fishing in Halsey Pond

SECTION I

TINY TREASURES

- ◆ Have one mile or less of trails
- ◆ Offer a small scale introduction to nature
- ◆ Are in the neighborhood or close by

Bye Preserve

Pound Ridge • 0.6 mile, 23 acres

As you enter the Bye Preserve on a narrow strip behind houses, the white-blazed trail heads downhill. It crosses a stream on stepping stones, follows a rocky gorge, and passes large boulders. At 0.4 mile the trail makes a sharp right turn. To the left, a trail leads into private property. The white trail reaches a junction which begins a loop. At the far end of the loop, there is a short connection to an unmarked woods road paralleling a stone wall and a property boundary. The walk down to, and then around the loop and back to the parking area, is 1.0 mile. In 2004, The Nature Conservancy transferred the property to Pound Ridge Land Conservancy with supporting conservation easements held by Westchester Land Trust.

DRIVING: From I-684, take Exit 4 (Route 172) and head east on Route 172. Drive through Bedford Village to where Route 172 ends at Route 137. Turn right onto Route 137 and go 2.4 miles. The preserve is on the left, just before the New York-Connecticut state line.

PUBLIC TRANSPORTATION: None available

For contact information, see Appendix, Pound Ridge Land Conservancy.

Carolin's Grove

Pound Ridge • 1.1 miles, 5 acres

A sense of serenity greets you as you drive into the parking lot at the entrance to Carolin's Grove. A large grove of Norway spruce planted in the 1930s gives a cathedral-like appearance to the site and invites visitors to pause, observe, and reflect. Robert Lawther donated the property to The Nature Conservancy in 1969 in memory of his wife, Carolin. In 2004, The Nature Conservancy transferred the property to Pound Ridge Land Conservancy with supporting conservation easements held by Westchester Land Trust.

The simple trail system resulted from the cooperative efforts of town, school, and a local not-for-profit organization, showing the whole to be far greater than the sum of the parts. The blue trail wraps around the town's ball and soccer fields and continues through the Pound Ridge Elementary School playground, providing the school with two outdoor learning areas.

From the parking lot on the side opposite a kiosk, the blue trail heads clockwise along a wood chip path. It passes white trail #1 at 0.1 mile. Reaching the edge of the woods, the blue trail skirts a ball field and heads down a paved service road. It turns right, passes a playground, and reenters the woods just before a second kiosk.

After passing white trail #2 at 0.4 mile, the trail loops around and passes it again at 0.6 mile. The blue trail reaches white trail #1. Passing through a Norway spruce grove, the blue trail ends in 0.9 mile at a service road into the soccer field. Parking is a short distance to the left.

DRIVING: From I-684, take Exit 4 (Route 172) and follow it east to where it ends at Route 137. Turn left and drive 0.3 mile to a parking area to the left.

PUBLIC TRANSPORTATION: None available

For contact information, see Appendix, Pound Ridge Land Conservancy.

Crawford Park and Rye Hills Park

Rye Brook • 0.8 mile, 43 acres

Separated by an ivy-covered concrete wall, Crawford Park and Rye Hills Park sit side by side on top of a hill in Rye Brook. The grounds of Crawford Park have gardens, benches, and a wildflower area. Paved paths are handicapped accessible.

Shanarock Farm was once the main family home of Edna and Everett Crawford, who purchased the 35.6-acre estate in the early 1900s. With development surrounding them, the Crawfords wanted to be sure the community maintained open space, and decided in 1955 to bequeath their estate. In keeping with their wishes, no announcement of the gift was made until Mrs. Crawford's death in 1974, when the estate became the property of Town of Rye. The mansion is an example of a big house of that period, surrounded by extensive landscaping, formal gardens, and outbuildings. Now, mature trees are along the vast expanse of lawn and the mansion is used for community events.

A 0.5-mile walking path is along most of the park's length, as well as ball fields. There are pedestrian access points on the road just before the crest of the hill and from Rye Hills Park and neighborhoods on two sides. Rye Hills Park has a wide 0.3-mile loop trail that offers pleasant places to sit, including a story circle and belvedere.

Stone story circle

DRIVING: From the northbound Hutchinson River Parkway, take Exit 29 (North Ridge Road) and turn right. If southbound, turn left onto North Ridge Road. It is a mile from the intersection of the northbound exit and North Ridge Road to the

Crawford Park entrance to the right. The road is one-way only through the park, with parking at the hilltop and near the exit to Lincoln Avenue.

Those with handicapped permits may continue past the entrance to Crawford Park and turn right onto Long Ledge Drive (Hidden Falls entrance). Turn left at Parkridge Court and take the next left into Rye Hills Park.

PUBLIC TRANSPORTATION: None available

For contact information, see Appendix, Rye (Town), Rye Brook.

Croton River Gorge Park

Croton-on-Hudson • 0.9 mile, 34.4 acres

Beginning in the parking lot for Silver Lake Park (resident permit required) at the end of Truesdale Drive, the Croton River Gorge Trail follows what is known as a "paper" road, a road that appears on maps, but has never been built. The wide trail is basically level, but at 0.3 mile, a narrow trail to the right descends steeply to reach Quaker Bridge Road. It is 0.2 mile along the road to Black Rock Park, where a Croton resident permit is required during the summer. Just past the trail which descends into the gorge, an unmarked trail heads uphill 0.2 mile to the parking lot behind the Carrie E. Tompkins Elementary School. A round trip from the end of Truesdale Drive to Cleveland Drive is 1.2 miles.

DRIVING: From Route 9, take the Croton Point Avenue Exit and turn inland (east) away from the river. After one block, turn left at a traffic light and take the first right onto Benedict Boulevard. When Benedict Boulevard reaches a traffic circle, take the second exit onto Truesdale Drive. Follow Truesdale Drive to its end where there is parking at Silver Lake Park. Alternately, take the third exit from the traffic circle and continue on Cleveland Drive for 1.5 miles to its end, where there is parking for five cars.

PUBLIC TRANSPORTATION: Beeline Bus #14 to Truesdale Drive

For contact information, see Appendix, Croton.

East Irvington Nature Preserve

East Irvington • 0.8 mile, 32 acres

High atop a ridge sits the East Irvington Nature Preserve. From the entrance, it is 0.1 mile to reach a viewing platform that overlooks a pond. Turn right and follow the gravel road for another 0.1 mile, arriving in 0.3 mile at an orange-blazed trail which eventually loops back to the gravel road. The gravel road is the access road to the water tower and another way to walk into the preserve. An intermittently marked trail from the orange trail descends 0.3 mile to Mountain Road, where 100 yards downhill is an unmarked trail leading into Irvington Woods.

DRIVING: From Route 9 at the Irvington/Tarrytown line, turn east onto Sunnyside Lane, 1.0 mile south of I-287 and 0.5 mile north of Main Street in Irvington. Follow Sunnyside Lane for 0.6 mile and turn left onto Taxter Road. Continue 0.7 mile further to the preserve entrance to the right.

PUBLIC TRANSPORTATION: None available

For contact information, see Appendix, Greenburgh.

East Rumbrook Park

Greenburgh • 0.7 mile, 51 acres

Ball fields dominate East Rumbrook Park, something of a diamond in the rough. Given its location in relation to the town, this little slice of forest is a way to escape large buildings and highway hum, particularly for a short hike.

At the far end of the parking lot past a barrier, a derelict paved road along the edge of the power line leads into a mixed hardwood forest. Just beyond the trailhead, to the right, a short side trail leads downhill to end at Rum Brook. At the next junction, the paved path continues straight to end in 0.1 mile at the power line. Turn right off the often overgrown paved path. At 0.4 mile, the path fords Rum Brook on stones, which in high water might not be sufficient to keep feet dry. The path turns away from the stream and passes behind houses. Numerous tracks lead to a set of wooden steps ascending into private property. The leftmost trail doubles back. An obscure trail leads to Route 9A across from the entrance to West Rumbrook Park with ball fields and wetlands.

DRIVING: From the Sprain Brook Parkway, take Dobbs Ferry Road/100B Exit and turn east. The entrance to the park is adjacent to the southbound exit ramp.

PUBLIC TRANSPORTATION: None available

For contact information, see Appendix, Greenburgh.

Five Ponds Trail

Waccabuc • 1.2 miles

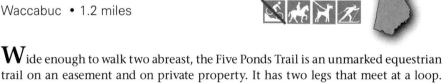

Wide enough to walk two abreast, the Five Ponds Trail is an unmarked equestrian trail on an easement and on private property. It has two legs that meet at a loop. A sign at the Grant Street entrance requests riders to stay off the trail when wet, implying that hikers should do the same.

From the entrance on Five Ponds Drive, the Five Ponds Trail descends on a woods road along a narrow right-of-way. It passes a tennis court to the right and then a large storm water retention pond. At 0.2 mile, it passes beneath a power line on a causeway through wetland. Heading uphill, the trail turns right. Straight ahead, a side trail goes uphill, turns right, and loops 0.3 mile to join the main trail.

From the turn, the Five Ponds Trail heads downhill, paralleling a stone wall with wetlands to the right. To the left, at 0.4 mile, is the other end of the loop side trail. Once past the ATT line, the trail is on private property. It passes to the right a side trail which follows a stone wall and the wetlands edge to rejoin the Five Ponds Trail close to Grant Lane. Both ends of the side trail are closed by a chain and sign: No Horses. The Five Ponds Trail passes a pond to the left at 0.6 mile, and then a gate, also to the left, at 0.8 mile. After crossing two branches of a stream, it reaches Grant Road (no parking).

DRIVING: From I-684, take Exit 6 (Route 35) and turn east onto Route 35 for 4.5 miles. Turn left onto Route 121. At 2.5 miles, turn right onto Chapel Road, opposite the end of Route 138. Drive a half-mile on Chapel Road and turn left onto Chapel Court. Take the first right onto paved Five Ponds Drive and drive to the end. The entrance is to the left, just before the cul-de-sac.

PUBLIC TRANSPORTATION: None available

For contact information, see Appendix, Lewisboro.

Fort Hill Park

Peekskill • 0.8 mile, 52 acres

Located on a hill near the center of Peekskill, Fort Hill Park is an unexpected oasis. Stone steps at the entrance and some paths attest to the fact that the park was at one time, more formal. During the American Revolution, Fort Hill was the site of a redoubt and five large barracks. Interpretive signs give a brief history of the role the area played in the conflict. A combination of intermittently marked and unmarked trails loops through former pastures and along old farm roads. One trail leads to a viewpoint with a limited view over the Hudson River. In 2007, in exchange for a 40-acre donation to expand the park, Ginsberg Development was given rights to build townhouses on adjacent property.

DRIVING: From Route 9, take the Route 6/202 Exit to Peekskill. Turn left onto Main Street. After a short distance, turn left onto Hadden Street, adjacent to a playground, and follow it to the end. Turn right, drive one block to Decatur Street, and turn left. The park entrance is to the left just before Orchard Street. Curbside parking has limited hours.

PUBLIC TRANSPORTATION: Beeline Bus #17 on Main Street

For contact information, see Appendix, Peekskill.

Guard Hill Park

Mt. Kisco • 0.5 mile, 17 acres

The single red-blazed trail in Guard Hill Park provides a stiff little climb to the top, which is overgrown with trees. During the American Revolution, observation patrols were stationed on Guard Hill, called a "commanding height" on maps made by Robert Erskine, General George Washington's cartographer. In 1981, Wilhelmine Kirby Waller donated the property to the Town of Bedford.

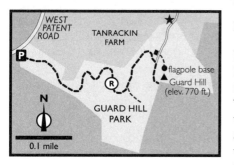

From the parking area, the trail begins between a fence and a stone marker. Logs and branches delineate the path for 0.1 mile before red blazes appear. The trail ascends, sometimes steeply, with frequent switchbacks. There are numerous large trees in the open woodland of mixed hardwoods and, at 0.3 mile, a view of a horse pasture. The trail continues to climb and reaches a radio tower and its access road at 0.5 mile.

To the left, 0.1 mile along the tower access road at the property boundary, there is a sweeping view over the nearby horse pasture. Another side trip is to bushwhack up to the top of the knob directly across from the radio tower. This is the site of an old tower with three stone piles and a conical structure, possibly once the base of a flagpole.

DRIVING: From I-684, take Exit 4 (Route 172) and turn west toward Mt. Kisco. Turn right onto West Patent Road and head north for 0.4 mile. Pass John Cross Road to the left; just beyond the stone walls of the entrance to #284 to the right, there is a small unmarked parking area. The only sign is a plaque on a rock, not noticeable from the road.

PUBLIC TRANSPORTATION: None available

For contact information, see Appendix, Bedford.

Halsey Pond

Irvington • 0.8 mile, 25 acres

Like a sentinel, the Beltzhoover Teahouse stands and overlooks Halsey Pond. This stone building is the largest remaining structure of Rochroane, the Beltzhoover Estate built in 1905. The New York State Office of Parks, Recreation and Historic

Preservation deemed it "architecturally and historically significant as rare examples of Gothic stone architecture associated with mid-nineteenth century picturesque landscape." It makes a perfect setting for a small wedding. Surrounded by houses and adjacent to a golf course, this tiny park has a wide variety of trees, shrubs, and wildflowers.

From the parking area at the end of Hamilton Road, an unmarked path heads uphill to Halsey Pond. The left hand fork leads to the teahouse with views over the pond. A wide level path circles the pond, with a catch and release policy for fishermen. The three additional access points for foot traffic are off Palister Road, Birch Lane, and Havemeyer Road, none of which have parking.

Beltzhoover teahouse

NEARBY PARKS: Old Croton Aqueduct, Juhring Estate

DRIVING: From Broadway (Route 9) just north of Mercy College in Dobbs Ferry, turn right onto Hamilton Road. Park at the end of the street, but take care not to block nearby driveways.

PUBLIC TRANSPORTATION: Beeline Bus #1W or #1T along Broadway at Ardsley and Clinton avenues

For contact information, see Appendix, Irvington.

Hunt Woods Park

Mount Vernon • 1.1 miles, 21 acres

Over the years, generations of children and countless dogs with their owners have enjoyed Hunt Woods Park. Laurel Brook runs through the park and flows into the Bronx River. In the 1920s, Westchester County purchased this land, now Hunt Woods Park, to be a right-of-way for the Cross County Parkway. However, instead of using the land, the county, wanting to cut costs, opted to align the parkway straight through Mount Vernon. A bridge was built over the Bronx River and the Bronx River Parkway. In December 1967, the land was transferred to the City of Mount Vernon.

Tall stately trees, some older than 250 years, grace two unmarked parallel trails. Although the area is densely populated, there is little road noise in the park because of its setting in a valley. The well-worn paths are often in the flood plain of Laurel Brook; after rain they may not be passable.

The trail begins at the end of a guardrail on Central Parkway in Mount Vernon and goes along a sewer line. Keep left at the first trail junction. The trail passes a cross trail and then Laurel Brook, which flows out of a culvert and along a course faced with rocks. At 0.3 mile, the trail reaches a wide intersection where a second trail joins and then splits off again, with each trail going over a wooden bridge.

Keeping left again, the trail heads slightly uphill, still paralleling Laurel Brook. The trail crosses the stream on cement block stepping stones and reaches what looks like a dead end at a stone wall at 0.5 mile. However, there are broad steps which go up to Gramatan Avenue. On the other side of the street, a flight of steps heads back down to the stream. This section has considerable evidence of flooding, and the path is narrower. The trail ends at ball fields, at 0.6 mile.

For a return trip, retrace your steps to cross Gramatan Avenue and back down the stairs. At the stream crossing on the concrete stepping stones, keep left, following the other path. The trail hugs the side of the valley, sometimes on a narrow path. It crosses a wooden bridge to reach the wide intersection. Go left, but almost immediately bear right at the Y intersection, continuing into Hunt Woods. The left branch continues 100 yards to end at Vernon Parkway. The main trail passes the cross trail mentioned earlier, and then a trail to the left out to the corner of Rhynas Drive and Central Parkway, where you can see your starting point to the right.

DRIVING: From eastbound Cross County Parkway, take Exit 8 (Route 22) toward North Columbus Avenue, Mount Vernon. Follow the parkway south, and turn left to head north on Columbus Avenue.* After two blocks, turn left onto East Devonia Avenue at 0.3 mile, then turn right onto Central Parkway. The park entrance is to the left adjacent to #112 Central Parkway (the first house); however, there is a No Parking sign. From westbound Cross County Parkway, take Exit 8 (Route 22). At the end of the exit ramp, turn left onto Columbus Avenue (Route 22). Follow the directions from *.

PUBLIC TRANSPORTATION: Beeline Bus #40 along North Columbus Avenue. Follow the preceding directions from East Devonia Avenue, above.

For contact information, see Appendix, Mount Vernon.

Leatherman's Ridge

Bedford Hills • 0.4 mile, 33 acres

The joint efforts of neighbors, the Town of Bedford, and the Westchester Land Trust preserved Leatherman's Ridge. On his route through Westchester County, the Leatherman frequented a cave on the site. (See sidebar about the Leatherman in Ward Pound Ridge Reservation, on page 309.) The only trail is a loop with a cross trail to allow for a shorter hike if desired. A well-used unmarked path under the power line is quite passable about 0.3 mile northwest of its intersection with the yellow trail. It continues southeast to end at a viewpoint.

DRIVING: From northbound Saw Mill Parkway, take the Bedford Hills Exit and turn left onto Route 117 (Cherry Street). At the intersection where Bedford Road goes right, continue straight ahead on Cherry Street.* In 0.2 mile, turn left onto Dwight Lane to park at the end. From southbound Saw Mill Parkway take the Bedford Hills Exit. Turn right onto Haines Road and then left onto Route 117 (Cherry Street) at the intersection with Bedford Road. Follow above directions from *.

PUBLIC TRANSPORTATION: Metro-North Bedford Hills Station. Walk south along Adams Street and turn right onto Route 117, following the driving directions from northbound Saw Mill Parkway. It is a little more than a half-mile to the trailhead.

For contact information, see Appendix, Bedford.

Henry Morgenthau Preserve

Pound Ridge • 1.1 miles, 35 acres

Four distinct forest communities (oak-hickory, red maple swamp, sugar maple forest, and white pine plantation) are at the Henry Morgenthau Preserve. Locations are identified in a brochure sometimes available at the kiosk.

In 1972, Ruth M. Knight donated twenty acres to establish the preserve in memory of her father, U.S. Ambassador to Turkey (1913-1916). Over the years, the preserve has grown with additions from donations and purchases.

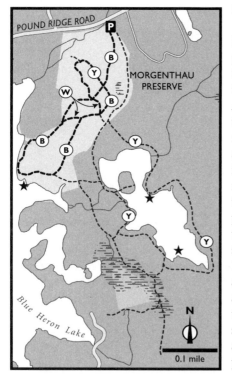

Blue Trail
Length: 0.7 mile Blaze: blue
From the entrance at the rear of the parking lot, the blue trail passes a kiosk and heads into the preserve, passing through a grove of young sugar maples. At 0.1 mile it splits, and to the right the yellow trail leads 0.2 mile toward a massive white oak. Continuing straight ahead, the blue trail passes the second intersection of the yellow trail to the right and a white trail to the left. Here, the trail goes through a white pine plantation established in the 1940s. The trail turns, descends, and follows the shore of Blue Heron Lake, created in 1940. It heads away from the lake, passes a fenced-in area called a deer exclosure, and makes a sharp left at 0.4 mile. This turn might be missed because the route straight ahead is more heavily trodden and leads to unmarked trails on private property. As the trail heads back to the

Blue Heron Lake

parking lot, it passes rock outcroppings and a glacial erratic at the intersection with the more southern of the two white trails. After passing the intersection with the northern white trail, the blue trail closes the loop. The yellow trail is straight ahead and the blue trail goes to the left and to the right. Turn right to return to the preserve entrance.

Unmarked Trails

Straight in from the parking lot behind the gate at the left of the entry trail just outside the preserve, a well-used unmarked woods road leads a quarter-mile to a lake. The woods road heads along the dam to numerous access points. In addition, there is an occasionally blazed yellow trail around the lake. Other unmarked paths connect the private property to the marked trails of the preserve.

DRIVING: From I-684, take Exit 4 (Route 172) and head east, passing through Bedford Village. The preserve entrance is approximately 2.9 miles from the Bedford Village Green. Marked with a small sign, the preserve is to the right, just past Tatomuck Road and opposite Meadowbrook Farm.

PUBLIC TRANSPORTATION: None available

For contact information, see Appendix, The Nature Conservancy.

Old Church Lane Preserve

Vista • 0.6 mile, 31 acres

In Old Church Lane Preserve, lush vegetation surrounds the lone trail as it winds its way in and around wetlands and through a moist acidic forest. The preserve began with a donation to the Open Space Institute (OSI) in the mid 1990s. Subsequently, OSI donated the land to the Westchester Land Trust. The donation protects the shrubby wetlands and surrounding woodland, habitat for sensitive amphibians such as wood frogs and spotted salamanders.

Just beyond the entrance, the trail passes four white pines growing together. It enters a wetland, crosses a stream, and heads up to the top of a ravine at 0.2 mile. The trail meanders through the forest with thick understory, predominantly mountain laurel. It heads downhill and crosses a stream. At 0.4 mile, the trail reaches a T junction with a woods road and turns left. It passes extensive wetlands to the left at 0.5 mile, and ends on Old Church Lane across from #28 at 0.6 mile.

NEARBY PARKS: Levy Preserve, Onatru Farm Park and Preserve

DRIVING: From I-684, take Exit 6 (Route 35) and turn east. Drive 9.1 miles and turn right at the traffic light on Route 123 (just before the New York-Connecticut state line). Follow Route 123 south for 1.8 miles and turn right onto Kitchawan Road. Drive 0.5 mile and turn left onto Old Church Lane. Another half-mile leads to parking to the left, across from #46.

PUBLIC TRANSPORTATION: None available

For contact information, see Appendix, Westchester Land Trust.

Pinecliff Sanctuary

Chappaqua • 0.5 mile, 7 acres

One might easily overlook tiny Pinecliff Sanctuary, set at the end of a cul-de-sac. Its 0.2-mile wheelchair accessible boardwalk travels around the wetlands and a pond. Both white and yellow trails form loops off the boardwalk for 0.2 and 0.1 mile, respectively.

Along the boardwalk

In 1969, the Stern and Arleo families donated seven acres to New Castle Land Conservancy (which later merged with Saw Mill River Audubon). The boardwalk was built in 1996 through a Westchester Community Development Block Grant with local support including volunteer labor.

DRIVING: From the Saw Mill Parkway, take Route 120 north towards Millwood. At

Pinecliff Road, turn right and continue to the end. Parking is limited.

PUBLIC TRANSPORTATION: Metro-North Harlem Line Chappaqua Station. Cross to the west side of the tracks and head north 0.6 mile on the sidewalk along Route 120. Take the third right onto Pinecliff Road and walk 0.2 mile to the end.

For contact information, see Appendix, Saw Mill River Audubon Society.

Ridgeway Nature Preserve

White Plains • 0.4 mile, 16 acres

Located on a sewer right-of-way, Ridgeway Nature Preserve offers views down onto a stream. To reach the preserve, park in Ridgeway Elementary School's parking lot (only if the school is closed) and walk along the east side of the ball fields. At the south end of the parking lot, a path heads along the edge of the school property behind the backstop, then downhill to the park entrance to the left. The wide trail looks down onto a stream with stonework channeling the water. It passes a strange stone structure with steps in the back. At 0.2 mile, the path turns right onto a trail that leads to a stone bridge downstream from a dam. Continue counterclockwise along the main trail to return to the parking lot.

NEARBY TRAIL: White Plains Greenway

DRIVING: From I-287, take the Bloomingdale Road Exit and turn left onto Bloomingdale Road, which becomes Mamaroneck Avenue. Pass Stepinac High School to the right and take the next right onto Ridgeway. Ridgeway Elementary School is to the left and, if not in session, park in the lot. No other parking is available.

PUBLIC TRANSPORTATION: Beeline Bus #60 on Mamaroneck Avenue and walk 2 blocks along Ridgeway to the Ridgeway Elementary School. Beeline #63 on Route 125 (Old Mamaroneck Road) and walk east on Ridgeway to Seeger Drive, a short dead end street just west of #165 Ridgeway. The park entrance is at the end of Seeger Drive.

For contact information, see Appendix, White Plains.

St. Paul's Chapel

Vista • 0.9 mile, 32 acres

All the trails at St. Paul's Chapel are blazed blue. They wander through the property, giving hikers a chance to enjoy laurel groves, wetlands, vernal pools, a balanced erratic, and a stream. The trails offer a walk that is both physically and spiritually satisfying.

Balanced glacial erratic

From the kiosk beside St. Paul's Chapel, the blue trail heads into the woods. It reaches an outdoor shrine to St. Francis at 0.1 mile and turns right. At the next intersection, turn right to return to the parking lot. Continue straight to head downhill, cross a rock field, and reach a balanced glacial erratic at 0.3 mile. At the next two intersections continue straight, as the trail will loop back to these two points. There are several streams which may be difficult to cross at high water. The trail ends at 0.5 mile at a high point, but no view.

NEARBY PARKS: Levy Preserve, Onatru Farm Park and Preserve

DRIVING: From I-684, take Exit 6 (Route 35) and head east for 9.1 miles. Turn right at the traffic light on Route 123, which is just before the New York-Connecticut line. Follow Route 123 south for 2.3 miles. St. Paul's Chapel is south of the intersection with Elmwood Road on the left side.

PUBLIC TRANSPORTATION: None available

For contact information, see Appendix, Lewisboro Land Trust.

Sculpture Garden at PepsiCo

Purchase • 1.1 miles, 168 acres

World class takes on new meaning at the Donald M. Kendall Sculpture Garden located at PepsiCo World Headquarters. The gardens are named for Donald M. Kendall, former chairman of the board and CEO of PepsiCo. He imagined an atmosphere of stability, creativity, and experimentation, reflecting his vision of the company. Set on a former polo field, the sculpture garden is also an arboretum, with both native and non-native trees and plants. The garden is open to the public; a map is available at the small visitors center.

The gardens immediately around the building (designed by Edward Durrell Stone) are formal and the surrounding grounds are on a grand scale. E.D. Stone, Jr. planned the extensive landscaping, with an understanding and appreciation of the forms, textures, colors, and scents of his trees, shrubs, and plants. Russell Page extended the garden from 1980 until his death in 1985. Thereafter, Françoise Giffinet continued to develop the garden.

A path winds 1.1 miles around the building, passing small groves of similar tree species, specialty gardens, and woodlands. The gold gravel covering the paved path is Russell Page's idea of a golden ribbon tying the garden's features together.

There are five sets of four-inch-high steps, both wide and long enough to allow the route to be handicapped accessible. The loop around the lake has no steps.

The art collection was begun in 1965. Featuring the work of major twentieth-century sculptors, by 2006 it had grown to include 45 pieces. Ten sculptures are in the courtyard of the building, while the others are in continuous view of the path. Benches are placed throughout the route, allowing for reflection, contemplation, and a chance to study the art from numerous angles.

Giant Trowel II by Claes Oldenburg

DRIVING: From eastbound I-287, take Exit 8E. Make a gentle left onto Westchester Avenue, and then another gentle left onto the ramp leading toward Anderson Hill Road. At the fork, continue toward the right on Anderson Hill Road to reach the PepsiCo entrance in 2.5 miles. From westbound I-287, take Exit 10 (Bowman Avenue/Webb Avenue). Follow Webb Avenue to Westchester Avenue. Turn right to follow Westchester Avenue for 0.2 mile, turning left onto Lincoln Avenue and continuing 2.1 miles to Anderson Hill Road. Turn right, and right again, at the entrance into PepsiCo. A security guard at the gate will direct you to parking. Maps are available at the visitors center.

PUBLIC TRANSPORTATION: Beeline Bus #12 can be used to reach or leave the site, but only on weekday mornings and evenings.

For contact information, see Appendix, PepsiCo.

Sparkle Lake Park

Yorktown • 0.5 mile, 37 acres

Beginning at the north end of the parking lot, the trail runs north above a sewer line along the edge of Sparkle Lake with sweeping views and opportunities to observe wildlife. At times the trail is close enough to the lake to allow fishing. It passes the end of the lake at 0.2 mile and an unmarked track heading 225 yards to private homes. At 0.3 mile, it passes a trail to the right which leads in 250 feet to a tot park, accessible from Douglas Drive. The sewer line heads uphill to end at London Road, near Curry Street. A paved handicapped accessible path heads south from the main parking lot along the beach. During summer months, this portion of the park is open only to Yorktown residents with swimming permits.

DRIVING: From the Taconic State Parkway, take the Route 202/35 Exit and head east. From the traffic light at the end of the northbound exit ramp, it is 1.2 miles to the traffic light at Granite Springs Road, across from the Mildred Strang Middle School entrance. Turn left at the light and continue for 1.3 miles to a T junction. Turn left, pass a large sign and the entrance to Yorktown Parks and Recreation, and turn left at the next entrance (with a smaller sign), in 0.2 mile. The trail begins at the north end of a larger parking lot adjacent to the Parks and Recreation office.

PUBLIC TRANSPORTATION: None available

For contact information, see Appendix, Yorktown.

Halle Ravine

POCKET PARKS

- Have one to two miles of trails
- Provide perfect opportunities for quick walks
- Are in nearby communities

Choate Sanctuary

Mt. Kisco •1.3 miles, 30 acres

A massive sugar maple and wetlands greet visitors as they enter Choate Sanctuary. Further into the sanctuary, there are rock cliffs and tall trees. This 23-acre sanctuary was established in 1972 by the heirs of Joseph H. Choate, Jr., the chair of a self-appointed committee to repeal the 18th Amendment (Prohibition). After the amendment's repeal, Choate was the first head of the Federal Alcohol Control Administration. In 1974, Geoffrey Platt gave three acres to the sanctuary in memory of his wife, Helen Choate Platt. The Swamp Loop Trail is on the four acres added in 1997 under a 99-year lease from the Town of New Castle.

TRAILS

Three short trails loop their way through Choate Sanctuary. Plan to get some exercise, because there are elevation gains and losses. Although the sanctuary is located near a main road, portions of the trails have no road noise.

White Oak Trail   *Length: 0.6 mile Blaze: white*

Beginning on Crow Hill Road, the White Oak Trail enters an extensive wetland and crosses a bridge. At 0.1 mile at a T junction with the Hickory Trail (yellow), the White Oak Trail turns right. At a second T junction, the White Oak Trail turns right to head uphill and, at 0.2 mile, splits. Heading clockwise, the trail continues to ascend. It turns right at a large erratic and passes a rock outcropping to the left. At 0.5 mile, the trail reaches the Swamp Loop Trail (blue), turns, and closes the loop at 0.6 mile.

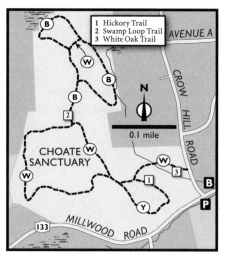

Hickory Trail
Length: 0.2 mile Blaze: yellow

From the junction with the White Oak Trail (white) the Hickory Trail parallels a stone wall, sometimes level with it. The trail turns, passes a ravine to the left, and ends at the White Oak Trail. Four species of Lycopodia are found in this area: ground cedar, ground pine, running pine, and shining club moss.

Swamp Loop Trail
Length: 0.5 mile Blaze: blue
From the White Oak Trail (white), the Swamp Loop Trail splits to form a loop. Going clockwise through an upland forest, the Swamp Loop Trail passes a white-blazed shortcut. At 0.2 mile, it descends to enter a red maple swamp, goes through banks of Christmas and New York ferns, and passes the other end of the side trail. Turning right, it ascends to close the loop at 0.5 mile.

Tulip tree

DRIVING: From the Saw Mill Parkway, take the Route 133/Mt.Kisco Exit. Head west on Route 133 for 0.5 mile to the Mt. Kisco Presbyterian Church to the left, opposite Crow Hill Road. Parking may be available in the church lot. Take care when crossing Route 133 and walking along Crow Hill Road. From the church parking lot, Choate Sanctuary is 100 yards up Crow Hill Road to the left. It is illegal to park along Crow Hill Road.

PUBLIC TRANSPORTATION: Beeline Bus #12, corner of Crow Hill Road and Route 133

For contact information, see Appendix, Saw Mill River Audubon Society.

Clark Preserve

Pound Ridge • 1.9 miles, 72 acres

Although one could say that the Clark Preserve majors in stone walls and minors in benches, there are many other things to see: ponds, wetlands, meadows, towering trees, rolling terrain. Even a short hike offers variety. Donated by Ben and Charlotte Clark, the preserve is part of the biotic corridor extending along the eastern portion of Westchester County that includes Ward Pound Ridge Reservation to the north.

TRAILS

In the Clark Preserve, trails have more than one blaze, except for three red trails, two of which are loops leading 0.1 and 0.3 mile from the red-blue trail to the edge of the property. The third red trail is a 0.1-mile connection between the yellow-blue trail and the red-blue trail. It is possible to follow either yellow or blue blazes for a loop hike.

Entrance Trail   *Length: 0.2 mile Blaze: red-yellow-blue*
From the entrance on Autumn Ridge Road, the red-yellow-red trail leads into the preserve. The yellow-red trail heads uphill to the left, while straight ahead the red-yellow-blue trail goes through the first of many stone walls and turns right. Stately trees tower over a grassy understory. At 0.2 mile, the entrance trail ends with the

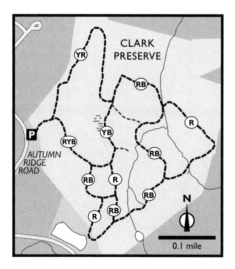

yellow-blue trail to the left and the red-blue to the right.

Red-Blue Trail
Length: 0.7 mile Blaze: red-blue
From the end of the entrance trail, the red-blue trail turns right and the character of the preserve changes; there are fewer large trees. A 0.1-mile red trail to the right leads to the town park on Brook Farm Road East and then loops back. At 0.1 mile, the red-blue trail turns right and a red trail heads left to connect to the yellow-blue trail. The red-blue trail passes the other end of the 0.1-mile red trail and heads downhill to cross a

stone wall. After crossing a wetland on a low bridge, the trail skirts it. Once across a stream on large rocks at 0.4 mile, the trail turns right. The red-blue trail passes a 0.3-mile red trail to the right and a 0.1-mile unmarked trail to the left leading to the yellow-blue trail. At 0.5 mile, the red-blue trail passes a bridge to the right, which is the other end of the previously mentioned red trail. The trail crosses a wet area on puncheon and a second bridge. It traverses a small field, enters another at 0.6 mile, and follows its left edge. The red-blue trail ends at a wide intersection, with the yellow-blue continuing straight and the yellow-red trail to the right.

Red Trail

Length: 0.3 mile Blaze: red
From the red-blue trail, the southern end of the red trail crosses a stream and then meanders through the woods. It passes a tree house at 0.1 mile, gradually turns, and crosses a bridge to end at the red-blue trail.

Yellow-Blue Trail

Length: 0.1 mile Blaze: yellow-blue
At the end of the entrance trail, the yellow-blue trail turns left. It passes a 0.1-mile red trail and turns left again. After passing an unmarked trail to a deformed birch tree, it ends at a wide intersection with the yellow-red trail and the red-blue trail.

Deformed birch tree

Yellow-Red Trail

Length: 0.3 mile Blaze: yellow-red
There are more elevation changes on the yellow-red trail than on the other trails. From the access trail, the yellow-red trail heads uphill. Cresting the hill, it turns right to go through a chainlink fence and join a woods road. From a rocky knob, it descends steeply and enters a cedar grove. It ends at a wide intersection with the red-blue and yellow-blue trails.

DRIVING: From I-684, take Exit 6 (Route 35) and turn east. In 3.8 miles, turn right onto Route 121 and go 2.9 miles to Route 137 (Stone Hill Road). Turn left, continue 1.4 miles, and turn right onto Autumn Ridge Road. It is 0.4 mile further to the entrance and parking to the left.

PUBLIC TRANSPORTATION: None available

For contact information, see Appendix, Pound Ridge Land Conservancy.

Croton Gorge Park

Croton-on-Hudson • 1.3 miles, 97 acres

The massive dam at the entrance to Croton Gorge Park never fails to impress. Whether there is a rainbow, water roaring down the spillway, or a delicate trickle barely covering the ledges of the spillway, it is always a spectacular sight. The New Croton Dam is also called the Cornell Dam because it was built on property once owned by A.B. Cornell and purchased from him in 1893. Completed in 1907, the dam stands more than 200 feet high. In 1964, for $95,000, New York City sold 97 acres to Westchester County for public use.

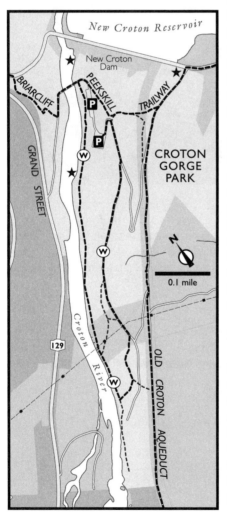

Walking along the Croton River is pleasant because the sound of rushing water in the river is soothing. One section of the River Trail is wide, allowing for walking two abreast. Longer hikes are possible. The Briarcliff Peekskill Trailway crosses through the park near the base of the dam; there are two side trails on the River Trail that connect to the Old Croton Aqueduct. The adjacent county-owned Stokes-Green property, a former estate, has unmarked woods roads.

River Trail

Length: 1.2 miles Blaze: white
Beginning by the bridge at the base of the dam, the River Trail heads downstream along the south side of the Croton River. Almost immediately, a side trail leads to the river, but then returns to rejoin the main trail. At 0.2 mile, the trail crosses a stone-lined channel, long unused, and then, at 0.4 mile, it crosses the flood plain of the Croton River. It heads away

from the river's edge to go under power lines at 0.5 mile, passing a trail which leads 0.1 mile uphill to the River Trail's return portion. It crosses a stone wall and turns left at a telephone pole. Straight ahead, the unmarked path leads to a springhouse and the end of the property.

At a driveway, a sign directs walkers to the Old Croton Aqueduct. The River Trail follows a gravel road and goes under the power lines at 0.9 mile. It passes two trails heading downhill to join the section of River Trail along the river. After passing through a white pine plantation at 1.1 miles, the River Trail again crosses the stone-lined channel. It crosses a bridge and passes between white pines lining the road. On the right at 1.2 miles, the trail ends at a sign for the

New Croton Dam

HERB CHONG

River Trail and a directional sign for the Old Croton Aqueduct. Close the loop by walking 0.2 mile past the Authorized Vehicles Only sign and through parking lots to the bridge at the base of the dam.

NEARBY TRAILS: Briarcliff-Peekskill Trailway, Old Croton Aqueduct

DRIVING: From Route 9, take the Croton Avenue Exit. At the end of the ramp, turn away from the river. Head uphill towards a traffic light at a T junction with South Riverside Avenue/Route 9A (not labeled) and turn left. Go 0.6 mile to turn right at Route 129 and continue 2.2 miles to the park entrance to the right.

Alternately, from the Taconic State Parkway take the Underhill Avenue Exit and head toward Croton. Underhill Avenue ends at a T junction with Route 129. Turn right and go 3.4 miles to the park entrance to the left, which is downhill from the road over the New Croton Dam (closed to vehicles).

PUBLIC TRANSPORTATION: None available

For contact information, see Appendix, Westchester County Parks.

Greenburgh Nature Center

Scarsdale • 1.4 miles, 32.5 acres

More than 40 tree species, 12 fern species, 75 fungus species, and 90 wildflower species call the Greenburgh Nature Center home. It is all the more amazing as the center is off a busy street and adjacent to a dense commercial area in central Westchester. Because the Greenburgh Nature Center is on both the Atlantic and Hudson River flyways, there are over 140 species of birds that either visit or nest on the property. Mushrooms and other fungi compose an integral part of the identified flora because a well-known amateur naturalist/mycologist, Sylvia Stein, had been active at the center.

The property was originally occupied in 1918 by Dr. Lewis Rutherford Morris, a direct descendant of Lewis Morris, who signed the Declaration of Independence. Some of the stone used to build the Manor House was quarried on-site. There is an admission fee to the Manor House, which contains a live animal display, a discovery room, a greenhouse, and a changing nature-arts exhibit.

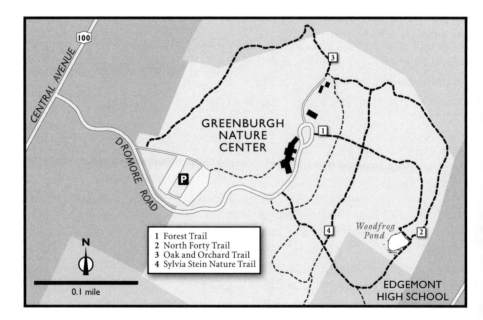

1 Forest Trail
2 North Forty Trail
3 Oak and Orchard Trail
4 Sylvia Stein Nature Trail

TRAILS

The compact trail system at Greenburgh Nature Center has numerous unmarked cross trails. Except for the Forest Trail, all trails are unmarked. In addition to the named trails, there are narrow paths in the rock garden behind the Manor House. Unmarked trails connect with a trail system at adjacent Edgemont High School.

Forest Trail   *Length: 0.4 mile Blaze: FT on white*

Beginning behind the Nature Center, numbered posts are along the Forest Trail, the main loop. The 0.6 mile of unmarked side trails either radiate from, or connect to, another part of the loop. The Forest Trail heads downhill to pass an unmarked trail to the left and then the 0.1-mile Sylvia Stein Nature Trail. The Forest Trail reaches a Y junction and turns left. A trail to the right leads to Edgemont High School.

The Forest Trail passes, to the left a trail which goes along Woodfrog Pond and later rejoins the Forest Trail. After following the edge of Woodfrog Pond, the Forest Trail reaches a T junction and turns left to cross a wooden bridge. To the right is the unmarked North Forty Trail. The Forest Trail crosses a small bridge at 0.2 mile, reaches a T junction, and turns right. It passes two unmarked trails to the right and Post #8 to the left. Just beyond Post #10, it passes an unmarked trail to the right, which leads 100 yards to the North Forty Trail. At Post #12, it passes the Sylvia Stein Trail again and then an unmarked trail mentioned earlier. It ends behind the Manor House near animal cages.

North Forty Trail   *Length: 0.3 mile*

Access trails on both sides of the bridge near Woodfrog Pond join to become the North Forty Trail. At 0.1 mile, this trail reaches the fence at Scarsdale Golf Course and turns left to parallel it. It passes an unmarked trail to the right and then a second, both of which lead back to the Forest Trail (FT on white). The North Forty Trail reaches a fireplace to the right at the service road and ends. The Oak and Orchard Trail begins to the right, goes through the turtle nesting area, and ends at the entrance road at 0.2 mile.

DRIVING: Take northbound Central Avenue (Route 100) to Dromore Road, one mile north of Ardsley Road and across from 455 Scarsdale Plaza. Follow Dromore Road to the visitors parking lot.

PUBLIC TRANSPORTATION: Beeline Buses #20 and #21 from the last stop (Woodlawn Cemetery/Jerome Avenue) of the #4 subway line in the Bronx and get off at Dromore Road. From the business district in White Plains, get off at South Healy Avenue.

For contact information, see Appendix, Greenburgh Nature Center.

Halle Ravine Nature Preserve

Pine Terrace Preserve

Pound Ridge • 1.4 miles, 38 acres

Clichés such as exceptionally scenic or picturesque just begin to describe Halle Ravine Nature Preserve. The majestic trees, babbling brook, and ravine are both restful and invigorating when one walks along the unmarked paths. The steep-sided ravine keeps visitors, as well as the stream, on course. The ravine has old growth hemlocks, which unfortunately are being damaged by the woolly adelgid. The preserve also has hardwood forests and wetland habitats.

In 1928, Hiram Halle purchased the property because of the ravine. Halle was a conservationist, philanthropist, inventor, businessman, and part owner of the Gulf Oil Company. He was instrumental in attracting businesses and wealthy residents to Pound Ridge in the 1930s. In 1968, the Halle Properties Corporation sold the land to The Nature Conservancy which, in 2004, transferred the property to the Pound Ridge Land Conservancy, with the supporting conservation easement held by Westchester Land Trust.

There is only one trail at Halle Ravine Nature Preserve. But there are places where it splits and offers the option to either travel along the stream or look down

Halle Ravine

upon it. From the entrance, the trail is along a woods road. It passes a kiosk and then a trail on the left leading into the ravine. At a quarter-mile, where the woods road continues into private property, the trail heads down log steps into the ravine. When it reaches a T junction, turn right and follow the stream through the narrow ravine. At the next junction, go straight. The two segments join again at 0.5 mile at a T junction after crossing a bridge. Follow the stream that is to your right. The trail becomes narrower and less worn. At a brief steep ascent, cross a stone wall and enter a section of Pine Terrace Preserve. The trail leaves the ravine to ascend up to a loop around a high point, unfortunately without a view.

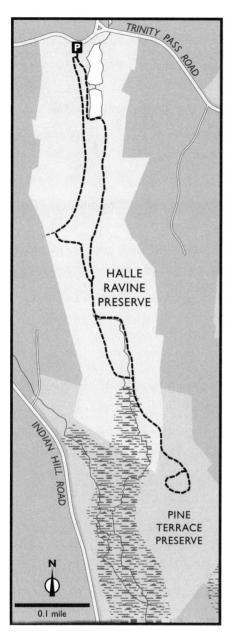

TRINITY PASS ROAD

P

HALLE
RAVINE
PRESERVE

INDIAN HILL ROAD

PINE
TERRACE
PRESERVE

N

0.1 mile

For the return trip, retrace your steps to descend the hill, then bear right whenever offered a choice, keeping the stream to your left. Follow the trail as it crosses a bridge and joins the original trail at the left fork at the Y junction. Go through the narrow portion of the ravine and, at the next intersection, cross the bridge to the right. Pass through another narrow portion of the ravine. After crossing the creek, head uphill on log steps with New York ferns lining both sides of the trail. The valley widens and the footpath becomes a woods road. Below, a small, but high, man-made dam is visible. At 1.8 miles, cross a larger dam on a stone bridge where knotted roots of a black birch drape over a portion of the dam. After passing the upper pond, continue uphill and, at 1.9 miles, reach the woods road near the kiosk.

DRIVING: From I-684, take Exit 4 (Route 172). Follow Route 172 through Bedford Village to Route 137 in Pound Ridge. Turn left onto Route 137 and turn north onto Route 124. At Trinity Pass Road, turn right. It is 0.7 mile to parking for 3-4 cars at a white gate, just before the intersection with Donbrook Road.

PUBLIC TRANSPORTATION: None available

For contact information, see Appendix, Pound Ridge Land Conservancy.

Horseman's Trail

Sleepy Hollow • 1.5 miles

In 1995, the Recreation and Parks Department of North Tarrytown (as Sleepy Hollow was then named), Historic Hudson Valley, and Sleepy Hollow Cemetery worked to build the Horseman's Trail, which connects two village parks, an historic cemetery, an historic site, and a state park. This trail is an example of how local groups can create an interesting walk in a town or village and connect open space via a road walk. It is also a section of the Hudson River Valley Greenway Trail.

HORSEMAN'S TRAIL

Beginning in Devries Park on the south side of the baseball field, the Horseman's Trail follows a chainlink fence and then parallels the Pocantico River. After rain the area is often wet, and muddy feet are unavoidable. The trail heads along a boardwalk, passing a fisherman's area. Turning right, it reaches the overflow parking lot for Philipsburg Manor at 0.2 mile. The Horseman's Trail turns left onto the walkway to Philipsburg Manor and passes through a gate behind the visitors center. The gate is locked from November through April and at times when the property is closed.

Cross the parking lot and turn left to head north on North Broadway (Route 9). To cross Broadway safely, use the crosswalk to reach the gates of Sleepy Hollow Cemetery at 0.6 mile. Inside the cemetery, follow Sleepy Hollow Avenue and turn right to cross the Pocantico River. Immediately after a bridge, turn right at a gate in the fence at 1.1 miles and enter woods. The path heads uphill along Sleepy Hollow Greenway to Douglas Park. Some side trails deadend at fishing spots on the river.

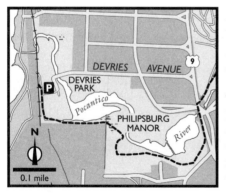

Walk north through Douglas Park, once part of Long View, the estate of William H. Douglas. During his lifetime, Douglas opened his property to friends and neighbors. Following his death in 1943, 17 acres became village parkland. This small park is the terminus of the Horseman's Trail and an additional point of access to the Old Croton Aqueduct. Gracing the park entrance are wrought iron gates; dedicated in October 2003, they were a gift of Giovanna Ceconi.

DRIVING: From northbound Route 9, pass the entrance to Philipsburg Manor and turn left onto Pierson Street, which becomes Bellwood Avenue. Turn left onto Devries Avenue, turn left ending in the park at a sign indicating the park is only for residents or by permit.

PUBLIC TRANSPORTATION: Metro-North Hudson Line Philipse Manor Station; Beeline Bus #13 along Route 9

For contact information, see Appendix, Sleepy Hollow.

Sleepy Hollow Cemetery

Sleepy Hollow • 87.5 acres

What do Samuel Gompers, Andrew Carnegie, Boyce Thompson, and Washington Irving have in common? These four men are among the more than 39,000 people who claim Sleepy Hollow Cemetery as their final resting place.

Vehicles move slowly through the grounds, which they do out of respect; however, it is mostly because the roads are narrow, winding, and twisty, particularly in older sections. Walkers have few worries about traffic and need only to decide where to walk and whom to visit. Dogs are permitted on leash.

A cemetery map is available at the office at the main gate and in a box at the south gate. The cemetery offers both daytime and evening tours. Advanced

Sleepy Hollow Cemetery

registration is required, and tickets are available for purchase online. The evening tour is a walk of about a mile. For more information, see www.sleepyhollowcemetery.org.

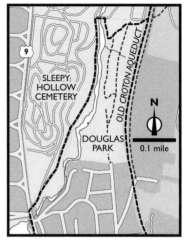

Mausoleums with ornamental trees are in the northern section of the cemetery. Sleepy Hollow Avenue parallels the Pocantico River; a walk along it provides a chance to enjoy flowing water as well as a break from looking at headstones. The modern cemetery is behind this area. Visitors are asked to respect services being held and those visiting graves.

The oldest section of the cemetery is adjacent to the Old Dutch Church of Sleepy Hollow, a separate not-for-profit. Both the church and the surrounding roughly three-acre burial ground are owned by the Reformed Church of Tarrytown, which still holds services there. This cemetery is the setting of Washington Irving's *Legend of Sleepy Hollow*. The characters in this story are not in the cemetery because they are fictitious. Friends of the Old Dutch Church offer free guided seasonal tours of the Old Dutch Burying Ground.

DRIVING: From northbound Route 9 in Tarrytown, head north toward Sleepy Hollow. The cemetery's south entrance is on the right just past Philipsburg Manor (an historic site). A walk-in gate is across the street from Palmer Avenue; the main gate is at the cemetery office 0.4 mile north of the south entrance. Parking is at the south entrance.

PUBLIC TRANSPORTATION: Metro-North Hudson Line Philipse Manor Station; walk east on Palmer Avenue, cross North Broadway, and enter the cemetery at the walk-in gate. Beeline Bus #13 runs along North Broadway.

For contact information, see Appendix, Sleepy Hollow Cemetery.

Juhring Estate

Dobbs Ferry • 1.2 mile, 47 acres

T ucked in behind a residential area and next to a golf course in Dobbs Ferry, the Juhring Estate–Shirley Elbert Memorial offers neighbors a pleasant place to walk. Although this former estate is near the Saw Mill River Parkway, little road noise penetrates the forest during leaf-on seasons.

Except for the occasionally marked yellow trail, all trails are unmarked, but an occasional old faded yellow blaze can be found. The 0.7-mile main trail crosses the property with a loop circling the park's high point. Side trails head off to roads, private property, or a party spot. Parking is only available at the Briary Road entrance, where a 0.1-mile entrance trail leads to the main trail.

DRIVING: From the Saw Mill River Parkway, take the Ashford Avenue Exit. Head west for 0.3 mile and turn right onto Briary Road to reach the entrance in 0.3 mile.

PUBLIC TRANSPORTATION: Beeline Bus #1C, 6, or 66 along Ashford Avenue to Briary Road. The park entrance is 0.3 mile uphill on Briary Road.

For contact information, see Appendix, Dobbs Ferry.

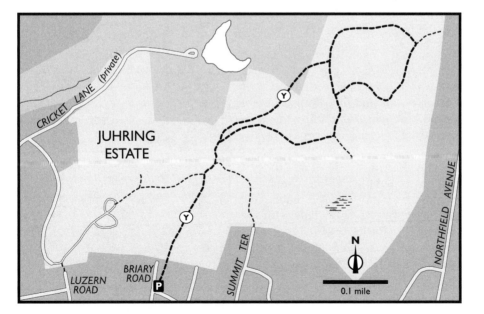

Koegel Park

Somers • 1.7 miles, 77 acres

A long curving driveway lined with stately trees is evidence that Koegel Park was once an estate. Although the pavement ends at a gate, the road obviously had once continued. Now called Green Way, it is a 30-foot-wide level, grassy path. At the end of Green Way is an open area with a chessboard table, so bring a friend and a chess set when you visit.

Tomahawk Chapel is adjacent to the park. The Putney family donated a half-acre plot on which the chapel was built in 1837 by Tom Miller, a local farmer. Many of the early residents of the area are interred in either the public burying ground to the west of the chapel or the Union Church Cemetery to the north.

TRAILS

A tiny network of trails wanders through mature upland forest with large deciduous trees. Koegel Park is at the top of a hill that slopes 140 feet down to the North County Trailway. Two short blue trails connect the red trail and the 0.2-mile Green Way, which in dry weather should be handicapped accessible. The park has a side trail to the North County Trailway, making longer hikes possible.

Red Trail   *Length: 0.7 mile Blaze: red*
Beginning at the signboard at the parking lot, the red trail leads into a picnic area on a wide woods road. It passes a blue trail which heads over to Green Way. It drifts downhill and, at 0.2 mile, passes a second blue trail also leading to Green Way. At 0.4 mile, the fence separating the park from the North County Trailway is in sight. Reaching a junction, the red trail turns right while the white trail continues straight. Heading uphill, the red trail reaches a T junction, with the white trail to the left. The red trail turns right, continues uphill to the parking lot, and ends beside the gate on Green Way.

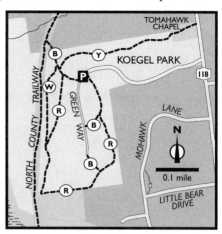

White Trail   *Length: 0.2 mile Blaze: white*

On a narrow path, the white trail parallels the fence along the North County Trailway. It reaches a blue trail to the left which leads 400 feet downhill to the North County Trailway. The white trail turns right and heads uphill. It passes the yellow trail to Tomahawk Chapel to the left before ending at the red trail.

Yellow Trail   *Length: 0.4 mile Blaze: yellow*

Beginning on the white trail, the yellow trail contours around the hill. It crosses stone walls and, at 0.3 mile, reaches a woods road behind houses. Passing between two cemeteries, the trail ends at Tomahawk Chapel.

CONNECTING TRAIL: North County Trailway

DRIVING: From the Taconic Parkway, take Route 6 east to Baldwin Place. Turn right onto Route 118 and go 1.3 miles to Koegel Park to the right.

PUBLIC TRANSPORTATION: Beeline Bus #16 or Putnam Area Rapid Transit (PART) to Somers Commons in Baldwin Place. Go to a small parking lot on the east side of the shopping center near Route 118. The entrance to the North County Trailway is on the far side of this parking lot. Turn right and head south on the trailway for a mile. To the left, shortly past a large rock, a paved path leads up to the blue trail in Koegel Park. (If you reach a bench on the right side of the trailway, you have gone too far and missed the path to the park.)

For contact information, see Appendix, Somers.

Larchmont Reservoir —
James G. Johnson, Jr. Conservancy

Wykagyl • 1.9 miles, 62 acres

Playing fowls or "fowl play" come to mind when visiting Larchmont Reservoir—James G. Johnson Jr. Conservancy. The reservoir and the surrounding land straddle the City of New Rochelle and the Town of Mamaroneck, but belong to the Village of Larchmont. The reservoir is a destination for birders.

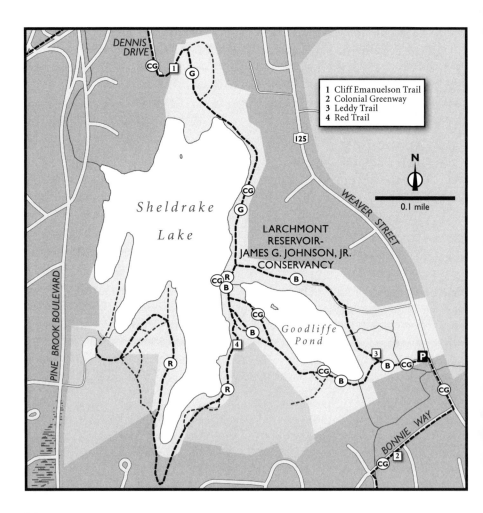

1 Cliff Emanuelson Trail
2 Colonial Greenway
3 Leddy Trail
4 Red Trail

HISTORY OF THE RESERVOIR

Playing fair, not foul, is the story of what is now known as the Reservoir and the merger of two organizations associated with it. A sawmill and grist mill were built along the Sheldrake River in the 1750s. By 1800, a cotton mill operated at the top of the falls above Garden Lake. In 1876, John T. Goodliffe constructed a dam to create a six-acre pond for his ice business. When Larchmont residents' wells became inadequate by the 1880s, the newly formed Larchmont Water Company purchased Goodliffe Pond, which was in New Rochelle, not Larchmont. Pipes were laid and water became available.

Flood control of the Sheldrake River and the need for more drinking water resulted in damming the river to create the Larchmont Reservoir. The first dam was completed in 1903, but by 1920, the reservoir could not supply enough water and a second dam had to be built. By the 1960s, as a consequence of increased pollution upstream, the water from Sheldrake Reservoir became too costly to purify. Because the Westchester Joint Waterworks supplied water to Mamaroneck and Harrison through the Delaware Aqueduct, a simple connection meant Larchmont could also buy water from the New York City system. By 1975, Larchmont no longer drew from the reservoir, which continued to be used for flood control.

With the reservoir closed, nature lovers still had an area to enjoy, although technically, entering the property was trespassing. However, other than nature lovers, Larchmont residents were not getting any benefit from the village's ownership of the reservoir. When the village board placed the property on the market in 1979, Local Involvement for Environment (LIFE) and Friends of the Reservoir opposed its sale. In 1984, the Larchmont Village Board dedicated the reservoir to be a conservation area in perpetuity. It was renamed the Larchmont Reservoir-James G. Johnson Jr. Conservancy.

LIFE and Friends of the Reservoir merged in 2001 to become the Sheldrake Environmental Center; a year later, the New York State Legislature approved the merger. Although its official name is Sheldrake Environmental Center, locally it is still referred to as The Reservoir.

TRAILS

Hikers should pay attention to the tags nailed to the trees, rather than the painted blazes remaining from the trail's previous locations and never removed. Because the trails are along the reservoir's shore, they are easy to follow. An all-terrain wheelchair is available upon request; contact the Engineer's Office, Village of Larchmont, 914-834-6210.

Leddy Trail   *Length: 0.6 mile Blaze: blue*

Longtime public works chief Tom Leddy was devoted to the Reservoir. A trail named in his honor circles Goodliffe Pond. The Leddy Trail and Colonial Greenway are co-aligned for 0.4 mile. From the parking lot off Weaver Street, the access trail crosses a stream and passes a kiosk on the way toward Goodliffe Pond. The access trail meets the Leddy Trail; turn left to go clockwise. The Leddy Trail passes a stone gatehouse, now converted to a bird blind. After passing a millstone to the

Goodliffe Pond

right, the trail follows the edge of the pond lined with stone blocks. At 0.1 mile, it heads up steps to a viewpoint and then over slab rock. Going downhill, the trail passes an unmarked trail leading to a private swim club. It heads along the shore of Goodliffe Pond and reaches a viewing platform at 0.3 mile. The Leddy Trail bears right, reaches a T junction at the base of the dam, and turns right. It crosses over the spillway on a wooden bridge. When the trail reaches the end of the dam, it turns right again. The Colonial Greenway continues straight. On a paved road, the Leddy Trail passes the Westchester Joint Waterworks, which pumps and treats water from the Delaware Aqueduct, and then the abandoned Larchmont Pump Station and Chemical Feed building.

At 0.5 mile, the LIFE Center Field Station is to the left; the former house of the reservoir superintendent is to the right where the Leddy Trail turns right to go downhill behind the house. On a wooden bridge it crosses Sheldrake River, the outflow from Goodliffe Pond. The Leddy Trail turns left to pass through a grove of trees and close the loop back at the kiosk.

Cliff Emanuelson Trail   *Length: 0.4 mile Blaze: green*
Named in 1998 for the environmental consultant who designed trails and bridges on the property in the mid-1970s, the Cliff Emanuelson Trail starts at the end of Dennis Drive. It passes a large stone structure resembling an extra large fireplace and heads downhill into the woods. At the bottom the trail splits, with an unmarked trail going left. At 0.1 mile, the trail crosses a wetland on a boardwalk. After passing an unmarked trail heading out to the edge of the shore, the trail passes the other ends of those unmarked trails.

The Cliff Trail goes downhill along the edge and through open areas with dense undergrowth of invasives. It passes homes overlooking the reservoir. At 0.3 mile, the trail heads to the right to follow the shore where numerous trails go out to the water's edge. It reaches the dam and heads down a ramp to the base where it ends at a junction with the Leddy and red trails as they turn onto the road toward Weaver Street.

Upper Red Trail   *Length: 0.7 mile Blaze: red*
Along the base of the dam, the red trail is co-aligned with the Leddy and Cliff trails. From the base of the dam, just south of the spillway, the red trail goes to the left up steps to the top of the dam. An unmarked trail to the right leads to a large rock overlooking the reservoir. The upper red trail continues more or less above the shore. It drops down to the shore at 0.3 mile to cross a bridge over an arm of the reservoir and then head back uphill. A rat's nest of trails with blazes of varying vintage crisscrosses the point. At 0.5 mile, the trail bears left at a Y junction and reaches steps down to the parking lot for New Rochelle tennis courts on Pinebrook Boulevard, where it ends. A 0.1-mile extension starts at the Lower Trail sign and passes a rock cliff to the left. It ends at the fence enclosing a protected area for nesting water fowl.

Colonial Greenway   *Length: 0.7 mile Blaze: blue with a white star*
Entering the property at the parking area on Weaver Street (Route 125), the Colonial Greenway is co-aligned with the Leddy Trail (blue) for 0.4 mile. It leaves the Leddy Trail at the base of the dam where it joins the Cliff Emanuelson Trail (green) to Dennis Drive. It is a 0.6-mile road walk to Ward Acres Park. At the end of Dennis Drive, cross Quaker Ridge Road, and turn left to follow the sidewalk. Turn right onto Broadfield Road to reach the entrance of Ward Acres Park across from William Ward Elementary School.

CONNECTING TRAILS & NEARBY PARK: Colonial Greenway, Leatherstocking Trail, Ward Acres Park

DRIVING: From the southbound Hutchinson River Parkway, take Exit 20 (Route 125) and turn left onto Route 125. *It is 0.7 mile from the traffic light at Hutchinson Avenue to Quaker Ridge Road on the right, and another 0.6 mile to the parking lot entrance on the right just past the Sheldrake Environmental Center sign. If northbound, take Exit 21 and turn right onto Hutchinson Avenue. At Weaver Street (Route 125), turn left and follow the directions from *.

PUBLIC TRANSPORTATION: None available

For contact information, see Appendix, Sheldrake Environmental Center.

Montrose Point State Forest

Montrose • 1.2 miles, 50 acres

Your eyes are not playing tricks on you when you see the New York State DEC sign for Montrose Point State Forest. Somehow a state forest seems out of place in heavily populated Westchester County. However, unlike other state forests, Montrose Point does not allow camping or hunting.

This state forest was once the site of the Montrose Brick Company; the land was heavily excavated for clay, and little soil was left in the raw clay pits. The exposed black rocks are igneous rocks which are part of the Cortlandt Complex and rarely seen on the earth's surface. In 2000, the former brickyard was purchased by the Trust for Public Land (TPL) and turned over to the New York State Department of Environmental Conservation. The following year, TPL purchased a conservation easement on adjacent property owned by the Kolping Society, a Catholic educational and action-oriented organization. In addition to protecting the Kolping Society property from being developed, the easement allows public access to the state forest from Montrose Point Road.

TRAILS

A part of RiverWalk, this small trail system wiggles its way through the woods to interesting destinations and views of the river. Bittersweet and honeysuckle vines cling to trees; there is dense wineberry and multiflora rose undergrowth.

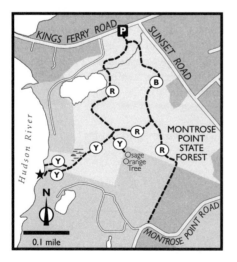

Red Trail

Length: 0.7 mile Blaze: red

Just past the kiosk at the parking area, the red trail turns right to head along an embankment. The trail descends to a bridge and then rounds the inlet. It crosses a second bridge and switchbacks uphill, turning away from the river. After reaching a seasonal view of the river, the trail heads downhill and turns left onto a woods road. At 0.3 mile at a T junction, it turns left, and the yellow trail is to the right. It reaches another

T junction and turns right. The blue trail to the left is a return route to the kiosk and parking. After crossing a bridge, the red trail goes uphill. It crosses a wetland on a 100-foot bridge, and enters Kolping Society property. Now on dry land, the trail passes through the easement, delineated by split rail fencing. The red trail crosses a driveway and reaches Montrose Point Road (no parking). Turn right and walk 0.2 mile along the road to George's Island Park.

Barrel-arch bridge

Blue Trail   *Length: 0.2 mile Blaze: blue*
Beginning at the kiosk at the entrance, the blue trail is a shortcut to Montrose Point Road. The blue trail leaves to the left and crosses three bridges before ending at a junction with the red trail at 0.2 mile.

Yellow Trail   *Length: 0.3 mile Blaze: yellow*
Almost immediately after beginning at the red trail, the yellow trail reaches a trail junction. Just ahead, a branch of the yellow trail goes over a barrel arch brick bridge and ends in 225 feet at a massive Osage orange tree, a species usually found growing farther south. To the right, the trail crosses a bridge, hugs a stone face covered with moss, and reaches a Y junction. The yellow trail to the right heads through a wet area and ends at a brick beach. The left branch of the yellow trail ends at a view of the Hudson River, the brick beach, and a marina.

CONNECTING PARK: George's Island Park

DRIVING: From Route 9, take the Route 9A/Montrose Exit and head north. Just past Roosevelt Veterans Hospital to the left, turn left onto Dutch Street. Go 0.6 mile to Sunset Road, turn right, and continue 0.9 mile to end at Kings Ferry Road. Turn left and head 100 feet to parking

PUBLIC TRANSPORTATION: None available

For contact information, see Appendix, New York State Department of Environmental Conservation.

Onatru Farm Park and Preserve

Vista • 1.9 miles, 101 acres

A large white farmhouse greets visitors to Onatru Farm Park and Preserve. Alice Lane Poor donated the property with house and outbuildings to the Town of Lewisboro because she wished to preserve the farming atmosphere of Lewisboro. Onatru is a nonsense word derived from "on a true farm"; it was made up by Mrs. Poor's father, Edward Lane. The farm fields are now ball fields, and the woodlands behind them are the park part of Mrs. Poor's gift. The woodlands across the street form the preserve. The farmhouse serves as a town office building.

TRAILS

The two blue-blazed trails in the park and in the preserve are on opposite sides of Elmwood Road. Both trails have sections that may be inaccessible in wet weather. Camping, with some restrictions and a permit, is allowed at the preserve. Applications are available through the Town Clerk's office, 914-763-3511.

Blue Trail (Farm Park)   *Length: 1.1 miles Blaze: blue*
Start from behind the buildings in the southeast corner of the furthest parking area. Follow Alice Lane to where the blue trail begins to the left at the second opening in a stone wall. The trail enters a former farm field, follows the edge, and turns left

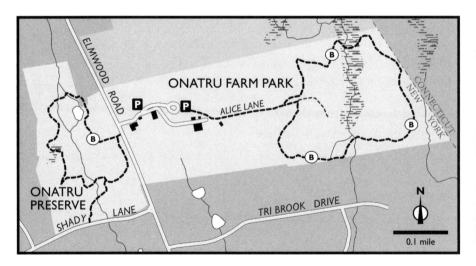

Alice Lane

at the corner of the field. About two-thirds of the way along the edge of the field, at 0.2 mile, the trail turns right to enter the woods. Check carefully here, the turn blaze is hard to see. As the trail winds its way through woodland and wetland, it crosses several streams. Crossing a wetland at 0.4 mile necessitates hopping from hummock to hummock. The trail heads uphill and wanders through the woods. At a stream crossing, hikers will again have to step from rock to rock and from hummock to hummock to keep their feet dry. At 0.9 mile, the blue trail goes through a hemlock grove and a Norway spruce grove, with a high chainlink fence and a baseball field on the other side of a stone wall. The trail reaches Alice Lane, turns left, and closes the loop at the starting point.

Blue Trail (Preserve)   *Length: 0.7 mile Blaze: blue*
In the preserve portion of Onatru Farm, the access trail starts almost directly across the street from the former farmhouse. Trees are labeled, including a log of a long-dead American chestnut. The trail crosses a field and enters the woods on a woods road. Turning right, it heads uphill and begins to wander through the woods, passing a man-made pond to the left. After crossing several streams, it turns left at 0.3 mile, passing several red oak trees growing together. The trail reaches a large sassafras tree, turns, and crosses a stone wall to enter a wetland at 0.5 mile. Before the trail climbs steeply uphill, there is a trail junction. Straight ahead, a spur heads 0.1 mile to end just west of #26 Shady Lane. To the left, the trail ascends steeply. It enters a field, passes a kiosk at 0.6 mile, and closes the loop at Elmwood Road.

NEARBY PARKS: Levy Preserve, Old Church Preserve

DRIVING: From I-684, take Exit 6 (Route 35) and turn east. Follow Route 35 for 9.1 miles and, just before the New York-Connecticut line, turn right at the traffic light onto Route 123. Continue south for 1.9 miles and turn left onto Shady Lane. At the T junction with Elmwood Road, turn left. Onatru Farm Park is to the right, 0.1 mile.

PUBLIC TRANSPORTATION: None available

For contact information, see Appendix, Lewisboro.

Reis Park

Somers • 1.8 miles, 80 acres ♿ 🚫 🚫 🚫 ⛷

The Somers Library, playground, and tennis courts greet visitors arriving in Reis Park. Further into the park are ball fields, with trails skirting their perimeters. The park is a bequest to the Town of Somers from Carolyn Wright-Reis, who died in 1967, leaving her property to the town. It was her wish that the land would be used for a park with space for a library.

TRAILS

The simple trail system at Reis Park effectively uses a small area to provide three trails with portions of a fitness course along each one. The gravel surface makes for easy jogging and walking. All three trails can be reached from the top of the wooden steps at the near end of the parking lot just past the ball field to the left. At the top of the steps, the first trail to the right is the yellow trail, the red trail is 30 feet further, and the blue trail is 40 feet beyond the red. The trails are all marked. Many short trails connect the parallel marked trails. Each of the three trails has stations for an advanced timber challenge course. To visit every one of the stations, it is necessary to walk all three trails.

A 0.3-mile trail connects the ball fields adjacent to the Somers Library to the soccer field at Van Tassel Park and Primrose School. For most of its length, its surface is crushed stone; it is handicapped accessible only from the soccer field to the edge of the field at Primrose School.

Yellow Trail   *Length: 0.7 mile Blaze: yellow*
The only complete loop, the yellow trail begins to the right from a grassy strip at the top of the wooden steps. Going counterclockwise, the trail gradually turns left through a forest with little understory. At 0.3 mile, the yellow trail heads downhill into an area with more shrubs and small trees. The red trail enters from the left at 0.6 mile and together they cross the mowed lawn around the end of the parking lot. The yellow trail crosses the road leading to the composting area, reaches the path from the parking lot at 0.7 mile, and closes the loop.

Blue Trail   *Length: 0.3 mile Blaze: blue*
The blue trail turns into open woods, with the red trail visible to the right. Slowly the understory changes and becomes denser. At 0.2 mile, the trail turns to parallel a stone wall. The red trail joins from the right; the two trails are co-aligned and

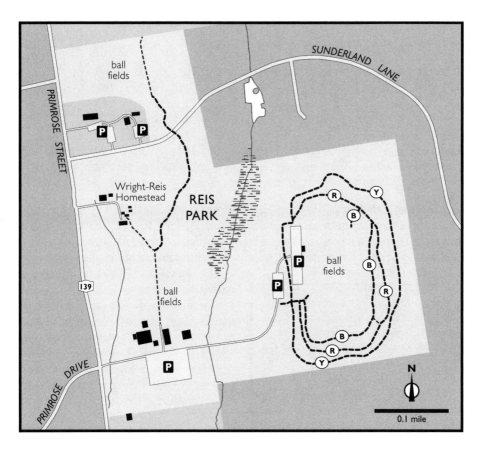

then split, with the blue trail turning left to end at the ball fields at 0.3 mile.

Red Trail

Length: 0.5 mile Blaze: red

The red trail parallels a stone wall on a woods road. Where the surface of the woods road becomes gravel, the trail turns and crosses the stone wall. It crosses exposed bedrock and heads downhill on dirt, only to change back to gravel. At 0.3 mile, the blue trail joins from the left and the path widens. The red trail meets and joins the yellow trail at 0.5 mile.

DRIVING: From I-684, take Exit 6 (Route 35) and go west to Route 100. Turn right and head north for 0.6 mile. Turn left at Route 139 and go 1.4 miles to the park entrance to the right. Drive past the library, playground, and tennis courts to the end of the road. Park at the first opportunity and head up the steps.

PUBLIC TRANSPORTATION: None available

For contact information, see Appendix, Somers.

Frederick P. Rose Nature Preserve
Rockshelter Preserve

Waccabuc • 1.8 miles, 105 acres

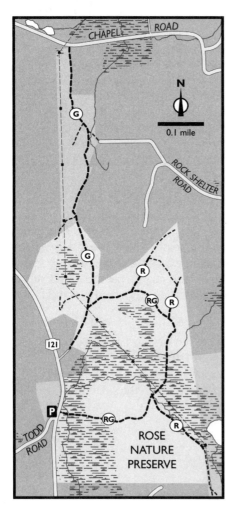

Near the entrance to the Rose Nature Preserve on North Salem Road (Route 121), large cinnamon ferns in the wetland create a primordial appearance. A visitor might half expect a pterodactyl to fly by or a brontosaurus to lift its head. But that impression quickly fades when the terrain changes to mixed hardwood forest with a grassy understory and later to mature hardwood forest.

The preserve is named in honor of the late Frederick P. Rose, head of one of New York City's oldest construction and real estate management firms. A philanthropist, he supported Yale University and the arts and music in New York City. He and his wife also funded the Rose Center for Earth and Science at the American Museum of Natural History. Their youngest son, Adam, donated 20 acres adjacent to several parcels of sensitive wetlands and hilly woods to prevent fragmentation of valuable habitat.

Green Trail
Length: 1.3 miles Blaze: green
From the entrance opposite Todd Road, the green trail winds through extensive wetlands. Even though the trail is on a raised roadbed, after heavy rain the trail might be impassable. The trail continues along a woods road, reaches a chainlink fence, and turns left at 0.2 mile. Ahead, an open upland field provides habitat and hunting grounds for red-tailed hawks and other raptors. Just before the trail crosses a stone bridge, red Lewisboro Horsemen's Association

Wetlands

(LHA) blazes appear on trees along with the green ones. Equestrians from adjacent property use these trails.

The green-red trail goes under a power line on a wooden bridge. It enters woods to head through an area with dense barberry understory. Crossing another stream, the trail heads uphill through open woods and then descends. At 0.4 mile, it passes rectangular open pits, with a mound of dirt beside each. These percolation test sites indicate that at one time this area had been considered for development.

After descending, the trail crosses a stream and reaches a Y junction. Ahead a red-blazed trail leads 0.1 mile to end at the property boundary near a private home. Turning left, the green-red trail continues on a woods road and crosses a stream at 0.6 mile. At a T junction, a red trail to the right leads to private property. There is a 0.1-mile trail which connects the two red trails. Heading left, the green-red trail reaches another T junction at 0.7 mile. To the left, an unmarked trail passes under the power line to reach the preserve sign at the end of a driveway. It is 0.1 mile along the driveway to Route 121; parking at Todd Road is 0.1 mile to the left.

To the right, the trail, now with only green blazes, is along a woods road. It passes stone walls and rock outcroppings while paralleling the power line. At 1.1 miles, it enters Rockshelter Preserve where a 200-foot trail leads to Rock Shelter Road (a private road, no parking). The green trail reaches a paved driveway at 1.2 miles and follows it to end at Chapel Road at 1.3 miles.

NEARBY PARKS: Five Ponds Trail, Long Pond Preserve, Old Field Preserve, Pine Croft Meadow

DRIVING: From I-684 take Exit 6 (Route 35) and go east for 4.3 miles to a traffic light where Route 121 turns left to leave Route 35. Follow northbound Route 121 for 1.6 miles to the intersection with Todd Road. Parking for 2 cars is on the north side of the intersection. The entrance is across the street.

Another access point, 0.1 mile farther north on Route 121, is through a shared driveway for #191 and #195. A third access point is up the driveway of 90 Chapel Road, immediately past the power line (no parking).

PUBLIC TRANSPORTATION: None available

For contact information, see Appendix, Westchester Land Trust.

White Plains Greenway

White Plains • 1.2 miles, 21.3 acres

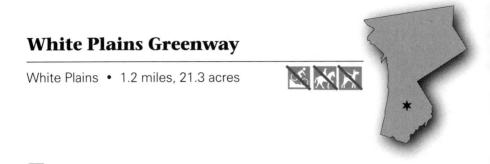

Even without a track, signal, or sign in sight, there is no doubt that the White Plains Greenway is on a former railroad right-of-way. Between 1912 and 1937, the New York, Westchester & Boston Railway went from Port Chester and White Plains to Mount Vernon, where the two lines joined and continued to 133rd Street in the Bronx. The railroad was part of the New York, New Haven and Hartford Railroad Company, purchased because the company's president was adverse to competition.

THE GREENWAY

From Gedney Way, the White Plains Greenway heads south on a deep layer of wood chips. At 0.1 mile, the trail curves to join what initially looks as if it might have been the railbed. However, the pathway continues to twist and turn through

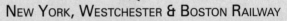

NEW YORK, WESTCHESTER & BOSTON RAILWAY

From the beginning, the New York, Westchester & Boston Railroad had financial and logistical problems. Filling in gullies and wetlands, cutting through rocks and hills, and building embankments, bridges, retaining walls, and viaducts contributed to the high cost of constructing the railroad. In addition, elaborate stations were constructed, not merely hastily built wooden sheds. Passengers had to transfer to a el into Manhattan because the trains did not go as far as Grand Central Terminal. The line did not own freight cars or carry much freight. Debt, too few passengers, and heavy investment meant that the line was not paying its way. The financial difficulties of the Depression made the situation worse, and rail service ended on December 31, 1937.

Even after the line shut down, it was hoped that service could eventually be restored. Those hopes were dashed when demand for scrap metal during World War II resulted in the removal of remaining wire gantries and tracks. Slowly and steadily, other features were removed or lost their identity. Underpasses along the route were filled in. Stations either found new uses or were razed. The railbed was built upon or became a parkway. In 2008, a few existing portions of the railbed could still be found in Nature Study Woods, Ward Acres, and White Plains Greenway. Using local maps and gathering knowledge of the railroad's exact route, it is possible to trace the line.

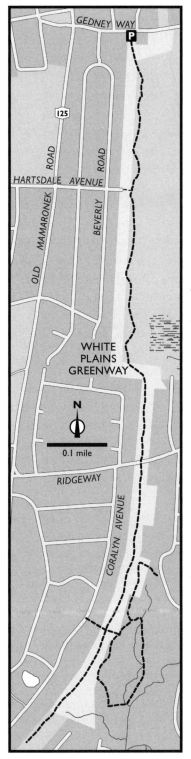

the woods amidst invasive vegetation including large patches of pachysandra, escaped from neighboring gardens. To the right at 0.3 mile, the Greenway passes a side trail heading out to Hartsdale Avenue. The Greenway turns right at 0.6 mile onto what was obviously the railbed. Continuing at-grade and above the wetlands, it passes the first of several concrete bases which had supported the electrical lines for the railroad. At 0.7 mile it heads downhill to cross Ridgeway. Abutments for a long-gone bridge loom overhead and there is an interpretive sign.

At the site of the former Ridgeway Station, concrete footings that once supported the station platform line the wide path. The trail is high above houses to the right, with woodlands to the left. It crosses an underpass, now filled in. Just before a second underpass at 1.0 mile, a path to the right leads down a trail out to Coralyn Avenue and to a path which goes through the underpass. At the other end of the underpass, a trail with red spray paint blazes runs along the base of the railbed embankment. Although it appears at the intersection that the trail makes a 0.5-mile loop with blazes going in both directions, the clockwise blazes soon stop. The Greenway's wood chip path continues along the high embankment. It ends abruptly at 1.2 miles at the Scarsdale-White Plains town line, where brush and wet soil fill a rock cut. A filled-in overpass at Reynal Crossing is barely visible.

DRIVING: From I-287, take the Bloomingdale Road Exit and turn left onto Bloomingdale Road, which becomes Mamaroneck Avenue. After passing Burke Rehabilitation Center to the left, turn right onto Gedney Way. Continue two blocks and cross a bridge. An entrance sign faces the road on the south side of the street.

PUBLIC TRANSPORTATION: Beeline Bus #60 on Mamaroneck Avenue and walk two blocks west on Gedney Way; Beeline Bus #63 on Route 125 (Old Mamaroneck Road) and walk two blocks east on Gedney Way.

For contact information, see Appendix, White Plains.

Marshlands Conservancy

SECTION III

MORNING STROLLS

- ◆ Have two to three miles of trails
- ◆ Provide more choice of trails
- ◆ Offer an hour or more of walking or hiking
- ◆ Are within a 10-15 minute drive

Burden Preserve

Mt. Kisco • 2.4 miles, 124 acres

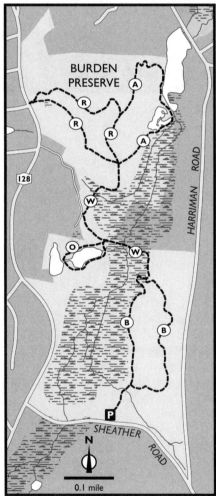

Variety is the word to describe Burden Preserve. Six ecosystems are packed into this 124-acre preserve: wetland, pond, stream, meadow, upland forest, and rock outcropping. With the variety of habitats, there are many opportunities for birding. The trails are laid out so that a hiker frequently passes from one habitat to another.

The Burden Preserve was once part of the estate of William A. M. Burden (1906-1984), an aviation finance consultant whose public service included a stint as U.S. ambassador to Belgium (1959-1961). In 2004, after a plan to build affordable housing failed when Mt. Kisco would not permit a development to connect to its sewage system, the Town of New Castle purchased the land. When New Castle acquired 12 acres to connect the pieces, it opened the preserve in 2008.

TRAILS

Extensive wetlands greet a hiker soon after entering Burden Preserve. Following wet weather, expect this area to be especially waterlogged, with lots of rivulets. The trail system is such that a hiker rarely has to retrace steps.

Blue Trail

Length: 0.7 mile Blaze: blue
From the parking area on Sheather Road, the blue trail passes a kiosk and heads into the wetlands along a path delineated by logs. At an intersection, turn left to follow the loop clockwise along the log-lined path. When necessary to protect wetland, the pathway is crushed stone.

The trail briefly follows a fence-line before reaching a T junction with the white trail at 0.4 mile. Turning right, it heads into the woods, goes uphill, and passes a cement structure and then a stone foundation. The blue trail gradually turns, reenters the wetlands, and closes the loop at 0.7 mile.

Aqua Trail   *Length: 0.5 mile Blaze: aqua*
Beginning on the red trail, just below the top of the hill, the aqua trail crosses a stone wall on a narrow path. Initially flat, it soon heads steeply downhill, descending even more steeply on a series of switchbacks. When the trail reaches a pond, it turns right to follow the shore, sometimes more closely than at others. The trail heads away from the pond along the berm of a breached dam. It turns away from the dam and former pond to end at the white trail at 0.5 mile.

Orange Trail   *Length: 0.2 mile Blaze: orange*
At the beginning of its clockwise circle of a pond, the orange trail passes an expanse of horsetails (*Equisetum*) which looks like a large green hair brush. The trail turns to pass another pond and continues to turn until, at 0.2 mile, it closes the loop.

Red Trail   *Length: 0.6 mile Blaze: red*
At the end of the white trail at a stone wall, the red trail heads left to cross a field. Following a wide path, it reaches a kiosk and a 100-foot trail to the intersection of Route 128 and Horseshoe Circle. The red trail turns, passes a stone foundation, and heads uphill along a path lined with multiflora rose and barberry bushes. Ascending more steeply, it goes over rock slabs to pass through a grove of large old red cedars. Immediately, the trail heads downhill, passing the aqua trail to the

left. The trunks of slender trees to the right are spattered with lichen. After passing through parallel stone walls, the red trail reaches the white trail and closes the loop.

White Trail
Length: 0.4 mile Blaze: white
From the junction with the blue trail, the white trail continues through the wetland. It turns at the end of cement fence posts and crosses a stream on a stone bridge. The white trail reaches an intersection with the orange trail and turns right. At 0.3 mile, the trail skirts the edge of a field and heads uphill, passing several scotch pines. After crossing a stone wall, it enters a second field. The trail ends with the red trail to the left and straight ahead. The aqua trail is to the right.

Lichen

DRIVING: From the Saw Mill River Parkway northbound, take Exit 34 (NY 133) and turn right onto Route 133 (West Main Street) towards Mt. Kisco. Southbound, take Exit 36 (Croton Avenue), turn left onto Croton Avenue, and then left again onto Route 133 towards Mount Kisco. It is 0.3 mile to the light at South Moger Avenue, just past the railroad tracks. Turn right onto South Moger Avenue (which shortly becomes Lexington Avenue) and, at 1.4 miles, cross Route 117. It is 0.8 mile to a left turn onto Sheather Road. Drive 0.1 mile to the parking area to the left.

PUBLIC TRANSPORTATION: None available

For contact information, see Appendix, New Castle.

Buttermilk Ridge Park
Glenville Woods Park Preserve
Tarrytown Lakes Park

Tarrytown, Eastview • 4.8 miles

Although Tarrytown Lakes Park, Buttermilk Ridge Park, and Glenville Woods Park Preserve are connected like beads on a string, they are quite different. Buttermilk Ridge Park is a linear path on a ridge that parallels the Saw Mill River Parkway. Glenville Woods Park Preserve, a former quarry and nursery, was part of a property slated for development. Tarrytown Lakes Park is a paved former right-of-way of the Putnam Division of the New York Central Railroad. The North County and South County trailways are near the first and last parks. Because Hackley School is responsible for the welfare of its students, please honor their request that its trails and grounds are closed to the public.

Buttermilk Ridge Park

Eastview • 2.3 miles, 114 acres

Long and narrow, county-owned Buttermilk Ridge Park parallels the Saw Mill River Parkway, whose noise is usually present. Stonework gracing the white trail dates from the 1930s. Mountain bikes are allowed on Buttermilk Ridge; unfortunately, some bikers consider it necessary to leave their mark in the woods and have spray painted routes on adjacent private property.

The white trail on Buttermilk Ridge begins near the road just before the gate at the base of the dam at Tarrytown Lake. It crosses a drainage ditch, heads steeply uphill, and crosses a former railbed. To the left, the railbed leads 0.1 mile to overlook the Saw Mill Parkway, which until 1931, it crossed. At 0.1 mile, the Buttermilk Ridge Trail turns to parallel the parkway below and then descends to it. The trail is not defined as it crosses a grassy area adjacent to the parkway. Just as the grassy area narrows, the trail heads into the woods. It reaches a built-to-grade road and, at 0.3 mile, heads downhill, along a road with wood posts that at one time supported guardrails. The posts stand like a sheaf of toothpicks for Paul Bunyan. The Buttermilk Ridge Trail reaches a height of land and then heads downhill once more. On another built-to-grade section, the trail crosses a small stream with a waterfall to the right, at 0.5 mile. The Buttermilk Ridge Trail reaches a stone belvedere (overlook) and then a section of stone pillars with wood railings, many of which have rotted away and left gaping holes in the pillars. At the end of these pillars, a stream passes under the stonework as the trail continues its ascent. It reaches the top of a rise at 0.8 mile and then heads downhill to reach a second belvedere, where WCPS 1933 is inscribed into one of the stones.

The trail continues through open forests often at-grade. At 1.1 miles, it passes a short unmarked trail leading 60 feet to the right to the trails in Glenville Woods. After passing over a stream, the trail is on a raised bed with stonework to the right. It ascends the hill via switchbacks, reaches a water tower at 1.6 miles, turns left, and descends. The white trail on Buttermilk Ridge ends at a woods road near a high tension power line.

The belvedere

PAUL MECK

DRIVING: From the Saw Mill River Parkway, take the Eastview Exit. Turn west toward the park-and-ride lot on the north side of the road. The white trail begins across the street, near the trail up to the dam.

PUBLIC TRANSPORTATION: None available

For contact information, see Appendix, Westchester County Parks.

Glenville Woods Park Preserve

Tarrytown • 1.5 miles, 37.5 acres

The Glenville Community Association, a neighborhood activist organization, worked to prevent what is now Glenville Woods Park Preserve from being developed. Without its intervention, a narrow right-of-way next to houses would have become a busy access road. The Town of Greenburgh, Trust for Public Land, and Open Space Institute negotiated with the Ginsburg Development Corporation and as a result, only 86 housing units were permitted to be built. In February 2001, the property was finally protected when the Town of Greenburgh, Open Space Institute, New York State, Westchester County, and private donations from the Glenville Community Association purchased the remaining property.

The Town of Greenburgh is developing this park so that a visitor heads further into the park, the more remote it seems. Dense vegetation and the hill block noise from I-287 and the Saw Mill River Parkway, adding to a feeling of remoteness. Part of Glenville Woods was once a nursery. Leaf duff has accumulated, almost covering the paved roads still lined with curbing. Some left-over nursery stock, including rhododendrons and leafy maples, tower over former roads.

Orange Trail   *Length: 0.6 mile Blaze: orange*

From the parking area on Old White Plains Road, the orange trail crosses an impressive rustic footbridge and rock faces which were quarried years ago. The wide gravel path parallels the bottom of the hill, eventually becoming a narrow footpath. It passes what was likely the blasting shack and heads uphill at 0.3 mile. After crossing a stream on a stone bridge, the trail continues uphill and heads into the former nursery. At a Y junction at 0.5 mile, the yellow trail begins to the left. The orange trail continues to the right through the former nursery. At 0.6 mile, it passes the other end of the yellow trail and then an opening in a stone wall to the right, where an unmarked path leads 60 feet to the white trail on Buttermilk Ridge. The orange trail ends where heavy vegetation blocks the trail.

Yellow Trail   *Length: 0.2 mile Blaze: yellow*

Beginning at the junction with the orange trail, the yellow trail makes a short loop through the former nursery. Leading off the yellow trail is a network of unmarked trails along the former nursery roads. One trail leads to the Bayer Corporation

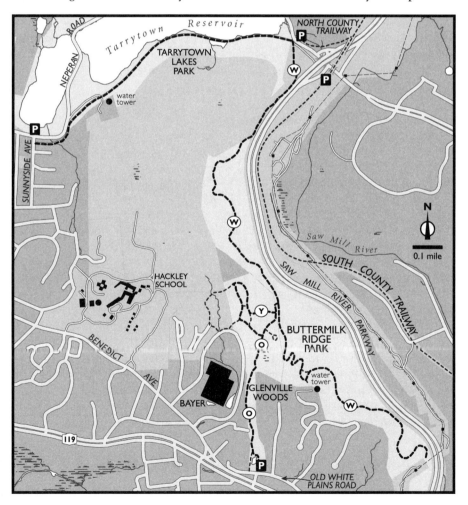

parking lot to provide park access for its employees, while another trail heads 0.4 mile to condominiums.

DRIVING: From the Saw Mill River Parkway, take the Route 119 Exit and head west. Turn right onto Dunnings Drive (across from 660 White Plains Road) and immediately turn right onto Old White Plains Road. Parking is to the left, next to the playground.

PUBLIC TRANSPORTATION: Beeline Bus #13 stops on Route 119, across from the parking lot.

For contact information, see Appendix, Greenburgh.

Tarrytown Lakes Park

Eastview • 1.0 mile, 21 acres

Sometimes referred to as the Tarrytown bike path, Tarrytown Lakes Park provides an easy walk with lake views in leaf-off season. From the gate by the building below the reservoir dam, the trail goes uphill for a short distance before leveling off. It passes a bench and then the first of four quarter-mile markers. After crossing the access road to the water tank, the pathway approaches Neperan Road. Although the former railbed is across the street and not the route of the paved path, the road crossing has poor line of sight and should not be used. The paved path curves left, parallels the road, and passes through a white pine grove. The path here is littered with pine needles, cushioning the pavement and making a quiet, soft footing. The path ends at Sunnyside Avenue at 1.0 mile.

MOVING A RAILROAD

This right-of-way was part of the Putnam Division as it passed through the Rockefeller estate. John D. Rockefeller, Jr. tired of the noise and soot of the locomotives; so in 1930 he paid to relocate the railroad, eliminating stops at Tarrytown Heights, Tower Hill, and Pocantico Hills. A new stop, Graham, was added. When the project was completed in May, 1931, 150 families had been displaced.

DRIVING: From the Saw Mill River Parkway, take the Eastview Exit. Turn west toward the park-and-ride lot on the north side of the road to park. The bike path begins across the street, just past the gate to the dam of the reservoir. Alternately, from Route 9 in Tarrytown, take Neperan Road 0.7 mile to the parking lot overlooking the reservoir. The bike path begins at the intersection of Neperan Road and Sunnyside Avenue.

PUBLIC TRANSPORTATION: None available

For contact information, see Appendix, Westchester County Parks.

Franklin-Fels Nature Sanctuary

North Salem • 2.7 miles, 204 acres

Don't be surprised to see equestrians on the trails at Franklin-Fels Nature Sanctuary. Nearby horse farms use the trail system to reach other farms. Consisting of deciduous woodlands, red maple swamp, and shrub swamp, the sanctuary offers easy walking, except for a portion of the blue trail. Tucked into a residential neighborhood, it is the perfect place for morning birding or an evening walk.

TRAILS

The trail system consists of a main loop, a side loop, and a shortcut. Many unmarked woods roads lead into private property and provide equestrian access. Two short

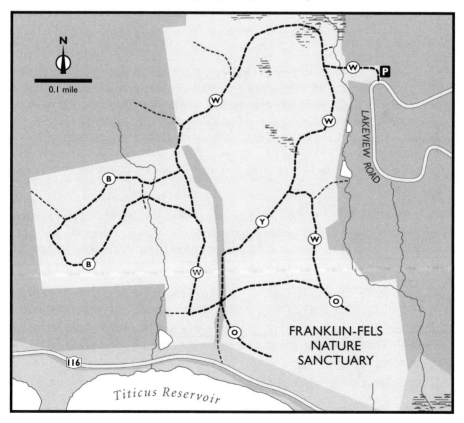

orange trails totaling 0.2 mile head to the sanctuary's edge.

White Trail   *Length: 1.6 miles Blaze: white*

Beginning at Lakeview Road, the white trail heads 0.1 mile through wetlands beside a huge stone wall and on puncheon to a bridge. It reaches a T junction with a woods road and the beginning of a loop. Turn left to go clockwise around the loop. The white trail crosses a stream on a causeway at 0.3 mile and heads left at 0.4 mile, where the yellow trail goes straight ahead. When the white trail makes a right turn, an unmarked trail leads left into private property. The white trail makes another right turn. Straight ahead an orange trail ends in the woods.

The white trail passes the other end of the yellow trail to the right at a five-way intersection at 0.8 mile. The leftmost trail is an orange trail which heads southeast to end at a wooden platform. To the right of the orange trail is an unmarked trail which goes downhill to Route 116. The white trail continues straight ahead and turns right at the next intersection, where an unmarked trail leads to private property. The white trail climbs steadily uphill, reaching the blue trail to the left at 1.0 mile. In 350 feet, it passes the other end of the blue trail, a well-used equestrian trail. Continuing uphill, just before and just after curving around the base of a large rock outcropping, the white trail passes to the left two more unmarked trails into private property. An unmarked woods road with heavy equestrian traffic heads left to a stream in the wetlands. The white trail closes the loop at 1.6 miles when it reaches the junction with the entrance trail.

Blue Trail   *Length: 0.7 mile Blaze: blue*

From the west side of the white trail loop, beside a stone wall, the blue trail on a narrow path is easy to miss. It crosses a stream and then immediately a woods road which connects to the other leg of the blue trail. Heading uphill steeply, it reaches a second woods road, turns left onto it, and immediately leaves to the right. At 0.3 mile, the blue trail goes over a rock outcropping with seasonal views of the reservoir. Continuing to head uphill, it curves away from the reservoir, reaches an equestrian trail along a woods road, and turns right. To the left, a woods road leads to private property, while the blue trail continues downhill, passes the woods road, and ends at the white trail.

Yellow Trail   *Length: 0.2 mile Blaze: yellow*

A shortcut across the white trail, the yellow trail heads southwest and goes downhill. After heading slightly uphill, it turns left to pass between two broken-down parallel stone walls to end at the white trail.

DRIVING: From northbound I-684, take Exit 8 (Hardscrabble Road) and turn right. From southbound I-684, take Exit 8, turn right, cross over I-684, and head east. Follow Hardscrabble Road for 2.4 miles and turn right onto Delancy Road. Continue 0.6 mile to Lakeview Road to the right. Parking for two cars is to the right, opposite #23.

PUBLIC TRANSPORTATION: None available

For contact information, see Appendix, Bedford Audubon.

Glazier Arboretum

Chappaqua • 2.2 miles, 48 acres

The long, narrow trail system in Glazier Arboretum offers opportunities to take either short or long hikes in a valley or along a ridge. Well-trod paths along the blue and red trails verify that Glazier Arboretum is a popular place to walk. On a mild, sunny winter day, hikers and dogs were enjoying exercise, fresh air, and sunshine. Mid-week days in summer provide many opportunities to enjoy the arboretum without seeing another person.

In 1919, Henry S. Glazier, Sr. purchased 85 acres from the George MacKay Estate. The property included a 1785 farmhouse, part of the original Quinby family property. Upon Glazier Sr.'s death, his two sons each inherited half the property. Henry, Jr. established the arboretum, which the Town Conservation Board now manages, so that homeowners would be able to learn how to improve their properties for living alongside local wildlife. Only the giant sequoia is labeled.

TRAILS

The view from the gate at the parking lot is a spreading open meadow. Trails form loops and can be followed in different combinations for a variety of walks. A 0.1-mile route through the meadow may vary from year to year. Some years it is brush-hogged to remove the woody vegetation, and in other years only a path is cut. Along the edge of the meadow next to Whippoorwill Road stands a giant sequoia. Not a towering specimen, it is only a few feet in diameter, with a smaller one next to it.

Giant sequoia

Blue Trail
Length: 0.8 mile Blaze: blue
From the road beyond the gate, the blue trail reaches a kiosk and splits to form a loop. The piece straight ahead is the shortest access trail to the interior. The section to the right

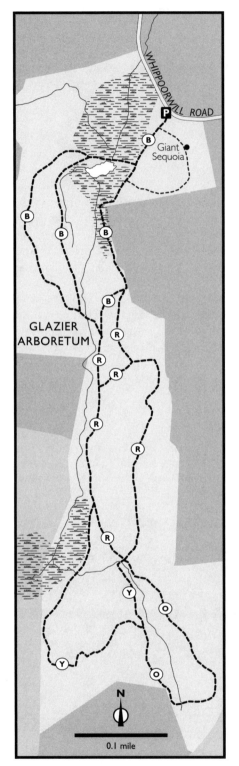

offers two choices: a trail on a ridge or another along a woods road.

Take the leftmost branch of the blue trail straight ahead. It reaches, at 0.1 mile, a long 60-foot boardwalk lined with tussock sedge and royal and cinnamon ferns. At 0.2 mile, it passes a junction with the red trail going off to the left. Shortly, the blue trail reaches the other end of the red trail and turns right to cross a stream on a causeway. In 75 feet, the blue trail splits. Take the left branch.

This branch of the blue trail gently ascends a ridge and, at 0.3 mile, passes a high rocky slope on the left. Descending, it reaches a grassy open area, where in August, goldenrod, black knapweed, and yarrow bloom in profusion. At 0.5 mile, it passes by the middle section of the blue trail and joins a woods road ending at the kiosk at 0.6 mile.

The so-called middle section of the blue trail is a level former farm road lined with barberry and multiflora rose bushes, which, unfortunately, obscure views of the pond. It provides a 0.2-mile-long shortcut that avoids the climb to the ridge mentioned above.

Red Trail *Length: 0.6 mile Blaze: red*
The red trail, a large loop beginning at the blue trail, ascends to a T junction. The split to the right is the shortcut to the other side of the loop and runs along 200 feet of washed-out woods road. Turn left and follow the woods road. The trail crosses a stream, reaches the orange trail at 0.3 mile, and 10 feet further, the yellow trail. Turning downhill, the red trail passes the other end of the yellow trail at 0.4 mile. It follows a stream with wetlands on the far side. At 0.5 mile, the red trail passes the cross trail mentioned above, to end at the blue trail.

Orange Trail   *Length: 0.4 mile Blaze: orange*

Accessible from the red trail, the orange trail heads steeply uphill along a rocky treadway paralleling a stream. At 0.2 mile, the orange trail descends into a valley. The orange trail crosses a bridge, turns right to go through a stone wall, and parallels the stream in the valley below, ending at a junction with the yellow trail.

Yellow Trail   *Length: 0.4 mile Blaze: yellow*

Heading into the far reaches of the arboretum, the yellow trail is accessible from the red trail in two places. From the junction of the red and orange trails, it goes steeply downhill and crosses a stream. Briefly in sight of the orange trail on the other side, the yellow trail follows the stream. After passing through a disturbed area, the trail crosses a bed of New York and cinnamon ferns. It parallels a stone wall and, at 0.2 mile, descends steeply. Crossing a stream, the yellow trail soon ends at a T junction with the red trail, at 0.4 mile.

NEARBY PARK: Whippoorwill Park

DRIVING: From the Saw Mill River Parkway, take the Roaring Brook/Readers Digest Exit east to Route 117 (Bedford Road). Turn right onto Route 117 and take the next left turn onto Whippoorwill Road. Continue 1.2 miles to the arboretum.

PUBLIC TRANSPORTATION: None available

For contact information, see Appendix, New Castle.

Hart's Brook Park and Preserve

Hartsdale • 3.2 miles, 123 acres

Picture perfect describes Hart's Brook Park and Preserve, located in the heart of lower Westchester. The open lawn of the former Gaisman Estate greets visitors and hints at what is to come. A tranquil pond, stately woodlands, flowing streams, and open fields entice visitors back for frequent visits. Rhododendrons and flowering trees are seasonal reasons to return. There are geological features along the woodland trails and opportunities for studying a variety of wildlife. Many tulip trees tower over the trails. A stone building near the pond silently attests to the opulence of a bygone era.

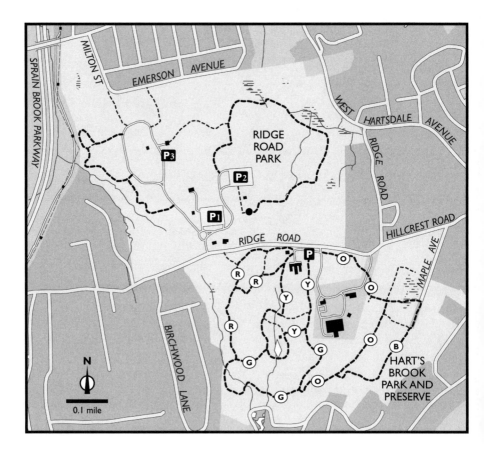

Henry Gaisman, of the Gillette Company, purchased 135 acres in 1932 and passed the title to the Archdiocese of New York with the understanding that he and his wife, Catherine, would reside there as long as they lived. After his death at 104 in 1974, Catherine continued to live on the property until 1995, when she moved to Connecticut. The Archdiocese wished to establish a convent for Sisters of Mercy and elderly nuns from other orders. Through a cooperative agreement in 1999, the Town of Greenburgh, Westchester County, and the New York State Office of Parks, Recreation and Historic Preservation purchased 124 acres. The remaining acreage in the center of the property was set aside for the convent. Currently, the Town of Greenburgh manages the park.

TRAILS

For the most part, the wide woodland trails are gently graded and wide enough for walking two or three abreast. Somehow they give the message: "relax and stroll, there's no need to hurry." Five connector trails add 0.3 mile to the miles of trails in the park. Conditions permitting, the trails are ideal for snowshoeing or cross-country skiing.

Red Trail   *Length: 0.6 mile Blaze: red*
Paralleling Ridge Road and passing in front of the caretaker's house, the red trail heads uphill. It passes an unmarked woods road to the left leading to another section of the red trail. The one to the right leads 200 feet out to the fence along Ridge Road, where there is a locked gate. Sometimes, exposed bedrock peeks up from the grass in the mowed path; at other times, a larger slab is visible.

After passing through a field, the red trail reenters the woods on a treadway with remnants of pavement. At a three-way intersection to the left, the red trail heads 0.1 mile back to the yellow trail near a barn and greenhouse. The right branch leads into a field. Straight ahead, the red trail descends through thick understory to end at a T junction with the green trail.

Yellow Trail   *Length: 0.7 mile Blaze: yellow*
Shaped like a U, the yellow trail loops down to a pond and back up. There are two unmarked connecting trails to provide shortcuts if needed. Starting at the parking lot, the yellow trail heads across the lawn, with greenhouses and a demonstration garden to the right. It crosses a short section of pavement before heading into the woods. After passing unmarked trails to the right, it reaches, at 0.2 mile, a V junction with the green trail to the left. Going right, the yellow trail reaches a second Y junction with the second of the shortcut trails leading to the right. Rhododendrons line the path, splendid in spring when in bloom and in winter when covered with snow. The trail begins its route around the pond and passes a stone warming-house to the right and a short trail to the pond.

Crossing the outlet of the pond at 0.3 mile, the yellow trail passes the green trail to the left. Curving to the right, it passes the ends of the cross trails, the first one at 0.5 mile. The yellow trail reaches the driveway to the barn at 0.6 mile and ends at the parking lot.

Springtime

Blue Trail
Length: 0.4 mile Blaze: blue

Beginning on a wide grassy strip near the orange trail, the blue trail follows a sewer line. It reaches a T junction with a paved road leading 270 feet to a barrier at Maple Avenue (no parking). The blue trail turns right to follow the paved road, which is lined with cut curbstones at 0.1 mile. Passing a fire hydrant, it turns right. Straight ahead, the mowed path is a shortcut to the orange trail. The blue trail jogs left up an embankment, graded to even off the slope. At a quarter-mile, it leaves the pavement to enter an established forest with little undergrowth. After a sharp right turn, it crosses a bridge, heads steeply uphill, and ends at the orange trail.

Green Trail
Length: 0.6 mile Blaze: green

Beginning near the southwest corner by the pond, the green trail reaches a Y junction where one branch of the red trail ends. The green trail turns left and heads downhill on a somewhat rough surface. At 0.1 mile, it crosses a bridge and goes uphill only to head downhill at 0.2 mile to cross a second bridge. It flattens out, crosses another stream on a causeway, and heads uphill. After passing the orange trail to the right at 0.4 mile, it continues uphill. At 0.5 mile, it makes a sharp left off the woods road onto a narrow footpath. Winding its way through dense forest, the green trail passes a rhododendron grove and ends at the yellow trail at 0.6 mile.

Orange Trail
Length: 0.6 mile Blaze: orange

From the junction with the green trail, the orange trail goes downhill on a woods road, which gradually steepens. It turns and follows a built-up graded path. It goes left at a Y junction with the blue trail and passes a grove of white pines. The orange trail passes a mowed path leading 0.1 mile to the blue trail. At 0.3 mile, it meets a T junction with a sewer line, where to the right is the other segment of the blue trail. The orange trail goes up the steepest grade in the park and reaches a mowed grassy path to the left leading to Marion Woods. The trail heads up stone steps and immediately turns right, passing the broad stone steps of the former Gaisman mansion. It turns again to head uphill, and reaches the park exit road at 0.4 mile. Turning right, the orange trail leaves the exit road and heads onto grass. It passes overgrown landscaping and continues its way across the lawn. The path is not defined, but the road to the parking lot is visible.

DRIVING: From the Sprain Brook Parkway, take the Route 100B Exit. At the end of the ramp, head east. At West Hartsdale Avenue (Route 100A), turn right and continue about 3 miles to Ridge Road. Turn right and follow Ridge Road for 0.3 mile to the entrance to the preserve to the left.

PUBLIC TRANSPORTATION: None available

For contact information, see Appendix, Greenburgh.

Ridge Road Park

Hartsdale • 2.0 miles, 236 acres

Where there's a will, there's a way—to find a nearby place to walk; if you live in Hartsdale, Ridge Road Park provides that opportunity. Sounds of picnickers and smells wafting from grills in three picnic areas greet walkers during summer weekends. Off-season and early or late in the day are better times to take advantage of the less-crowded park roads and the small trail system. Parking areas #2 and #3 are gated and locked late in the day; however, the exact times are not posted. The park property was acquired by the county in 1925. Later, in 1942, the Works Progress Administration (WPA) financed and built the stone picnic shelter.

Relatively level unmarked trails traverse dense woods with numerous large tulip trees, including one approximately 120 feet off-trail with a circumference of about 15 feet. Logs, looking like scrawny collapsed versions of a split rail fence, line the trails. Pallets or boards serve as bridges over wet areas. An 0.8-mile trail circles the area including the octagonal picnic pavilion. On the west side, there is a 0.5-mile trail accessible from the road leading from the gate for picnic area #3. Two 0.1-mile access trails go to Emerson Avenue and Milton Street (no parking). A road walk around the picnic area is 0.5 mile.

DRIVING: From the Sprain Brook Parkway, take the Route 100B Exit. At the end of the ramp, head east. At West Hartsdale Avenue (Route 100A), turn right and continue about 3 miles to Ridge Road. Turn right and follow the signs to the park entrance to the right.

PUBLIC TRANSPORTATION: None available

For contact information, see Appendix, Westchester County Parks.

Hilltop Hanover Farm and Environmental Center

Yorktown Heights • 2.5 miles, 183 acres

When Westchester County purchased Hilltop Hanover Farm in 2003, they did more than just save the farm. Their objectives were to preserve open space, protect drinking water, and establish an environmental resource center. The Department of Planning is responsible for managing and developing the property. All recreational use also has an environmental education component.

The old stone walls, both surrounding and within the property, indicate early farm field patterns and suggest that the land was farmed in the late eighteenth century. Croton Heights Road and Hanover Street are known to have existed before the American Revolution. Dairy operations began about 55 years ago, but when the economy turned sluggish in the early 1990s, the breeding operation was discontinued. When the owners tried to sell the farm in the mid-1990s, the remaining cows were sold.

Hilltop Hanover Farm is still a working farm, but with scaled-back operations: a privately owned herd of Merino sheep, a vineyard, beehives, and vegetable gardens. The county does not allow the use of pesticides on the property; anyone farming has to adhere to this limitation. These partners are helping promote responsible environmental and sustainable agricultural practices.

TRAILS

Beginning on Hanover Street across from the farm buildings is a trail network through open woods. An unmarked trail leads 0.3 mile from Hanover Street past a kiosk to a second kiosk at the beginning of the Hilltop Loop. A 0.1-mile unmarked trail and three short unmarked trails divide Hilltop Loop.

Hilltop Loop   *Length: 1.7 miles Blaze: blue*
From the second kiosk on the entrance trail, walk clockwise around the Hilltop Loop and head downhill. The trail crosses a bridge over the outlet stream from the pond and turns left to reach the top of the dam. After briefly hugging the edge of the pond and passing several picnic tables, it turns away from the pond. At a T junction, the trail turns left onto a woods road, which, to the right, is a 0.1-mile shortcut ending on Hilltop Loop. At 0.2 mile, the trail ascends. At an intersection with the yellow and green trails, the blue trail turns left. The aptly named Vernal Pond Trail (yellow) heads straight, to end in 350 feet at Hilltop Loop; the Rock Pass Trail (green) goes right for 0.2 mile, also ending at this blue trail.

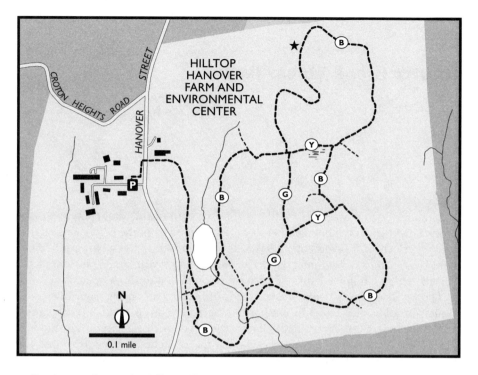

Passing under rock cliffs, Hilltop Loop wanders uphill and down to reach a viewpoint at 0.7 mile. It descends and, at 1.0 mile, passes to the right the Vernal Pond Trail and a vernal pond. The Hilltop Loop heads uphill and turns left as it passes the Campfire Circle Trail (yellow), which leads 460 feet downhill to end at the Rock Pass Trail. Hilltop Loop heads downhill, crossing and joining woods roads as it goes. At 1.5 miles, it turns right onto a woods road and passes a breached dam. The trail crosses a stone wall and to the right passes Rock Pass Trail (not blazed going north) and an unmarked woods road that leads back to the pond. Hilltop Loop enters a field and, at 1.7 miles, closes the loop at the kiosk.

DRIVING: From the northbound Taconic State Parkway, take the Millwood/Route 100 Exit. At the end of the exit ramp, turn left onto Campfire Road. At the traffic light at Route 100, turn right. Head north for 3.9 miles and turn left onto Route 118. Hanover Street is the first right turn and Hilltop Hanover Farm is 1.4 miles to the left.

From the southbound Taconic State Parkway, take the Underhill Avenue Exit and turn left. Go 2.0 miles, turning right at the second light to stay on Underhill Avenue. Continue 0.2 mile to a stop sign and turn right onto Hanover Street. Hilltop Hanover Farm is 1.6 miles to the right.

PUBLIC TRANSPORTATION: None available

For contact information, see Appendix, Hilltop Hanover Farm and Environmental Center.

Hunter Brook Linear Park

Huntersville • 2.1 miles, 56 acres

Although the entrance trail is along a grassy strip in full sun, visiting Hunter Brook Linear Park on a hot summer day offers respite from the heat, thanks to the cooling effects of flowing water and the shade of towering trees. However, do not limit your visit to hot summer days. The park provides year-round pleasant places to walk, either along the banks of a stream or on a loop through uplands.

The wooded area is composed of stands of beech, oak, maple, and tulip trees. Hunter Brook is also home to mink, muskrat, native brook trout, sunfish, frogs, and salamanders. An agreement between the developer of adjacent housing and the Town of Yorktown, in conjunction with the Westchester Land Trust and the Yorktown Land Trust, has made Hunter Brook Linear Park possible.

TRAILS

In some sense, there are two trail systems at Hunter Brook Linear Park—one on each side of a broad, swift flowing stream which is a tributary of the Croton Reservoir.

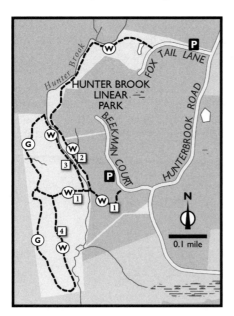

White Trail
Length: 1.6 miles Blaze: white
From the trailhead on Beekman Court, white trail #1 curves 0.1 mile downhill along a grassy strip. It reaches a large steel bridge over Hunter Brook, where to the right, white trail #2 heads upstream. Continuing over the bridge, white trail #1 passes white trail #3 to the right, then a kiosk, then white trail #4 to the left, ending at the green trail at 0.3 mile.

On the east side of Hunter Brook, white trail #2 is on a woods road, leaves the woods road, and crosses a wooden bridge over a feeder stream at 0.2 mile. Veering away from Hunter Brook, it crosses a stone wall, passes a triple tulip tree, and parallels the stream once again. It makes a sharp right turn at 0.6 mile to head uphill while the stream continues to run its course below. The trail enters an open area and, at 0.8 mile, ends on Fox Tail Lane across from a utility box. Hunterbrook Road is 0.1 mile to the left.

Also heading upstream along Hunter Brook, white trail #3 is on the west side of the brook and passes through a grove of Norway spruce with drooping branches. It goes through a stone wall and ends at the green trail on the preserve boundary at 0.3 mile. On the opposite side of Hunter Brook, white trail #2 is visible, but to reach it, return and cross the steel bridge.

White trail #4 leaves white trail #1 and heads south. It crosses stone walls, parallels Hunter Brook, and ends at 0.3 mile at the green trail.

Along Hunter Brook

Green Trail
Length: 0.6 mile Blaze: green

From the south end of white trail #4, the green trail begins and baying hounds on adjacent Southern New York Beagle Club can be heard. The green trail parallels that property, then turns to head south. At 0.4 mile, it passes to the right an unmarked trail which returns to the bridge over Hunter Brook. After crossing a big trench, the trail heads through an area with deep gullies and descends steeply to end at white trail #3.

DRIVING: From the Taconic State Parkway, take the Route 202 Exit and head west. At 0.6 mile, turn left onto Pine Grove Court. Immediately turn right onto Old Crompond Road. Go 0.3 mile and turn left onto Hunterbrook Road. It is 1.5 miles to a right turn onto Beekman Court. Parking is to the left at 0.1 mile in a small pullout beside a small sign: Trail Head Parking Area. The trailhead is 200 feet back along the road at a sign between two driveways. An alternative entrance is on Fox Tail Lane, 1.1 miles from the intersection of Old Crompond and Hunterbrook roads (no parking).

PUBLIC TRANSPORTATION: None available

For contact information, see Appendix, Yorktown.

Lenoir Preserve
Untermyer Park

Yonkers • 2.5 miles

If you think Lenoir Preserve and Untermyer Park are too small for a lengthy walk, you are wrong! In addition to small networks of trails through former estates, they each have a trail descending to the Old Croton Aqueduct State Historical Park, which makes longer walks definitely possible.

Lenoir Preserve

Yonkers • 1.3 miles, 39 acres

Like many former estates, Lenoir Preserve has benefited from the common practice of wealthy landowners to import and plant specimen trees. Portions of the formal gardens have been converted to a butterfly garden and community gardens. From the front of the mansion, it is possible to watch fall bird migrations. The nature center runs programs and is headquarters for the Hudson River Audubon Society.

The Lenoir mansion dates from the 1850s when it was built for Samuel Tilden, who also owned a home at what is now Untermyer Park. Aldenwold, another mansion on the northern part of the property, burned in 1979. Westchester County purchased the Lenoir parcel in 1976 and Aldenwold after the 1979 fire.

Gate in stone wall

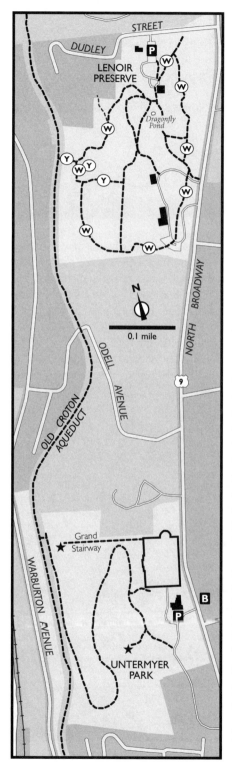

TRAILS

The trails in Lenoir Preserve beg you to explore. The 0.4-mile handicapped accessible pathway connects the Hawk Watch, Dragonfly Pond, Butterfly Garden, and stone gazebo. From the gardens, the yellow trail descends 73 steps to reach the Old Croton Aqueduct at 0.1 mile.

White Trail
Length: 0.8 mile Blaze: white
Beginning at the nature center, the white trail follows a path with some remnants of pavement. It turns left along the paved path, passes European beeches, and enters a field. The white trail turns left onto a woods road at 0.2 mile and crosses the driveway to the mansion. It crosses the lawn and driveway again, and upon reaching a gate in a wall, turns right. Paralleling the wall, the white trail heads downhill, crosses a paved path at 0.4 mile, and descends on steps. It levels out and at 0.6 mile, joins the yellow trail coming from the right. The two trails are co-aligned for 130 feet until the yellow trail continues downhill to end at the Old Croton Aqueduct; the white trail turns right and heads steeply uphill. It passes a trail to an adjacent apartment building and a man-made pond. Ascending more steeply, it ends at a learning circle near the paved path.

DRIVING: From the Saw Mill River Parkway take Exit 9 (Executive Boulevard). Follow Executive Boulevard west for 0.9 mile to North Broadway. Turn right, continue 0.3 mile to Dudley Street, and turn left. The park entrance is to the left shortly after the turn.

PUBLIC TRANSPORTATION: Beeline Bus #6 to Dudley Street

For contact information, see Appendix, Westchester County Parks—Lenoir Preserve.

CONNECTING THE PARKS

To reach the Old Croton Aqueduct from Lenoir Preserve, take the paved path to the right of the nature center and turn right. Pass the Butterfly Garden and head toward the formal garden. Follow the yellow trail down to the Old Croton Aqueduct. Walk south on the Aqueduct 0.6 mile to Untermyer Park and take a stroll through that property. An alternate return route is along North Broadway, avoiding the steep descent and ascent to the Old Croton Aqueduct.

Untermyer Park

Yonkers • 1.2 miles, 33 acres

Set high on a bluff overlooking the Hudson River, Untermyer Park is hardly unpretentious. The mansion is long gone, but the park offers places to walk in its Grecian Gardens, a Beaux Arts landscape design at its best when flowers are blooming. Plan your hike so that you can picnic and attend Untermyer Performing Arts Council events during summer months. The gardens are handicapped accessible.

The Untermyer Estate was known as Greystone when it was built in 1892 by John T. Waring, industrialist and philanthropist. The second owner was Samuel J. Tilden, former governor of New York and an unsuccessful 1874 presidential candidate. The third owner, Samuel Untermyer, a lawyer, lived there for over 40 years. He bequeathed the estate to Yonkers to be used as a public park. The original villa stood where St. John's Riverside Hospital is now.

The major trail is a wide woods road from the left entrance of the parking lot. It passes a stone gazebo which was built for the wedding of Untermyer's daughter. Switchbacking downhill, it ends at the stone pillars at the Old Croton Aqueduct in 0.8 mile. The broad stone staircase leading down from the gardens toward the river and the stone gazebo are

The Grand Stairway

settings where a child's imagination can run wild.

DRIVING: From the Saw Mill River Parkway, take Exit 9 (Executive Boulevard). Follow Executive Boulevard west to North Broadway and turn left. The park is to the right, just south of St. John's Riverside Hospital.

PUBLIC TRANSPORTATION: Beeline Bus #6 on North Broadway

For contact information, see Appendix, Yonkers.

Marshlands Conservancy

Rye • 2.7 miles, 170 acres

Packed into Marshlands Conservancy's 170 acres is a network of unmarked trails through a mowed field, a deciduous forest, and a salt marsh. There are many opportunities to watch wildlife as the trails loop through woods and along the shore. Given the number of cross trails, there are many possible hikes. The trails leading out onto the spits into Long Island Sound have many birdwatching opportunities; waves lapping the shore encourage visitors to meander. Because the shore and Route 1 are essentially fences to keep walkers from going astray, Marshlands Conservancy is a good place to practice navigational skills.

The Jay Heritage Center is the large white house overlooking the meadow. John Jay, the first chief justice of the United States, grew up on the farm on the property. He is buried in the fenced-in Jay Cemetery on land still owned by his descendants.

DRIVING: From the New England Thruway, take Exit 19 (Playland Parkway). Take

Milton Harbor

the first right off the parkway, turn left, and then right at the next intersection. In 0.3 mile, merge with the Boston Post Road. Continue 0.5 mile to the entrance to Marshlands Conservancy to the left just past the Rye Country Club.

PUBLIC TRANSPORTATION: Metro-North New Haven Line Harrison Station. Cross Halstead Avenue and walk down Purdy Street. Turn left onto Park Avenue and at the end turn right onto Boston Post Road. The entrance to Marshlands Conservancy is about 200 yards to the left. The total walk is a mile.

For contact information, see Appendix, Westchester County Parks—Marshlands Conservancy.

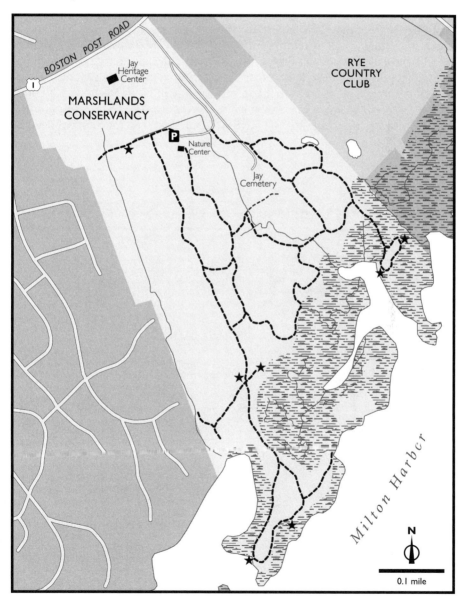

Merestead

Mt. Kisco • 2.7 miles, 130 acres

Galileo, Rembrandt, and Merestead have something in common: they are all known by a single name. It is quite obvious on a visit to Merestead why it could not possibly be called Merestead Park. The understated elegance of the buildings and grounds typifies the lifestyle of the social elite in the early 1900s. The Georgian Revival style brick mansion overlooks a vast expanse of lawn. A grass tennis court, swimming pool, and a croquet court adjoin the house. The springhouses on the farm have arched openings. In 1984, Merestead was placed on the National Register of Historic Places.

TRAILS

Thanks to a 2003 Youth Conservation Corps project, 3,200 feet of old hiking trails

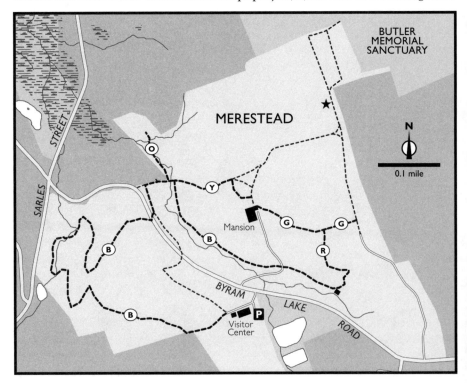

Carriage House (Visitor Center)

at Merestead were restored, and 3,000 feet of new trails were built. Merestead's trail system has both marked and unmarked trails. The latter, mainly on farm roads, add 0.5 mile to the trail system, and have the only views in the park. The blazed trails often pass through fields which, whenever they have not been mowed recently, have tall grass obscuring the treadway and making it hard to follow. Trail descriptions tell hikers where to look and go in these situations. At the far end of the farm fields, a Bedford Riding Lanes Association (BRLA) trail enters the woods in the Butler Memorial Sanctuary.

Blue Trail
Length: 1.2 miles Blaze: blue

From the far end of the front of the Carriage House, the blue trail turns left. It heads uphill, following the right edge of the field to the far corner where it enters the woods. Blue blazes once again appear on trees. The trail passes through a white pine plantation. At 0.1 mile, the trail turns right through a wide opening in a stone wall and heads downhill. After crossing a stone wall at 0.3 mile, it turns left and descends to follow another stone wall. At 0.4 mile, the trail turns left and goes over a crumbling section of the wall it had been following. After crossing a stream on a bridge, the trail turns right, crosses a second bridge over a seasonal stream, and then crosses a third stream on large rock slabs.

At 0.6 mile, the blue trail reaches two fence posts and turns right. It contours along the base of a low ridge to the left. After gaining some elevation, the trail switchbacks to the left and continues to the top of the ridge. At 0.8 mile, it enters a field and heads northeast towards a tree in the middle of the field. It passes a cedar

History of Merestead

Merestead is the Scottish word for farmland. Its woods and rolling fields were part of a working farm and estate of William Sloane II of the W & J Sloane home furnishings store. He purchased two pieces of property in 1905 and hired the architectural firm of Delano and Aldrich to design a house built the following year. Its furnishings came from the store, but were not custom-made. Although the Sloanes lived there only from May to November, it was their legal residence and they established ties to the community. Mrs. Sloane helped to create Northern Westchester Hospital (1916) and to establish Leonard Park (1917). After Sloane's death in 1922, his widow considered selling the property, but their only child, Margaret, urged her to keep it.

When Mrs. Sloane died in 1962, her daughter, now Mrs. Robert L. Patterson, Jr., inherited the property which they used on weekends. In 1983, the Pattersons moved there permanently. Mrs. Patterson contacted the Westchester Department of Parks with a "shot in the dark" letter, in regard to bequeathing her property for preservation as a park and historic house museum. She considered Merestead a jewel in a green necklace connecting the Butler property, Marsh Sanctuary, and Leonard Park. Upon Mrs. Patterson's death in 2000, the county began transforming Merestead from a private estate into a public park and museum. Reserved tours of the main dwelling have been available since January 2007.

The Patterson gift preserved open space and a house that had only two owners. The contents of the house show how life changed for the wealthy in the twentieth century. Servants' quarters are part of the house because it required 12 people to run it. A linen room, silver safe, and butler's pantry were necessary parts of housekeeping. To learn more about Merestead and the people who lived there, see: www.westchestergov.com/parks/naturecenters05/merestead.htm.

tree and heads down toward Byram Lake Road.

The blue trail turns left onto Byram Lake Road and heads 40 feet to an opening through the stone wall to the right. It descends stone steps to a field, turns left, and stays close to the left edge of the field. A BRLA trail coming from farther east along the field merges into the track. Frequent horse traffic tramples the grass and makes the route more visible. At 0.9 mile, the blue trail reaches a tree-lined woods road, turns right, and descends. Just before a bridge over a stream, a BRLA trail leaves to the left across the north edge of a large field to end at Sarles Street. Soon after, the orange trail begins to the left, heading in a northwesterly direction along the brook for 0.1 mile. The blue trail, co-aligned with a BRLA trail, continues straight and crosses a stream on a stone arch bridge. On the far side of the bridge, the blue trail turns right, and the BRLA and yellow trails head straight.

Paralleling the stream, the blue trail heads uphill. At 1.1 miles at a Y junction, an unmarked trail heads left uphill to the gardens south of the main house. The blue trail veers right, staying within sight of the brook and ending at the paved driveway. Ahead, the red trail leads 0.2 mile through a shallow valley to connect to the green trail near the utility line. The driveway leads back to Byram Lake Road and the parking lot.

Green Trail   *Length: 0.2 mile Blaze: green*

Serving as a connector trail to unmarked trails, the green trail begins at the back of the mansion. It climbs stairs to a large tree with long, low-hanging branches. The trail veers right and passes a pet cemetery with a fire hydrant set conspicuously in the center. After passing under a utility line, it passes the red trail to the right. The green trail enters a field, passes a Chinese lantern, and ends at a T junction with a farm road.

Yellow Trail   *Length: 0.2 mile Blaze: yellow*

Connecting the blue trail with the mansion, the yellow trail starts on the far side of the mansion at the staff parking area. It heads north on a woods road. When the road begins to veer slightly to the right, the yellow trail becomes a poorly-defined path on grass to the left of the road. It passes an old fireplace surrounded by trees on the right. The trail turns left at the edge of the field and is co-aligned with a BRLA trail. It heads towards a large isolated tree, stays to its right, and then hugs the forest edge on the right. On entering the forest, the trail descends to end at the blue trail. The BRLA trail continues straight ahead with the blue trail.

NEARBY PARKS: Butler Memorial Sanctuary, Marsh Memorial Sanctuary, Meyer Preserve

DRIVING: From I-684, take Exit 4 (Route 172) and head west. In 1.5 miles, turn left onto Sarles Street. Continue 1.5 miles to the stop sign at Byram Lake Road. Turn left and drive for 0.4 mile. Parking is across the street from the main driveway.

PUBLIC TRANSPORTATION: None available

For information, see Appendix, Merestead.

Herbert L. Nichols Preserve

Armonk • 2.4 miles, 87 acres

Easy is one word to describe the trails in the Nichols Preserve. But a second description should include varied. The preserve has forests, meadows, wetlands, man-made ponds, and abandoned roads, all of which create a landscape perfectly suited to rambling leisurely and watching wildlife. These ecosystems are typical of those found in southern New York and southwestern Connecticut. In season, the ponds harbor water fowl, turtles, and frogs. The abandoned roads, broad meadows, and former orchards provide many opportunities for birding. Over a hundred varieties of wildflowers fill the fields.

Prior to European settlement in 1640, the Siwanoy tribe of the Wappinger Nation lived in what is now the Town of Greenwich. By the early 1700s, Quakers settled in the area around what is currently Nichols Preserve. The close proximity to New York City assured a ready market for local produce. The area was farmed until the 1870s, when opportunities for farming moved west. From 1908 to 1910, Herbert L. Nichols, Sr. purchased property. He and his son of the same name dug

A meadow is just ahead

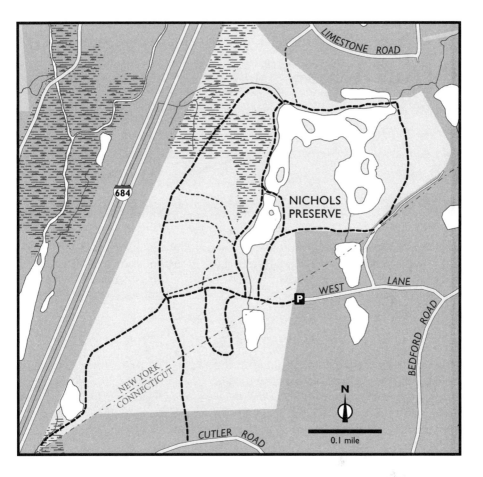

ponds and planted trees and wildflowers. In 1968, Herbert L. Nichols, Jr., Henry Metcalf, and Harriet Underhill donated 44 acres to The Nature Conservancy in honor of Herbert L. Nichols. Subsequent donations by Mr. Nichols in the 1970s and 1980s increased the preserve to its present size. In 2002, The Nature Conservancy transferred the preserve to the Greenwich Riding and Trails Association.

No trails are blazed. Nichols Preserve is a good place to learn to follow a map, because it is bounded by I-684 and private property. Unfortunately, noise from I-684 is ever present. With sufficient snow, the wide woods roads and open fields are suitable for cross-country skiing.

DRIVING: From I-684, take Exit 3 and head north on Route 22. Turn right onto Route 433 and drive 0.7 mile. After the Connecticut line, make the first right turn onto Bedford Road. Turn right onto West Lane (a private road) and continue to the end, with parking in front of the gate. There is also an entrance on Cutler Road (no parking).

PUBLIC TRANSPORTATION: None available

For contact information, see Appendix, Greenwich Riding and Trails Association.

Old Field Preserve

Waccabuc • 2.8 miles, 112 acres

In Westchester County, it is hard to find open fields in which to walk, but Old Field Preserve has five! The preserve is part of a 22,000-acre biological corridor stretching from North Salem through Lewisboro to Pound Ridge. This open space is particularly important for wildlife because of its combination of meadows, old fields, wetlands, and woodlands. Pictures of the current season's plants and animals are posted at the kiosk.

TRAILS

Easy walking is the name of the game on the trails at Old Field Preserve. An open field greets hikers, and a mowed farm road follows the edges of the fields. Because of the high water table in the woods, there are many places for feet to get wet. Several sections of the fields are suitable for cross-country skiing. However, the section of the blue trail from Waccabuc River Lane to Bouton Road has steep sections and is likely to be used by horses even in winter.

From 1679 to 1776, Old Field Preserve was part of Van Cortlandt Manor. In 1776, Enoch Mead settled in the area. His descendants farmed until 1974, when Arthur Houlihan purchased the property and farming ceased. In 2003, this open

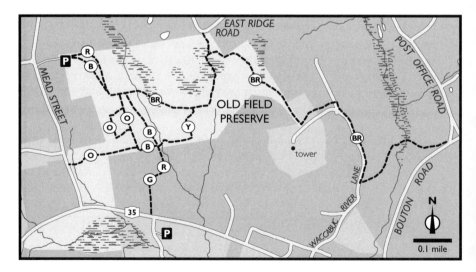

space was preserved thanks to the efforts of Westchester Land Trust, the Town of Lewisboro, Wolf Conservation Center, New York State, and Westchester County. It is jointly owned by the town and the county, with New York State holding a conservation easement. Westchester Land Trust created a management plan to maintain the fields.

The preserve has two trails blazed blue. Because one of them is blazed red as well, indicating that it is also part of the Lewisboro Horsemen's Association (LHA) trail system, it will be referred to as the blue-red trail.

Blue-Red Trail (to Bouton Road) *Length: 1.7 miles Blaze: blue-red*

Serving as the main trail through the preserve and crossing private property, the blue-red trail begins at the kiosk at the entrance on Mead Street. The red blazes are along the edge of the field, while the blue blazes follow a mowed path. They join at 0.1 mile and are co-aligned except for a short split. Leaving the field, the trail crosses through a stone wall at 0.2 mile and turns left at a woods road. After passing the orange trail, the blue-red trail passes the blue trail to Route 35 in 100 feet. The blue-red trail crosses a wet area on puncheon and enters a field on a mowed path. To the right, a 0.2-mile yellow trail heads into a field and an orchard to join the blue trail.

The trail enters the woods again at 0.5 mile and veers left crossing a wet area.

It makes a sharp right turn at 0.7 mile as it passes an orange-blazed side trail to the left leading 330 feet to East Ridge Road (no parking). At 1.0 mile, the blue trail reaches a road to an omni (communication) tower, part of the Federal Aviation Administration navigation system. Turning left, the blue trail descends as it crosses a field and turns right to follow Waccabuc River Lane. At 1.3 miles, the blue trail leaves the road and descends, sometimes steeply. After crossing the driveway to Hazelnut Farm, the blue trail turns right, only to join the red trail again in 60 yards. At 1.5 miles, the blue trail crosses a bridge and a driveway to end at the corner of Bouton and Post Office roads.

Puncheon along the blue-red trail

Blue Trail (to Route 35)   *Length: 0.4 mile Blaze: blue*

Starting on the blue-red trail 0.2 mile from the kiosk, the blue trail to Route 35 heads south on a mowed path. In winter, the many shrubs harbor small mammals. Occasional deer tracks may be seen. Club mosses are hidden in the grass. The blue trail passes the yellow trail to the left at 0.2 mile. Now marked with Westchester Land Trust and LHA blazes, the blue trail heads steeply downhill above a stream. It ends at Route 35 across from the Lewisboro Town Park.

Orange Trail   *Length: 0.5 mile Blaze: orange*

Beginning at the blue trail, the orange trail heads south into a field. A side trail loops 0.1 mile into scrubby trees and returns to the orange trail. At a T junction, the orange trail turns right, while a blue spur trail to the left leads to the blue trail (to Route 35). The orange trail enters the woods at 0.3 mile, descends steeply to cross a stream, and ends at Mead Street (no parking).

NEARBY PARKS: Lewisboro Town Park, Ward Pound Ridge Reservation

DRIVING: From I-684, take Exit 4 (Route 35) and head east 5.6 miles to Mead Street. Turn left and drive 0.4 mile. Schoolhouse Road is to the left across the street from a grass-and-gravel road into the parking area, which is often muddy.

PUBLIC TRANSPORTATION: None available

For contact information, see Appendix, Lewisboro.

Pine Croft Meadow Preserve

Waccabuc • 0.4 mile, 9 acres

*S*ummertime and the livin' is easy comes to mind on a visit to Pine Croft Meadow Preserve during the summer. Yet for an insect or a butterfly, nothing could be further from the truth. They are busy gleaning sustenance from flowers and plants and in turn, are the prey of birds and other insects. The preserve is home to both resident and non-resident songbirds, American kestrels, small mammals, and thousands of non-bothersome insects. This small preserve shows that landscape management practices make a real difference in protecting a scarce habitat and the rural character of northeast Westchester County. The family of Emory Katzenbach donated this land in his memory. The trails at Pine Croft are mowed paths through the meadow and change from year to year. The quarter-mile gravel road is included as a trail for observing birds and insects.

DRIVING: Follow the directions for Old Field Preserve; continue 0.6 mile further to Pine Croft Meadow Preserve, to the left, just past the Waccabuc Country Club.

PUBLIC TRANSPORTATION: None available

For contact information, see Appendix, Westchester Land Trust.

Long Pond Preserve

Waccabuc • 0.7 mile, 39 acres

Bring a budding naturalist with nature guides and plan to spend several hours at Long Pond Preserve. The five ecosystems (lake, meadow, forest, stream, and wetland) have something for everyone to identify. It is particularly appealing on a hot summer day when the meadows are abuzz with butterflies, and the cool forest beckons with access to the lakeshore. The property had been in the Mead family from 1650 until 1970 when it was donated to The Nature Conservancy (TNC), thanks to a group of local residents and the Studwell Foundation representing the family.

From Mead Street, the single trail marked with green TNC tags on trees enters the preserve. It descends to follow a berm which had supported a power line through wetlands. The trail turns south along the edge of a wet meadow and then enters the forest at 0.2 mile. It parallels the lakeshore and passes the remains of ice-cutting operations at 0.4 mile. It ends at 0.5 mile at the edge of the property. A loop in the preserve and unmarked paths add another 0.2 mile of trails.

DRIVING: Follow the directions for Old Field Preserve, but continue an additional 0.9 mile to the preserve located to the right across from the Mead Memorial Chapel. The entrance is to the right of a wood gate marked Private. From the entrance, a welcome sign is visible down the hill. Parking is on the west side of the road in several pullouts, just south of the entrance before reaching the chapel.

PUBLIC TRANSPORTATION: None available

For contact information, see Appendix, The Nature Conservancy.

Meadow

Oscawana Island Park

Cortlandt • 2.9 miles, 161 acres

T here are many reasons to hike in Oscawana Island Park: a river view, a walk along a stream, and wide trails. In addition, it is a great place to learn navigation skills. The park is the former McAndrew Estate, purchased by Westchester County in 1958 and under an agreement, managed by the Town of Cortlandt.

The two sections of Oscawana Island Park offer different experiences. The section adjacent to the Hudson River provides a pleasant walk over the railroad tunnel to the edge of the river and a view. There are wetlands, birds, and in early fall, monarch butterflies resting on their trip south. From December 1 to March 1, the park is closed because bald eagles roost there overnight.

The upland section is on the east and north sides of Furnace Dock Road. This section is a good place to become comfortable with unmarked trails because the property is bounded by two roads and Furnace Brook. It is a place that begs to be explored. Oscawana's network of unmarked trails passes remnants of many structures. What their use was is fodder for speculation. A yellow-orange brick

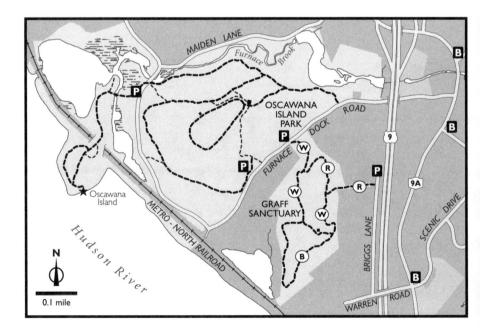

Tree that swallowed a pipe

building without a door or windows is especially curious. Its architecture is best described as 1950s comfort station. Other points of interest are a breached dam adjacent to wetlands where its pond once existed, a pump house with remnants of a pump, and a race track. There are miles of fence built with steel pipe. Occasionally, a tree grows around a section of pipe, looking as if it had swallowed a piece.

Trees along the main route through the park are labeled with both common and Latin names. There are many non-native species; if you are interested in learning to identify trees, this park is a good place to start.

DRIVING: Take Route 9 to the Route 9A Montrose/Buchanan Exit and turn south onto Route 9A. Turn right onto Furnace Dock Road (west), across from a shopping center, and follow it toward the river. There are parking spots along the road. However, to reach parking for the river portion of the park and another access point, follow the road toward the river and then turn to parallel it. A parking area is to the left, 1.1 miles beyond the turn.

PUBLIC TRANSPORTATION: Beeline Bus #14 stops at the shopping center across the street from Furnace Dock Road.

For contact information, see Appendix, Cortlandt.

Graff Sanctuary

Crugers • 1.1 miles, 30 acres

Tucked behind private homes, Graff Sanctuary provides a quick walk in the woods on a hillside with tree-filtered views out over the Hudson River. Three trails go through an oak forest that includes shagbark hickory and tulip trees. In 1975, Howard Graff donated the property to the National Audubon Society, which transferred ownership to the Saw Mill River Audubon Society (SMRAS) in 1991.

Jack-in-the-Pulpit Trail *Length: 0.3 mile Blaze: red*
As the access trail from Briggs Lane, the Jack-in-the-Pulpit Trail begins at an SMRAS sign and heads close to private property. At 0.1 mile, at a T junction with the Tulip

Structure of unknown origin

Tree Trail (white), it turns right, ascends, and then steeply descends to end at the Tulip Tree Trail.

Tulip Tree Trail   *Length: 0.4 mile Blaze: white*

From the entrance on Furnace Dock Road, the Tulip Tree Trail heads steeply downhill, passing a trail leading left into private property. Reaching the end of the Jack-in-the-Pulpit Trail (red) at 0.1 mile, the Tulip Tree Trail heads gradually uphill. It crosses a small causeway and then passes the end of the River View Trail (blue). It passes a structure of unknown origin, reportedly sealed for safety. There are steps up to a cement platform, which provides a view, probably better when there were fewer trees. The trail turns left and passes the other end of the River View Trail at 0.3 mile. Winding through woods and over a stream, the Tulip Tree Trail ends at a parking spot on Briggs Lane.

River View Trail   *Length: 0.4 mile Blaze: blue*

Beginning on the Jack-in-the-Pulpit Trail (red), the River View Trail passes an unmarked side trail to the Tulip Tree Trail (white), then winds its way through open woods. It follows a stone wall and heads downhill at 0.2 mile. Turning, it parallels the river, offering views along the way and ending at the Tulip Tree Trail.

DRIVING: From Route 9A, just north of Croton-on-Hudson, turn left onto Warren Road, opposite Scenic Drive. Cross the bridge over Route 9 and immediately turn right onto Briggs Lane. Parking is at the end of the road beyond the last driveway. Walk up the driveway of #20 to the trailhead into the sanctuary. A second entrance is on Furnace Dock Road, 0.5 mile from its intersection with Route 9A. Limited parking is on the right, across from the sign.

PUBLIC TRANSPORTATION: Beeline Bus #14 stops at the corner of Route 9A and Scenic Drive. Graff Sanctuary is across the street between the two entrances to Oscawana Island Park on Furnace Dock Road.

For contact information, see Appendix, Saw Mill River Audubon Society.

Pound Ridge Town Park

Pound Ridge • 2.2 miles, 342 acres

Pound Ridge residents who take time to venture from the swimming pool, tennis courts, and playground can find rewards on the 0.6-mile network of unmarked trails in the park. Pine Terrace Preserve extends to the east towards the Halle Ravine Preserve. There is no visible boundary between these entities. Although the trails in Pound Ridge Town Park are not blazed, Shelly's Walk and Bud's Way are easily followed. The network of unmarked trails, some frequently used by runners, includes the Fred Zwick Fitness Trail. At the access road to the town hall, a 1.1-mile bike path extends south, ending at Scott's Corners.

Bud's Way   *Length: 0.1 mile*
Directly across from a No Parking sign at the paddle tennis court, Bud's Way begins at a break in the stone wall. The wood chip path curves down to the right and is

1 Bud's Way
2 Shelly's Walk

0.1 mile

paddle tennis
pool
tennis
BEECH HILL LANE
baseball
volleyball
basketball
P
POUND RIDGE
TOWN PARK
N
Town Hall
WESTCHESTER AVENUE
to Scott's Corner
FANCHER ROAD
137

either lined with logs or set on a boardwalk. It ends near private property at a sign for Bud's Way.

Shelly's Walk   *Length: 0.4 mile*
A handicapped accessible path wends its way along the shore of a rehabilitated pond. It is named in memory of Shelly Satin, a long-time Pound Ridge resident and community advocate. The numerous benches provide places to sit and watch activity in the water. Interpretive signs explain water quality and wildlife habitat. Once past the outlet to the pond, the path curves along a wetland and ends at the access road to the town hall. A wood chip path on the west side of the pond is 0.1 mile.

DRIVING: From I-684, take Exit 4 (Route 172). Head east through Bedford Village on Route 172 to where it ends at Route 137. Turn right and continue 0.5 mile to the park entrance to the left.

PUBLIC TRANSPORTATION: None available

For contact information, see Appendix, Pound Ridge.

Pruyn Sanctuary

Millwood • 3.0 miles, 92 acres

When driving on Route 133, there is little to indicate the existence of a trail system at Pruyn Sanctuary located at #275, a modest white house set back from the road. In 1966, Dr. F. Morgan Pruyn and his wife Agnes donated 16 acres to the Saw Mill River Audubon Society to establish the Gedney Brook Sanctuary, as it was then known. In 1978, Dr. Pruyn purchased an additional 31 acres to prevent its being developed and then donated it to the Audubon Society. Later the Pruyns bequeathed their own property to Audubon, further enlarging the sanctuary. Their residence is now the office of Saw Mill River Audubon. In 1990, the sanctuary was renamed in the Pruyns' honor.

TRAILS

Taking your time is what you do at Pruyn Sanctuary. Narrow trails, wide woods roads, boardwalks, and former gardens offer hikers and birders access to upland woods, wetlands, and rocky hilltops. Steeper sections provide vigorous exercise, while the gentle terrain fosters strolling as well as brisk walks. In particular, the boardwalks with access into extensive wetlands encourage an even slower pace.

Fern Trail   *Length: 1.0 mile Blaze: white*
Starting out as a woods road from the entrance at Woodmill Road, the Fern Trail is the main route into the sanctuary. The trail passes a kiosk, visible from the entrance, and then the junction with Ridge Walk (blue). The woods road ends at a T junction with the Pruyn Trail (green) on a boardwalk to the right. The Fern Trail turns left. At 0.2 mile, it passes through a section of a felled three-foot diameter tree. The Fern Trail reaches an intersection with the other end of Ridge Walk to the left and the Pruyn Trail to the right.

At 0.4 mile, the Fern Trail passes to the left a white-blazed side trail which first loops uphill and then back down. At the Y junction with the Swamp View Trail (red), the Fern Trail bears left. It heads uphill along a woods road, crosses through many stone walls, and passes the other end of Swamp View Trail entering from the right. The Fern Trail is now mainly on woods roads. At 1.0 mile, it ends at a driveway, which leads to parking for two cars at Seven Bridges Road. A sign for the sanctuary is near the mailbox for #59 Seven Bridges Road.

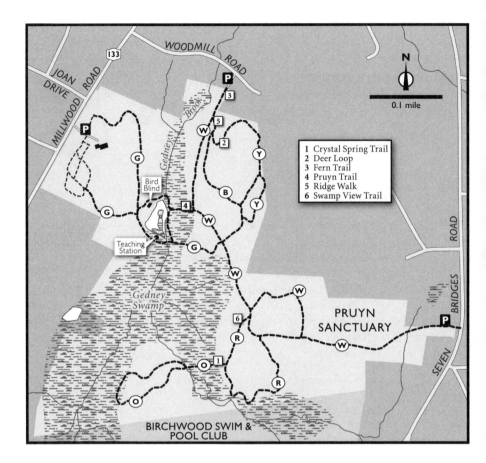

Crystal Spring Trail
Length: 0.3 mile Blaze: orange

At the beginning of the Crystal Spring Trail on the Swamp View Trail (red), the boardwalk passes large ferns growing from hummocks in the wetland. The trail heads slightly uphill at the end of the boardwalk. At the trail junction, proceed counterclockwise to go around the loop. After passing a rock outcropping off to the left, the trail descends to reach a boardwalk and a stone foundation with an intermittent spring. Leaving the boardwalk, the trail gradually turns up a rise. When it reaches a swim club, the Crystal Spring Trail turns sharply left and heads uphill. It then turns and steeply descends to close the loop.

Deer Loop
Length: 0.3 mile Blaze: yellow

In the more rugged section of the sanctuary, Deer Loop begins at a Y junction with Ridge Walk (blue) and heads steeply uphill. It passes a private tennis court and skirts the edge of the property. At a Y junction, it bears left and continues uphill. The right fork leads 350 feet downhill to form a loop. At 0.2 mile, the Deer Loop descends and reaches a T junction with Ridge Walk. The 350-foot segment mentioned above is uphill and to the right.

Pruyn Trail   *Length: 0.9 mile Blaze: green*

Although the Pruyn Trail can be accessed near the Audubon offices in the former Pruyn home, walking along the boardwalk as it crisscrosses Gedney Swamp is more interesting. The cross trails allow varied routes.

Starting at the junction of the Fern Trail (white), 0.2 mile from the entrance on Woodmill Road, the Pruyn Trail is on a boardwalk through most of the wetlands of Gedney Swamp. At the next trail junction, the Pruyn Trail turns right, and after passing a bird blind, it reaches a T junction at 0.1 mile. Turn left and almost immediately turn right to head uphill. At 0.4 mile, the trail reaches the mowed area of the former lawn where there is a choice of several unblazed routes. Use whichever route to the driveway seems most pleasing, and then take the grassy path heading into the woods. At 0.5 mile, the Pruyn Trail turns right, and heads downhill, briefly parallels a stone wall, and descends gradually. At 0.7 mile, the Pruyn Trail passes the trail to the bird blind and continues straight ahead. At the next intersection, turn left. The trail continues on a boardwalk through the wetlands and passes the cross trail mentioned above. The boardwalk ends, but soon begins again and winds through the wetlands. The Pruyn Trail ends at the Fern Trail at 0.9 mile.

Ridge Walk   *Length: 0.2 mile Blaze: blue*

Starting 250 feet from the entrance on Woodmill Road, Ridge Walk heads uphill for 100 feet to bear right at a Y junction with Deer Loop (yellow). Paralleling the Fern Trail (white) while heading uphill, the Ridge Walk reaches the top of the ridge at 0.1 mile. It descends to meet the Deer Loop and turns right downhill to pass, almost immediately, the other end of the Deer Loop. Continuing downhill through a large rock outcropping to the left, the Ridge Walk ends at an intersection with both the Pruyn Trail (green) and the Fern Trail.

Swamp View Trail   *Length: 0.3 mile Blaze: red*

From the Fern Trail (white), the Swamp View Trail heads along a shelf above wetlands, following a stone wall. At a break in the stone wall at 0.1 mile, it reaches the Crystal Spring Trail (orange). The stone wall ends, but the Swamp View Trail continues to the left, up a rise, and across a seasonal wet area. After heading uphill, it turns back to the stone wall, crosses it, and ends at the Fern Trail.

DRIVING: From the Taconic State Parkway, take the Route 100 Exit. Head north on Route 100 to the traffic light at Station Place at a shopping center, and turn right. Continue 0.5 mile further and at the next intersection turn right where Route 133 joins Route 120. In 0.6 mile, when Route 120 bears right, keep left and stay on Route 133. Turn right in 0.5 mile at Woodmill Road. Follow Woodmill Road to the end. Park to the right, taking care not to block the entrance or nearby driveways.

PUBLIC TRANSPORTATION: None available

For contact information, see Appendix, Saw Mill River Audubon Society.

Edith G. Read Wildlife Sanctuary

Rye • 2.2 miles, 179 acres

If "Virginia is for Lovers," then the Edith G. Read Wildlife Sanctuary is for birders. Whether you are a novice or an experienced birder, take advantage of this site, where sightings are posted daily at the Visitors Center. Occasional birders on an early spring visit saw a nesting great horned owl, bufflehead ducks, and three wild turkeys within a few minutes. Recognized as an Important Birding Area by the Audubon Society of New York, it is also a place to stroll through forest, field, and shoreline. Boardwalks meander through wet areas in the forest.

When the property was purchased in 1925 to build Playland, a salt marsh was

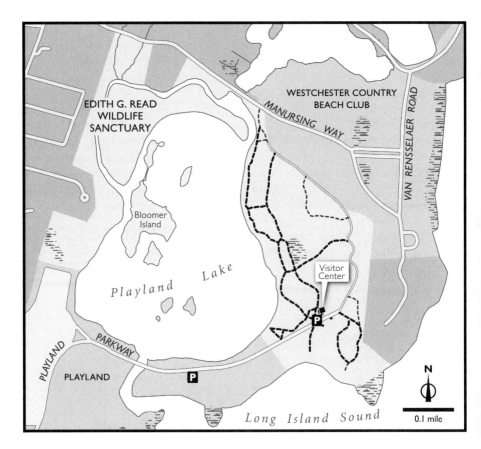

Long Island Sound

dredged for landfill and a brackish lake was created. Sixty years later, the county set aside the lake, adjacent shoreline, woodlands, and fields to establish a wildlife sanctuary. It was named to honor Edith Read, an environmental advocate also active in the 1920s during the early development of Westchester County parks.

Unmarked trails loop around the property, sometimes along the shore of Playland Lake (with a bird blind), and at other times through woods. During growing seasons, trails through fields and meadows are mowed and clearly visible. Benches and boardwalks are strategically placed. A portion of the gravel road near the Education Center is handicapped accessible. The approach to the Long Island Sound shoreline is a boardwalk south and east of the parking lot and also through a mowed path, if the thick reeds have been cut.

NEARBY PARKS: Playland, Rye Town Park, Oakland Beach

DRIVING: From the New England Thruway (I-95), take Exit 19 (Playland Parkway). Follow the Parkway to the Playland entrance, directly ahead at the third light. Continue around two traffic circles to reach a parking lot. Drive through the lot, head to the far right corner, and turn right. The road ends at the sanctuary. A parking fee is charged May through September.

PUBLIC TRANSPORTATION: Beeline Buses run seasonally to the Playland bus terminal: #75-Rye Railroad Station; #76-Portchester, Rye; #91-New Rochelle, Mt. Vernon, Yonkers; #92-White Plains Express. An 0.8-mile walk leads to the sanctuary.

For contact information, see Appendix, Westchester County Parks—Read Sanctuary.

Rye Nature Center

Rye • 2.8 miles, 47 acres

Tucked away from busy Boston Post Road, the Rye Nature Center is located on what had been the Parson family estate. Its original 35 acres were acquired by the City of Rye in 1945. Two additional parcels of land (2 acres, 10 acres) were added through purchase and donation. Rye Nature Center was the first nature center to be designated an Urban Wildlife Sanctuary by the National Institute for Urban Wildlife. Owned by the City of Rye, it is currently operated by Friends of Rye Nature Center.

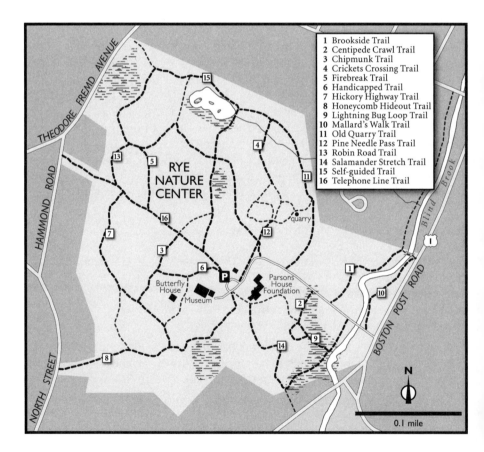

1 Brookside Trail
2 Centipede Crawl Trail
3 Chipmunk Trail
4 Crickets Crossing Trail
5 Firebreak Trail
6 Handicapped Trail
7 Hickory Highway Trail
8 Honeycomb Hideout Trail
9 Lightning Bug Loop Trail
10 Mallard's Walk Trail
11 Old Quarry Trail
12 Pine Needle Pass Trail
13 Robin Road Trail
14 Salamander Stretch Trail
15 Self-guided Trail
16 Telephone Line Trail

Reflection

Its small size makes the Rye Nature Center a great place to learn about the outdoors. The compact trail system travels through rocky outcroppings, wetlands, fields, and streams. Free guidebooks for the two self-guided nature trails are available at the office. Aside from the nature trails, there are no blazed trails, but the property is small and fenced in, so you cannot accidentally wander into someone's back yard. Thus, the Rye Nature Center is an excellent place to practice navigation skills.

The two nature trails have numbered posts keyed to basic ecological information. As they pass through different habitats, these trails offer interesting things to observe. Because of the many connector trails, it is easy to make a walk as long or as short as one would like.

DRIVING: From I-287, take Exit 11 (Rye) and head south on US 1 (Boston Post Road). The Rye Nature Center is to the right at 1.1 miles. Pedestrian access gates are on Boston Post Road, Hammond Road/Theodore Fremd Avenue, and North Street.

PUBLIC TRANSPORTATION: Metro-North New Haven Line Rye Station. Walk along Purchase Street to Boston Post Road (US 1) and turn right, a 0.5-mile walk.

For contact information, see Appendix, Rye Nature Center.

Betsy Sluder Nature Preserve

Armonk • 2.0 miles, 70 acres

A narrow entrance between a gated community and an industrial park is not at all indicative of what lies ahead in Betsy Sluder Nature Preserve. Woods roads and narrow paths wind their way through beech-maple forest and schist outcroppings. In early spring, the many vernal pools are full of frogs singing to attract mates.

TRAILS

The trails are ostensibly blazed, but consider the park to be a network of unmarked trails offering plenty of exercise. Although the elevation gains are slight, it seems that no sooner does a trail go up, than it goes down.

Red Trail   *Length: 0.8 mile Blaze: red*

As the main trail through the preserve, the red trail is on a narrow right-of-way through wetlands. Eventually, the red trail widens and becomes a woods road. Aside from an occasional short level section, it plods its way slowly uphill for its entire length. At 0.2 mile, the red trail passes the white trail, which leads 0.1 mile uphill to the blue trail. Red blazes are found along the trail after it goes by a bench overlooking Agnew Pond. Continuing more steeply uphill, the trail passes the blue trail to the right and passes under a massive boulder jutting out over the trail. At

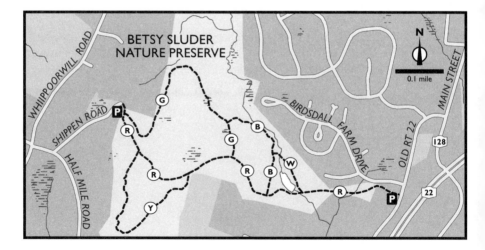

0.4 mile, it passes the green trail to the right, then wetlands. The yellow trail is to the left at 0.5 mile and 0.6 mile, respectively, with the other end of the green trail at 0.7 mile, just beyond a large boulder. The red trail passes an unmarked trail to the left that heads to Shippen Road. The red trail then continues to the property boundary where it ends.

Blue Trail   *Length: 0.3 mile Blaze: blue*
Starting from the green trail, the west end of the blue trail goes up a small rise and then along a stream. After passing the end of the white trail, which can be easily missed, the blue trail turns away from the stream and toward a large rock outcropping to the right at 0.2 mile. Continuing downhill, it ends at the red trail at 0.3 mile.

Green Trail   *Length: 0.5 mile Blaze: green*
It is not easy to find the green trail. On the red trail, just before it reaches the unmarked trail to Shippen Road, look for a large boulder to the right where the green trail heads downhill on a woods road. Veering right, it passes a vernal pool where, in wet weather, the trail may be submerged in spots. At 0.2 mile, it curves slowly right, circling a high point of large rocks. It passes the blue trail to the left, flattens out, and ends at the red trail.

Yellow Trail   *Length: 0.4 mile Blaze: yellow*
As it wends its way through open forest, the yellow trail goes up and down. Starting from the east junction on the red trail, the yellow trail passes the first of many vernal pools at 0.2 mile. At the top of a rise, the trail turns right in view of a large house. At 0.3 mile, the trail turns left and heads up over a rise. The yellow trail passes between two vernal pools and ends at the red trail.

DRIVING: From I-684, take Exit 3 and head south on Route 22. Turn right onto Route 128 and take the first left, Old Route 22. The preserve entrance is to the right just past a gated community on Birdsall Farm Drive. An alternative entrance off Shippen Road has parking for 5 to 8 cars. The west entrance is 50 feet up the private driveway of 11 Shippen Road and to the right.

PUBLIC TRANSPORTATION: Beeline Bus #12 stops near the intersection of Route 22 and Old Route 22.

For contact information, see Appendix, North Castle.

Sunny Ridge Preserve

Ossining • 2.8 miles, 77 acres

The name Sunny Ridge seems to put a smile on your face and makes you want to visit this town preserve. Once there, you will find many reasons to return. First, there are two lovely ponds close enough to the entrance to entice even a timid hiker. And for those who wander farther back into the preserve, there is a view out toward distant hills. Along the trails are many spots to interest budding naturalists, so bring nature guides when you visit.

In 1999, a local resident gave 33 acres to the Town of New Castle to protect wetlands and wildlife habitat. The town subsequently purchased adjacent parcels, one of which had been slated for development. The land in the area was once part of the estate of David T. Abercrombie, founder of Abercrombie & Fitch, a store for outdoorsmen. His stone castle, Elda, still stands on adjacent private property.

TRAILS

The trail system is well laid out in a series of loops off the white trail, making it possible to vary return trips. Many of the trails not along woods roads are lined with logs, making it easy to see where the paths lead. Some blazes have white borders, more noticeable on trees with dark bark. Aside from the white trail, all trails are short. The green, purple, and two red trails are described to be hiked southbound as return trips from the white trail.

White Trail   *Length: 0.8 mile Blaze: white*

As the main trail, the white trail connects Route 134 to Spring Valley Road. At the preserve's entrance on Route 134, the trail heads north on a woods road and passes a kiosk. The white trail goes by the southern red trail to the left and then a vernal pond to the right. After passing the yellow trail to the left at 0.1 mile, the white trail heads through barberry and wineberry bushes on a woods road. At an old foundation, the trail leaves the woods road to the left. An unmarked trail straight ahead leads to a dam and a pond.

After heading downhill, the white trail crosses a seasonal stream and then climbs steeply up Motts Hill along a path lined with logs. At 0.3 mile, the white trail reaches a T junction with the yellow trail and turns right. The narrow trail soon curves to the left and heads up log steps. Logs line the trail as it becomes a woods road. At 0.4 mile, it reaches a junction with the northern red trail to the left

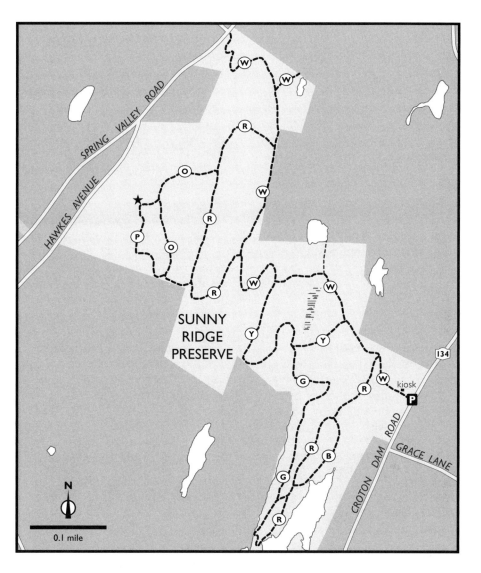

and then passes it again at 0.6 mile. The white trail heads downhill to a Y junction with white blazes going both ways. The trail to the right ends 200 feet ahead at a crude stone wall. The left fork heads downhill and snakes its way via switchbacks and steps to end at Spring Valley Road across from Glendale Road (no parking).

Blue Trail   *Length: 0.1 mile Blaze: blue*
As a side trail off the southern red trail, the blue trail provides an alternate route to the first pond. No matter in which direction it is hiked, the blue trail goes uphill from the southern red trail along a ridge and then down again to rejoin it.

Green Trail   *Length: 0.3 mile Blaze: green*
From the yellow trail, the green trail heads south, crosses a stream on stepping

stones, and continues through a flat area. It makes a sharp right at a large pit at 0.1 mile and then heads up steps to a small ridge. It reaches the southern red trail (near the ponds) at 0.3 mile.

Orange Trail   *Length: 0.3 mile Blaze: orange*
Both ends of the orange trail are connected to the northern red trail. At the uppermost intersection with the northern red trail, the orange trail heads uphill along a woods road. The purple trail is to the right at 0.1 mile. After passing the second junction with the purple trail at 0.2 mile, the orange trail turns left. It ends at 0.3 mile at a T junction with the northern red trail, where to the left is the other end of the orange trail.

Purple Trail   *Length: 0.2 mile Blaze: purple*
Both ends of the purple trail are connected to the orange trail. From the far end of the northern red trail, where the orange trail meets the purple trail, it heads uphill and makes a sharp left. The short spur leads to a view of an adjacent ridge in the foreground and a distant ridge in Harriman Park on the west side of the Hudson River. After reaching the top of the ridge, the purple trail turns left and descends to end at a T junction with the orange trail.

Red Trail (northern)   *Length: 0.4 mile Blaze: red*
A loop off the white trail, the northern red trail is located near the top of Motts Hill. It heads uphill, shortly joins a woods road, and then goes by, at 0.1 mile to the right, the orange trail. After bypassing the other end of the orange trail, it heads left, passing piles of neatly stacked logs. At 0.4 mile, the northern red trail ends at a T junction with the white trail.

Pond on the southern red trail

Red Trail (southern)   *Length: 0.4 mile Blaze: red*

Shortly past the preserve entrance, the southern red trail goes off to the left. It heads uphill to meet the blue trail at 0.1 mile and then descends on steps filled with crushed stone. After crossing a wet area on a boardwalk, the southern red trail meets the other end of the blue trail at 0.2 mile and arrives at a junction with red blazes in two directions. Take the path to the right which soon passes the green trail, travels downhill on steps parallel to the stream, and then uphill to overlook the pond. After reaching a stone-faced concrete dam, the trail turns and follows the shore. It reaches the second pond and, at 0.4 mile, loops back to the junction mentioned above.

Yellow Trail   *Length: 0.3 mile Blaze: yellow*

Beginning 0.1 mile from the entrance on Route 134, the yellow trail heads west downhill on crushed stone. It crosses a stream on stepping stones and turns right at a T junction with the green trail. After passing through an opening in a stone wall, the yellow trail follows another wall and, at its end, turns left uphill. At the top, it follows a ridge with a ravine to the left. Along the route are casket-sized rectangular pits, used in percolation tests for septic fields. The yellow trail ends at the white trail which heads uphill either to the left or to the right to return to the entrance on Route 134.

NEARBY TRAIL: Briarcliff Peekskill Trailway

DRIVING: From Route 9A, take Route 134 east for 0.5 mile. The preserve is to the left just past Grace Lane. Parking is opposite and 100 yards east of Grace Lane. This entrance is 2.5 miles west of the Taconic Parkway's Route 134 Exit. Another entrance is at Spring Valley and Glendale roads (no parking).

PUBLIC TRANSPORTATION: None available

For contact information, see Appendix, New Castle.

Sylvan Glen Park Preserve

Mohegan Lake • 2.6 miles, 180 acres

Sylvan Glen Park Preserve, tucked away on a hillside in northern Westchester, is a place where a visit provides more than just a walk in the woods. This preserve protects an abandoned nineteenth-century granite quarry. In its heyday, Mohegan Granite supplied honey-colored stone to the Cathedral of St. John the Divine, the approaches to the George Washington and Whitestone bridges in New York City, and the Senate Office Building in Washington, D.C.

TRAILS

Remnants of quarrying operations are found in several locations at Sylvan Glen. There are building foundations, a nineteenth-century lime kiln, discarded granite columns, polished blocks, old machinery, and cables. Observe caution when

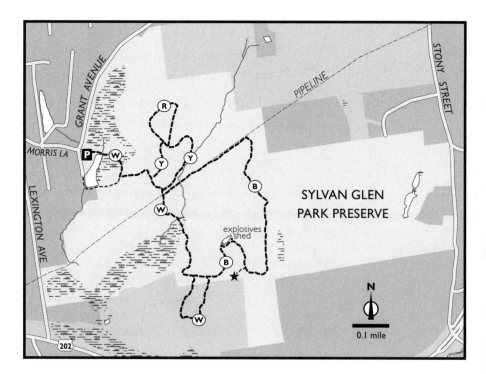

looking down into the quarry and stay back from the edge. Leave artifacts for others to enjoy.

Turtle Pond Trail
Length: 0.9 mile Blaze: white

From the parking lot, the Turtle Pond Trail leads through a wetland, passes an outdoor classroom and a pond, and turns left to head uphill. The Sylvan Brook Trail (yellow) leaves to the left to loop around and end at the Turtle Pond Trail. After crossing the gas pipeline at 0.3 mile and reentering the woods, the Turtle Pond Trail passes through a white pine plantation. It turns right onto a woods road and crosses Sylvan Brook in a wet area adjacent to wetlands. A stone foundation is visible to the left. The trail bears left, leaves the woods road, makes a sharp right turn, and parallels the road. To the right are more foundations associated with the quarry; interpretive signs give their history. The Turtle Pond Trail passes the end of the High Quarry Trail (blue), which heads steeply uphill to the left on a woods road. At 0.6 mile, the trail turns left and begins to ascend. It reaches the end of the quarry at a talus heap. At 0.9 mile, the Turtle Pond Trail terminates at the High Quarry Trail.

Grant Lookout Trail
Length: 0.3 mile Blaze: red

Beginning on the Sylvan Brook Trail (yellow), the Grant Lookout Trail heads uphill and, at 0.1 mile, descends. It passes a small quarry pit to the left and ends at the Sylvan Brook Trail.

High Quarry Trail
Length: 1.1 miles Blaze: blue

The High Quarry Trail begins on the Turtle Pond Trail (white) and heads steeply uphill. At 0.1 mile, the Turtle Pond Trail ends to the right, while the High Quarry Trail continues uphill to reach the edge of the quarry. Pieces of abandoned quarry equipment are scattered along the trail. After leaving the quarry rim, the trail passes under a rock bridge. There is a water-filled quarry to the left as the trail turns right and passes a stone shed, once housing explosives. The trail goes through a stone wall, then turns to parallel it. At 0.3 mile, the trail reaches an unmarked side trail leading to a view down into the pit and the only unobstructed view in the park—a view to the west. After passing more stone walls on a relatively level woods road, at 0.8 mile the trail turns sharply left, descending toward the gas pipeline. Turning left again, the High Quarry

Explosives shed

History of the Quarry

About 1895, an outcropping of golden granite was discovered on the hills north of present-day Route 202 near Mohegan Lake. Known as Peekskill Granite, it is part of the Ordovician Cortlandt igneous complex which also underlies Blue Mountain Reservation.

Under the name Mohegan Granite, various owners operated the quarry. In 1925, Bruno M. Grenci and Thomas H. Ellis acquired the property and its quarrying operations. They modernized the machinery using diesel-electric generators instead of less dependable steam engines and built a narrow gauge cable railway, which eliminated the need for oxen. At the time, the company was the largest employer in Yorktown, using hundreds of workers for quarrying and carving stone. The granite eagles atop Arlington Memorial Bridge on the Potomac River attest to the craftsmanship of their workers.

Although operations continued through the Great Depression, they ended with the advent of World War II in 1941. A lack of manpower coupled with the lower cost of newer construction materials (steel, glass, aluminum) sounded the company's death knell. The property lay dormant for years until, in 1981, it was purchased by the Town of Yorktown from Norman Van Kirk of Red Bank, New Jersey. When enough adjoining property was acquired, the town opened the preserve. Eagle Scout projects have enhanced trails and created interpretive signs.

Trail, now without blazes, follows the pipeline downhill. At the base of the descent, the trail crosses a small stream and reaches an orange-and-white pylon where it ends at the Turtle Pond Trail.

Sylvan Brook Trail   *Length: 0.3 mile Blaze: yellow*
From the Turtle Pond Trail (white), the Sylvan Brook Trail passes one end of the Grant Lookout Trail (red) at 0.1 mile and shortly the other end of that same trail. The Sylvan Brook Trail parallels a stream and ends at the Turtle Pond Trail near the gas pipeline.

DRIVING: From the Taconic State Parkway, take the Route 202 Exit and turn west. At the traffic light at 1.8 miles, turn right onto Lexington Avenue and drive 0.6 mile uphill to Morris Lane. Turn right and go 0.2 mile to a parking lot directly ahead at the bottom of the hill.

PUBLIC TRANSPORTATION: Beeline Bus #12 to Lexington Avenue in Crompond. Walk 0.6 mile uphill to Morris Lane, turn right, and walk 0.2 mile to a parking lot directly ahead at the bottom of the hill.

For contact information, see Appendix, Yorktown.

Warburg Park

Millwood • 2.4 miles, 32 acres

$\mathbf{A}$ wide gravel road greets visitors to Warburg Park, but a walk along it is short, unless there's an interest in examining the Town of New Castle's composting area, with its wood chip mountains. The park's trails do, however, go through several habitats with vernal pools and a large pond. Warburg Park is a cooperative venture of the Town's Conservation Board and its Recreation and Parks Commission.

In 1948, James and Bessie Rosenberg donated a 37-acre landlocked parcel to New York State in honor of Felix M. Warburg (1887-1937), philanthropist, banker, and proponent of an Arab-Jewish state. When the Taconic State Park Commission decided the area was not large enough to be a state park, the state transferred it to the Town of New Castle in 1963. The town negotiated with Con Edison and

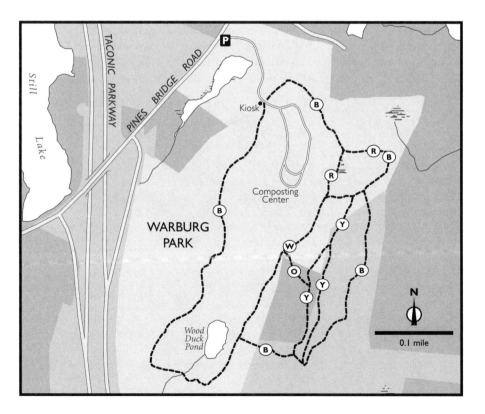

finally, in 1988, acquired an adjoining 57-acre parcel, which gave access from Shinglehouse and Pinesbridge roads. Part of this additional land is used for town composting operations.

TRAILS

Easy on the feet is the best way to describe trails in Warburg Park, passing as they do through mixed hardwood forest. To the left of the access road on the Perimeter Trail, a small network of trails makes many short hikes possible. A 100-foot orange trail connects the white trail to the Ridge Valley Loop.

Perimeter Trail
Length: 1.3 miles Blaze: blue

Where the Perimeter Trail crosses the access road, go counterclockwise and pass a kiosk with a map. The trail heads up to reach a ridge and zigzags as it follows a stone wall. Leaving the stone wall, it follows the edge of the ridge looking down into the valley and at a pond. At 0.3 mile, the trail descends to where road noise from the Taconic State Parkway is audible. Turning away from the parkway, the trail heads steeply downhill to pass the white trail to the left at the end of a stone wall.

The Perimeter Trail crosses a stream and turns away from the pond. At 0.7 mile, the Ridge/Valley Loop (yellow) enters from the left to join the Perimeter Trail for 100 feet before heading to the left up onto the ridge. The Perimeter Trail continues to climb over the flank of the ridge, turns, and goes up a valley. It turns again, away from the ridge, and then heads downhill, passing a vernal pool. The red trail joins from the left at 1.0 mile and together they enter the next valley. The trails go uphill steeply with the town composting site visible. The red trail leaves to the left. The Perimeter Trail reaches a woods road, turns left, and ends at 1.3 miles at the access road.

SPRING PEEPERS

That intense chirping sound so often heard in the early spring woods is made by one of the smallest native frogs—spring peepers. These harbingers of spring, like wood and tree frogs, survive winter's coldest weather frozen hidden under the damp leaf litter at water's edge, where they do not eat, breathe, or even have a heartbeat. As temperatures rise, these creatures literally come to life, the males singing loudly as they call to mates. By the end of March, the forest abounds with this serenade from the fresh water of vernal pools.

Most animal species avoid freezing and adapt to the cold either by migrating, hibernating, growing dense extra coats of feathers or fur, or burning calories to maintain body warmth. In almost every animal, freezing can cause tissue damage. Spring peepers effectively counteract the cold winter temperatures by creating special antifreeze composed of sugars or sugar alcohols. As ice forms in the frogs' cells, this compound draws water out, leaving behind the anatomical equivalent of thick maple syrup. Once the warmer weather arrives, peepers "spring" back to life and sing!

Red Trail   *Length: 0.3 mile Blaze: red*

The red trail is a short loop providing access to the white and yellow trails. For half its length, it is co-aligned with the Perimeter Trail (blue). From the beginning of the red trail on the Perimeter Trail, go right (counterclockwise), following only red blazes. The red trail passes the white trail to the right, then the Ridge/Valley Loop (yellow) at 0.1 mile. At a T junction, the red trail turns left to join the Perimeter Trail which enters from the right. The co-aligned trails circle back to where the red trail started.

Ridge/Valley Loop   *Length: 0.5 mile Blaze: yellow*

The Ridge/Valley Loop is a trail of contrasts. From the junction with the red trail, head south, and at the point where the trail splits, go left. Almost immediately the trail heads up onto the ridge, narrow enough in places to see both sides. The trail reaches a T junction with the Perimeter Trail (blue) at 0.2 mile. It turns right, joining this blue trail for 100 feet before leaving it to head up the wide valley with outcroppings on the ridge just traversed. At 0.3 mile, the trail reaches an orange trail which heads 100 feet straight ahead to join the white trail. The Ridge/Valley Loop, however, turns right and right again to parallel the ridge. It closes the loop at a T junction.

White Trail   *Length: 0.3 mile Blaze: white*

Starting out on the Perimeter Trail (blue), the white trail first leads to a pond, then passes below a high rock outcropping on the left. Large pieces of metamorphic rock with contoured bands have tumbled down the hillside. Taconic Parkway noise abates as the trail heads up the valley. After crossing into another valley at 0.2 mile, the white trail passes the orange trail to the right. Within sight of compost piles and with the smell of wood chips in the air, the white trail ends at the Perimeter Trail at 0.3 mile.

DRIVING: From northbound Taconic State Parkway, take the Pinesbridge Road Exit and turn right. The park is on the right, just past houses. From southbound Taconic State Parkway, exit at Route 133, turn right, and pass under the parkway. Turn left to go northbound on the parkway, following the directions above.

PUBLIC TRANSPORTATION: None available

For contact information, see Appendix, New Castle.

Mount Holly Sanctuary

SECTION IV

AFTERNOON JAUNTS

- Have three to five miles of trails
- Offer varied habitats
- Provide enough trail miles for aerobic exercise
- Are within a 15-30 minute drive

Brinton Brook Sanctuary

Croton-on-Hudson • 4.3 miles, 129 acres

Tucked away from busy Route 9, Brinton Brook Sanctuary is surrounded by an apartment complex, a golf course, and a power line. But surprisingly, there is a variety of wildlife to be found in the open meadows, old orchard, edge environments, red maple swamp, hemlock groves, dry ridge hardwood forest, and rocky slopes. The varied terrain offers opportunities to take easy or vigorous hikes.

The tract was originally owned by Laura and Willard Brinton. In 1957, following her husband's death, Laura Brinton donated 112 acres to the National Audubon Society so the land would be permanently protected as a wildlife refuge. After her death, an additional 17 acres were donated by Ruth Brinton Perera, a niece.

TRAILS

A series of loops and connector trails offers many options for exploring the sanctuary. The interconnected 0.2 mile of wide farm roads near the sanctuary entrance provide an easy stroll and a short introduction to using unmarked trails. The meadows are mowed to prevent the forest's encroaching on the field ecosystem. Although not considered part of the trail system at Brinton Brook, there is a 0.5-mile path under the high tension power line adjacent to the property.

Pond Loop Trail   *Length: 1.3 miles Blaze: yellow*
Heading clockwise from the sanctuary's main entrance, the Pond Loop Trail passes through an open meadow and an old orchard near former farm roads. At 0.3 mile, it reaches Red Maple Swamp and a pond, where an unmarked side trail leads 0.1 mile to building #23 at the Amberlands apartment complex.

Leaving the woods road, the trail runs along an embankment. It passes the Turkey Trail (blue) to the left at 0.5 mile and again at 0.6 mile. Turning right, the Pond Loop Trail begins its return to the entrance. It passes the Hemlock Spring Trail (red) at 0.9 mile, an unmarked farm road at 1.0 mile, and the Hemlock Spring Trail again at 1.1 miles. The Pond Loop ends at the parking lot.

Coyote Trail   *Length: 0.4 mile Blaze: green*
From the Turkey Trail (blue), the Coyote Trail heads uphill. At 0.1 mile, it passes an unmarked trail that connects to the Highland Trail (white) and travels between two glacial erratics at the junction. At 0.3 mile, it turns right as it joins the Highland Trail. The Coyote Trail ends at an intersection with the Hemlock Spring Trail (red) at 0.4 mile, where the Highland Trail turns left.

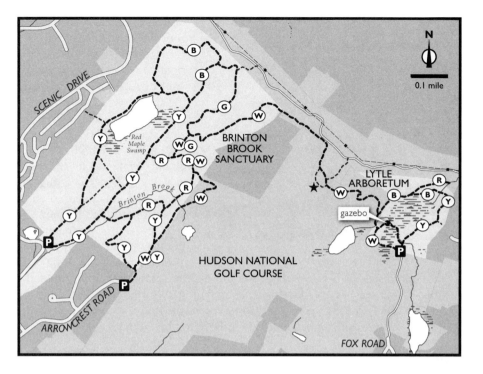

Hemlock Spring Trail

Length: 0.5 mile Blaze: red

Beginning on the Pond Loop Trail (yellow), the Hemlock Spring Trail follows above the brook. At 0.1 mile, it passes the Laurel Rock Trail (yellow) at Split Rock Spring, which was designed by Willard Brinton. The trail climbs gradually to the ridge and at 0.2 mile, again passes the Laurel Rock Trail. Continuing to climb, the trail crosses three seasonal streams before descending. The Highland Trail joins from the right and together they pass stone ruins and then the Coyote Trail (green) at 0.4 mile. Continuing downhill, the Hemlock Spring Trail ends at the Pond Loop Trail. To the left, it is a 0.4-mile return to the sanctuary's main entrance.

Highland Trail

Length: 1.1 miles Blaze: white

From the parking spots on Arrowcrest Road, outside the entrance to the Hudson National Golf Course, the Highland Trail parallels the golf course. Hikers should stay on the path. Within sight of parking, the trail joins the Laurel Rock Trail (yellow) entering from the left. The trails are co-aligned until the Laurel Rock Trail leaves to the left at 0.2 mile. A large sign noting that Lytle Arboretum is 2 miles away is not correct. The trail has been rerouted to avoid a private holding; it is 1.5 miles from the entrance on Arrowcrest Road to the Lytle Arboretum.

The Highland Trail crosses a stream and gradually drifts downhill away from the ridge. It turns to descend, passing a massive glacial erratic off to the right just outside the sanctuary. At 0.5 mile, the Highland Trail reaches a T junction with the Hemlock Spring Trail (red) and turns right to join it. Continuing downhill, they pass stone ruins before reaching the end of the Coyote Trail (green) to the

Split Rock Spring

right. The Hemlock Spring Trail continues straight ahead and the Highland Trail turns to the right. At 0.6 mile, the Highland Trail turns right again to leave the Coyote Trail. It traverses a ridge, with a stone wall visible along the side of the next ridge, and heads downhill. A large glacial erratic is to the right at 0.8 mile. After crossing the power line maintenance road, the trail heads uphill again.

Once across a stream, the Highland Trail enters a Norway spruce grove at 1.0 mile. It climbs uphill steadily between the power line and the golf course. At 1.1 miles, the Highland Trail reaches a T junction where the unmarked trail leads left along the power line back to the Coyote Trail. To the right, the trail continues, now as the Village of Croton Trail, and ends at Lytle Arboretum in 0.4 mile.

Laurel Rock Trail   *Length: 0.5 mile Blaze: yellow*
Starting on the Hemlock Spring Trail (red) at the Split Rock Spring, the Laurel Rock Trail traverses some of the more rugged terrain in the sanctuary. The trail heads uphill sometimes more steeply than at others. At the top of the ridge at 0.3 mile, it turns left to join the Highland Trail (white). To the right, it is 300 feet to the parking on Arrowcrest Road, just outside the entrance to the golf course. The Laurel Rock Trail leaves the Highland Trail to the left at 0.4 mile and heads downhill to end at the Hemlock Spring Trail.

Turkey Trail   *Length: 0.5 mile Blaze: blue*
From the northeast corner of the pond on the Pond Loop Trail (yellow), the Turkey Trail heads through a hardwood forest of black birch, hickory, and oak. As it nears the edge of the property, the trail reaches the highest point in the park near power lines from Indian Point. At the junction with the Coyote Trail (green) at 0.3 mile, it passes through parallel stone walls to end at the Pond Loop Trail.

NEARBY PARKS: Graff Sanctuary, Oscawana Island Park

DRIVING: From Route 9, north of Croton-on-Hudson, take the Senasqua Road Exit and head north on Route 9A. Pass the Sky View Nursing Home to the left at 0.3 mile and turn right at a sign for Brinton Brook Sanctuary. Follow the gravel road up a private drive to parking.

PUBLIC TRANSPORTATION: Beeline Bus #14 stops at Warren Road, 0.2 mile north of the access road. It is a 0.3-mile road walk to the sanctuary from Route 9A.

For contact information, see Appendix, Saw Mill River Audubon Society.

Village of Croton Trail

Croton-on-Hudson • 0.4 mile

Negotiations during the construction of the Hudson National Golf Course resulted in the Village of Croton Trail, which joins Brinton Brook Sanctuary to the Jane E. Lytle Memorial Arboretum. From the Highland Trail in Brinton Brook Sanctuary, the trail continues uphill steadily. At a Y junction, white blazes go in both directions and the segments are of equal length. The trail to the right heads towards the golf course and passes through a stand of phragmite reeds to reach a bench with a view across the golf course to the Hudson River. The chimneys seen here are the remains of a former property owner's mansion. The trail rejoins the main trail as it descends through a series of switchbacks to end at the Link Trail in the Lytle Arboretum at 0.4 mile.

For contact information, see Appendix, Croton.

Jane E. Lytle Memorial Arboretum

Croton-on-Hudson • 0.8 mile, 20 acres

Connected to Brinton Brook Sanctuary via the Village of Croton Trail, the Lytle Arboretum is a trailhead for a longer walk. The arboretum can be enjoyed in its own right, as wildlife viewing opportunities are plentiful on this tiny trail system. The main entrance into Lytle Arboretum is along a golf course right-of-way, so remaining on the road is important to avoid being hit by a golf ball. The trail system is a loop with spurs going out to the alternate entrances: one to Brinton Brook Sanctuary and the other to Hixson Road (no parking). Each of the trails in this 0.8-mile trail system has a name, so walkers can find an area of the arboretum which allows them to view a particular type of wildlife. The Beech Trail (yellow) goes 0.2 mile through a beech forest. It finishes at the Marshlands Trail (blue) which continues for 0.2 mile to end at the white trail, the Link Trail, and the Village of Croton Trail. Rubin's Trail (red) goes 0.1 mile to a stream. The 0.1-mile Boardwalk Trail crosses wetlands (handicapped accessible to the gazebo).

DRIVING: From Route 9 in Croton-on-Hudson, take either the Senesqua Road Exit or Route 9A Exit onto South Riverside Drive. Turn right, then left onto High Street, ending at a T junction with Old Post Road. Turn right and take the first left onto Lounsbury Road. Continue uphill and turn right onto graveled Fox Road. Pass through the Hudson National Golf Course right-of-way to the parking lot.

PUBLIC TRANSPORTATION: Beeline Bus #14 stops at Old Post Road and at Lounsbury Road, where a 0.7-mile walk on a narrow road leads to the parking lot.

For contact information, see Appendix, Lytle Arboretum.

Brownell Preserve
Marx Tract

Goldens Bridge • 4.1 miles, 228 acres

Off Route 138 behind private property is Brownell Preserve, a Town of Lewisboro park. A half-mile east on Route 138 is the Marx Tract, preserved open space of the North Salem Open Land Foundation (NSOLF). Connected via an ATT cable line, the two tracts preserve 118 and 110 acres respectively. The gentle terrain, woods roads, and ATV tracks are suitable for snowshoeing and cross-country skiing.

Thanks to a bequest from Lewisboro residents Katharine and George Brownell, in 1984 the town acquired open space for wildlife habitat and passive recreation. George Brownell served as a diplomatic envoy to Mexico and India during the Truman Administration.

TRAILS

A 50-foot entrance trail leads into Brownell Preserve. It ends at the ATT cable line which is the spine of the trails in the Brownell Preserve and also leads to the Marx Tract. Trails in the Brownell Preserve are blazed with colored tags. At the Marx Tract, an unmarked woods road leads 0.4 mile north from the small parking lot on Route 138.

Thick hairy vines wind their way up many trees. Do not touch! These vines are poison ivy and are as toxic as the leaves.

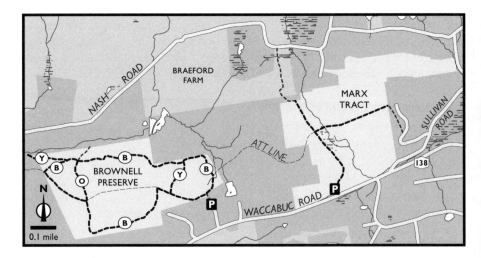

ATT Line

Length: 1.8 miles Blaze: none

Widely-spaced numbered orange posts mark the ATT line. There are three sections totaling 0.5 mile where the blue trail utilizes the ATT line. It is 0.5 mile between the two preserves along the ATT line and another 0.4 mile to the eastern edge of the Marx Tract.

Blue Trail

Length: 1.8 miles Blaze: blue

In order to form a loop through the preserve, the blue trail utilizes the ATT line, but at times is not marked with blue blazes. From the entrance to the preserve, head clockwise around the loop. There is one blue blaze along the ATT line as it heads left. At 0.1 mile, it passes a yellow trail to the right providing a 0.2-mile

Poison ivy vine

shortcut to the other side of the loop. Just past a stone wall, the blue trail turns left off the ATT line. After heading steadily uphill, the trail slowly curves into an area with little understory except for barberry bushes. At 0.5 mile, the forest closes in a bit and the trail turns right to join a woods road. The blue trail reaches the ATT line at 0.7 mile and turns left. Straight ahead is the orange trail which heads downhill, paralleling a stream and stone wall to end in 0.2 mile at the blue trail.

The ATT right-of-way does not have blue blazes, but at 0.9 mile, at ATT post #468, the blazes reappear as the trail turns to head downhill. It passes a large sugar maple to the left and the yellow trail, which descends for 0.1 mile to end at a breached dam. At 1.1 miles, the blue trail intersects the orange trail to the right. Going uphill, the blue trail crosses a series of seasonal streams and passes a large boulder at 1.3 miles. Continuing uphill, the blue trail turns to cross a seasonally wet area. Just beyond a stream crossing at 1.6 miles near the property boundary, it passes the yellow trail to the right which heads uphill 0.2 mile to the ATT line. After going left and crossing a stone wall, the blue trail turns to follow it. The blue trail ends at the ATT line, where to the right, it is a 0.1-mile walk back to the entrance road. To the left, it is 0.5 mile to the Marx Tract.

DRIVING: From I-684 take Exit 6 (Route 35) and head east on Route 35 for 0.1 mile. Turn left onto Route 22 and go 1.9 miles. Make a right turn past a shopping center and follow signs to Route 138. Turn right onto Route 138. For Brownell Preserve, continue 2.1 miles to Harriet Lane to the left, with parking for two cars at the end. The Marx Tract is 0.5 mile past Harriet Lane, opposite #78. Neither entrance has a sign near Route 138.

PUBLIC TRANSPORTATION: None available

For contact information, see Appendix, Lewisboro.

Franklin D. Roosevelt (FDR) State Park

Yorktown • 3.4 miles, 841 acres

Not to be confused with the FDR home in Hyde Park, Franklin D. Roosevelt (FDR) State Park is a large multi-use park with picnic tables, boat rentals, and a swimming pool. There are two distinct user groups. In season and on weekends, picnickers arrive by car and busload, filling the park with sounds of people enjoying the outdoors, and smells wafting from grills. During weekends in spring and fall, there are often road races and walkathons. But on weekdays and off-season weekends, local residents walk, jog, or bike along the park roads. Small children use the empty parking lots to practice riding their bicycles.

TRAILS

Aside from a few scattered disks nailed to trees, the trails at FDR are by and large unmarked. There are 6.8 miles of trails to walk in the park, half of which are roads and sidewalks. The remaining miles are in the woods away from crowds.

A winter walk with man's best friend

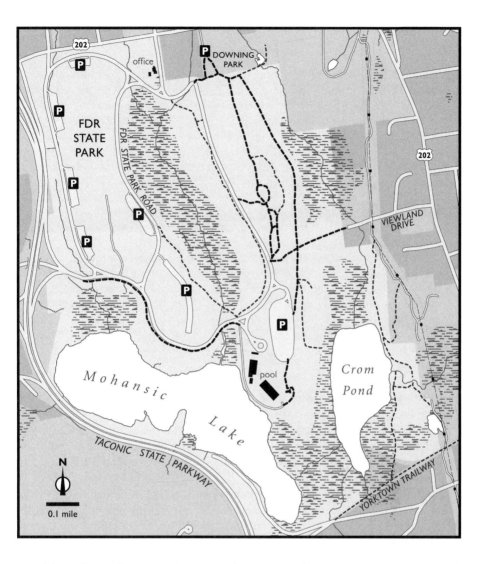

Athletes from adjacent Yorktown High School, walkers, and joggers use several tried-and-true loops: 1.9 miles along the paved park road, 0.9 mile around the swimming pool area, 0.6 mile on the paved path from the entrance to the swimming pool, and a 3-mile loop on gravel and paved park roads.

Old roads along the back edge of the park and well-worn paths leading into wetlands near Crom Pond provide other places to walk. The loop consisting of two somewhat parallel trails is 0.9 mile and being relatively level, is ideal for cross-country skiing. These areas are a distance away from the swimming pool and picnicking crowds and make for more interesting woodland forays.

Local entrances give access to the less developed parts of the park. Viewland Drive (no parking) provides access to the parallel trails on the east side of the park. Just east of the Baldwin Road Exit of the Taconic State Parkway is access and parking, either west along former Mohansic Avenue or east on unmarked well-

History of FDR Park

New York State acquired the land which now comprises FDR Park as two pieces. Purchased in 1908, the area south of the lake was to be used for the New York State Training School for Boys. The State Hospital Commission acquired the land north of the lake. Because both Mohansic Lake and Crom Pond are in the New York City watershed, there was concern over possible pollution of the city's water supply. Results of a study concluded that there indeed was a potential problem and, as a result, the land was given to the county in 1922. It was used for a Civilian Conservation Corps camp during President Roosevelt's administration. Many park buildings reflect that influence. To serve the proposed facility, a rail spur from the Putnam Division in Yorktown Heights was planned but never completed. All that remains is a partially constructed railbed, some of which is underwater in adjacent wetlands.

In 1957, Governor Averell Harriman signed a bill which returned the lands east of the Taconic State Parkway to the state to be developed as a state park. The land west of the Taconic became county-owned Mohansic Golf Course. A portion of the county property was given to the Town of Yorktown and is now Downing Park. Until 1982, FDR Park was known as Mohansic Park. To celebrate the 100th anniversary of FDR's birth, the New York State Office of Parks, Recreation and Historic Preservation renamed the park in his honor.

established paths. Former Mohansic Avenue was cut off when the Taconic State Parkway was widened to six lanes in the 1960s; it is still used by fishermen to reach their boats on Mohansic Lake. The route to the east is through woods and wetlands, but because there is no bridge across the outlet from Crom Pond, these trails do not connect to the network heading south from Viewland Drive.

DRIVING: From the Taconic State Parkway, take the FDR Park Exit. There is an entrance fee daily in season and on weekends during spring and fall. Parking for Yorktown residents is available at Downing Park off Route 202, east of the Taconic State Parkway just past the bus entrance to FDR Park. The FDR trails are accessible from behind the wood barriers in the rear of Downing Park.

PUBLIC TRANSPORTATION: Beeline Bus #10 to Route 202 at Strang Boulevard near the blocked-off entrance, or #15 to the commuter parking lot near Downing Park (not on Sundays).

For contact information, see Appendix, FDR Park.

Gedney Park

Millwood • 3.4 miles, 126 acres

If you think Gedney Park is only a playground, sledding hill, and fishing pond, you are quite mistaken. Do not allow the entrance to the park fool you because opportunities to observe wildlife are not apparent when one first arrives. Having passed the park many times in the 40 years we have lived in Westchester County, we were amazed to find 3.4 miles of trails through wetlands, woodlands, and several edge environments.

TRAILS

The trail system in Gedney Park surrounds several of the Town of New Castle's ball fields. There are some relatively flat sections with gentle ups and downs and some short steep sections. In addition to three interpretive trails, there is a handicapped accessible paved path running from the parking lot to a fishing pier on the lake, and also a half-mile of unmarked trail with short access trails.

Blue Trail   *Length: 0.6 mile Blaze: blue*
To the right, just past the gate on the access road to the ball fields, the blue trail co-aligned with the red trail heads uphill. At an intersection they split, with the blue trail going right to climb steeply uphill. It passes an unmarked trail to the right, which heads downhill, passing rusted rope tow pulleys and reaching the top of the sledding hill in 0.1 mile. The blue trail heads over the crest of the hill and reaches a junction where the red trail enters from the right. The joint trail goes straight, heading downhill. It enters a soccer field, turns left following the edge of the field, and then turns left again to leave the field. Heading uphill, it skirts the base of the hill and closes the loop at 0.6 mile.

Red Trail   *Length: 1.6 miles Blaze: red*
There are many marked and unmarked side trails along the red trail. Just past the gate to the right side of the access road to the ball fields, the joint red/blue trail heads uphill. At an intersection, the blue trail turns right, while the red/blue trail continues straight ahead, skirting the base of the hill. It enters the soccer field at 0.2 mile, turns right to go along its edge, and then turns right again to head uphill. At a trail junction at 0.3 mile, the blue trail continues straight while the red trail bears left and heads downhill. The red trail reaches a T junction at 0.5 mile and turns right. The red trail to the left provides access in 150 feet to the soccer field.

At the next intersection, the red trail makes a sharp left, while the unmarked trail straight ahead leads to the Catskill Aqueduct and the access road under the power line. Well inside the woods, the red trail circles ball fields. Passing over a wet area on a bridge at 0.9 mile, the red trail is within sight of baseball fields and then turns away, reaching a woods road. To the right is the cul-de-sac at the end of Barnes Lane. To the left, it is 0.2 mile to the white trail. Heading uphill, the red trail reaches a trail junction at 1.1 miles; the yellow trail continues straight ahead downhill.

The yellow and red trails turn left together as they head downhill. After crossing a stream at 1.4 miles, they reach a trail junction where the yellow trail goes right and the red trail bears left. The red trail makes a sharp right turn at 1.5 miles. Straight ahead is a short side trail leading down to the road; its red blazes begin soon after the intersection. The red trail bears right and descends to reach a grassy area south of the pond. Red blazes go in both directions on the wood chip path. To the right, the red trail heads to the road where a walk to the left along the road closes the loop at the red/blue trailhead. To the left, the red trail follows the wood chip path. Just before the white nature trail begins, the red trail heads left uphill 60 yards to create a loop at the intersection mentioned above.

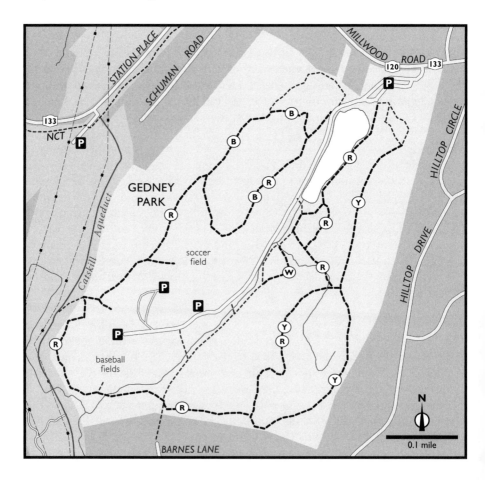

At the pond

Yellow Trail   *Length: 0.8 mile Blaze: yellow*

Behind the playground at the top of the sledding hill, the yellow trail begins at the edge of the woods. At 0.2 mile, it reaches a Y junction where it goes in both directions. Heading clockwise to the left, the yellow trail follows the base of a hill and crosses stone walls before it climbs uphill steeply. It passes a split rail fence and reaches the red trail at 0.5 mile. The yellow trail turns right to join the red trail and at 0.6 mile they head downhill together. After crossing a stream, the joint trail splits. The red trail continues to the left and the yellow turns right to close the loop at the Y junction mentioned above.

INTERPRETIVE TRAILS: Thanks to Eagle Scout projects, there are three interpretive trails at the park. The 0.2-mile white trail focuses on wetlands and is just south of the pond. Signs on a 0.1-mile red trail along the edge of the pond describe how Native Americans lived, hunted, and gathered food. A 0.1-mile yellow trail behind the playground features woodland descriptions.

NEARBY TRAIL & PARK: North County Trailway, Pruyn Sanctuary

DRIVING: From the Taconic State Parkway, take the Route 100 Exit. Head north on Route 100 to the traffic light at a shopping center at Station Place (Route 133) and turn right. Continue for 0.5 mile and at the next intersection turn right where Route 133 joins Route 120. The entrance is to the right in 0.3 mile.

PUBLIC TRANSPORTATION: Beeline Bus #15. The nearest bus stop is at the junction of Station Place and NY 100 in Millwood. Follow the sidewalk to Route 133/120 and turn right to walk 0.3 mile along the road to the park entrance.

For contact information, see Appendix, New Castle.

George's Island Park

Montrose • 3.1 miles, 204 acres

$\mathbf{A}$t first glance, George's Island Park appears to be a picnic park and boat launch. But, hidden off to the side, trails connect to other parks, making longer hikes through the woods possible. In winter, the Hudson River is a favorite feeding spot for bald eagles. From the end of the parking area straight ahead as one enters, late afternoon visitors with binoculars can view eagles roosting in the trees on Dugan Point. Of course there is no guarantee of seeing them on any particular day.

TRAILS

RiverWalk, Westchester County's portion of the Hudson River Valley Greenway Trail, is the spine of the trail network. The entrance road splits RiverWalk. The section

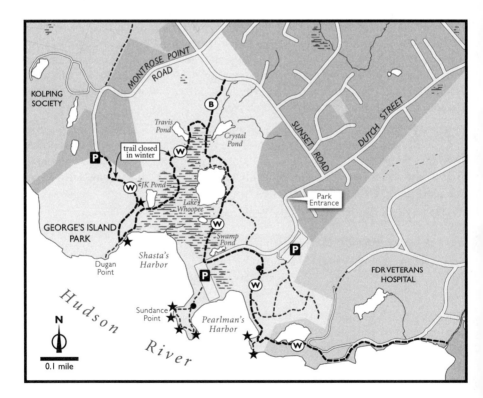

to the north is a woodland walk; the section to the south has river views. Both have RiverWalk blazes at trailheads and trail junctions, but are accessed from different parking lots. The connecting piece goes 0.2 mile along the entrance road from the picnic pavilion closest to the entrance, to a mowed path to the right of the parking lot. There is 0.5 mile of unmarked trail south of the parking lot. Although there are no handicapped accessible trails, the parking lots by the river

Rejected bricks

offer broad views. Near the picnic pavilion overlooking the river, the 0.2 mile of unmarked paths lead to more river views.

RiverWalk (northbound)   *Length: 1.3 miles Blaze: white*

In the parking lot at the far end of the entrance road, a post in the grass on the north side indicates the entrance to RiverWalk. At 0.1 mile, the wide path first passes to the right a road leading back to the maintenance building and then Lake Whoopee to the left. The trail winds its way through woods and at 0.3 mile, heads onto a short causeway and up and down several steep hills. At 0.4 mile, RiverWalk reaches the blue trail to the right. This trail was established as a winter route so that hikers do not disturb bald eagles roosting for the night on Dugan Point.

RiverWalk crosses a bridge and, at 0.5 mile, heads through an area littered with bricks. High above a former clay pit filled with water, the trail descends to a bridge over its outlet. Much of this area has a thick understory of invasive plants, proof that the soil was once heavily disturbed. After crossing a bridge at 0.8 mile, the trail passes large black walnut trees and a pond. It reaches a rock face and the woodland opens up. From a beach at 0.9 mile, there is a view. At low tide it looks as if one might walk back to the parking lot along the beach. However, it is not possible to do so without getting wet, muddy feet because of the fast-moving outflow from Lake Whoopee.

The trail follows the shore and at 1.0 mile, turns right to head steeply uphill. It reaches a woods road along a ledge with views down to a pond. Continuing uphill, it leaves the woods road and crosses through an area covered with myrtle and Christmas fern. At 1.2 miles, it turns right onto a closed paved road and heads slightly downhill to parking for three cars on Montrose Point Road. RiverWalk continues past George's Island Park. It follows Montrose Point Road 0.2 mile to the trail through Kolping Society property toward Montrose Point State Forest.

RiverWalk (southbound)   *Length: 0.3 mile Blaze: white*

In the parking lot to the left of the entrance booth, follow along the access road toward the picnic pavilion. However, instead of going to the pavilion, head slightly left of the pavilion and down a mowed path with remnants of old paving still

History of George's Island

The Kitchawonk Indians summering in the area harvested oysters. There are shell middens along the trail on the south part of the park. Removing material from archeological sites is illegal.

Obviously the park is currently not an island, but at one time it was. Gormley's Brick Manufactory once was located here. The shoreline and parts of RiverWalk are still sprinkled with bricks, evidence of the enormous industry situated here a century ago. The ponds and Lake Whoopee were all part of brick-making operations. At that time, all African-American brickyard workers were called George, hence the name George's Island. The county purchased property for a park in 1966.

A common practice among brick manufacturers was to imprint bricks with the company name. The Gormley bricks littering the area are rejects. Some were fused together in the kiln, while others are broken or deformed. These bricks should be left in place for others to see.

visible. Almost at the river, the trail turns left, passing one unmarked trail to the right and two to the left. At 0.2 mile it crosses a bridge, turns left at a Y junction, and then left again at a T junction to head uphill. Take time to explore the short unmarked trail to the right which leads to shell middens and views out over the river. At 0.3 mile, the trail reaches a gate at the FDR Veterans Hospital, where it skirts a pond and continues on a walkway along the river's edge.

Winter Route   *Length: 0.1 mile Blaze: blue*

Beginning at 0.4 mile where the northbound RiverWalk makes a sharp left turn, the blue trail goes straight. It heads uphill, crosses a berm, and reaches Sunset Road. To continue on the winter route, turn left onto Sunset Road. At 0.3 mile, turn left onto Montrose Point Road. The trail to Montrose Point State Forest is at 0.5 mile and the parking area is 0.8 mile from where the trail reaches Sunset Road.

CONNECTIONS: RiverWalk continues north to Montrose Point State Forest, while southbound RiverWalk connects to the 0.5-mile section along the shore at FDR Veterans Hospital. The trail at the VA hospital is open to staff, residents, and the public.

NEARBY PARK: Montrose Point State Forest

DRIVING: Take Route 9 to the Route 9A Exit (Montrose). Head north on Route 9A for 1.3 miles. Turn left onto Dutch Street and follow it 0.9 mile to the park entrance.

PUBLIC TRANSPORTATION: Metro-North Hudson Line Cortlandt Station. Walk 0.5 mile through the parking lot. Turn right and continue 0.5 mile north along Route 9A. At Dutch Street turn left and walk 0.9 mile to the park entrance.

For contact information, see Appendix, Westchester County Parks—George's Island.

Mildred E. Grierson Memorial Wildlife Sanctuary
Marion Yarrow Preserve
Mount Holly Preserve

Katonah • 4.0 miles, 147 acres

The saying "the whole is greater than the sum of the parts" is descriptive of three preserves collectively called the Indian Brook Assemblage by The Nature Conservancy. Grierson Sanctuary and Yarrow Preserve are contiguous properties; Mount Holly Preserve is a short distance away. Together, the three provide birding and wildlife watching opportunities in a primarily mixed upland forest.

Mildred E. Grierson Memorial Wildlife Sanctuary
Marion Yarrow Preserve

2.4 miles • 18 and 78 acres

With ponds, wetlands, and a cascade, the Grierson and Yarrow preserves invite multiple visits, especially if one comes with nature guide in hand. The property was once farmland, as evidenced by the many stone walls. With Mount Holly Preserve and Mount Holly Sanctuary nearby, it is easy to have a full day's excursion.

In 1974, Stanley Grierson donated 18 acres to The Nature Conservancy in memory of his mother, Mildred E. Grierson. Two years later, Mr. and Mrs. Wilson P. Foss donated 47 acres in memory of Mrs. Foss's mother, Marian Yarrow, creating the Yarrow Preserve. An additional 31 acres are a conservation easement held by The Nature Conservancy.

TRAILS

Wide, well-blazed trails with signs make hikers feel welcome. These short, clearly laid-out trails have created a user-friendly network. There are three entrances, but only the one at the Lake Trail has parking. Horses are allowed on all trails except for the Falls Trail.

Lake Trail   *Length: 0.9 mile Blaze: green*
From the entrance on Mount Holly Road, the Lake Trail (or Lake Loop) heads into the Yarrow Preserve. The trail reaches a junction at 0.1 mile, the beginning of a loop. Turn right to follow the trail counterclockwise. The Lake Trail, also referred to as the Maple Trail, has numbered posts keyed to a brochure, which

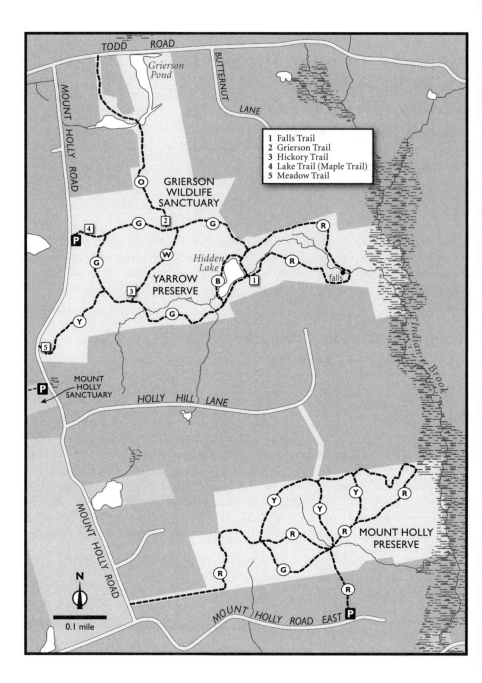

At 0.2 mile, the Lake Trail passes to the right the 0.2-mile Meadow Trail (yellow) to Mount Holly Road (no parking). It passes the Hickory Trail (white) to the left, a connection to the other side of the loop in 0.1 mile. Continuing downhill, the Lake Trail crosses a rock culvert across a stream. It heads uphill and passes wetlands to the left. At 0.4 mile, the trail skirts the edge of the property and crosses a bridge.

unfortunately may not always be available at the kiosk near the entrance.

Hidden Lake

At 0.5 mile, the Lake Trail passes one end of the Bass Trail (blue) to the left, which leads 0.1 mile around the other side of Hidden Lake. After passing the Falls Trail (red), the Lake Trail follows a woods road over the dam at the outlet of Hidden Lake. At 0.6 mile, it reaches the Bass Trail again to the left and then the Falls Trail to the right. Continuing on the woods road, the trail heads uphill and leaves the woods road leading to the right into private property. The Lake Trail rejoins the woods road and continues uphill. At 0.8 mile, it passes the Hickory Trail to the left and the Grierson Trail (orange) to the right. Heading downhill, the Lake Trail levels off, crosses a stone wall, and closes the loop. The preserve entrance on Mount Holly Road is straight ahead.

Falls Trail *Length: 0.6 mile Blaze: red*

Beginning on the Lake Trail (green) loop, the Falls Trail crosses numerous stone walls and heads downhill. It turns left to cross a stream with the cascade to the left. Heading uphill, it crosses a feeder stream to the left and leaves the main stream. At 0.4 mile, the trail reaches the top of a rise only to head downhill briefly before heading back uphill. Crossing a stone wall, the Falls Trail ascends steeply and ends at the Lake Trail.

Grierson Trail *Length: 0.4 mile Blaze: orange*

Beginning on the Lake Trail (green), the Grierson Trail heads north through open forest and then proceeds downhill. At 0.2 mile, it descends more steeply and passes through an area blanketed with ferns. The trail enters a wetland and crosses a bridge. After passing a rock outcropping to the right, the trail continues downhill to end at Todd Road (no parking).

DRIVING: From I-684, take Exit 6 (Route 35) and head east for 1.8 miles. Turn left onto North Salem Road and follow it to Mount Holly Road. Turn right at the Y junction and continue 1.2 miles to where Mount Holly Road makes a sharp left. The preserve is to the right, 0.8 mile past the turn.

PUBLIC TRANSPORTATION: None available

For contact information see Appendix, The Nature Conservancy.

Mount Holly Preserve

Katonah • 1.6 miles, 51 acres

Two narrow rights-of-way provide access to Mount Holly Preserve. Not to be confused with its larger neighbor, the Mount Holly Sanctuary, this preserve offers an opportunity for a quick walk. Part of the preserve was once a dairy farm; just less than half the property is meadow slowly returning to forest. The forested area is mixed second growth hardwood. Indian Brook runs along the eastern side of the property, and the adjacent wetlands form another habitat on preserve property. Large rock outcroppings and cliffs of a six-million-year old Fordham gneiss are found at the eastern portion of the preserve. In 1975, Mrs. Francis R. Dunscombe's donation to The Nature Conservancy established Mount Holly Preserve. Two easements provide access.

TRAILS

Think of the red trail as a tree with branches reaching upward. The two pieces of the North Trail (yellow) connect those branches and thus allow for loop hikes. At most intersections there are signs, but it helps to refer to the map. The South Trail (green) is a 0.1-mile connection between portions of the red trail.

Main Trail   *Length: 0.5 mile Blaze: red*
From the parking on Mount Holly Road East, an access trail (red) leads into the preserve. Heading right and immediately after crossing a stream on a bridge, the Main Trail first passes the end of the North Trail (yellow) and then the North Trail Extension (yellow). The Main Trail continues downhill passing a large spring to the right. It turns sharply left at 0.3 mile and heads very steeply uphill along switchbacks on a section not open to horses. At 0.5 mile, it ends where the North Trail Extension enters from the left, turns, and continues straight ahead.

Red Trail   *Length: 0.5 mile Blaze: red*
Directly ahead from the access trail, the red trail heads across an open area and passes the North Trail (yellow) to the right and the South County Trailway (green) to the left. It crosses a stone wall and goes through another open area at 0.2 mile. Heading uphill through woods, it turns left and descends. It turns left again and

passes through barberry bushes behind houses. Entering a narrow right-of-way easement, it heads slightly uphill and crosses a stone wall. The red trail descends on stone steps to end at Mount Holly Road (no parking).

North Trail & North Trail Extension *Length: 0.5 mile Blaze: yellow*
Use either the North Trail or the North Trail Extension as a way to reach the top of the ridge without the large elevation loss and a long climb along the Main Trail (red). The North Trail begins to the left immediately after the bridge near the entrance trail from Mount Holly Road East. It heads up to the ridge, turning left at a T junction with the end of the North Trail Extension to the right. Passing through former meadows, it turns to end near a stone wall at the red trail.

The North Trail Extension connects the North Trail with the red trail. It starts on the Main Trail, 0.1 mile east of the bridge. It goes to the top of the ridge, turns left at the junction with the Main Trail, and ends at the North Trail.

DRIVING: From I-684, take Exit 6 (Route 35) and head east for 1.8 miles. Turn left onto North Salem Road and follow it to Mount Holly Road. Turn right at the Y junction and go 1.2 miles to where Mount Holly Road makes a sharp left. Continue straight ahead on Mount Holly Road East for 0.4 mile to reach parking to the left for two cars.

PUBLIC TRANSPORTATION: None available

For contact information, see Appendix, The Nature Conservancy.

John E. Hand Park

Teatown • 3.1 miles, 112 acres

A hike up Bald Mountain in John E. Hand Park is nothing like the storyline accompanying Mussorgsky's *A Night on Bald Mountain*, in the Walt Disney film *Fantasia*. Instead, a graded woods road winds its way gracefully to the base of the mountain where a trail circles to the top with limited views. In 1992, Westchester County acquired this land to protect Bald Mountain. Later, in 1995, the park was named to honor the late John E. Hand, a county legislator from Yorktown.

TRAILS

Although Hand Park is riddled with mountain bike trails, there is easy walking along the green-blazed woods road. In addition to the marked trails, there are 1.6 miles of easy-to-follow bike trails. Other bike tracks switchback up the northwest side of Bald Mountain. However, they are not pleasant hiking and thus are not included in the total trail miles.

Green Trail   *Length: 1.1 miles Blaze: green*
From the parking area on Blinn Road, an unmarked woods road heads slightly uphill through multiflora rose and barberry bushes. At 0.2 mile, it passes to the left the first of many unmarked mountain bike trails. Just past where the barberry bushes no longer crowd the trail at 0.4 mile, there are green blazes on trees. The trail continues its gradual ascent and makes a sharp right turn at 0.5 mile. After the trail crosses a stone wall, an unmarked bike track enters from the left. Easily missed as one heads uphill, it is clearly seen when heading downhill as it veers right to wind its way 0.8 mile back to Blinn Road. At 0.7 mile, a second unmarked bike path leaves to the right and snakes its way 0.8 mile uphill to rejoin the green trail.

The green trail ascends and at 1.0 mile crosses an unmarked trail. To the left is an unmarked short steep route up Bald Mountain, while to the right is the other end of the second bike path mentioned above. The green trail heads downhill slightly and at 1.1 miles, ends at a stone wall. To the left, a white-blazed trail ascends 0.2 mile to the top of Bald Mountain with its seasonal views. Straight ahead is New York City Department of Environmental Protection property, where a hiking permit is required. As of 2008, it has no developed trails.

NEARBY TRAIL & PARK: Briarcliff Peekskill Trailway, Teatown Lake Reservation

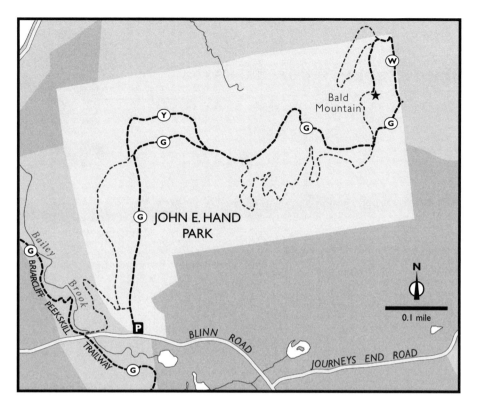

DRIVING: From the Taconic State Parkway, take the Route 134 Exit and turn west towards Ossining. Just past the southbound entrance ramp, turn right onto Grant Street, immediately passing a small house to the left. Do not make the hard right turn onto Illington Road. Instead, at the stop sign turn right onto Spring Valley Road. Continue 0.6 mile and turn right onto Blinn Road. At 1.6 miles, turn right into the small parking area for three or four cars.

PUBLIC TRANSPORTATION: None available

For contact information, see Appendix, Westchester County Parks.

Hardscrabble Wilderness Area

Pleasantville • 3.8 miles, 235 acres

Nestled on ridges and valleys near the Taconic Parkway, the trails in Hardscrabble Wilderness Area are a series of interlocking loops allowing several ways to vary a hike. Although the only view is southwest over the power line, tall trees and shade provide a pleasant place to take an invigorating stroll or a relaxing meander. Mountain bikers using the park help keep paths open and have established numerous unmarked trails paralleling the blazed trails.

The amount of stonework in the park is incredible. With the exception of two wooden bridges, all stream crossings are stone; some are fords while others are stepping stones or causeways. The trails are well-defined by logs along the sides in many places, and often have rock cairns. At two points on the white trail there are beautifully constructed cairns, sculptures rather than just piles of rocks.

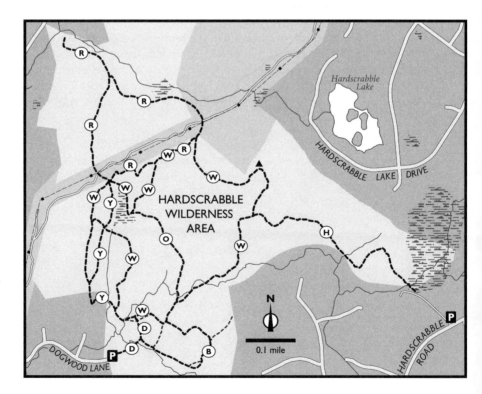

TRAILS

The trail system passes through mixed deciduous forest with little understory. There are towering tulip trees and spreading white oaks. Aside from red cedars at higher elevations, there are almost no evergreens. Even in mid-September, wildflowers can be found. In summer, butterflies and bees hover around goldenrod where the red trail crosses under the power line. The two access trails into the park are named for their respective access roads.

Dogwood Trail   *Length: 0.1 mile Blaze: black D on white*

Starting from the parking area at the end of Dogwood Lane, the Dogwood Trail passes one end of the blue trail. It turns slightly left at a junction with an unmarked trail and ends at the white trail at 0.1 mile.

Hardscrabble Trail   *Length: 0.5 mile Blaze: black H on white*

From a grassy triangle to the right near the end of the private drive, the Hardscrabble Trail heads along a woods road. It continues into the woods to the right of the sign and passes wetlands to the right as it follows a stone wall. Leaving the woods road, it turns right and skirts a hill. At 0.2 mile, it turns right again, where an unmarked trail leads straight into private property. After crossing a stream, the Hardscrabble Trail heads onto a woods road between stone walls. It goes uphill and then down to meet the white trail.

Blue Trail   *Length: 0.3 mile Blaze: blue*

One end of the blue trail is about 100 yards from the beginning of the Dogwood Trail, just past the stream crossing. It heads uphill, passing an unmarked trail to the left. Following above a stream to the right, it continues uphill before turning to descend and end at the white trail.

Orange Trail   *Length: 0.3 mile Blaze: orange*

The orange trail provides a shortcut across the white trail, eliminating the climb over the high point in the park. Going counterclockwise from the intersection with the Dogwood and white trails, it is 0.1 mile to the orange trail to the left. A smaller path leads to a wooden bridge over the stream. The trail passes a large white oak with gnarled stubs where widely spreading branches once grew, evidence that this woodland was pasture at one time. After leaving a large wetland at 0.1 mile, the wide level trail passes a rocky outcropping and ends at the white trail.

Red Trail   *Length: 0.8 mile Blaze: red*

The red trail is a loop that can be reached from the white trail in three places, all near the power line that splits the park. The southernmost point is at the intersection of the red, yellow, and white trails near the power line, reached from either the yellow or white trails. Going counterclockwise, take the red trail uphill, paralleling the power line in the woods and switchbacking up a steep section. When the white trail joins from the right, the trail is blazed both red and white until it reaches another T junction at a quarter-of-a-mile. The trails split, with the white trail going right and the red trail turning left, passing through a stone

Rock cairn

wall and heading down steps. The red trail then goes under the power line and reenters the woods at 0.3 mile. As it heads downhill, it parallels wetlands. At 0.5 mile, the trail reaches a rock cairn and a red-blazed spur trail, leading downhill 0.1 mile to the edge of the property near houses. The red trail goes uphill, crosses a stone wall at 0.6 mile, and heads under the power line. At 0.8 mile, it closes the loop.

Yellow Trail

Length: 0.3 mile Blaze: yellow

From a Y junction with the white trail, 150 feet from a wooden bridge in the park, the yellow trail crosses a seasonal stream. It passes a rock outcropping to the right and turns to go up along its top. The yellow trail continues uphill and crosses the white trail at 0.2 mile. After passing another rock outcropping, the yellow trail ends at an intersection with both red and white trails.

White Trail

Length: 1.5 miles Blaze: white

The longest trail in the park, the white trail is a loop with all other trails branching from it. From the end of the Dogwood Trail (black D on white) at a T junction, go counterclockwise around the loop. The white trail soon heads left at a Y junction and the blue trail continues straight. The white trail then goes uphill and, at 0.1 mile, passes the orange trail to the left. Continuing to climb, the white trail crosses a stream. At 0.3 mile, the stream below to the left has a small collapsed dam, now part of a stone wall. Reaching a Y junction with the Hardscrabble Trail (black H on white) at 0.4 mile, the white trail turns left and continues uphill.

The trail reaches a stone bench beside a rock cairn sculpture at the high point in the park, where unfortunately, there is no view. Shortly it passes a second rock cairn, massive and not easily missed. The white trail descends, and noise from the Taconic State Parkway can now be heard. The white trail reaches an intersection at 0.8 mile where the red trail is straight ahead. Turning left, the white trail is co-aligned with the red trail, but the trails split at 0.9 mile, with the white trail heading left along a ridge and then down to meet the orange trail. At 1.0 mile, the white trail reaches a low point and then ascends to a confusing intersection at 1.1 miles. Going clockwise to the left are a yellow trail, the continuation of the white trail, the red trail entering from the power line, and finally the red trail heading out and paralleling the power line into the woods. The white trail makes a gentle descent. At 1.2 miles, it turns sharply left where a wide unmarked trail continues straight ahead, eventually joining the yellow trail.

The white trail crosses the yellow trail, heads into wetland, crosses a stream, and heads uphill. Meeting the yellow trail for the last time at 1.4 miles, the white trail turns left. In this area, there are a number of unmarked trails created by bikers to avoid a rocky section and make their ride easier. After crossing a wooden bridge, the white trail closes the loop at the Dogwood Trail.

DRIVING: From southbound Taconic State Parkway, take the Pleasantville Road Exit, turn left, and head towards Pleasantville. Just after passing under the power lines, turn left onto Dogwood Lane. From northbound Taconic State Parkway, take the Pleasantville Road Exit, turn left, and then right onto Dogwood Lane. Go 0.2 mile to the end of Dogwood Lane with parking for 4 or 5 cars near a kiosk.

To reach the entrance on Hardscrabble Road from the Taconic Parkway, take the Pleasantville Road Exit toward Pleasantville. Turn left onto Hardscrabble Road. It is 0.8 mile to #309 to the left, where there is a parking area for 3 or 4 cars. Walk 0.1 mile along the driveway to where the Hardscrabble Trail begins to the right at the end of a grassy area opposite a utility pole.

PUBLIC TRANSPORTATION: Beeline Bus #19 stops on Pleasantville Road, 0.5 mile east of Dogwood Lane opposite the Briarcliff schools. Walk up Dogwood Lane to the end.

For contact information, see Appendix, Mount Pleasant.

Hillside Park & Hillside Woods

Hastings-on-Hudson • 4.9 miles, 98 acres

Well-loved describes adjacent Hillside Park and Hillside Woods, collectively referred to as Hillside. Hillside Park was the property of the Jewish Mental Health Society, acquired by the Village of Hastings in 1941. The Trust for Public Land purchased Hillside Woods in 1993 to prevent its being developed. It is jointly managed as a park by Westchester County and the Village of Hastings. A stone wall which divided the Lefurgy and Birnie/Smith farms is the property line between the two parks. The well-trod paths coming from adjacent streets verify that over the years many feet have visited these two parks. Consider walking to get there, because parking is limited. Places to park are at Hillside Elementary School near Lefurgy Avenue and at the tennis courts off Farlane Drive.

Sugar Pond

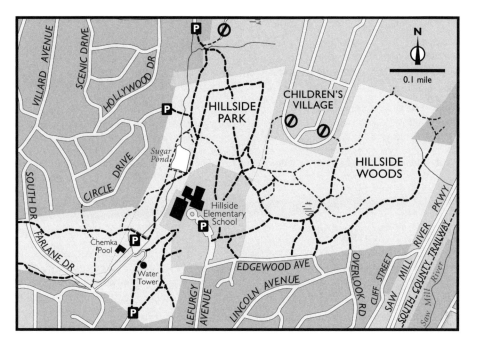

TRAILS

The trails in Hillside are not just trails to come for a walk with or without a dog. Some are the routes children take to school, while others provide access to the swimming pool, tennis courts, or ball fields. As of 2008, the trails at Hillside are sporadically blazed, mostly with yellow paint. Thus, it is best to use a map to navigate. As they wind their way through the two parks, wide paths and woods roads allow for walking two or three abreast. In the northeast portion of the park, the trails intersect Children's Village trails which are blazed and have signs, but are not open to the public. The trails at Hillside are part of the Hastings Trailway, but they are not connected to sections of the trailway in other parks.

Algonquin Trail   *Length: 0.5 mile Blaze: occasional yellow*

The Algonquin Trail was allegedly a Native American route between the Hudson River and Long Island Sound. There is no historical confirmation that what is at present known as the Algonquin Trail is indeed that route.

The Algonquin Trail begins just south of a vernal pool, near the unmarked entrance at Edgewood Avenue. At a T junction, the trail goes right, descends, and passes a short trail out to Taft Street and Edgewood Avenue. Continuing downhill, it parallels a ravine to the left. Tree limbs line the steeply descending trail. To the right, rock outcroppings with folded layers to the right are Fordham gneiss. After crossing a third brook, the trail turns left at 0.4 mile at two black birch trees with a large stump at the base of one of them. The trail first descends steeply into a ravine and then ascends towards the bluffs to reach a T junction. To the right, the trail leads to Children's Village. To the left, the red trail with occasional blue blazes heads back to the trails in Hillside Woods.

DRIVING: From the Saw Mill Parkway, take Farragut Parkway west to Hastings. Turn right onto Hillside Avenue which is immediately north of the middle school. Head uphill and, at a traffic island, turn left onto Rosedale Avenue. Cross the intersection with Farlane Drive and enter the park by the tennis courts.

PUBLIC TRANSPORTATION: Beeline Bus #6 on Route 9. It is a 0.4-mile walk from the Old Croton Aqueduct to the tennis courts.

For contact information, see Appendix, Hastings.

Hastings Trailway

Three tiny segments of the Hasting Trailway are located between houses in Hastings. Lefurgy Park is a narrow pathway wedged on the side of a hill; it provides a 0.2-mile pedestrian access between Mount Hope Boulevard and Fairmont Avenue. The park is named for Isaac Lefurgy, a tax collector and wealthy landowner who deeded property to establish the First Reformed Church in 1850.

Pulvers Woods has 0.3 mile of trails which go through an open forest with no understory. It is two blocks from the intersection of Farragut Avenue and Farragut Parkway at Green and Rose streets. John Henry Pulver was a farmer, who in the 1830s, founded the white dolomite marble quarry between the Old Croton Aqueduct and what is now Draper Park.

A quarter-mile of trails wind their way through Ravendale Woods. Accessed through narrow rights-of-way, Ravendale Woods is located one block from the Farragut Avenue Exit of the southbound Saw Mill River Parkway.

Hudson Highlands Gateway Park

Cortlandt • 4 miles, 352 acres

Located in the northwest corner of Westchester County adjacent to Putnam County, Hudson Highlands Gateway Park (Gateway) is rich both in Revolutionary War history and biodiversity. Its viewpoints were once signal hills manned by troops quartered in nearby Continental Village. Some trails are on Revolutionary-era roads. In the early 1800s, the Clinton family operated a dairy farm on the property. During the mid 1900s, parts of its eastern and western edges were quarried for their glacial till and subsequently abandoned. In 2000, Scenic Hudson Land Trust, New York State, and Westchester County together purchased the property which was slated for development. Under a cooperative arrangement, the Town of Cortlandt manages the park.

A 2002 ecological analysis of Gateway found the area to be one of the most ecologically diverse properties in Westchester County. Its topography of ridges, rock outcroppings, slopes, and vales form a variety of habitats. Bordered by Annsville Creek and Sprout Brook, the park also contains meadows, wetlands, and minor and seasonal streams. Birds frequent the more open areas of the former gravel pits, while the core of its intact forest allows migrant birds a place to rest or breed. The vernal pools are home to frogs and salamanders. Reptiles living on the property include eastern box turtles, spotted turtles, worm snakes, black rat snakes, and black racers.

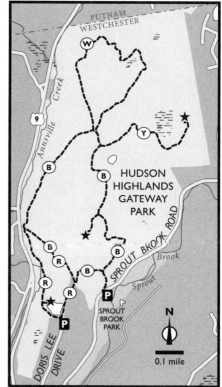

TRAILS

The trail system of Hudson Highlands Gateway Park was developed to minimize its impact on wildlife. The trails were designed to utilize existing woods roads and avoid going too close to vernal pools. The four trails pass through a meadow, succession forest, wetlands, and uplands. Unfortunately, illegal ATV use has widened woods roads and damaged narrow trails.

Upland Trail
Length: 1.8 miles Blaze: blue

Beginning from the kiosk at Sprout Brook Road, the Upland Trail heads uphill crossing a stream to a T junction at 0.1 mile to begin a loop. Going counterclockwise, it passes a bench and heads uphill leaving the former gravel pit. After passing a Revolutionary War-era road to the right, it continues uphill. At 0.4 mile, the Upland Trail reaches a side trail leading 0.1 mile to a lookout used during the Revolutionary War. Unfortunately, as of 2008, the seasonal view includes the Sprout Brook Landfill, the Jan Peek Bridge over Annsville Creek, the Indian Point power plant, as well as the Hudson River.

The Upland Trail works its way uphill and down, and at 0.7 mile, passes the Hudson Overlook Spur Trail (yellow) to the right. The Upland Trail goes through a stone wall to join the Vernal Pool Trail (white) to the right. These two trails are together briefly until the Vernal Pool Trail leaves to the right. Heading downhill, the Upland Trail crosses a stream just upstream of a small seasonal cascade. It then parallels a stone wall on a gullied woods road, marked on old maps as Old Revolutionary Road. It passes through laurel at 1.0 mile, leaves an eroded section of the gully, and returns to the old road when the terrain flattens out.

At 1.3 miles, the Upland Trail turns left to join the Annsville Creek Trail (red). It passes a foundation to the left and massive rock outcroppings, some of which have tumbled down the hill. It goes through a rock cut and passes a vernal pool which drains onto the trail further downhill. At a T junction at 1.6 miles, the Upland Trail turns left and the Annsville Creek Trail turns right. The Upland Trail crosses a stream, heads downhill, and closes the loop at 1.8 miles. The return route to the parking lot is to the right.

Annsville Creek Trail
Length: 0.8 mile Blaze: red

From the parking area at the end of Doris Lee Drive, a short access trail goes through a gate in a split-rail fence to reach the Annsville Creek Trail. Going counterclockwise from the sign, the trail passes a pond to the left and then continues through a wet area. At the intersection with the Upland Trail (blue), the Annsville Creek Trail turns left to join it.

Heading uphill, the two trails pass a rock outcropping to the

A pleasant view

right. At 0.3 mile, the co-aligned trails go over a rise and head downhill. After passing rock outcroppings, the trail reaches a small open area with a foundation to the right. At 0.4 mile, the trails split with the Annsville Creek Trail turning left and the Upland Trail turning right. After entering a former gravel pit, the Annsville Creek Trail passes the first of several paths to Route 9. It crosses a wetland on wood chips or puncheons. Turning away from Route 9 to cross a bridge, the trail parallels Annsville Creek at 0.6 mile. It heads uphill on a broad woods road and reaches a side trail leading 60 feet to an overlook of a pond. The Annsville Creek Trail then goes along the shore of the pond, and closes the loop at the park sign.

Hudson Overlook Spur Trail   *Length: 0.5 mile Blaze: yellow*
From the Upland Trail (blue), the Hudson Overlook Spur Trail heads downhill, sometimes steeply. It makes a sharp right turn, passes a vernal pool to the left at 0.3 mile, and descends to cross a stream at 0.4 mile. Going uphill, the trail passes slab rock to the left. It then turns left to go steeply uphill to a lookout used during the Revolutionary War, but now marred with views of RESCO's ash dump and the Indian Point nuclear power plant.

Vernal Pool Trail   *Length: 1.1 miles Blaze: white*
Reached from the Upland Trail (blue), the Vernal Pool Trail is a loop. It goes through a low ravine at 0.1 mile and a forest with sparse understory. At 0.3 mile, it heads up onto a rock outcropping. Turning left to leave the outcropping, it ascends, slowly curving to the left. After passing a large vernal pool to the left, the trail works its way right and, at 0.5 mile, heads steeply downhill. It crosses a stream and then a second stream just above a small seasonal cascade to the right. Paralleling the stream briefly, the Vernal Pool Trail crosses a stone wall, immediately turns left, and heads uphill. It passes through an area covered with mixed ground pine and tree club moss. At a T junction with a woods road at 0.8 mile, the trail turns left. To the right, a woods road heads downhill to Route 9. The Vernal Pool Trail crosses another stone wall and goes gradually uphill. It passes through a former meadow at 1.0 mile, reaches the Upland Trail, and turns left to join it, closing the loop.

DRIVING: From Route 9 at the Annsville Circle, just north of Peekskill, go north 0.6 mile and turn right onto Roa Hook Road at a traffic light. When Roa Hook Road ends at Highland Avenue, turn right and take an immediate left onto Sprout Brook Road. Go 0.3 mile to parking to the right, just past the parking lot for the athletic fields in Sprain Brook Park. The entrance to Hudson Highlands Gateway is on the opposite side of the road, through a gap in the guardrail.

To reach the Annsville Creek Trail off Doris Lee Drive, follow the directions from Annsville Circle. But instead of turning right, cross Highland Avenue and turn left onto Old Albany Post Road, which parallels Highland Avenue. Turn right onto Doris Lee Drive to end at the parking lot.

PUBLIC TRANSPORTATION: None available

For contact information, see Appendix, Cortlandt.

Hunt-Parker Memorial Sanctuary

Lake Katonah • 4.3 miles, 318 acres

Home to a wide variety of birds, the Hunt-Parker Memorial Sanctuary is also a great place for short or long hikes. The diverse habitat includes open meadow, wetland, and upland forest. Field guides would be helpful in learning about flora and fauna in the area.

James Ramsey Hunt made the original gift in memory of his son of the same name. Later, gifts from other family members enlarged the sanctuary. In 2001, Mary Welsh Parker's bequest added 100 acres; her 1720s farmhouse, Bylane, is now headquarters for the Bedford Audubon Society.

TRAILS

At the Hunt-Parker Sanctuary, intersections are marked with colored bands on trees. Orange trails provide sanctuary access for neighbors. With trails of different lengths, it is easy to spend as much time as one would like enjoying the outdoors, either busily walking or just quietly observing. In 2007, the sanctuary closed portions of several trails to reduce habitat fragmentation and to eliminate unnecessary parallel trails. The yellow trail into Mt. Holly Sanctuary is 275 yards north on North Salem Street. A full day of hiking is possible by visiting these two sanctuaries.

Valley Brook Trail   *Length: 0.8 mile Blaze: white*

There are three sections of the Valley Brook Trail which, prior to 2007, were connected. All sections either begin or end at the Katonah Ridge Trail (blue).

Starting at the kiosk adjacent to the parking area, the Valley Brook Trail turns left to follow a boardwalk with an eight-foot-wide stone wall to the left. At 0.2 mile, the trail crosses a buried telephone cable line. At the junction with the Katonah Ridge Trail, the Valley Brook Trail turns right to join the Swamp Maple Trail (yellow). Almost immediately, the Swamp Maple Trail leaves to the right. The first segment of the Valley Brook Trail ends at the Katonah Ridge Trail.

Other sections of the Valley Brook Trail are 0.3-mile shortcuts along the Katonah Ridge Trail. Section #2 passes an oak tree with a large burl. Section #3 is *Burl*

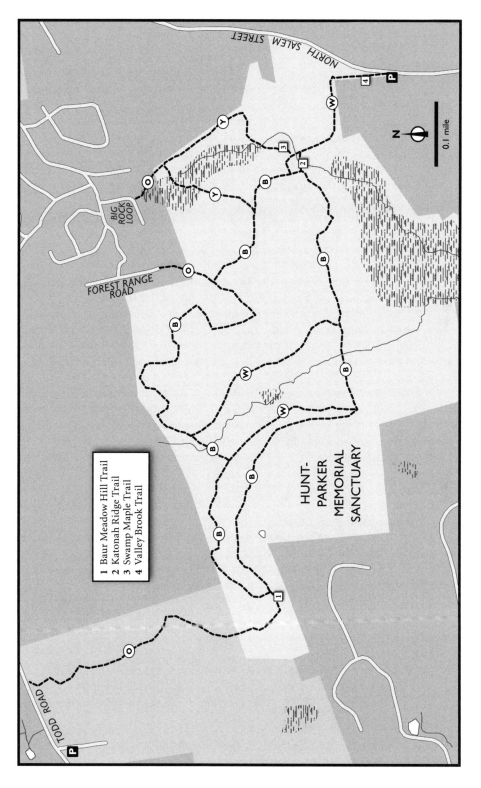

NORTH SALEM STREET

BIG ROCK LOOP

FOREST RANGE ROAD

HUNT-PARKER MEMORIAL SANCTUARY

TODD ROAD

N

0.1 mile

1 Baur Meadow Hill Trail
2 Katonah Ridge Trail
3 Swamp Maple Trail
4 Valley Brook Trail

parallel to Section #2 and eliminates a three-quarter-mile segment of the Katonah Ridge Trail.

Baur Meadow Hill Trail   *Length: 0.6 mile Blaze: orange*
The Baur Meadow Hill Trail is accessible from the farthest end of the Katonah Ridge Trail (blue) and from Todd Road. From a high point on the Katonah Ridge Trail, the Baur Trail heads downhill through open woods without understory. At 0.4 mile, the trail reaches open fields and continues to descend. The field and edge environments support plants and animals not found in other areas of the sanctuary. About 50 butterfly species live in the meadow at various times, from spring through fall. At 0.6 mile, the trail reaches Todd Road.

Katonah Ridge Trail   *Length: 2.4 miles Blaze: blue*
As its name implies, the Katonah Ridge Trail leads to the highest areas of the sanctuary. From the junction with the Valley Brook Trail (white) and the Swamp Maple Trail (yellow), the Katonah Ridge Trail heads straight ahead. At the next intersection, go straight heading clockwise around the loop. The Katonah Ridge Trail continues through the wetland on puncheon. At 0.4 mile, it passes section #2 of the Valley Brook Trail and at 0.7 mile, section #3. Continuing uphill, the trail reaches the Baur Meadow Hill Trail (orange) at 1.0 mile. The Katonah Ridge Trail turns to descend steeply. It passes section #3 of the Valley Brook Trail at 1.3 miles and crosses a bridge. Section #2 of the Valley Brook Trail is to the right at 1.5 miles.

From the high point of the sanctuary at 1.7 miles, the Katonah Ridge Trail descends. At a T intersection, it turns left at 1.9 miles and then turns right at 2.1 miles where an orange trail leads 0.1 mile to Forest Range Road, a local road (no parking). The Katonah Ridge Trail passes the Swamp Maple Trail to the left at 2.3 miles, and closes the loop at 2.4 miles at the junction of the white, yellow, and blue trails.

Swamp Maple Trail   *Length: 0.5 mile Blaze: yellow*
Although there are bridges over the wetlands, you could get wet feet on the Swamp Maple Trail. Beginning at the intersection of the Valley Brook Trail (white) and the Katonah Ridge Trail (blue), the Swamp Maple Trail crosses wetlands on bog bridges. At 0.3 mile, it turns left where a 0.1-mile orange-blazed connector trail heads straight to Big Rock Loop, a local road (no parking). The Swamp Maple Trail ends at the Katonah Ridge Trail.

NEARBY PARKS: Grierson Wildlife Sanctuary, Mount Holly Preserve, Mount Holly Sanctuary, Rose Nature Preserve, Yarrow Preserve

DRIVING: Take I-684 to Exit 6 (Route 35). Turn east onto Route 35. In 1.0 mile, turn left onto unpaved Mt. Holly Road. At the T junction, turn left onto North Salem Street. The entrance is to the left, 0.1 mile from the turn, with parking for 3 cars.

PUBLIC TRANSPORTATION: None available

For contact information, see Appendix, Bedford Audubon.

Kitchawan Preserve

Kitchawan • 4.9 miles, 208 acres

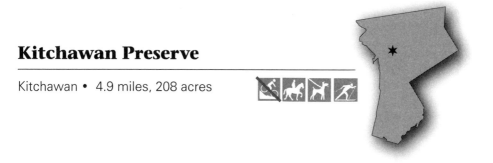

Extremely popular with people who enjoy taking man's best friend on a hike, Kitchawan Preserve is dog heaven. Without a dog, you might just feel out of place, but the woods roads offer ample opportunities to stroll and chat with other hikers. Although posted signs state that dogs must be kept on a maximum six-foot leash, unfortunately this law is rarely heeded.

Kitchawan Preserve supports a diversity of flora and fauna in a variety of habitats, largely because of its size and its location next to the New Croton Reservoir. In 2008, sightings of a fisher, a member of the weasel family extremely rare in Westchester, points to the health of the preserve's intact forest habitat. Vernal pools grace the preserve, providing breeding habitat for many species of amphibians and invertebrates. The old fields are excellent areas to view butterflies

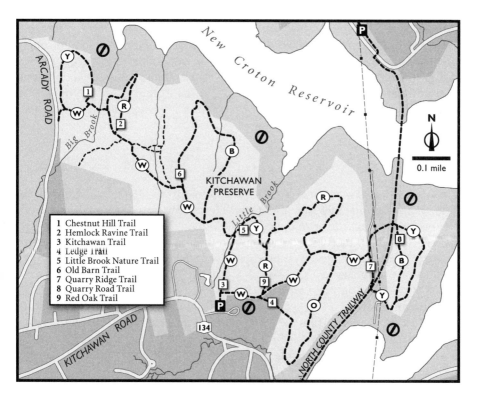

1 Chestnut Hill Trail
2 Hemlock Ravine Trail
3 Kitchawan Trail
4 Ledge Trail
5 Little Brook Nature Trail
6 Old Barn Trail
7 Quarry Ridge Trail
8 Quarry Road Trail
9 Red Oak Trail

The land in what is now Kitchawan Preserve was home to the Kitchawonks, who deeded it to Stephanus Van Cortlandt in 1683 and it became part of Van Cortlandt Manor. The bricks manufactured near the North County Trailway were used to build chimneys and foundations for Woods House, a summer retreat for Fernando Woods, a colorful New York City mayor in the 1850s.

The Van Brunt family donated 223 acres of their land in 1956 to the Brooklyn Botanic Garden (BBG). Three years later a laboratory building and facilities were completed. Through funds raised by the Kitchawan Auxiliary, a research and teaching greenhouse were added in 1968. During the 1970s and early 1980s, BBG, as the site was often called, held special projects on location with school groups.

In 1989, BBG sold 208 acres to Westchester County to preserve the open space, but retained 15 acres including the buildings and greenhouses. The buildings lay dormant and the greenhouse fell into disrepair until October 1998, when they were purchased by the Weston Charitable Foundation and Kitchawan Institute. Once renovated, the buildings were used to host community meetings which focused on human rights, environmental concerns, and sustainable development. In 2001, Kitchawan Institute sold the property to the Warren Institute, a not-for-profit organization conducting medical research.

on meadow wildflowers as well as a diversity of field and shrub-dwelling birds. Two prominent riparian habitats are the gems of the preserve. One stream passes through a beech forest with old trees, where the flute-like songs of thrushes reverberate on summer evenings. Local lore reports that the hemlock ravine is original forest where the trees have never been cut. Many majestic old-growth hemlocks are in the steep ravine of Big Brook. Forest birds such as kinglets, brown creepers, and wood warblers can be heard overhead in spring. Although many of Kitchawan's diverse native wildflowers have been lost due to deer overpopulation, a few lady's slippers still bravely grow in some sites.

TRAILS

The trails at Kitchawan Preserve traverse land that in the 1890s was still pasture. Some trails continue into New York City DEP watershed lands along the reservoir. However, these trails are open only to those who hold permits. Along the northern boundary of the preserve are stone walls built around the turn of the twentieth century. These well-built stone walls capped with flat rocks delineate the watershed of the New Croton Reservoir.

Kitchawan Trail   *Length: 1.5 miles Blaze: white*
A short access trail leads from the parking area to the Kitchawan Trail which serves as a spine to access other trails in the preserve. To the right, the trail ends at the North County Trailway in 0.6 mile; the section continuing straight ends at Arcady Road in 0.9 mile.

Bridge over Little Brook

To the right at the end of the access trail, the Kitchawan Trail follows a wide and well-used woods road. At 0.1 mile, it first passes the junction with the Ledge Trail (orange) to the right and then the Red Oak Trail (red) to the left. Continuing uphill at 0.3 mile, it reaches the Red Oak Trail a second time and then the Ledge Trail again. Heading downhill, the Kitchawan Trail reaches the power line right-of-way and its service road at 0.5 mile. To the right is the Quarry Ridge Trail (yellow). The Kitchawan Trail briefly follows the power line access road and then turns right. The access road continues straight to eventually enter New York City DEP watershed lands. After passing under the power lines, the Kitchawan Trail reaches the North County Trailway, where it ends at 0.6 mile.

At the end of the access trail, the Kitchawan Trail heads straight, follows Little Brook, and reaches a bridge. Straight ahead the Little Brook Nature Trail (yellow) connects to the Red Oak Trail in 0.2 mile. The Kitchawan Trail turns left to cross Little Brook and turns left again to head steeply uphill. As it enters an orchard and the first of four fields, it passes the Old Barn Trail (blue) immediately to the right. Once in the field which had been the Brooklyn Botanic Garden's demonstration garden, the Kitchawan Trail turns right and follows a well-worn path. Entering the next field, at 0.4 mile it passes the Old Barn Trail and passes into the third field. An unmarked equestrian trail leaves to the left, as does a second one, just past where the trail exits the last field at 0.6 mile.

The Kitchawan Trail turns left at the intersection with the Hemlock Ravine Trail (red). Descending, it turns left to cross a stone wall, while straight ahead is the other end of the Hemlock Ravine Trail. The Kitchawan Trail crosses Big Brook on large stones at 0.8 mile. Heading uphill, it wanders through the woods as it passes the Chestnut Hill Trail twice and ends at Arcady Road at 0.9 mile (no parking).

Chestnut Hill Trail   *Length: 0.3 mile Blaze: yellow*
Beginning near Big Brook on the Kitchawan Trail (white), the Chestnut Hill Trail parallels stone walls which border DEP lands. Bearing left as it climbs, the trail leaves the stone walls behind. Passing the base of rock outcroppings, it continues through open forest to end at the Kitchawan Trail.

Hemlock Ravine Trail   *Length: 0.3 mile Blaze: red*
From the Kitchawan Trail (white), the Hemlock Ravine Trail heads along a well-worn woods road. It reaches a stone wall delineating the DEP watershed property and makes a U-turn to parallel the wall. It turns right, descends to meet a woods road, and turns left. Heading slightly uphill and avoiding a wet area, the Hemlock Ravine Trail ends at the Kitchawan Trail.

Ledge Trail   *Length: 0.6 mile Blaze: orange*
Beginning on the Kitchawan Trail (white), the Ledge Trail gently curves left and passes an occasional rock cairn. It heads uphill onto a ledge where the traffic below on Route 134 is both audible and visible. The Ledge Trail follows a stone wall briefly and heads uphill. At 0.5 mile, it passes through a low ravine and ends at the Kitchawan Trail at 0.6 mile.

Old Barn Trail   *Length: about 0.7 mile Blaze: blue*
From the Kitchawan Trail (white), the Old Barn Trail follows along a woods road through open woods and reaches the foundation of an old barn at 0.2 mile. The two large Norway spruces are part of what once was the summer home of Fernando Wood, a colorful New York City mayor of Tammany Hall fame in the 1850s. His home overlooking the Croton Reservoir was demolished long ago.

The Old Barn Trail turns left onto a path through barberry bushes. It crosses a narrow stream on stepping stones and heads uphill. Paralleling the stone wall boundary of DEP watershed property, the trail skirts the base of a hill while continuing its ascent. It turns left to join a woods road at 0.4 mile. Passing a stone fireplace to the left, the Old Barn Trail descends into a former orchard. It ends in a field at the Kitchawan Trail.

Quarry Ridge Trail   *Length: 0.5 mile Blaze: yellow*
Beginning at the power lines on the Kitchawan Trail (white), the Quarry Ridge Trail goes under the lines. It crosses the North County Trailway at 0.1 mile while still in the power line right-of-way. At the far side of the right-of-way, the Quarry Ridge Trail turns to enter the woods. To the left is the Quarry Road Trail (blue), a 0.2-mile shortcut to the North County Trailway which passes an old quarry, likely to have supplied stone for building the old Putnam Division.

At that intersection, the Quarry Ridge Trail passes a large sugar maple. The trail follows the quarry rim on top of the ridge and at 0.4 mile heads downhill. A dense low understory of invasive plants thrives in the break in the forest canopy. The trail passes the Quarry Road Trail again and ends at the North County Trailway.

Red Oak Trail   *Length: 0.6 mile Blaze: red*
Beginning on the Kitchawan Trail (white), the Red Oak Trail goes through a stone

wall and along a woods road. It passes the Little Brook Nature Trail (yellow) and then at 0.2 mile, an unmarked trail into New York City DEP watershed lands. The Red Oak Trail skirts along the base of a hill to the right and heads uphill. It levels off at 0.5 mile and turns left to end at the Kitchawan Trail.

CONNECTING TRAIL: North County Trailway

DRIVING: From the Taconic State Parkway, take the Route 134 Exit and turn east. Continue past the entrance to the IBM T. J. Watson Research Center. The preserve entrance is 1.2 miles to the left just beyond a sharp right-hand turn.

PUBLIC TRANSPORTATION: None available

For contact information, see Appendix, Westchester County Parks.

Lasdon Park, Arboretum & Veterans Memorial

Somers • 4.9 miles, 234 acres

Considering all the beautiful parks in Westchester County, it cannot be said for certain that Lasdon Park is the most beautiful. To decide for yourself, visit this well-manicured park in the spring when trees and ornamental plants are in bloom and the place is ablaze with color. It is difficult to capture the beauty of the park in a picture and easy to claim photographs do not do the place justice. Located on the former estate of William and Mildred Lasdon, the park has a massive lawn rolling up from Route 35 with a lone sugar maple standing sentinel beside the entrance road.

Lasdon Park is multifaceted; it is the horticultural hub of Westchester County with offices for horticultural groups, rooms for both horticultural and botanical art, and a volunteer-run plant shop offering information and selling garden-related items. The park contains four inspirational memorials, special collections of trees, William Lasdon's azalea garden, magnolia grove, and dwarf conifer collection, and the Chinese Friendship Garden, a gift from the People's Republic of China. A walk at Lasdon Park can be a special interest stroll through these collections or an easy hike along blazed woodland trails.

A portion of the park is fenced to prevent marauding deer from devastating the vegetation around the house, formal gardens, and major tree and plant collections. The greenhouses, shop, and Veterans Museum are part of this enclosure because of their proximity to the house, now the park office.

Three groups are active in the park: the Friends of Lasdon Park and Arboretum, the Vietnam Memorial Committee, and the Vietnam Veterans of America, Westchester County Chapter 49.

HISTORY OF LASDON PARK

In 1939, William and Mildred Lasdon purchased what was originally called Cobbling Rock Farm and used it as a summer residence. William Lasdon had established a major pharmaceutical company and was well known for his philanthropy. Because of his interest in horticulture, Lasdon imported many tree specimens found on his worldwide travels and had them planted on his country retreat. As part of its efforts to preserve open space, Westchester County purchased the Lasdon estate in 1986 for $4.2 million. Since its acquisition, the county has retained much of the design of the formal grounds and has embellished the collections.

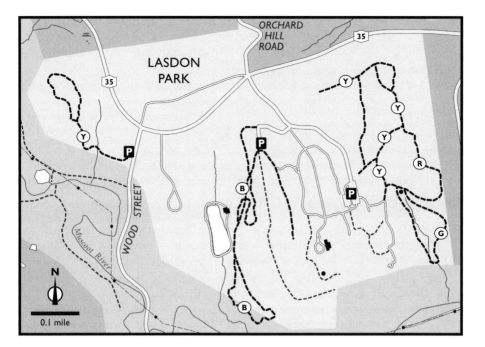

BLAZED WOODLAND TRAILS

All the blazed woodland trails except for the green trail were part of the equestrian trail system at the Lasdon Estate and are suitable for cross-country skiing. A detailed map is available at a pavilion at the upper parking lot. The red, green, and yellow trails can be reached from the lower main parking lot by following the handicapped accessible path past the Merchant Marine Memorial and turning left onto a woods road, a walk of 0.1 mile. The blue trail is accessible from the parking lot for the Chinese Friendship Pavilion and the Famous and Historic Tree Trail.

Yellow Trail   *Length: 0.5 mile Blaze: yellow*
From the handicapped accessible path, the yellow trail continues along a woods road, passing the junction with the red trail to the right. Continuing through open forest, it passes an unmarked trail to the left leading to the upper parking lot. At the end of the red trail at 0.2 mile, the yellow trail goes left through a white pine plantation. It passes a trail to the right near a Lasdon Arboretum sign, reaches a T junction with a woods road, and turns left. After passing an unmarked woods road that leads 0.2 mile back to the parking lot, the yellow trail crosses two seasonal streams and ends at 0.5 mile at the lawn.

To reach the trail system on the west side of the entrance road from the end of the yellow trail, head uphill directly towards the crown of the sugar maple on the entrance road. After reaching the tree, turn slightly left toward a green sign and a utility line. The Trail of Famous and Historic Trees begins just past the leftmost utility pole. Alternately, continue on the paved road to the parking lot for the Chinese Friendship Pavilion and the Famous and Historic Tree Trail.

Red Trail   *Length: 0.3 mile Blaze: red*

From the junction with the yellow trail, the red trail passes a gazebo which surrounds a small pool. It heads along a woods road through deciduous trees with sparse understory, turns left, and leaves the carriage road. The trail then goes through a stone wall, passes a rounded glacial erratic, and ends at the yellow trail.

Green Trail   *Length: 0.4 mile Blaze: green*

Beginning at the gazebo on the red trail, the green trail is a loop. To the right of the gazebo, the green trail heads straight downhill through an open area. It parallels a stream and turns to cross it at 0.2 mile. Heading uphill, the green trail reaches a woods road and turns left. The trail passes through an open area to close the loop back at the gazebo.

Blue Trail   *Length: 0.6 mile Blaze: blue*

Think of the blue trail as a lollipop, a long stem with a loop on the end. It starts at the parking lot for the Chinese Friendship Garden. After passing the woods road following the outer fence, the blue trail goes on an unpaved road and crosses the Trail of Historic Trees. Passing through a Chinese arch, it crosses a grassy area alongside a pond and heads into the woods on a woods road. When the trail splits at 0.3 mile, go counterclockwise. The blue trail heads uphill through an open forest and passes the ruins of two buildings. It turns right off the woods road and descends steeply. Turning onto a woods road, it goes through a bank of New York ferns. As it heads uphill, the trail gradually turns, crosses a small bridge over a seasonal stream, and closes the loop.

SPECIALIZED WALKS

Name your favorite plant and there is likely to be a collection of it in the arboretum. Unmarked trails in or around the special collections encourage a slow pace and offer opportunities for contemplation, reflection, or taking photographs.

ONGOING BOTANICAL RESEARCH

The Lasdon Arboretum is more than just a collection of trees and shrubs; there is ongoing botanical research at the site. In 1992 following the discovery of three acres of American chestnut trees on the property, Lasdon Arboretum became a location for research with the American Chestnut Foundation to develop a variety of the species that would be resistant to chestnut blight. Since that time, trees have been collected from sites around the country. Planted on five acres, these trees provide additional material for genetic research.

Lasdon Arboretum is also doing research to combat the butternut canker, an imported fungus affecting the butternut tree. They are partners with the New York State Department of Environmental Conservation and the U.S. Department of Agriculture.

Dogwoods are threatened as well. More than 80 trees from around the world have been planted at the arboretum as part of a research project.

Azaleas in bloom

Chinese Friendship Pavilion & Culture Garden   *Length: 0.3 mile*
The Friendship Pavilion is the focal point of the garden. Situated on four acres, it recognizes the close ties between Westchester County and Jingzhou in the People's Republic of China. A trail with many benches encircles a pond.

Blue Star Memorial By-Way   *Length: 0.4 mile*
Accessible to the handicapped, this section of the park honors U.S. armed forces as well as veterans of wars fought by the United States. Busts, statues, and memorial trees line the route.

Famous and Historic Tree Trail   *Length: 0.4 mile*
Along a gravel path, trees have been planted to honor people and events in American history. Interpretive signs provide information about the person or event, the tree's relevance, and its species. Access is either through the field on the west side of the drive or from the blue trail.

Mildred D. Lasdon Bird and Nature Sanctuary   *Length: 0.5 mile*
In 1976, William Lasdon donated 22 acres to the county to establish the Mildred D. Lasdon Bird and Nature Sanctuary in memory of his wife. It is home to many birds, including 20 species of breeding warblers. From the parking lot, the trail goes along a mowed strip and downhill to cross a causeway. It enters the woods and splits into a loop; the faint yellow blazes are more easily seen going counterclockwise. After crossing stone walls and passing through an expanse of hay-scented ferns at 0.3

mile, the trail closes the loop at 0.5 mile. To reach the sanctuary from Lasdon Park, head west on Route 35; make the first left turn onto Wood Street. A small parking area to the right is visible from Wood Street.

UNMARKED WOODS ROADS

The woods road following the west side of the outer perimeter of the fence is 0.4 mile long. A 0.6-mile gravel and dirt road system is inside the fence, as well as the 0.3-mile connection to the American chestnut trees northwest of the mansion. There are numerous short paths that meander through collections, offering walks of various lengths.

NEARBY PARK: Muscoot Farm

DRIVING: From I-684, take Exit 6 (Route 35) west for 3.6 miles to the park entrance to the left.

PUBLIC TRANSPORTATION: None available

For contact information, see Appendix, Westchester County Parks—Lasdon Park, Arboretum & Veterans Memorial.

Along the Muscoot River

Somers • 1.3 miles

Just south of the entrance to the Lasdon Bird and Nature Sanctuary on Wood Street, an unmarked fisherman's path heads north along the Muscoot River, passing a non-functioning dam. The quality of the footpath varies over the 0.9-mile northerly walk to Route 35.

Another fisherman's path begins on Pinesbridge Road, a short distance south of the junction with Route 35. It heads along the south side of Hallocks Mill Brook and then on the west side of the Muscoot River where the two join. The path leads 0.7 mile to the dam and continues another 0.7 mile further south. The Muscoot River is the outflow of the Amawalk Reservoir. High or swift flowing water prevents safe river crossings.

Leon Levy Preserve

Vista • 4.9 miles, 386 acres

$\mathbf{T}$here are many words to describe the Leon Levy Preserve; tranquil, scenic, and peaceful are just three. However, to the residents of Lewisboro, as of 2006, protected is another word to add to the list. The property contains a ravine with 25-foot high cliffs, extensive wetlands, and hardwood forests. It harbors a variety of wildlife and protects drinking water. A mansion in ruins and overgrown with vines adds to the charm of the preserve. Stone walls are throughout the property.

Known locally as the Bell property, the preserve is named in memory of its principal benefactor. Leon Levy's love of Lewisboro and for nature came together in the purchase of watershed property that local residents had wished to protect since 1996. Levy, a Wall Street investor and founder of Oppenheimer Funds, died in 2003. Through the Jerome Levy Foundation, his widow, Shelby White, and his brother, Jay Levy, provided $5 million of the $8.3 million purchase price.

TRAILS

The woods roads on the property have become hiking trails and are wide enough to allow walking two or three abreast. Extensive stonework is apparent on the many at-grade raised roadbeds. The 2.1 miles of unmarked woods roads traverse the preserve and connect to adjacent private property.

White Trail   *Length: 0.5 mile Blaze: white*
From parking spaces by the entrance sign, the white trail heads 300 feet to a T junction where it splits. Heading north from that junction towards Route 35, the trail goes uphill and passes the ruins of a stone building to the left. It ends at the blue trail at 0.2 mile.

From the aforementioned T junction at the access trail, the other branch of the white trail turns left towards Lake Kitchawan Drive. The white trail follows the base of a hill to the right and wetlands to the left, sometimes at-grade. It reaches a hairpin turn with extensive stonework and ascends to end at the blue trail.

Blue Trail   *Length: 1.1 miles Blaze: blue*
Beginning at the park boundary near Route 35 at a chain across a woods road, the blue trail heads south. It passes the white trail to the left at 0.1 mile and then a paved road, now in disrepair, which leads up to the site of the mansion. At 0.4 mile, a woods road to the right heads 0.5 mile to a radio tower. After passing a

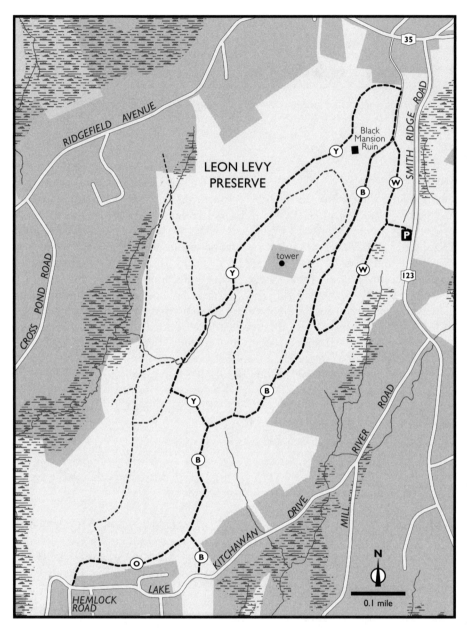

vernal pool to the left, the blue trail reaches a Y junction with the white trail at 0.5 mile. Just past the intersection to the left, extensive stonework on the white trail is visible below through the trees. The trail passes a rock outcropping, heads downhill, and crosses a ravine on a stone viaduct. At 0.8 mile, the blue trail passes the south end of the yellow trail as it continues through open woods. At 1.0 mile, the trail turns left off the woods road. Straight ahead, the orange trail follows the woods road. The blue trail descends, crosses stone walls and a stream, and ends at Lake Kitchawan Drive.

Orange Trail *Length: 0.3 mile Blaze: orange*

From the blue trail, the orange trail heads south, skirts houses, turns away from them, and crosses through a field. To the right is a nest of ATV tracks, some of which connect to other unmarked woods roads in the preserve. The orange trail ends at the corner of Hemlock Road and Lake Kitchawan Drive.

Yellow Trail *Length: 0.9 mile Blaze: yellow*

From behind the carriage house on the northern edge of the property, the yellow trail heads uphill on a woods road. It reaches pavement, turns right, and passes through what was once a lawn beside the former mansion. The trail reenters the woods and turns right at a Y junction with an unmarked trail. The yellow trail reaches a small field and goes straight across an intersection. After passing through a narrow row of trees, it crosses a second field with an unmarked trail to the right. At the far end of the second field, an unmarked woods road to the left connects in 0.6 mile to the blue trail. The yellow trail enters a wooded area with small trees at 0.3 mile and heads downhill.

At 0.6 mile, the trail reaches a T junction and turns left through a stone wall. The unmarked woods road to the right heads downhill 0.4 mile into private property. The yellow trail reaches a stone wall, turns left, and parallels it. Straight ahead through the stone wall, an unmarked woods road heads towards other unmarked woods roads often marred with ATV tracks. The yellow trail crosses a stream, turns, and crosses a stone wall. At 0.8 mile, it turns left just before reaching a stone wall, continues through the open woods, and ends at the blue trail.

DRIVING: From I-684, take Exit 6 (Route 35) and turn east. Continue 9.1 miles and turn right at the traffic light onto Route 123 just before the New York-Connecticut line. The Levy Preserve is to the right, 0.3 mile from the turn. Parking is available at a pullout to the left, just before the sign for the preserve and at a tiny parking spot to the right just beyond the sign.

PUBLIC TRANSPORTATION: None available

For contact information, see Appendix, Lewisboro.

Stone viaduct

Marsh Memorial Sanctuary
Leonard Park

Mt. Kisco • 2.7 miles, 156 acres

Consider Marsh Memorial Sanctuary to be a comeback kid. Although the sanctuary had appeared in lists of parks, several visits to Marsh Sanctuary on Route 172 revealed no evidence of any activity. In early 2008, a more thorough look at the wetlands on Sarles Street did reveal a derelict boardwalk. On subsequent visits in the spring, it was noted that sanctuary signs had been posted and trails were open. Walkers and birders welcome the opportunity to visit Marsh Sanctuary.

The Leonard family purchased the property just before 1900 and gave it to Martha Leonard, thespian and gardener. She created gardens and an amphitheater, holding plays and concerts there from 1911 to 1921. Norman and Cornelia Marsh bought the property in 1956. They donated it as a memorial to their 10-year-old daughter, Cornelia, thus protecting wetlands near the corner of Sarles Street and Byram Lake Road. During the 1970s and 1980s, the sanctuary was a summer camp. The amphitheater was renovated in 1990. Since then, new properties have been added and have protected other habitats. Open to the public, the sanctuary is privately owned. It is managed by Marsh Sanctuary Inc., a not-for-profit organization.

TRAILS

Trails at Marsh Memorial Sanctuary traverse diverse habitats: woodland, wetland, meadow, stream, and pond. The trails are blazed with a silhouette of a heron on a colored tag. The background color is listed first, and then the color of the heron is listed next. For example, the white/red trail is a white tag with a red heron. Marsh Sanctuary has three trailheads: Brookside parking area on Route 172, Field parking area on Sarles Street, and South Trail parking on Sarles Street.

BROOKSIDE PARKING AREA
Driving by on Route 172, one does not see the white columns of the amphitheater or the stonework in the garden. Both give a sense of refinement from a bygone era. The red/dark blue trail connects to Field parking on Sarles Street.

Red/Dark Blue Trail   *Length: 0.4 mile Blaze: red/dark blue*
Heading out of the parking area and skirting the amphitheater, the red/dark blue trail climbs steeply uphill on a wide woods road. Leveling off, it passes the junction with the red/yellow trail. At 0.2 mile, the trail heads downhill through open woods, then ends at the driveway to the stable at 0.4 mile.

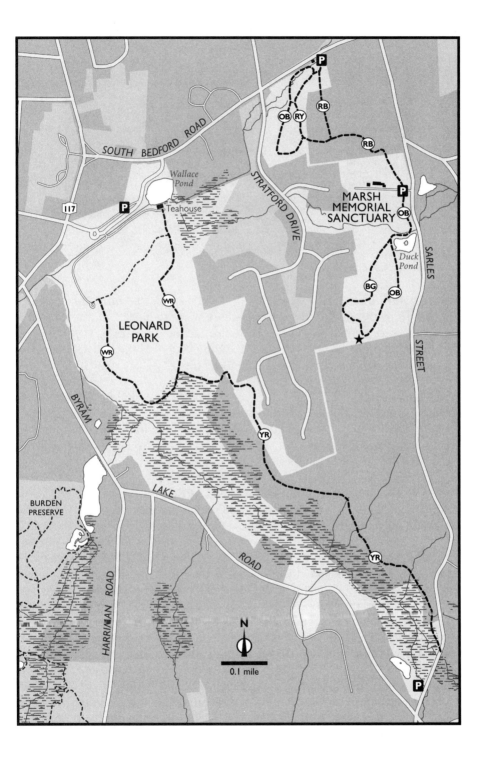

Chicken coop

Orange/Dark Blue Trail *Length: 0.3 mile Blaze: orange*
Starting from the amphitheater stage, walk toward Route 172. On a stone slab, the trail crosses a stream, follows it downstream, and recrosses it. The trail turns and passes an unmarked trail to the left leading 90 feet to the red/yellow trail. It ascends along switchbacks to end at 0.3 mile at the red/yellow trail.

Red/Yellow Trail *Length: 0.2 mile Blaze: red/yellow*
Beginning at the red/blue trail, the red/yellow trail passes the orange/dark blue trail. Descending, it passes an outdoor stone kitchen and to the left, an unmarked trail to the orange/dark blue trail. The red/yellow trail turns onto a road lined with stones and ends at the amphitheater.

FIELD PARKING AREA
A former chicken coop overlooking a meadow and a kiosk greet visitors. The 0.4-mile red/dark blue trail connects to trails at Brookside parking.

Orange/Black Trail *Length: 0.5 mile Blaze: orange/black*
Beginning at the kiosk and chicken coop in a grassy area, the orange/black trail crosses a bridge over a stream. It goes along the shore of a large pond at 0.1 mile and turns left at a junction with the light blue/green trail. Turning away from the pond, the trail enters a field and heads uphill. Entering and leaving fields, it continues uphill and enters woods at 0.3 mile. It heads uphill steeply to reach the top at 0.4 mile and then a view where it ends at the light blue/green trail.

Light Blue/Green Trail *Length: 0.2 mile Blaze: light blue/green*
From the top of the hill at the orange/black trail, the light blue/green trail overlooks fences of houses below. It enters a field and descends, ending near the pond and the orange/black trail.

SOUTH TRAIL PARKING AREA

On Sarles Street, two pullouts provide parking for the yellow/red trail, which connects to the white/red trail in Leonard Park.

Yellow/Red Trail
Length: 1.1 miles Blaze: yellow/red

Beginning across from 286 Sarles Street, the yellow/red trail enters a mature forest and contours above wetlands. The trail crosses a stream and, at 0.2 mile, leaves the wetlands. It goes through stone walls and crosses a stream as it generally drifts uphill. At 0.6 mile, New York ferns carpet the area surrounding the trail. The trail skirts below a house and crosses a stream at 0.8 mile. From there, its path is adjacent to a wetland before ending at the white/red trail in Leonard Park at 1.1 miles.

NEARBY PARKS: Merestead, Burden Preserve

DRIVING: Take I-684 to Exit 4 (Route 172) and head west. Field parking: go 1.5 miles and turn left onto Sarles Street. At 0.3 mile, turn right to park in an open field. South Trail parking: it is another 1.1 miles for roadside parking south of #286. Brookside parking is beyond Sarles Street; turn left into the parking area at a barn with a Marsh Sanctuary sign.

PUBLIC TRANSPORTATION: None available

For contact information, see Appendix, Marsh Memorial Sanctuary.

Leonard Park

Mt. Kisco • 1.0 mile, 120 acres

At Leonard Park behind a teahouse on Wallace Pond, one marked and several unmarked trails co-exist with a Frisbee golf course. Well-used trails and paved paths provide additional places to walk.

White/Red Trail
Length: 0.7 mile Blaze: white/red

The trail begins at the teahouse on a well-trod path. At picnic tables, an unmarked trail leads over to the sledding hill. At 0.2 mile, the white/red trail turns left at a Y junction and crosses a ridge. It passes wetlands and follows the base of a hill in open forest. At 0.5 mile, it passes the red/yellow trail heading to Sarles Street in 1.1 miles. Unmarked trails to the right lead either to parts of the Frisbee golf course or back onto the main trail. The white/red trail ends near Frisbee golf basket #9.

DRIVING: From I-684, take Exit 4 and head west on Route 172 for 1.6 miles. The park is located just before the junction with Route 117.

PUBLIC TRANSPORTATION: None available

For contact information, see Appendix, Mt. Kisco.

Mount Holly Sanctuary

Katonah • 3.4 miles, 208 acres

Having Mount Holly Sanctuary all to oneself during the middle of the week is a delightful experience. There is no shortage of things to hear and see. In season, ponds resonate with choruses of frogs. Birdsong and leaves rustling in the wind are uninterrupted by human noise.

Until the twentieth century, the land that is now the Mount Holly Sanctuary, except for its steepest parts, was farmed. In 1975, the threat of development led concerned citizens to join together to purchase the land from the estate of Edward A. Norman. The numerous stone walls add to the beauty of the place. Mount Holly Sanctuary is not to be confused with the smaller Mount Holly Preserve, located across and down Mount Holly Road.

TRAILS

Trod by both horses and humans, the trails of Mount Holly Sanctuary provide access to a topography that lends itself to a variety of hiking experiences. The two main trails begin at the parking area on Mount Holly Road. The Pond Trail and the steep portion of the North Main Trail are closed to horses. The entrance to the white trail into Hunt-Parker Memorial Sanctuary is 275 yards south on North Salem Road. A full day of hiking is possible by visiting these two sanctuaries.

South Main Trail   *Length: 1.3 miles Blaze: blue*
From the parking area on Mount Holly Road, the South Main Trail (blue) and the North Main Trail (red) head past the kiosk. At 0.1 mile, they go through a stone wall and split at a T junction, with the South Main Trail heading left. It heads along the edge of the property and then goes gently downhill, crossing numerous stone walls. The trail reaches and briefly joins the North Main Trail at 0.7 mile and continues to descend. At 0.8 mile, the South Main Trail crosses the ATT right-of-way and heads more seriously downhill.

The North Main Trail briefly joins the South Main Trail for a second time at a stone wall at 0.9 mile; they separate at a Y junction, with the South Main Trail going left. Continuing downhill, the South Main Trail passes the Pond Trail (yellow) to the left, crosses the inlet to a lake on stepping stones, and then joins the North Main Trail for the third and last time. They descend together past houses to the entrance at Todd Road (no parking).

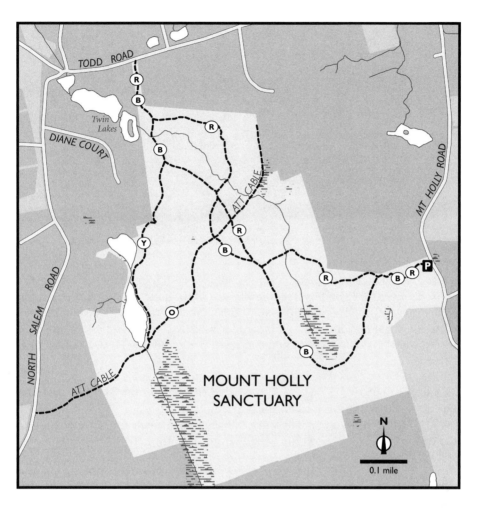

North Main Trail
Length: 1.1 miles Blaze: red

From the entrance at Todd Road, the North Main Trail and the South Main Trail (blue) head uphill. At 0.1 mile they split, with the North Main Trail going left and heading steeply uphill. At 0.4 mile, it crosses a stream and is briefly co-aligned with the South Main Trail. Continuing uphill, it crosses the ATT right-of-way at 0.5 mile and joins the South Main Trail a second time. The North Main Trail goes gradually uphill and through barberry bushes at 0.7 mile. After reaching the crest of the hill, the trail crosses stone walls and skirts the edge of the property. It joins the South Main Trail for the last time at 1.0 mile. Together they go through a stone wall and end at the parking area on Mount Holly Road.

Pond Trail
Length: 0.5 mile Blaze: yellow

Starting 1.0 mile from the entrance at Mount Holly Road along the South Main Trail (blue), the Pond Trail immediately heads uphill, passing a No Horses sign. It passes an unmarked trail to the left at 0.1 mile and then descends. The Pond Trail follows the edge of wetlands on a woods road partially paved with stones. At

Wetlands

0.4 mile, the Pond Trail reaches a pond and passes a trail to the left, occasionally marked orange. The Pond Trail reaches the end of the pond at 0.5 mile, turns right, and crosses the outlet on a causeway. At this point the trail has occasional yellow blazes, but can be followed uphill along a woods road. It reaches a Y junction with the left branch leading 0.3 mile to the ATT right-of-way toward North Salem Road.

ATT Right-of-Way   *Length: 0.9 mile Blaze: occasional*

The first section starts near 143 North Salem Road on an unmarked route along the ATT right-of-way. It parallels a driveway and horse fields to the right. Leaving the right-of-way, it goes downhill where a trail enters from the right. It reaches the Pond Trail (yellow) at 0.4 mile.

The second section starts at a No Horses sign and takes the unmarked trail to the right with occasional orange posts. Heading slightly uphill, the trail joins the phone line once again at 0.2 mile. Skirting the edge of a seasonally wet open area, the path is marked with ATT phone line signs. It passes the South Main Trail (blue) at 0.3 mile and then the North Main Trail (red). Crossing a stream at 0.4 mile, the right-of-way passes a vernal pool and shortly after, an unmarked trail at 0.5 mile. At the crest of the hill, it is necessary to retrace steps because houses on adjacent private property block the way.

NEARBY PARKS: Hunt-Parker Memorial Sanctuary, Grierson Sanctuary, Yarrow Preserve, Mount Holly Preserve

DRIVING: From I-684, take Exit 6 (Route 35) and head east for 1.8 miles. Turn left onto North Salem Road and follow it to Mount Holly Road. Turn right at the Y junction and continue 1.2 miles to where Mount Holly Road makes a sharp left. The entrance and parking for three cars is just beyond the intersection with Holly Hill Lane. There is no parking at the entrances on North Salem and Todd roads.

PUBLIC TRANSPORTATION: None available

For contact information, see Appendix, The Nature Conservancy.

Rockwood Hall

Sleepy Hollow • 3.1 miles, 88 acres

Rockwood Hall is small enough that with a special friend and a picnic lunch, you can find a spot in the shade of a sycamore, maple, or weeping beech tree and hide from other visitors. Yet it is so large you can visit many times and still find other interesting spots among the many nooks and crannies. Exotic trees, wide paths, and sweeping views make it an enjoyable place to spend the day.

TRAILS

Carriage roads of this former estate circle the property, providing a path which overlooks the Hudson River to the Palisades. Although none of the paths are blazed, navigation is easy and there is something interesting around every corner.

HISTORY OF ROCKWOOD HALL

In 1886, William Rockefeller (1841-1922), brother of John D. Rockefeller, purchased Rockwood, a 200-acre estate overlooking the Hudson, intending it to be his summer home. Accounts vary as to whether he made extensive renovations to the original castle or demolished it to build Rockwood Hall, a 204-room mansion. Frederick Law Olmstead designed the landscape, which includes many unusual ornamental trees. Rockefeller had a carriage road system built. After his death in 1922, his heirs unsuccessfully tried to sell the property to an individual buyer. Eventually, a group purchased the estate and converted it to a country club, which went bankrupt in 1936. A year later, John D. Rockefeller, Jr. bought the estate, leasing the property to a country club, which also was short-lived.

Having no real use for the buildings, Rockefeller had them razed in 1941-1942 and dumped into the Hudson. In 1946, he deeded the property to his son Laurance. IBM purchased 80 acres in 1970 for its world trade center. In the early 1970s, New York State leased the property as a public park for one dollar a year. Laurance Rockefeller underwrote the cost of maintenance. In 1999, he donated the land to the state as part of Rockefeller State Park Preserve. Only the foundation of the mansion and a gatehouse along Route 9 remain of the estate buildings. For more information about Rockwood Hall, click on "properties" at http://archive.rockefeller.edu/faqs.

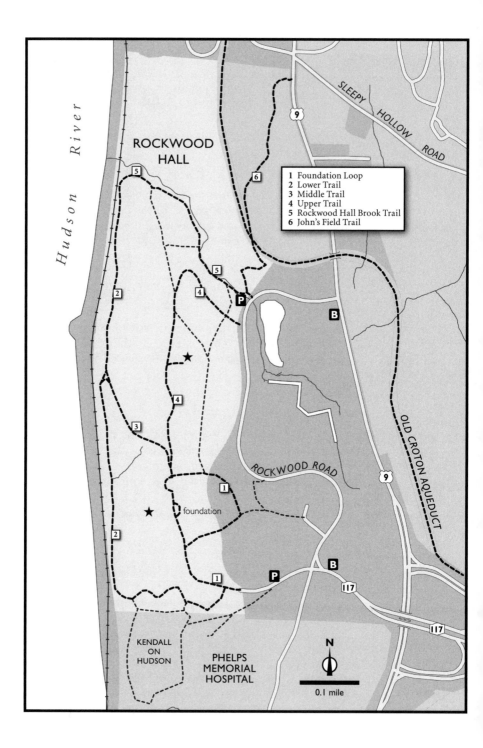

1 Foundation Loop
2 Lower Trail
3 Middle Trail
4 Upper Trail
5 Rockwood Hall Brook Trail
6 John's Field Trail

ROCKWOOD HALL

Hudson River

SLEEPY HOLLOW ROAD

OLD CROTON AQUEDUCT

ROCKWOOD ROAD

foundation

KENDALL ON HUDSON

PHELPS MEMORIAL HOSPITAL

N

0.1 mile

A perfect picnic spot

Thirteen numbered posts are located on Rockwood Hall trails. By calling 914-517-5570 on a cell phone and keying in the number of the post, visitors can learn about the history and landscape of Rockwood Hall.

Foundation Loop   *Length: 0.6 mile*

Beginning at the end of the parking lot, the Foundation Loop heads uphill. It goes right at a junction where the Lower Trail goes left. Continuing uphill on a surface of paving stones, it passes a massive weeping beech tree to the right at 0.2 mile. Just past the tree, a road which is the return portion of the loop, heads downhill. Straight ahead are the stone walls that once surrounded William Rockefeller's mansion. There are sweeping views over the river. On the opposite side of the mansion's foundation, the Foundation Loop turns right and goes downhill along the paved road. It curves past copper beeches with an expansive lawn behind them. After passing through stonework that once surrounded buildings, the paved path turns to head uphill. Although the mansion is gone, a sense of grandeur that once existed is still present. The Foundation Loop reaches the road near the weeping beech to close the loop.

Lower Trail   *Length: 1.0 mile*

Beginning near the parking lot at the junction with the Foundation Loop, the Lower Trail heads through a rockcut and passes an entrance to Kendall-on-Hudson. At the bottom of the hill at 0.2 mile, it goes by another entrance and then turns right to parallel the Hudson River with limited views to the Palisades. At 0.6 mile, the Lower Trail passes a junction with the Middle Trail which heads uphill to connect with the Upper Trail. The Lower Trail ends at the Rockwood Hall Brook Trail.

Rockwood Hall Brook Trail   *Length: 0.3 mile*

At the north end of the park, the Rockwood Hall Brook Trail goes along a gravel road at the edge of the field. It passes the mowed path leading to the Upper Trail and then enters woods. Heading uphill, it parallels Rockwood Hall Brook and goes through several small rhododendron groves. In quick succession, the trail crosses five bridges. It then passes a gravel road to the left which leads 0.1 mile to the Old Croton Aqueduct. The Rockwood Hall Brook Trail ends on a paved road. It is 300 feet farther uphill to parking and the Upper Trail.

Upper Trail   *Length: 0.5 mile*

From the far side of the foundation of the mansion and off the Foundation Loop, the Upper Trail heads north, almost immediately passing the Middle Trail to the left. Heading uphill on paving stones, it goes through a wooded area which obscures the view. The path becomes gravel when it reaches an open field. It descends with views out over the Hudson River.

The Upper Trail passes a large flat rock outcropping to the right at 0.3 mile. This solid rock platform is just before a mowed path which leads 0.3 mile over the hill and back to the Foundation Loop. To the left 150 feet farther, another mowed path heads downhill for 0.2 mile toward the Rockwood Hall Brook Trail. Both mowed paths offer sweeping views across the Hudson River. The Upper Trail curves to the right, enters the woods, and continues downhill. It ends at a gate on the access road that runs along the border of the property.

CONNECTING TRAIL & NEARBY PARK: Old Croton Aqueduct, Rockefeller State Park Preserve

DRIVING: From the Taconic State Parkway or Route 9A, take Route 117 west to Rockwood Road, where it ends at the parking area. Alternately, from Route 9 just north of Tarrytown and south of the junction with Route 117, take the entrance road to Phelps Memorial Hospital and follow it to the right all the way through the hospital facility and its parking areas, to Rockwood Road. Turn left to park.

PUBLIC TRANSPORTATION: Take the Metro-North Hudson Line to Scarborough Station. Walk south for 0.3 mile on River Road to Creighton Lane. Turn right and rejoin River Road briefly at the intersection with the Old Croton Aqueduct just before reaching Route 9. Turn right again and head south on the Old Croton Aqueduct for 0.6 mile to Rockwood Hall. Beeline Bus #13 goes to Rockwood Road, just past the parking areas of Phelps Memorial Hospital.

For contact information, see Appendix, Rockefeller State Park Preserve.

St. Matthew's Church Woodlands

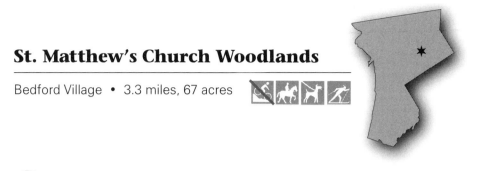

Bedford Village • 3.3 miles, 67 acres

Comprised of Ketchum Sanctuary and The Glebe, St. Matthew's Church Woodlands has been set aside for reflection and quiet enjoyment of nature. Ketchum Sanctuary is former pasture now woodland nestled between ridges in Bedford and surrounded by private estates. In 1971, Mrs. Kerr Rainsford donated 26 acres to The Nature Conservancy in memory of Arthur Ketchum, pastor of St. Matthew's Episcopal Church, 1923-1957. In 2002, The Nature Conservancy conveyed the property to St. Matthew's Church, which welcomed the responsibility of caring for the property. The Woodlands Commission of the church marked the existing trail in Ketchum Sanctuary and also established new trails. In The Glebe, they used a woods road and blazed a connecting trail segment to create a loop. ("Glebe" means land that provides revenue or belongs to a parish church.)

TRAILS

The trails in St. Matthew's Church Woodlands have benches for rest and thoughtful contemplation, though they are often moved and thus not always to be found in the spot described. A Bedford Riding Lanes Association (BRLA) trail goes through private land and links the two parcels. There is 0.9 mile of other BRLA trails, which either provide access to or crisscross the property.

Bridge over Beaver Dam River

The Glebe Trail
Length: 0.6 mile Blaze: blue
A large sign welcomes visitors to St. Matthew's Church Woodlands where the Glebe Trail begins. Go clockwise to follow the loop, heading downhill and passing a short woods road into the leaf composting pile. The trail goes by an outdoor chapel with a large bell and wood benches where services are held in summer. At 0.2 mile, the Glebe Trail passes the access trail to Ketchum Sanctuary, which crosses the bridge over Beaver Dam River. Heading

upstream on a woods road, the Glebe Trail intersects with BRLA trails as it follows the brook. At 0.4 mile, it leaves the woods road, goes through a stone wall, and joins and then leaves a BRLA trail. The Glebe Trail turns right, paralleling the edge of the parking lot to close the loop at the welcome sign.

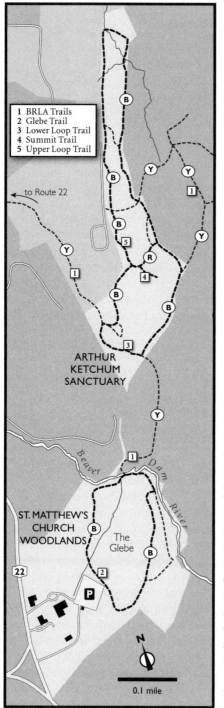

1 BRLA Trails
2 Glebe Trail
3 Lower Loop Trail
4 Summit Trail
5 Upper Loop Trail

BRLA Sanctuary Access Trail
Length: 0.3 mile Blaze: BRLA

Just past the outdoor chapel on the Glebe Trail, the access trail for pedestrians crosses a bridge over Beaver Dam River, where the BRLA signs point to a ford slightly downstream. Immediately, a trail onto private property, with a red sign No Riders, leaves to the left. The BRLA trail heads to the right and uphill to meet the Lower Loop Trail, where again, there is a No Riders sign. The BLRA signs continue to the right as the trail goes counterclockwise on the Lower Loop Trail of Ketchum Sanctuary.

Lower Loop Trail
Length: 0.5 mile Blaze: blue

At the end of the BRLA Sanctuary Access Trail, the Lower Loop Trail goes both straight and to the right. Continue straight ahead on the Lower Loop Trail, climbing steeply uphill. The trail curves right and at 0.1 mile at a Y junction, a BRLA trail goes off to the left and descends to reach Route 22 in 0.6 mile. The Lower Loop Trail continues uphill, crosses another BRLA trail, and turns right at a T junction at 0.2 mile. It passes a rock outcropping and then a riding ring and horse jumps on private land downhill to the left. At 0.3 mile, it reaches a Y junction with the Upper Loop Trail (blue) to the left and the Summit Trail (red) to the right, connecting in 0.1 mile to another segment of the Lower Loop Trail. Turn right onto the Summit Trail.

At the end of the Summit Trail, turn right at the T junction with the Upper and Lower Loop trails. The Lower Loop Trail heads steeply downhill along the upper edge of one of two parallel stone walls. At a T junction with a BRLA trail, it turns right and closes the loop at the BRLA Sanctuary Access Trail.

Upper Loop Trail   *Length: 0.9 mile Blaze: blue*

Aside from two small sections, the Upper Loop Trail is off-limits to equestrians. The Upper Loop Trail begins on the Lower Loop Trail. Proceding clockwise, the Upper Loop Trail crosses a BRLA trail and squeezes through a stone wall. It reaches a road and turns to parallel it. Leaving the road, it heads downhill at 0.2 mile. The trail crosses a BRLA trail and then two seasonal streams with adjoining wetlands. After passing a pair of large stones at 0.4 mile, it turns to parallel a stone wall. At a T junction with a BRLA trail, the Upper Loop turns right onto a BRLA-blazed woods road and then turns right again at 0.5 mile to reenter the wetlands. After crossing two bridges in quick succession, the Upper Loop Trail works its way to higher ground. Another BRLA trail enters from the right, but splits off at a Y junction where the Upper Loop Trail goes left. The trail goes over a stone wall and turns left. The BRLA trail continues right for 100 yards to the Summit Trail (red). Going slightly uphill, the Upper Loop Trail parallels a stone wall and ends at a junction of the Lower Loop and Summit trails at 0.9 mile.

NEARBY TRAILS: Bedford Riding Lanes Association

DRIVING: From I-684, take Exit 6 (Route 35). Head east on Route 35 for 0.3 mile and turn right onto Route 22. It is 3.7 miles to St. Matthew's Church. Follow the driveway to parking lots in the rear where a large white sign welcomes visitors.

PUBLIC TRANSPORTATION: None available

For contact information, see Appendix, St. Matthews Church.

Silver Lake Preserve

Harrison • 4.3 miles, 236 acres

Although near a heavily populated section of Westchester County, Silver Lake Preserve surprisingly has areas where no road noise can be heard. What is now the preserve was part of a military action on Merritt Hill in the Battle of White Plains, October 28, 1776. A monument erected in the parking lot on Old Lake Street explains its historical significance.

Silver Lake Preserve is also the site of Westchester's first free black community, which included houses, a church, school, and cemetery. The Hills, as it was called, was established on a land grant from the Purchase Friends Meeting (Quakers), who voluntarily had freed their slaves. Many residents were literate and recorded their views in letters to family members. Their 6.5-acre cemetery, Stony Hill Cemetery, is now owned by the Mt. Hope A. M. E. Zion Church of White Plains. It contains the remains of approximately 200 residents as well as many Civil War veterans.

TRAILS

Stone steps, bridges, and paved areas are along the trails in Silver Lake Preserve. Although in disrepair, they add an element of grace and elegance to the preserve. There are 1.3 miles of unmarked trails, not including a rat's nest of ATV tracks near the yellow trail.

Blue Trail   *Length: 0.6 mile Blaze: blue*
Beginning at the north end of the parking lot, the blue trail heads downhill into the woods. At an intersection at 0.1 mile, where the yellow trail goes both ways, the blue trail turns left. The two trails continue to descend, reaching a trail junction at a double tulip tree; the blue trail turns left and the yellow trail joins the white trail. Heading gradually uphill, the blue trail enters a field and turns left. It follows the edge of the field as it continues to ascend. To the right, a cannon commemorates the Battle of Merritt Hill. The trail reenters the woods on a narrow path at 0.5 mile. It parallels the road and closes the loop when it reaches the parking lot entrance.

White Trail   *Length: 1.6 miles Blaze: white*
At the double tulip tree junction at the bottom of the hill, the blue trail splits to the left when the yellow trail joins the white trail. The co-aligned trails round the end of the lake. At 0.1 mile, the yellow trail turns right and the white trail goes straight and up broad steps as it passes an unmarked trail to the right.

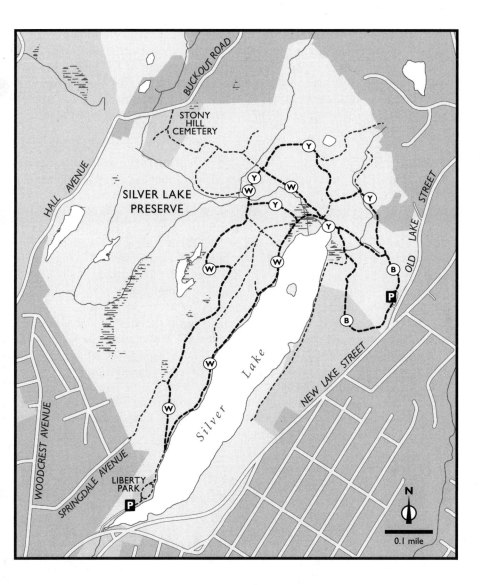

The white trail goes along the lake, passing numerous fishing spots; unmarked trails head uphill to the right. The trail crosses a stream at 0.4 mile and continues along the shore of the lake, until at 0.7 mile, it turns sharply right to head uphill away from the lake. Straight ahead, the unmarked trail leads 0.1 mile to Liberty Park. The white trail heads uphill gradually at first, and then more steeply, at times on steps. It passes an unmarked trail to the left leading 0.2 mile to Springdale Avenue (no parking). The trail levels off and passes a vernal pool. At 1.0 mile, the white trail crosses a stream and continues uphill. This section contrasts dramatically with the level path along the lake. At an intersection, the trail makes a sharp left; straight ahead the unmarked trail goes 0.1 mile to join an unmarked trail leading to the lake.

Curving to the right, the white trail goes through rock outcroppings on both sides of the trail. Descending, it reaches an intersection where an unmarked trail leads 0.1 mile down to the lake. It reaches the yellow trail at 1.4 miles, turns left to join it, and crosses a stream. Passing a fireplace, it reaches a Y junction and turns right; the yellow trail continues straight. Descending on steps on a graded path, the white trail closes the loop at 1.6 miles, joining the yellow and white trails coming from the right.

Yellow Trail   *Length: 1.0 mile Blaze: yellow*

Beginning on the blue trail heading north from the parking lot, the yellow trail is a loop with sections co-aligned with the white and blue trails. To go counterclockwise around the loop, turn right and leave the blue trail. The yellow trail skirts the bottom of a hill. It heads left when an unmarked trail heads north into a valley. After descending stone steps, the yellow trail turns right at an intersection where an unmarked trail continues 250 feet downhill to the lake. As the yellow trail ascends on stone steps, it passes, to the right, rock outcroppings with surfaces pitted from flowing water. The trail continues uphill and reaches an unmarked woods road leading 0.2 mile through a valley.

Descending, the yellow trail at 0.4 mile enters a rat's nest of former ATV trails which loop onto each other. From one of the ATV tracks, an unmarked trail leads 0.2 mile to the Stony Hill Cemetery. At 0.5 mile, the white trail joins from the left and large flat rocks pave the treadway of the co-aligned trails. The two trails pass a fireplace surrounded by a stone wall and then cross a stream on large flat stones. At a T junction at 0.6 mile, the yellow trail turns left and the white trail continues straight, heading downhill. At 0.7 mile, the yellow trail turns left to join the white trail entering from the right. At lake level, the trails together cross two

Stone fireplace

inlet streams and reach a junction where the loop portion of the white trail begins to the left. The two trails reach the blue trail at 0.8 mile, where the white trail ends; the yellow trail joins the blue trail to the left and continues uphill. At 1.0 mile, the yellow trail closes the loop at the intersection where the blue trail heads up to the parking lot.

CONNECTING PARK: Liberty Park, at the south end of Silver Lake, connects to a trail on the west side of the lake. The park was established in July 2003, to honor three White Plains residents who died in the 9/11 disaster. The City of White Plains has a 30-year lease from Westchester County, which owns the property. Anyone may use the park, but the boat launch is open only to White Plains residents. The paved patterned macadam path is handicapped accessible.

DRIVING: From I-684, take Exit 2 (Route 120) and proceed south for a mile. Turn right onto Lake Street and continue for 1.8 miles; turn right onto Old Lake Street. A parking lot is to the left.

PUBLIC TRANSPORTATION: Metro-North Harlem Line White Plains Station or Metro-North New Haven Line Harrison Station. Beeline Bus #5 leaves from those stations and stops at Liberty Park.

For contact information, see Appendix, Westchester County Parks.

Tibbetts Brook Park

Yonkers • 3.3 miles, 161 acres

Opened to the public in June 1927, Tibbetts Brook Park was Westchester County Park Commission's first large-scale developed recreational facility. Woodland buffer surrounds its large grassy fields, lake, pond, and brook. An historic gazebo, restored in 2003, and a bathhouse grace the center of the park. The stone and stucco bathhouse with its gabled roof line is a singular style of architecture; throughout the building is neo-classical ornamentation. To avoid crowds using the park to picnic, swim, and play ball, visit Tibbetts Brook Park either off-season or on weekdays.

The park is named for George Tippet, (variant spellings include Tibbetts, Tibbitts, and Tibbit), a settler in the Colonial period. An adjacent landowner, Jacobus Van Cortlandt, needed water power for his grist and saw mills. In 1718, the men agreed to dam Tippet's Brook, flooding a portion of both properties. The mills, in what is now Van Cortlandt Park, operated from about 1690 until 1915.

Across the lake

TRAILS

Walking in Tibbetts Brook Park is along unmarked paved paths and park roads, all easily accessible from the parking lots, neighboring streets, Old Croton Aqueduct, and South County Trailway. A loop around the large lake is 1.1 miles. The loop at the park's north end is 0.9 mile and a loop around the entire park is 2 miles.

There are three access trails from Tibbetts Brook Park to the Old Croton Aqueduct. A paved path at the north end of the park is 0.2 mile; another at the park

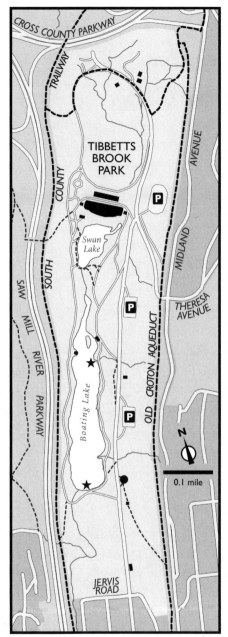

entrance is 0.1 mile. The third, a 0.1-mile unpaved path is in the southern portion, near restrooms. The 0.8-mile road walk from the entrance booth goes south to the pedestrian entrance at Jervis Road. Several paths on the west side of the park lead to the South County Trailway.

CONNECTING TRAILS: Old Croton Aqueduct, South County Trailway

DRIVING: From the Saw Mill River Parkway, take Exit 4 (Cross County Parkway) and stay in the right lane to get off at the next exit, Yonkers Avenue. At the end of the exit ramp, turn right onto Midland Avenue. The park entrance is 0.5 mile on the right. A Westchester County resident's pass is required in-season.

From westbound Cross County Parkway, take Exit 3 (Yonkers Avenue East). At the second light, turn right onto Midland Avenue. The park entrance is to the right in 0.5 mile.

PUBLIC TRANSPORTATION: Beeline Bus #7 along Yonkers Avenue at the north end of the park, or #4 at McLean Avenue near the Old Croton Aqueduct

For contact information, see Appendix, Westchester County Parks—Tibbetts Brook Park.

Turkey Mountain Nature Preserve

Yorktown Heights • 3.4 miles, 125 acres

*O*n *a Clear Day You Can See Forever* is the title of a 1965 musical; those words come to mind when enjoying the view from the top of Turkey Mountain—that is, of course, if the day is clear. A sweeping view to the south and east shows the Croton Reservoir and the Manhattan skyline in the distance.

From Colonial times until 1917, what is now Turkey Mountain Nature Preserve was owned by members of the Griffen family. Lydia Locke purchased 400 acres of

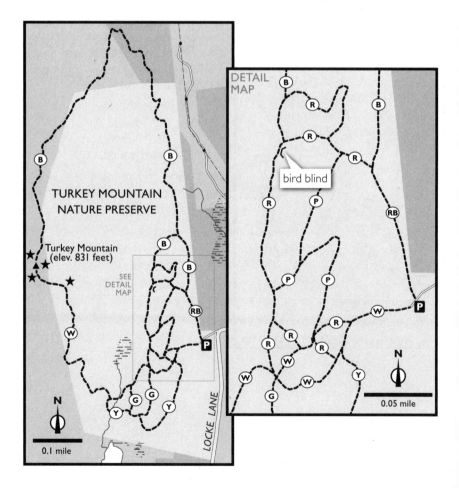

the property and created Loch Ledge, a preserve. In 1951, she sold 125 acres to the Child Services League (Queens) for a boys' summer camp after Yorktown refused her offer to sell them land for a school. The camp operated from 1957 until 1964, when it closed because of financial difficulties. The following year, the Save Turkey Mountain Committee formed to explore ways to preserve open space. The Town of Yorktown agreed to spend $30,000 to match contributions from two families. In 1969, the property was acquired with a restriction that it was to be used as an outdoor education and hiking facility.

TRAILS

A hike in Turkey Mountain Preserve should include a vigorous hike to the top and a slow amble on the 1.1 miles of intertwined trails adjacent to the parking lot. Many of the trails at the bottom were part of the former camp and wander past a few remnants. Maps posted near trail junctions help negotiate the rat's nest of trails. For someone interested in plants, there is a lot to see within the variety of habitats. The preserve is also a great area to learn or practice map-reading skills.

Blue Trail   *Length: 1.4 miles Blaze: blue*
One of two trails to the summit of Turkey Mountain, the blue trail begins on the north side of the parking lot and initially is co-aligned with a segment of one of the red trails. Shortly past the parking lot, the two trails pass a kiosk. When the trails split, the red trail leaves to the left. On level terrain for the first 0.1 mile, the blue trail passes a blue-blazed side trail on the left leading in 0.1 mile to the network of red trails. At 0.3 mile, the blue trail crosses a series of seasonal streams. It works its way uphill, at first gradually then more steeply, and at 0.5 mile, begins its assault on the hill. Climbing over rocks, it reaches the ridge at 0.8 mile. On

Rocks on the ridge

fairly level terrain, the trail traverses the ridge. Underfoot in some places is dark gray slab rock which looks like the hide of an elephant complete with wrinkles. The blue trail reaches expansive views at the top of Turkey Mountain. It ends at three concrete pillar bases, where the white trail begins.

White Trail   *Length: 0.7 mile Blaze: white*
As the white trail leads steeply down from the top of Turkey Mountain there are occasional sections leveling off slightly. At 0.2 mile, the trail crosses a log bridge. After passing the yellow trail to the right, the white trail is on a boardwalk as it traverses wetlands and a stream. To the right at 0.5 mile, the trail passes the 0.1-mile green trail which provides an alternate route and then in quick suggestion a red trail to the left, the end of a green trail to the right, and a white trail to the left. After a gentle rise, the trail passes to the right the trail to the classroom. Now on a woods road, the white trail goes by another red trail to the left, the yellow trail to the right, and a final red segment to the left, before ending at the kiosk in the parking lot.

Yellow Trail   *Length: 0.3 mile Blaze: yellow*
Beginning on the white trail shortly beyond the entrance, the yellow trail heads through an open area, passes a massive tulip tree on the left, and reaches the green trail at 0.2 mile. The two trails are co-aligned for a short distance but then split, with the yellow trail going straight ahead to end at the white trail.

NEARBY TRAIL: North County Trailway

DRIVING: From the Taconic State Parkway, take the Underhill Avenue Exit and turn east towards Yorktown Heights. At the first light, turn right onto Route 118. Go 1.9 miles, until there are signs for Croton Heights Road on the left and Locke Lane on the right. Turn right onto the dirt road to reach parking.

PUBLIC TRANSPORTATION: Beeline Bus #12 on Route 118

For contact information, see Appendix, Yorktown.

Twin Lakes Park
Nature Study Woods

Eastchester • 7.0 miles, 220 acres

At the entrance to Twin Lakes Park, it is obvious that this park is for equestrians. But there is plenty of room for everyone to walk. Nature Study Woods also allows equestrians, but there are no stables adjacent to this park and thus less horse traffic. In Twin Lakes, two stables are on county property: River Ridge Equestrian Center and Twin Lakes Farm. The latter is an indoor riding rink. The Hutchinson River Parkway goes through Twin Lakes Park.

Twin Lakes Park is named for two lakes used as reservoirs to control flooding on the Hutchinson River. The land, which became Twin Lakes Park and Nature Study Woods, was purchased in 1924 and 1927 as part of the Hutchinson River Parkway. Unmarked trails vary in width, and many small trails connect wider ones.

From 1917 to 1937, the New York, Westchester & Boston Railway went through Nature Study Woods and a small portion of Twin Lakes Park. Indications of the railroad's presence include a concrete stub, which shows a center divider where tracks once were, scattered gravel, the straight at-grade path, concrete litter in Reservoir #2, and a large concrete trestle, which supported a viaduct. For additional history of the railway, see the sidebar about the railway in White Plains Greenway, page 46.

TRAILS

At Twin Lakes and Nature Study Woods, the trails are primarily along woods roads. Many narrow equestrian trails in Twin Lakes Park connect the woods roads. The Hutchinson River Pathway (Hutch Pathway) and the Colonial Greenway go through both parks and are sometimes co-aligned. Inside the parks, the Hutch Pathway and Colonial Greenway are blazed; for the former, blazes are often faded or missing. There are an additional 2.9 miles of unmarked trails and woods roads.

Colonial Greenway   *Length: 2.6 miles Blaze: blue with white star*
Entering Twin Lakes Park from the north, the Colonial Greenway is co-aligned with the Hutchinson River Pathway for the first 0.3 mile. Together they pass through a grassy triangle intersection, bearing left. At the next intersection, where the Hutch Pathway goes left, the Colonial Greenway turns right. It crosses trails heading right, which eventually either lead back to the parking lot for the stables or head left towards Reservoir #3. At 0.6 mile, it reaches the reservoir and parallels the shore. The Colonial Greenway turns toward California Road, and at 1.0 mile,

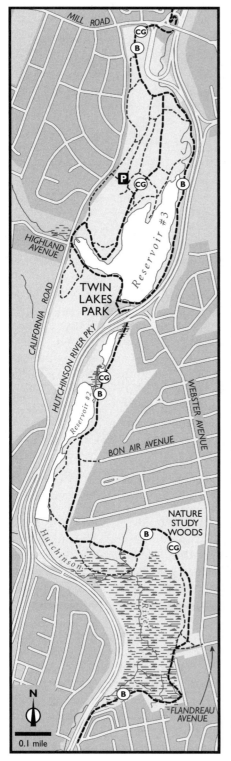

0.1 mile

passes an entrance across from Highland Avenue (limited parking). Turning away from California Road, it continues to follow the shore. A 0.3-mile unmarked path loops up a hill and returns. Noise from the Hutch is audible and across the reservoir, cars are visible.

At 1.2 miles, the Hutch Pathway joins the Colonial Greenway at the Reservoir #3 dam. The co-aligned trails cross a bridge over an entrance ramp to the Hutch, head down a ramp, and cross a bridge below the dam. After passing under the Hutch where the Hutchinson River runs through a concrete channel to the left, at 1.4 miles the pathway enters an area blanketed with invasive plants. It reaches Reservoir #2 and then parallels it. To the right, a short 0.2-mile trail goes through a flood control area to reach a dam. At 1.8 miles, the pathway passes an unmarked trail to the left leading to Bon Air Avenue. Entering Nature Study Woods, the pathway is routed along a railbed. To the right at 2.0 miles, a lone trestle of the former New York, Westchester & Boston Railway looms high overhead. Just beyond the trestle, at a Y junction, an unmarked trail to the right heads 0.2 mile out into the flood plain of the Hutchinson River.

The co-aligned trails pass a stone outcropping to the left. Numerous unmarked trails join and leave the co-aligned trails. The Colonial Greenway is a wide path as it goes through a large intersection at 2.6 miles and heads towards Webster and Flandreau avenues.

Hutchinson River Pathway
Length: 3.1 miles Blaze: blue
See Linear Corridors, pages 353-354

CONNECTING TRAIL: Colonial Greenway

DRIVING: To reach Twin Lakes from the southbound Hutchinson River Parkway,

Reservoir #3

take Exit 18W (Mill Road). Go 0.1 mile and *turn left at California Road. It is 0.5 mile to the entrance of River Ridge Equestrian Center at Twin Lakes Park. Public parking is to the left. From the northbound Hutchinson River Parkway, take Exit 17 (North Avenue) and go left at the end of the ramp. At the next traffic light, bear left onto Mill Road. Follow the directions from * above.

To reach Nature Study Woods from the northbound Hutchinson River Parkway, take Exit 16 and turn right onto southbound Webster Avenue. Go 0.8 mile to the park entrance to the right across from 822 Webster Avenue. From the southbound Hutchinson River Parkway, take Exit 18E (Mill Road East) toward New Rochelle. At 0.3 mile, make a slight right onto North Avenue. Follow North Avenue 1.1 miles and turn right onto Rosehill Avenue. Go 0.2 mile and turn left onto Webster Avenue. It is 0.4 mile to the park entrance to the right, across from 822 Webster Avenue.

PUBLIC TRANSPORTATION: For Twin Lakes, none available; for Nature Study Woods, Beeline Bus #45 on Webster Avenue and Bus #53 on New Rochelle Road

For contact information, see Appendix, Westchester County Parks.

Ward Acres Park

New Rochelle • 3.5 miles, 62 acres

For many years, Ward Acres was a haven for dog owners who liked to walk their pets off-leash. Wide trails, former farm fields, and adjacent woodlands became their playground. In time, some dog owners began taking care of the park. Litter decreased, as did vandalism. However, because of the excessive number of unleashed dogs, in 2007 New Rochelle officials passed a regulation which imposed a fee for dogs using the park and restricted the hours they were allowed to be off-leash. Although the high fee for non-residents was eventually reduced, in 2008 the issue was still contentious. As of July 2008, a three-acre fenced-in dog park where dogs are allowed to run off-leash is in the first field by the park's main entrance on Broadfield Road.

Ward Acres Park was originally part of a 100-acre farm purchased in 1912 by Robert Ward of the Ward Baking Company. His son, William B. Ward, added 300 acres, and at his death in 1929, left it to his wife and their five children. One son, Jack, raised thoroughbred horses and by 1940 had established his own company, American Saddle. A small equine cemetery is along the white trail. In 1956, Mrs. Ethel Ward donated 13.3 acres where the William B. Ward Elementary School was built, across the street from the park's main entrance. Gradually the farmland was sold, including a piece to New Rochelle as a site for the Albert Leonard Middle School. The final acreage with house and barns was sold to the city in 1962, for use as a passive recreational park, the largest in New Rochelle.

Part of the route of the New York, Westchester and Boston Railroad went through Ward Acres. To find the railbed in the north part of the park, look for a level bed often built at-grade. To learn more about the railway, see sidebar in White Plains Greenway, page 46.

TRAILS

Delineated by three roads, Ward Acres Park has marked trails and a network of unmarked wide mowed paths and woods roads. Although the terrain is flat, large numbers of visitors make it unsuitable for cross-country skiing. The snow becomes pock-marked with many footprints, and after being packed down may be icy.

Marked trails are mostly narrow paths rimming the park. The 1.7 miles of unmarked trails crisscross unmowed former farm fields now overgrown. Frequent traffic on these pathways has kept invasives somewhat at bay. Other unmarked trails follow stone walls or are near the remaining farm buildings.

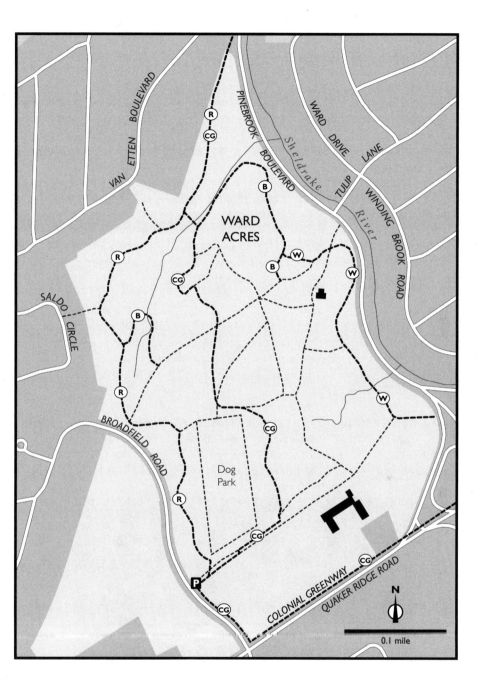

There are three major intersections of unmarked trails. One intersection is just past the kiosk on Broadfield Road at the main entrance. Two prominent intersections are along a wide woods road dividing the wetlands from more open woodland: one where the Colonial Greenway enters the wetlands and the other a convergence of five trails.

Red Trail *Length: 0.6 mile Blaze: red*

At the main entrance across from William Ward B. Elementary School on Broadfield Road just before the kiosk, the red trail heads north, enters the woods, and passes access points to Broadfield Road. At 0.2 mile, it makes a sharp left as it passes a large sugar maple to the right. It turns around the end of a stone wall and crosses a 0.2-mile-wide unmarked woods road leading across the park into the network of unmarked trails. The red trail heads onto the bed of the former New York, Westchester & Boston Railway. It passes a structure thought to be an abandoned power station and parallels a stream.

At 0.3 mile, the red trail turns left to leave the stream and a blue trail goes right for 0.1 mile to end at the previously noted wide woods road across the park. The red trail passes a rock face to the left and crosses a tiny stream on a bridge. It reaches a junction where the Colonial Greenway enters from the right. The two trails are co-aligned; crossing on an 80-foot boardwalk, they pass a large tulip tree and continue along another boardwalk. Passing back yards and heading up a short rise, they reach Pinebrook Boulevard at 0.6 mile.

Blue Trails *Length: 0.2 mile Blaze: blue*

From the wide woods road across the park, the blue trail heads north. It passes the white trail to the right and crosses a convergence of small streams. After making a sharp left turn, the trail runs between a stream to the right and a berm to the left. The blue trail ends at the Colonial Greenway. Another 0.1-mile blue trail is on the west side of the park.

Colonial Greenway *Length: 0.6 mile Blaze: blue with white star(s)*

Across from the William Ward Elementary School, a Colonial Greenway sign is at the main entrance. This section of the Colonial Greenway enters Ward Acres and parallels a stone wall with a trail in the field on its other side. This field is a fenced-

Stone wall

in dog park. Turning left to go through the stone wall, the trail enters a new field and heads north. Just after entering the woods, the trail turns left to round the corner of a stone wall, and at a junction, turns right to parallel another stone wall. It crosses a wide intersection and heads down to cross a bridge into a wetland. Heading through dense vegetation, the Colonial Greenway turns right, left, and then left again, to cross a bridge at 0.4 mile and join the red trail. Wood chips and boardwalks make it possible to keep feet dry crossing the wetlands. The Colonial Greenway leaves Ward Acres Park utilizing the shoulder of southbound Pinebrook Boulevard to join the Outer Loop of the Colonial Greenway in 0.6 mile.

White Trail   *Length: 0.3 mile Blaze: white*

Beginning at Pinebrook Boulevard near an exit ramp, the white trail enters the woods at a large sign. Turning to parallel Pinebrook Boulevard, the white trail passes the thoroughbred horse cemetery to the left. With headstones set so close, it is likely that the horses were cremated. The trail crosses a stream on a stone bridge and continues along a raised bed. To the left, it passes an unmarked trail leading back to the fields. At 0.2 mile, the trail curves toward the road and passes three stone slabs set upright like posts of a guardrail fence. Turning away from Pinebrook Boulevard, it crosses a driveway to a vacant house on the property, and then a field. At 0.3 mile, the white trail ends at the blue trail. To the right, the blue trail continues 0.2 mile further to end at the Colonial Greenway. To the left, the blue trail ends in 75 feet at the wide woods road across the northern part of the park.

NEARBY PARK & TRAILS: Larchmont Reservoir, Colonial Greenway, Leatherstocking Trail, Hutchinson River Pathway

DRIVING: From the southbound Hutchinson River Parkway, take Exit 20 (Route 125), turn left onto Route 125, and continue for 0.8 mile. *Turn right onto Quaker Ridge Road; go 0.5 mile and turn right onto Broadfield Road. Parking is on the road, across from the William B. Ward Elementary School. If northbound, take Exit 21 and turn right onto Hutchinson Avenue. At Route 125, turn left and follow the directions from *.

PUBLIC TRANSPORTATION: None available

For contact information, see Appendix, New Rochelle.

Whippoorwill Park

Chappaqua • 3.5 miles, 167 acres

With trails that traverse the valleys and ridges of a soaring hardwood forest, Whippoorwill Park offers a great place to spend part of a day. There are opportunities for wildlife observation along a pond, near a wetland, and in a mixed hardwood forest. Even in winter with significant snow cover, the park's trails are used. Visitors are encouraged to hike along marked trails but also to bushwhack through the rugged terrain. There is little or no road noise because the park is in a valley shielded by large wetlands and a ridge bordered by undeveloped private land below road level.

Whippoorwill Park was once part of Henry Berol's 500-acre estate, which included a game preserve. Berol, an avid quail hunter, was head of the Eagle Pencil Company. In 1966 he sold his estate, which was divided into a park and a residential area.

TRAILS

Trails in the park are marked with colored square plastic tags and are accessible from the parking lot via the red trail. Although no parking is available from Whippoorwill Lake Road and Kitchel Road at the blue and white trails, there is pedestrian access. There are also 1.1 miles of unmarked trails and woods roads; all but one lead off the blue trail. Because some go into private property, please respect landowners and do not trespass.

Red Trail   *Length: 0.4 mile Blaze: red*
From the parking lot, the red trail heads downhill along a narrow path. Soon after reaching the valley floor, the red trail passes the blue trail to the right and then continues straight when the yellow trail turns left. The red trail climbs uphill, reaches the ridge top, parallels a stone wall, and descends. Leveling slightly, the trail goes through a stone wall. As it descends, it passes barberry bushes to the left and another stone wall to the right. At 0.4 mile, the red trail ends at a T junction with the blue trail.

Blue Trail   *Length: 0.9 mile Blaze: blue*
At the bottom of the descent from the parking lot, the blue trail begins to the right. It skirts the edge of an extensive wetland and contours around the base of a hill. At 0.2 mile, as it rounds the hill which now has steep slopes, there is an

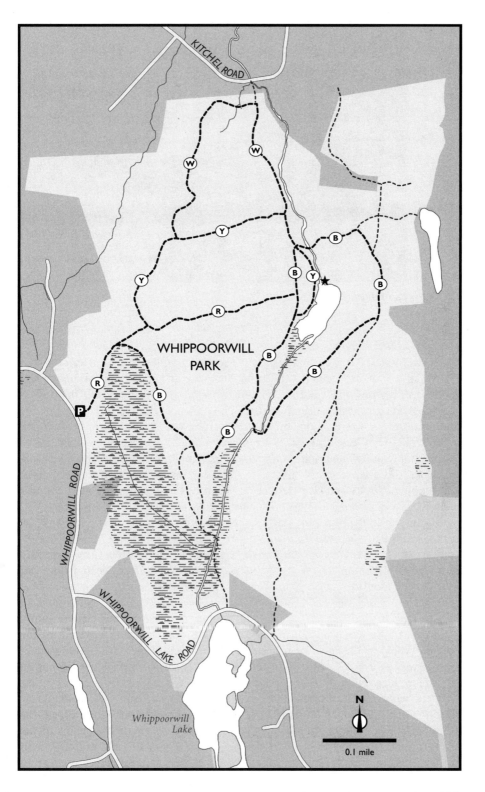

Dam in winter

unmarked side trail leading 0.2 mile to Whippoorwill Lake Road and, in 180 feet, a branch of that same trail.

To the right at 0.3 mile, at an easily missed intersection, the blue trail splits to form a large loop around a pond. Going clockwise and continuing straight along the base of the hill, the trail has views of the pond. At a Y junction at 0.5 mile, it reaches the yellow trail for the first time. The blue trail heads left, leaves the lake, and passes the red trail to the left next to a stone wall. The blue trail crosses the yellow trail at 0.6 mile and makes a right turn onto a woods road, which crosses an outlet stream of the pond on a rock bridge. Except for an occasional airplane overhead, this area seems completely removed from the world beyond the park. Ascending gradually, the blue trail leaves the woods road and turns right. Straight ahead is an unmarked trail into private property.

Bearing right, the blue trail reaches a massive downed tulip tree. Turning right, it heads uphill along a woods road, only to turn right again and leave the woods road at 0.8 mile. As the trail descends, the pond becomes visible once more, but only in leaf-off season. The trail crosses the inlet stream on a bridge and closes the loop at a T junction.

White Trail   *Length: 0.5 mile Blaze: white*

A sign on the yellow trail indicates that the white trail is a nature trail, focusing on trees found in the area. Signs beside the trees include information about their uses as well as a map indicating where they are generally found. The humorous signs make it easy to learn to identify tree species. From a junction with the yellow trail, the white trail first gradually goes downhill, then crosses a small stream. At the bottom of the hill, an unmarked track leads to a bridge along Kitchel Road. The white trail heads uphill to parallel a cascading stream. It ends at the yellow trail at 0.5 mile near an old earthen and rock dam, a remnant of Colonial times. A short path off the white trail leads to the base of this former dam and spillway.

Yellow Trail   *Length: 0.5 mile Blaze: yellow*

Heading uphill from a junction with the red trail, the yellow trail joins a woods road and continues uphill. At 0.2 mile, it passes the white trail on the left and descends between a stone wall to the right and barberry bushes to the left. At the base of the hill at 0.3 mile, the yellow trail turns right at a T junction with the white trail to the left. At the junction with the blue trail at 0.4 mile, be alert: the blue trail goes either straight ahead or left. The yellow trail crosses the blue trail and follows the stream. It reaches a dam with a breached spillway, then hugs the lakeshore until meeting the blue trail again at 0.5 mile, where it ends.

NEARBY PARK: Glazier Arboretum

DRIVING: Take the Saw Mill River Parkway to the light at Readers Digest Road and cross the railroad tracks. Stay on Readers Digest Road until it ends at Route 117 (Bedford Road). Turn right onto Bedford Road and head south. At Whippoorwill Road, turn left and continue 1.0 mile to the park.

PUBLIC TRANSPORTATION: Beeline Bus #19 stops just north of the intersection of Route 117 and Whippoorwill Road. A one-mile road walk leads to the park.

For contact information, see Appendix, New Castle.

Iona Island from Anthony's Nose

SECTION V

DAY TRIPPERS

- ◆ Have five to ten miles of trails
- ◆ Encompass greater variety of habitats
- ◆ Provide sufficient trails for a full day of hiking
- ◆ Are worth longer than a half-hour drive

Baxter Tract

North Salem • 6.3 miles, 167 acres

From the parking area on Baxter Road, former farm fields in the Baxter Tract stretch as far as the eye can see, and even further. The grassy fields close to Baxter Road are mowed, and you can walk anywhere. Deeper into the property, fields are flush with wildflowers in the summer and only a path is kept mowed.

North Salem is often described as "horsey," and one should expect to see horses and to give them the right of way. Model airplanes may not be flown in the fields. Dogs can be off leash, but not on weekends and legal holidays when more visitors frequent the trails. Snowshoeing and cross-country skiing are permitted.

Baxter Tract is the largest of the properties owned by the North Salem Open Land Foundation (NSOLF), a conservation trust founded in 1974. As of 2008, the Foundation owns 750 acres and holds conservation easements on another 210 acres. These tracts offer opportunities for exercising, observing wildlife, and enjoying scenic vistas.

In the Baxter Tract, the rolling terrain and wide sky make for pleasant walking. However, on hot summer days the sun can be brutal, even with sunscreen and a hat. The mowed paths in the fields may vary from year to year and are not always exactly as shown on the map. Sometimes mowed paths are found on both sides of a stone wall. There are so many places to walk, varying a route is easy.

The hike around the lake is 1.0 mile and passes evidence of an old steeplechase race track. A stand for viewing the turf races was next to the large white oak perched on the knoll with a split rail fence along its top. It is 2.6 miles to follow the perimeter of Baxter Tract which has few distinguishing landmarks on the property, making it difficult to describe a hike in detail. The fields are level and it is only in the southern area of the tract that there are any noticeable elevation changes. Those wishing to explore the far reaches of the tract can use the edge of the property as a guide.

Standing sentinel

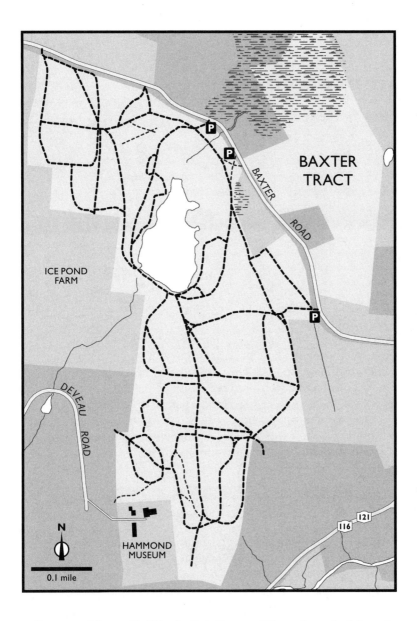

BAXTER
TRACT

ICE POND
FARM

BAXTER ROAD

DEVEAU ROAD

N

0.1 mile

HAMMOND
MUSEUM

116 121

DRIVING: From northbound I-684 take Exit 7, turn right at the end of the exit ramp, and turn left onto Route 22. Once on Route 22, turn right at Route 116 (Titicus Road) and follow it for 3.7 miles. Turn left onto June Road and drive 0.9 mile. Turn right onto Baxter Road and drive 0.4 mile. Parking is available to the right, opposite #107 and #67. If driving from southbound I-684, take Exit 8 and follow Route 22 south. At the intersection with Route 116, where Route 22 heads right, follow Route 116 to the tract, using the directions above.

PUBLIC TRANSPORTATION: None available

For contact information, see Appendix, North Salem Open Land Foundation.

Beaver Dam Sanctuary

Katonah • 7.8 miles, 171 acres

S cenic and lovely are the words to describe Beaver Dam Sanctuary. There are mowed fields for easy walking. Expect to see horses, or evidence of horses, because the sanctuary trails are part of the Bedford Riding Lanes Association (BRLA) trail system.

The numerous stone walls crisscrossing the property attest to the land's first uses as pasturage and cropland. The occasional large trees with spreading crowns were shade trees for livestock, indicating which fields once served as pasture rather than being cultivated.

Established in 1969, with an original purchase of 14 acres containing Broad Brook and Beaver Dam River, the sanctuary has grown through gifts and purchases. Jan and Parker Montgomery and Marilyn and Kelly Simpson, along with other Bedford residents, established a not-for-profit corporation. Marilyn Simpson donated large sections of land, including a broad meadow named in her memory.

Beaver Dam River, a fast-flowing, wide stream running through the property, flows north into the Muscoot Reservoir. Upstream from the sanctuary, streams are stocked every year. Fishing is permitted in season.

Beaver Dam River

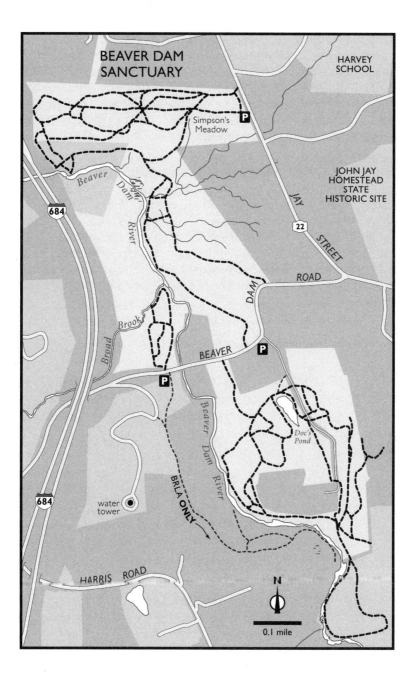

BEAVER DAM
SANCTUARY

HARVEY
SCHOOL

Simpson's
Meadow

JOHN JAY
HOMESTEAD
STATE
HISTORIC SITE

684

Beaver

Dam

River

JAY

22

STREET

DAM

ROAD

Broad

Brook

BEAVER

Beaver

Dam

River

Doc's
Pond

684

water
tower

BRLA ONLY

HARRIS   ROAD

N

0.1 mile

TRAILS

Hiking at the Beaver Dam Sanctuary is either on flat terrain for a long distance or on short steep sections. Because all trails within the sanctuary are marked with yellow BRLA signs, hikers should pay close attention to their routes. The many fords of Beaver Dam River are primarily suited to equestrians and almost guaranteed to get hikers' feet wet. Fields are mowed annually; as a result, the exact location and mileage of trails across the fields may vary from year to year. Some sections of the trail system are open only to BRLA members. Please stay off trails posted as such, unless you have purchased a BRLA yearly pass. For membership information, contact BRLA www.bedfordweb.net/brla/.

CONNECTING PARK & TRAILS: John Jay Homestead, BRLA trail system

DRIVING: From I-684, take Exit 6 (Katonah) and travel east on Route 35. Turn right onto NY 22 and head south. Look for an entrance to the sanctuary on the right, just past the Harvey School entrance to the left. An option is to drive to Beaver Dam Road, 1.4 miles south of the intersection of Routes 35 and 22, where Beaver Dam Road becomes a dirt road almost immediately. Head downhill and park on the left side, where the road makes a sharp right turn. More parking is available at the entrance to the northern portion of the sanctuary, 0.2 mile west on Beaver Dam Road.

PUBLIC TRANSPORTATION: None available

For contact information, see Appendix, Beaver Dam Sanctuary.

Butler Memorial Sanctuary

Mt. Kisco • 6.6 miles, 352 acres

In Westchester, the best place to watch fall hawk migration is Butler Memorial Sanctuary. The Robert J. Hammershlag Hawkwatch, erected there in 1972, was rebuilt and expanded in 1994. With grandstand-style seats, the hawk watch overlooks I-684 in the valley below. It might lack hot dogs, popcorn, and rooting fans, but during fall migration, there are many visitors, including experts who help identify and describe the species being seen and counted. From the bleachers, Long Island Sound 10 miles away is visible.

In 1954, Anna Butler donated 225 acres to The Nature Conservancy in memory of her husband, Arthur, an amateur naturalist and astronomer. He planted evergreens and laid out many of the trails throughout the sanctuary. In 1957, the Walter Huber family added 20 acres. The purchase of another 107 acres increased the sanctuary to its present size.

TRAILS

As the trails traverse up and down through the ridge and swale topography of Butler Memorial Sanctuary, hikers experience various forest communities, including mixed hardwoods dominated by oak, hickory, or hemlock. The ages of the trees vary and include younger white pine and Norway spruce plantations. Wet areas are mostly red maple swamps.

Each intersection displays a green arrow showing the shortest route back to the parking lot. There are six short white trails, totaling 0.8 mile. Five of them serve as connectors to the other trails and one leads to the viewpoint at Sunset Ledge. These are described in relation to the trails they connect. Thus, the white trail which connects the red trail with the yellow trail is mentioned at an appropriate place in the trail description.

Red Trail   *Length: 1.3 miles Blaze: red*
Beginning at the kiosk near the sanctuary entrance, the red trail passes junctions with the yellow trail to the left and orange trail #2 to the right, in quick succession. The blue trail merges from the left at 0.1 mile, and after crossing a stone wall, leaves to the right. Gently contouring around a broad knob, the red trail climbs upward to pass the white trail, which leads down 0.1 mile to the yellow trail. Continuing to contour, the red trail crosses the blue trail at 0.6 mile in a broad saddle, then

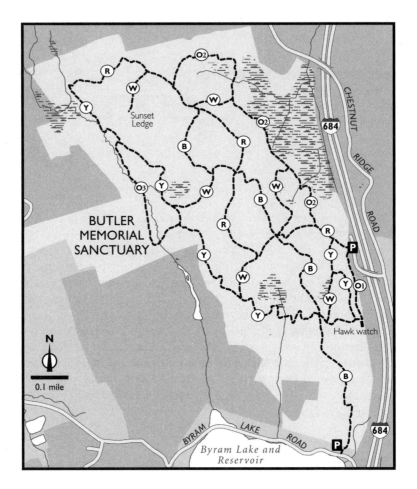

contours around another. At 0.8 mile, the red trail reaches the end of the blue trail on the left, and then immediately passes the white trail leading 0.1 mile downhill to orange trail #2. The red trail passes the end of orange trail #2 to the right. At 1.0 mile, it passes the white trail to the left, which then deadends in 0.1 mile at the view at Sunset Ledge. The red trail continues gently downhill along a woods road to end at the yellow trail, at 1.3 miles.

Blue Trail   *Length: 1.3 miles Blaze: blue*

Running the length of the sanctuary, the blue trail begins across the road from the northeast end of Byram Lake at Byram Lake Road, where parking for two cars is available 100 yards to the west. The sign at the sanctuary entrance is visible at the stone wall approximately 100 yards from the road.

From the trailhead, the blue trail heads uphill for about 500 feet along switchbacks and through stone walls. At 0.3 mile, it follows the low line of a hollow and gently ascends along a woods road. After crossing the yellow trail at 0.4 mile, it crests a low ridge and descends, crossing a seasonal stream at the bottom. The blue trail continues to descend and follows a stone wall to the right, where the forest floor is covered with grass. It enters a mixed pine and hemlock forest, and then merges with the red trail, entering from the right at 0.7 mile. When the trails split, the blue trail goes right. It soon goes left at a Y junction with the white trail, which gradually descends to reach orange trail #2.

At 0.8 mile, on a path often icy and treacherous in winter, the blue trail climbs steeply at first, then less so. It descends to cross the red trail at 1.1 miles, and the white trail which leads downhill 0.2 mile to the yellow trail. The blue trail ascends out of the hollow and contours around the shoulder of the hill. It heads between rock outcroppings and ends at a T junction with the red trail, at 1.3 miles.

Orange Trails   *Length: 1.4 miles Blaze: orange*
There are three orange trails: #1 leads to the hawk watch, #2 parallels the red trail as an alternate route, and #3 is a side trail off the yellow trail.

From the south end of the parking area, following signs to the hawk watch, orange trail #1 rises steadily to reach the hawk watch bleachers at 0.2 mile, where it ends.

Orange trail #2 begins on the red trail 0.1 mile from the parking lot. It parallels wetlands and wiggles through a few sharp turns. At 0.2 mile, it passes a white trail to the left which climbs uphill for 0.2 mile to reach the blue trail. Orange trail #2 passes a rocky crag to the left, then a stand of tall tulip trees. It joins a woods road contouring around the hill. Large ferns line the path, and beyond are extensive wetlands. The orange trail passes a junction with a white trail that heads 0.1 mile uphill to the red trail. At 0.6 mile, it reaches a junction with another woods road defined by stone walls on both sides, where it turns left. Wetlands are on the left as the trail heads on a woods road alongside a stone wall. Notice the large old

Fallen tulip tree

tulip trees with interesting shapes. After passing an open meadow to the right, the orange trail ends at a T junction with the red trail, at 0.8 mile.

Well within the sanctuary, 1.3 miles from the entrance via the yellow trail, orange trail #3 is an alternate route along the yellow trail. Descending from the southern junction with the yellow trail, orange trail #3 almost immediately crosses a stone wall. Roots of a large beech are visible as they spread across the forest floor. Aggressively growing outward, the roots have tried to gain a secure foothold in the earth. Crossing wetland, the trail turns right, crosses a stream, and then parallels it to end at the yellow trail, at 0.4 mile.

Yellow Trail
Length: 1.8 miles Blaze: yellow

Starting to the left of the red trail near the entrance kiosk, the yellow trail wanders uphill and down. Heading south, it climbs gradually and passes a white trail, which eliminates 0.2 mile and the climb up to the hawk watch. The yellow trail contours around a low rock ridge and continues the climb. At a junction, the yellow trail turns right. Be alert here, because the short stub to the left is also yellow-blazed and leads to the hawk watch. As the yellow trail drops down the ridge to the west, road noise from I-684 gradually disappears.

At 0.4 mile, the yellow trail passes the other end of the white trail mentioned above. Almost immediately, the yellow trail crosses the blue trail and briefly rises only to descend steeply via switchbacks. At the bottom, the yellow trail crosses a wetland outlet; this can be tricky to manage when water levels are high. The trail heads uphill to cross the ridge overlooking a wide wetland strewn with dying hemlocks, and then descends. At 0.8 mile, it passes the white trail leading 0.1 mile uphill to the red trail.

The yellow trail ascends and turns right, passing ruins to the right. It reaches a junction with the orange trail #3 on the left at 1.3 miles, and then another white trail to the right which ascends to connect in 0.2 mile to the blue trail. The yellow trail passes through a stone wall and crosses the outlet of the wetlands on stepping stones. It heads uphill and, at 1.4 miles, descends. It passes the other end of orange trail #3 on the left at 1.6 miles. After crossing a small stream on boulders, the trail parallels a larger stream. To the right, a boulder field tumbles down from Sunset Rock. At 1.8 miles, the yellow trail ends at the red trail.

NEARBY PARKS: Westmoreland Sanctuary, Merestead

DRIVING: From I-684 take Exit 4 (Route 172) and turn west toward Mt. Kisco. At 0.3 mile, turn left onto Chestnut Ridge Road. Head south for 1.2 miles, turn right, and cross the bridge. Parking for the sanctuary is at the end of the road, where the entrance is on the left.

PUBLIC TRANSPORTATION: None available

For contact information, see Appendix, The Nature Conservancy.

Camp Smith Trail

Peekskill • 3.7 miles, 216 acres

Without a doubt, the most rugged trail in Westchester County is the Camp Smith Trail, rewarding a hiker with many panoramic views along its route. This strenuous trail, best approached with a car shuttle, has a net elevation gain of 1,100 feet when hiked from south to north. Hikers are more inclined to savor the views when hiking uphill in this direction, even though the hike has less elevation gain if walked the opposite way.

Because the state park property is narrow as it passes through Camp Smith National Guard Training Site, hikers may see military personnel engaged in tactical maneuvers. Although there is buffer land between the trail and the practice ranges, hikers are asked to remain on the trail.

Anthony's Nose is an excellent spot for watching raptors, including peregrine falcons, which nest on the Bear Mountain Bridge. Bald eagles winter on Iona Island; they can often be seen perched on snags at the southern end of the island.

Iona Island

Visitors to the Camp Smith Trail look down on Iona Island with its old buildings and network of roadways. Owned by the Palisades Interstate Park Commission, the island is part of the National Estuarine Research Reserve. In 1849, C. W. Grant, M.D. purchased the island and developed extensive vineyards, which eventually produced the Iona grape. Later, the island was a summer resort, using Dr. Grant's mansion as a hotel. From 1900 until after World War II, the island was a naval arsenal with about 140 buildings. In 1911, the road causeway was built; repairs were made in 1983. Currently, the few remaining buildings are storage facilities for Palisades Interstate Park.

A variety of plants and animals live on or visit Iona Island. Bald eagles nest on Round Island, the bump at the island's southern tip. Prickly pear cactus is found growing on south-facing rocky slopes. Deer, five-lined skinks, wetland birds, and waterfowl make their homes there.

TRAIL

The blue-blazed Camp Smith Trail starts behind the historic Bear Mountain Bridge toll house, 0.7 mile north of the entrance to Camp Smith on Bear Mountain Road, Route 6/202. The toll house is the Town of Cortlandt Visitor Center and open in season. At first, the trail parallels the road, climbing steadily. It then drops steeply through a rock field and turns left before reaching a massive cliff. At 0.3 mile the trail crosses a breached earthen dam. Staying within sight and sound of the road, it works its way gradually uphill, crossing small ridges. At 0.6 mile, it begins a serious ascent of Manitou Mountain, soon climbing very steeply on a series of rock steps. It turns left, climbs more gradually, and reaches a viewpoint to the south. Turning right, it crosses the top of an open rock face.

The Camp Smith Trail drops slightly and resumes its steady ascent of Manitou Mountain, all the while turning west toward the river. It passes through a gully as it approaches viewpoints on the brow of the mountain. Two scrub pines beckon hikers to sit and savor the view of Iona Island. At 0.9 mile, the trail turns away from the river and passes through the aftermath of an extensive fire in 1993. It turns left toward a rock outcropping with views, and then turns right and away from the views to begin its descent. The rock steps, switchbacks, and sidehill construction make it possible to safely descend the extremely steep talus slope.

At 1.2 miles, the Camp Smith Trail reaches the bottom of the slope, crosses a flat area, turns gradually left, and arrives at a small rock outcropping with a view. From the viewpoint, the trail leads inland and turns once again towards the river for another westerly view. Leaving the view, the trail continues the gradual descent, crossing intermittent brooks. At 1.9 miles, it reaches a parking area on Route 6/202

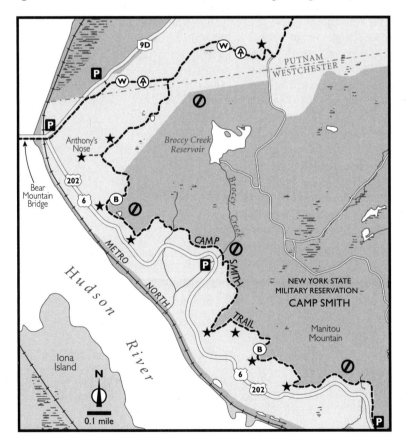

Iona Island from Two Pines View

at a large bend in the road, 2.2 miles north of the entrance to Camp Smith.

Continuing north to Anthony's Nose, the trail crosses Broccy Creek and heads gradually uphill, paralleling the road. After turning away from Route 6/202, it joins and leaves woods roads and crosses streams. Rising out of a ravine, the trail turns right at 2.4 miles, onto a rock outcropping with views of the Hudson River, Iona Island, and Bear Mountain-Harriman State Park. Paralleling the river high over the road, the trail first drops slightly then begins to climb steeply. At 2.7 miles, another rock outcropping with a view offers an excuse to stop before tackling the remaining unrelenting assault up Anthony's Nose. Along the last 0.4 mile, there are both seasonal and year-round views from open rock slabs. The trail drops down off the summit to join a woods road. Straight ahead, a woods road leads to panoramic views of the Hudson River, the Bear Mountain Bridge, and Bear Mountain-Harriman State Park. A right turn takes hikers to the Appalachian Trail (white), where the Camp Smith Trail ends at 3.7 miles. From that junction, Route 9D is 0.6 mile downhill to the left.

CONNECTING TRAIL: Appalachian Trail

DRIVING: Take Route 6/202 north from the traffic circle located just north of Peekskill. The toll house is on Route 6/202, 0.7 mile north of the entrance to Camp Smith. Parking is available along Route 6/202 at the toll house and at the hike's midpoint. Access to the trail's northern terminus is via the Appalachian Trail with parking along Route 9D just north of the Bear Mountain Bridge.

PUBLIC TRANSPORTATION: Metro-North Hudson Line to Peekskill Station. A 2.5-mile taxi ride gets you to the trailhead at the toll house. After the hike, follow the southbound Appalachian Trail, 2.0 miles downhill and across the Bear Mountain Bridge to the Bear Mountain Inn, a stop for the Short Line Bus to Manhattan's Port Authority Bus Terminal. For bus schedules, call 800-631-8405.

For contact information, see Appendix, Hudson Highlands State Park.

Cranberry Lake Preserve

Valhalla • 6.7 miles, 190 acres

It is not surprising that you will find visitors at Cranberry Lake Preserve all year round, because here in the midst of suburbia is a tranquil environment with a glacial lake, cranberry bogs, and abandoned quarrying operations. In addition, there are opportunities for enjoying views, birding, or a cascade. Portions of the preserve are lightly used, offering a chance of solitude to those desiring it.

In early spring, from many vernal pools, the choruses of spring peepers can be considered either a cacophony or a symphony, depending on your point of view. Hot summer days are made more tolerable by a walk in these woods. When fall colors are at their peak, a stroll through the woods is also a feast for the eyes. In winter, with adequate snow, some parts of the preserve are better for snowshoeing than for cross-country skiing.

TRAILS

Because many of the trails start at the Nature Center and lead to the lake, most hikes will involve walking first downhill and then uphill to return to the starting point. Generally the trails are wide, with room for walking two abreast. Green blazes show the return route to the Nature Center.

There are two main loops at Cranberry Lake Preserve: a red one and a blue one. The History Trail (purple) uses portions of the red trail. In addition to the two main loops, one of many yellow trails starts from the Nature Center and serves as a spine from which other trails emanate. Numerous short trails make it possible to shortcut either the red or blue trails. Connecting trails are mentioned where they leave or join one of the major trails.

Yellow Trail   *Length: 0.6 mile Blaze: yellow*
At the Nature Center, the yellow trail goes through a gate and heads downhill along a woods road. It passes two white trails on the left and then a sign for an orange trail; all of these trails lead down to the Littoral Trail (blue) by the lake. The trail narrows slightly and passes, at 0.2 mile, a red trail which joins from the right. Marked with both yellow and red blazes, the woods road also gains blue blazes when the blue trail joins from the left. The woods road passes an orange trail to the left which continues on a boardwalk along the lake, passing a root cellar and foundation before rejoining the yellow trail in 0.1 mile.

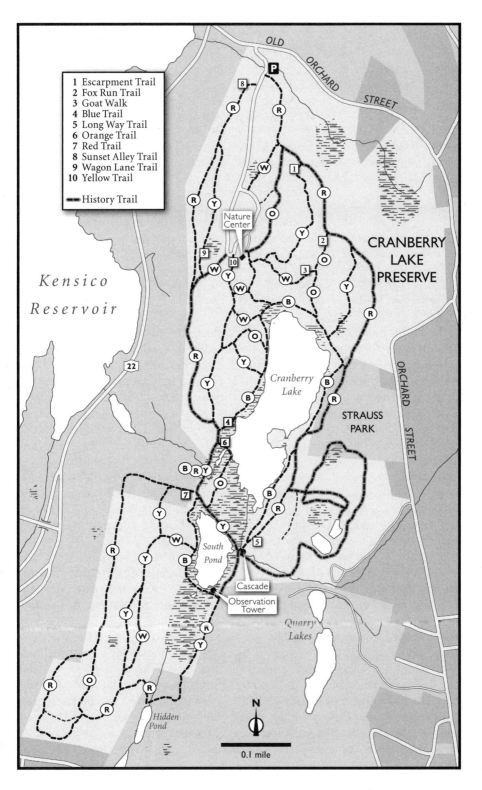

1 Escarpment Trail
2 Fox Run Trail
3 Goat Walk
4 Blue Trail
5 Long Way Trail
6 Orange Trail
7 Red Trail
8 Sunset Alley Trail
9 Wagon Lane Trail
10 Yellow Trail
▬ ▬ History Trail

*Kensico
Reservoir*

CRANBERRY
LAKE
PRESERVE

*Cranberry
Lake*

STRAUSS
PARK

Nature
Center

South
Pond

Cascade
Observation
Tower

*Quarry
Lakes*

*Hidden
Pond*

OLD ORCHARD STREET

ORCHARD STREET

N

0.1 mile

History of Cranberry Lake Preserve

Stone walls and an abandoned root cellar are evidence of the long-gone agricultural past of what is now Cranberry Lake Preserve. The rocky terrain of the area's many small farms was really not well-suited to agriculture. From 1912 to 1917, the preserve was a quarry, furnishing rock and gravel to build the Kensico Dam, a part of New York City's water supply system. The project employed hundreds of skilled laborers, many of whom were recent immigrants from Italy. Seventeen miles of railroad track connected the quarry and rock crusher to the dam construction site. Along the History Trail (purple), hikers can find what remains of the quarrying operations: a rock crushing plant, stone-cutting sheds, railroad beds, and footings for derricks.

In the early 1900s, small farms were purchased and merged to form one large estate, which changed hands several times. In the 1940s, Nathan Straus III, owner of WMCA, the last family-owned radio station in New York City, purchased the property. He subsequently sold a portion to Westchester County in 1967. The preserve opened to the public in 1973 and became a biodiversity reserve area in 1999.

At the bottom of the hill, just before a turn, the red trail leaves to the right. Shortly beyond the turn, at 0.3 mile, the blue blazes leave to the right. With only yellow blazes, the trail continues on a causeway between two lakes. To the left, the orange trail, mentioned above, ends. The yellow trail is joined from the left by both the red and blue trails, and together they reach a bench at a cascade. The well-marked woods road turns right, and at 0.5 mile, the blue trail leaves to the left. At 0.6 mile, at the property boundary, the yellow trail ends at a Y junction, and the red trail turns off to the right.

Blue Trail   *Length: 1.0 mile Blaze: blue*

Forming a loop around two lakes, the blue trail has boardwalks and short bridges. From the junction with the yellow trail, which leads 0.3 mile from the Nature Center along a woods road, the blue trail turns left heading clockwise. It continues uphill to reach a viewpoint over Cranberry Lake. The trail passes a narrow yellow trail leading uphill to the Nature Center. The blue trail clambers down rocks to follow the shoreline and passes both an orange trail and a white trail also heading back to the Nature Center. After skirting a vernal pool to the right at 0.2 mile, the blue trail passes an orange trail and then a yellow trail which lead to the red trail.

The blue trail turns away from the lake and continues uphill, passing a large rock with a view at 0.4 mile. The red trail is 20 feet away. Hugging the shore on a rocky path, the blue trail passes a wooden Adirondack-style chair set there to overlook the lake. Quarry tailings and the cement supports of a long-gone structure are found uphill to the left. At 0.5 mile, the red and blue trails join and then split. The blue trail heads right, following the shore on a narrow rocky path with rock outcroppings to the left. At 0.7 mile, the trails rejoin for the last time, cross a brook, and reach a small scenic cascade with a bench.

To the right is the yellow trail, heading back to the Nature Center. The blue, red, and yellow trails pass quarry tailings and extensive cement walls which once supported the stone crusher. Here, orange slashes on trees to the left mark the boundary of White Plains watershed property. At 0.8 mile, the blue trail turns right and passes an observation tower. After crossing a wet area on a 240-foot boardwalk, the trail turns to follow the lakeshore. It goes through a series of stone wall enclosures and passes a white trail leading in 300 feet to a short yellow trail. The blue trail continues to follow the lakeshore and ends at the yellow trail returning to the Nature Center in 0.3 mile.

Red Trail   *Length: 2.6 miles Blaze: red*
As the trail that travels around the perimeter of Cranberry Lake Preserve, the red trail begins just inside the gate into the preserve, about 100 feet from the parking lot outside of the gate. The trail heads west to parallel a stone wall marking the boundary with New York City watershed lands. To the left, the trail passes a yellow trail leading in 0.2 mile to the white trail, an alternate access trail for the Nature Center. Then, at 0.2 mile, the red trail passes the above-noted white trail.

At a massive stone outcropping, the red trail turns right to pass through a stone wall. To the left, a large impressive slab looks as if it is glued to the hillside. Now heading downhill, the red trail reaches the yellow trail at 0.5 mile and turns right to join it on a woods road. This red/yellow trail soon meets the blue trail entering from the left. The three trails together pass the orange trail going out to a boardwalk along the shore of Cranberry Lake before passing an old stone cellar and foundation.

At a bend in the road at 0.7 mile, the yellow and blue trails curve left and the red trail turns right. The red trail immediately heads uphill following a stone wall marking the boundary between the New York City watershed lands and the preserve. To the left is a yellow trail which heads 0.3 mile to rejoin the red trail. After making a sharp left, the red trail, with seasonal views down to Kenisco Reservoir, continues beside the stone wall. At 1.0 mile, it turns right, while the orange trail continues straight ahead, becoming a 0.1-mile shortcut across a loop in the red trail. Continuing to follow the stone wall, the trail turns left where an unmarked path heads straight to private property. The trail climbs up a rise and turns left again. At 1.2 miles, it turns right at an intersection with the orange trail noted above.

The red trail briefly parallels the bed of the railroad which once moved stone from the quarry to the construction site. The trail joins the railbed briefly and then descends steeply downhill to turn right where a yellow trail is straight ahead. At 1.4 miles, the red trail crosses the end of Hidden Pond on a large mat of tangled tree roots. It joins a woods road, turns left to head downhill, and turns right to pass through a seasonal wet area. Reaching a gravel path, the red trail turns left. When an unmarked woods road enters on the right, the red trail turns left to join the yellow trail at the base of the quarrying operations, a place where quarry tailings tumble down cement walls, and all three trails become part of the History Trail, (purple). At 1.6 miles, the blue trail joins from the left. The trail, now blazed red, blue, and yellow, continues on the gravel road. At a bench by a cascade, the red/blue trail continues straight ahead, while both the History and yellow trails head left.

The red/blue trail turns left over a small bridge and immediately splits, with the red trail bearing right uphill through laurel. At 1.8 miles, it reaches and joins the History Trail at an open spot with views of Cranberry Lake over the wetlands. To the right, the History Trail leads into the abandoned quarry. Heading downhill, the red trail joins the blue trail briefly, then splits off to the right. It travels under the cliffs where a derelict tipple, a machine used in quarrying operations, looms overhead. Leaving the quarrying area, the red trail travels through woods, mostly on woods roads. It passes, at 2.2 miles, a yellow trail and then an orange trail, both of which lead down to the blue trail. At 2.4 miles, the red trail passes another yellow trail leading past an escarpment en route to the blue trail in 0.2 mile. At the junction with the orange trail, the History Trail turns left to follow it for 0.2 mile back to the Nature Center.

Continuing on the woods road, the red trail turns right at a T junction, while the white trail heads back 0.1 mile to an overflow parking area near the Nature Center. The red trail heads towards the entrance road, where it closes the loop at 2.6 miles.

History Trail   *Length: 1.9 miles Blaze: purple*

In addition to explaining the story of quarrying operations to build the Kensico Dam, the History Trail relates the importance of Kensico Reservoir's watershed. For the most part, the History Trail blazed purple follows existing trails in a clockwise direction, as described in a brochure available at www.westchestergov.com/parks/Trailways.htm—click on Cranberry Lake History Trail map.

From the Nature Center, follow the orange trail to the red trail at 0.2 mile, and turn right. At 0.6 mile, the History Trail leaves the red trail, crosses a railbed, and enters the quarry. It loops around the quarry floor on a path outlined with rocks, and returns to the railbed. Heading along the railbed, it leads to the top of the quarry. Because there are no paint blazes on the rocks and no signposts, it is tricky to follow the route down from the top of the quarry. Once down from the top, turn right near the two ponds and head left past a decrepit tennis court. The History Trail rejoins the red and blue trails beside the cascade at 1.3 miles. A side trip to the crusher follows the red/yellow trail, adding 0.1 mile to the hike.

The return trip to the Nature Center is first via the yellow trail along the causeway, and then following the red trail after it joins and then leaves the yellow trail. Passing along stone walls marking watershed property, the red trail reaches the white trail. The History Trail turns right and follows the white trail to close the loop at the Nature Center at 1.9 miles.

NEARBY TRAIL: Bronx River Pathway

DRIVING: From the Bronx River Parkway at the Kensico Dam in Valhalla, use Route 22 north. Once past the dam, make the first right turn onto Old Orchard Street and again the first right to enter the preserve.

PUBLIC TRANSPORTATION: None available

For contact information, see Appendix, Westchester County Parks—Cranberry Lake Preserve.

Croton Point Park

Croton-on-Hudson • 6.3 miles, 504 acres

Like an onion, Croton Point Park's history has many layers. Located on a peninsula jutting out into the Hudson River (designated an American Heritage River), Croton Point has more human history than any other Westchester County park. Humans have been using Croton Point for about 6,300 years.

Native Americans summered there harvesting oysters, as evidenced by shell middens located throughout the park. It is possible that they stayed longer or returned to the same sites on a regular basis. Colonial documentation indicates the Kitchawonks built a palisaded village at the entrance to what was then Teller's Point, now known as Croton Point. To the right of the entrance road from the bluffs on Croton Neck, they would have seen Henry Hudson's ship, the *Half Moon*, anchored in Haverstraw Bay, north of Teller's Point. In 1899, an archaeological study for the American Museum of Natural History found extensive earthworks on the western portion of the bluffs.

William and Sarah Teller acquired the southern point and possibly all of the area in about 1682. They are believed to be the first white settlers in the Town of Cortlandt. The southern tip became known as Sarah's Point, later renamed Teller's Point. In 1804, Robert Underhill purchased 250 acres from Elijah Morgan and Robert McCord, sons-in-law of the Tellers. At Underhill's death, his two sons inherited the property. One son, Dr. Robert Underhill, acquired an 85-acre tract, gave up his medical practice in New York, took up farming, and eventually established a reputation as an agriculturalist. He developed the high quality Croton grape, with a flavor valued for wine, but unfortunately difficult to grow.

In 1837, the second son, William, established a 165-acre brickyard on the point; it was one of 34 brickyards along the Hudson River in the Town of Cortlandt. Marked with W.A.U., the bricks were advertised to have a "fine edge and durable qualities." A village with a store, tavern, and school grew up around the brickyard which was located in the present-day parking lot near the picnic pavilion. Some buildings of that era remain: two wine cellars, a barn, carriage house, and school. The wine cellars are the barrel-vaulted brick structures built into the hillside along the exit road from the cabins.

Westchester County purchased Croton Point and opened the park in 1924, with a children's camp opening the following year. In 1964, the camp closed and moved to Mountain Lakes Park. The bathing beaches on the point were a way of cooling off during hot summer days. They were closed when the Hudson River became too polluted for swimming, but have reopened for swimming on summer weekends.

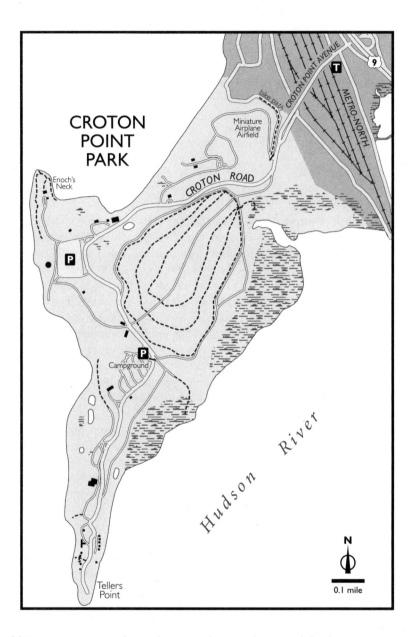

CROTON
POINT
PARK

Enoch's
Neck

Miniature
Airplane
Airfield

CROTON ROAD

CROTON POINT AVENUE

METRO-NORTH

bike path

9

T

P

P

Campground

Tellers
Point

Hudson River

N

0.1 mile

In addition to camping, the park rents cabins at the site of the former camp.

Croton Point Park includes the Croton landfill. When the county acquired the property, 70 acres were set aside for a landfill. Originally a wetland, the landfill closed in 1986, and capping operations were completed in 1995. Before it closed, the landfill was often referred to as the Croton dump, a misnomer, because at a dump, garbage is left exposed to weather and scavengers, but at a landfill, garbage deposits are covered daily with a layer of soil.

Croton is named for the sachem, Kenoten, meaning "wild wind." If you have ever visited the shoreline in Croton Point Park on a wind-whipped winter day, you know why the Native Americans did not winter there. However that same wind is refreshing during summer months. Weather aside, the park has many walking opportunities with expansive views of the Hudson River and Croton Bay.

TRAILS

There are no marked trails at Croton Point, and much of the walking is along gravel roads. From the upper parking lot across from the gate to camping, it is 0.8 mile out to Tellers Point. Before reaching a view south to the Tappan Zee Bridge, the road passes English or common yew trees planted by Robert Underhill near his house. They have grown to an impressive size.

Once the feeding ground for thousands of seagulls, the capped landfill is now a 113-acre meadow. With 360-degree views out over the Hudson River, it offers opportunities for observing eagles, owls, and in summer, butterflies. It is a 1.3-mile walk around the base of the landfill.

From the main parking area, the walk up to the nature center, around Enoch's Neck, and back to the circular picnic pavilion is 0.7 mile. It passes through several shell middens as it drops down to the water level and then goes high above the shore.

The road behind the park office leads up to the picnic area on the bluffs of Croton Neck. The model airplane field located there is for members of the Miniature Airplane Association of Westchester. Signs caution about low-flying aircraft. Although the bluffs are natural, the airplane field is a capped landfill. A

Wine cellar entrance

0.3-mile path heads down off the capped landfill to the bike path to Discovery Cove, but should not be used when the airfield is active.

CONNECTING TRAILS: CrOssining Bridge, the bike path to Discovery Cove

DRIVING: From Route 9, take Croton Point Avenue, turn west towards the river, and follow signs into the park.

PUBLIC TRANSPORTATION: Metro-North Hudson Line, Croton-Harmon Station. Walk up the entrance road to Croton Point Avenue, turn left, and follow signs to the park. It is a mile walk from the train station to the park office. From there, it is 0.6 mile along the base of the landfill or 0.8 mile along the road to the gate at the campground. The road to the nature center is 0.4 mile from the park office.

For contact information, see Appendix, Westchester County Parks—Croton Point Park.

Graham Hills Park

Pleasantville • 9.6 miles, 431 acres

Wedged between the Taconic State and Saw Mill River parkways, Graham Hills Park is a popular mountain biking destination with narrow trails geared to experienced bikers. It is recommended that hikers should visit the park during weekdays, avoiding weekends and evenings, especially during the summer. The varied and sometimes steep terrain provides interesting snowshoeing in winter; the gentler portions are good for cross-country skiing.

In 1785, Dr. Isaac Gilbert Graham, a surgeon's mate in the Revolutionary War, settled in the area now bearing his name. At one time, the hamlet of Graham Hills was a station on the Putnam Division of the New York Central Railroad. The county acquired the property in 1963, dedicating it in 1973.

TRAILS

There are lots of opportunities for exercise at Graham Hills Park. In addition to the 7.0 miles of marked trails, there are 2.6 miles of unmarked twisty bike trails. The park is bounded by houses and two parkways, making it really hard to accidentally stray off the property. The 2.6 miles of unmarked trails are not shown on the map because their exact locations may vary.

Blue Trail   *Length: 3.6 miles Blaze: blue*
The blue trail serves as both entrance trail and main trail. At the entrance, and for a portion of the loop near the entrance, the trail is blazed blue and yellow. From the parking lot, the blue trail heads downhill and crosses a bridge over a wet area. Immediately after crossing a bridge, it passes the first junction with the orange trail to the right. At 0.2 mile, the orange trail briefly joins the blue trail from the left and then leaves to the right. The blue trail reaches a trail junction at 0.4 mile where blue and yellow blazes go to the left and blue blazes go to the right. The blue trail to the right crosses the top of a deep ravine and then descends on a woods road. Noise from the Taconic State Parkway is audible. At 0.5 mile, a red trail heads to the right 0.1 mile to connect with several unmarked trails.

Continuing downhill, the trail passes a stone foundation with steps leading down into it, and then passes through an open area before reentering the woods. It is on a woods road parallel to a fence marking the boundary between the park and the Taconic State Parkway. Leaving the woods road, the trail heads uphill briefly. At 0.9 mile, it passes the end of the blue/white trail which connects, in 0.2 mile,

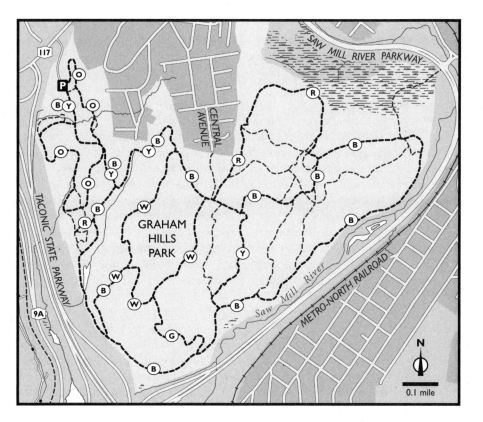

uphill to the white trail. The blue trail descends to parallel the parkway, passing the green trail to the left. After crossing a stream, the blue trail, at 1.4 miles, passes the junction with the yellow trail to the left, which rejoins the blue trail on top of the ridge. The blue trail passes an unmarked trail to the left, descends steeply, and levels off at 1.5 miles. Another unmarked trail goes left at 1.7 miles. The blue trail reaches a foundation in a cedar grove at 1.9 miles. After passing a second foundation at 2.2 miles, the trail curves away from the parkway and road noise diminishes. At 2.4 miles, a 0.3-mile unmarked woods road to the right leads to a traffic light on the Saw Mill River Parkway at Thornwood.

The blue trail passes a series of unmarked trails to the left as it ascends the ridge. At 2.6 miles, it passes the red trail on the right and reaches an open gravel area, a former motocross area with many unmarked trails. After crossing a stone wall, the trail reaches a high point, leveling off slightly. It then heads steeply uphill at 2.8 miles, passing a well-initialed beech tree. The trail alternately climbs and levels off. After passing a yellow trail to the left at 2.9 miles, the blue trail passes the red trail to the right. Almost immediately, an unmarked trail to the right leads to an entrance off Central Avenue (no parking) and a white trail leaves to the left. After descending sometimes steeply over rocky terrain and passing through an open area, the blue trail again passes the white trail to the left at 3.1 miles. The blue trail acquires yellow blazes at 3.2 miles and makes a left turn along a woods road with wetlands to the left. At 3.6 miles, the blue trail closes the loop.

Green Trail   *Length: 0.4 mile Blaze: green*

Starting 0.9 mile from the section south of the blue trail split, the green trail provides access between the white and lower blue trails. At 0.1 mile it begins to climb and ends a third of the way around the southern part of the white trail.

Orange Trail   *Length 1.3 miles Blaze: orange*

Wiggling its way up and down hills, the orange trail passes through a network of unmarked trails. For most of its length, the noise of the nearby Taconic State Parkway is present, even in leaf-on season. From the parking lot, the orange trail almost immediately passes the first of many unmarked trails. It turns left at a Y junction and parallels a fence marking the boundary between the park and the Taconic State Parkway. At 0.2 mile, it turns away from the fence. Reaching the blue trail at 0.8 mile, the orange trail jogs left then right. It turns right at a Y junction and passes through extensive wetlands. Crossing a bridge at 1.0 mile, it passes the exposed braided roots of a tulip tree, showing how far the stream has undercut the bank. The trail heads uphill passing an unmarked trail leading to the parking lot. At 1.2 miles, it turns back, parallels the entrance road, and ends at the parking lot.

Red Trail   *Length: 0.8 mile Blaze: red*

Traversing some very steep terrain, the red trail begins off the north fork of the blue trail. At 0.2 mile, the red trail turns left at a T junction and descends, sometimes steeply. At a T junction at 0.7 mile, it turns right and reaches a woods road. It turns left at the next junction and reaches the blue trail at 0.8 mile, where it ends.

White Trail   *Length: 1.0 mile Blaze: white*

Going from north to south, the white trail begins off the north fork of the blue trail 0.4 mile from where the blue trail splits. It travels through open woods, and gradually descends to the blue/white trail at 0.5 mile. Ascending, the white trail reaches the green trail at 0.8 mile, then returns to end at the blue trail.

Yellow Trail   *Length: 0.4 mile Blaze: yellow*

Serving as a connection across the blue trail, the yellow trail starts from the lower blue trail 1.0 mile from where the blue trail splits. The yellow trail heads right at a Y junction. Ascending the hill, it alternates between steep and gradual, sometimes passing over rocky terrain.

NEARBY TRAIL: North County Trailway

DRIVING: From the northbound Taconic State Parkway, take the Route 117 Exit and turn right. The park entrance is the first right turn. From southbound Route 9A, take the Route 117 Exit and turn left at the top of the ramp. The park entrance is to the right, past the Taconic ramps.

PUBLIC TRANSPORTATION: Metro-North Harlem Line Pleasantville Station. Walk south to Bedford Road, cross the road, and follow it to the next intersection, where Bedford Road turns left. It is 0.9 mile from the station to the park entrance.

For contact information, see Appendix, Westchester County Parks.

Irvington Woods
V. Everit Macy Park

Irvington • 5.6 miles, 272 acres

Can you keep a secret? Bordering the Saw Mill River Parkway to the west is V. Everit Macy Park and its neighbor, Irvington Woods. Little visited, the two parks provide a delightful way to spend some part of the day outdoors in woodlands. Because most of the trails are on the west side of the hill, there is little noise from either the New York State Thruway or the Saw Mill River Parkway.

Once inside the parks, it is difficult to tell where one park ends and the other begins. The two parks are owned and managed by different entities. The Village of Irvington owns Irvington Woods, while Westchester County owns V. Everit Macy Park, managed by the Town of Greenburgh. To complicate matters, some of Irvington Woods is on Irvington Reservoir lands and other parts are on property purchased by the village and the county from a developer as part of a deal to preserve open space. There are two composting sites on the Irvington Woods property, and woods roads go through them.

The V. Everit Macy Park has three sections: ball fields and picnic facilities, Great Hunger Memorial Park at Woodland Lakes, and the hills west of the Saw Mill River Parkway, where a trail system connects with Irvington Woods. Great Hunger Memorial Park is adjacent to the South County Trailway; the picnic area has no trails.

A member of the wealthy Macy family, V. Everit Macy, was Commissioner of Public Welfare, the first commissioner of any kind in Westchester County; he later served as Commissioner of Parks. It was under his guidance that the Grasslands complex was transformed from a poorhouse to a complex of hospitals and a correctional facility. As a businessman, he assembled a chain of newspapers that ultimately became the *Journal News*. What is now V. Everit Macy Park was originally called Woodlands Park, and was later renamed in his honor.

TRAILS

Because there are few places to park and no convenient public transportation, the number of people using these two parks is low. Those who do use them enjoy the solitude along a variety of trails ranging from wide tracks in open woods to narrow paths. Most of the wide trails are the results of ATV incursions. ATVs are no longer a problem, although the evidence of their destructive activity remains. Thanks to five Eagle Scout projects, the trails have been improved and blazed.

Neighbors can walk into the parks easily; however, parking is in short supply at

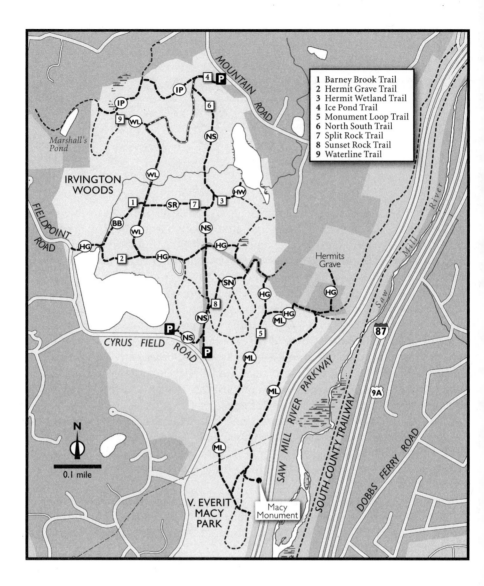

all access points except two. There is parking on Mountain Road for the Ice Pond Trail, and on Cyrus Field Road and the lower compost road for the North South Trail. Fieldpoint Road lacks parking for access to the Hermits Grave Trail.

There are four short trails at Irvington Woods. The Barney Brook Trail starts on the Water Line Trail and heads downhill alongside Barney Brook for half its distance, ending at the Hermits Grave Trail at 0.1 mile. The Hermits Wetlands Trail leads 0.1 mile from the North South Trail to the Hermits Wetlands. The Split Rock Trail goes 0.1 mile between the North South Trail and the Waterline Trail to pass a massive glacial erratic, split so that one can walk through it. Sunset Rock Trail heads off the North South Trail to an overlook at 0.1 mile.

Ice Pond Trail
Length: 0.5 mile Blaze: IP

From the parking area on Mountain Road, the Ice Pond Trail heads through a gate and downhill along the access road to a compost site. The road goes left, and the Ice Pond Trail continues curving right, passing a pillar to the right. At 0.2 mile, the Ice Pond Trail passes an unmarked trail to the right which leads in 0.2 mile to Riverview Road. It passes the Waterline Trail to the left at 0.3 mile, with the ice pond to the right. Shortly, an unmarked trail to the left curves for 0.2 mile to connect back to the Waterline Trail. The Ice Pond Trail passes Marshalls Pond with a stone retaining wall and iron pipe fencing along its edge and, at 0.5 mile, reaches a paved driveway overlooking the ball fields of Irvington High School. To the right is a driveway leading down to the high school.

Hermits Grave Trail
Length: 0.8 mile Blaze: HG

Beginning at Fieldpoint Road (no parking), the Hermits Grave Trail heads downhill through a grove of Norway spruce to the shore of the Irvington Reservoir. It crosses a bridge and passes the Barney Brook Trail (BB) to the left. The Hermits Grave Trail heads uphill then turns away from the reservoir. It passes the Waterline Trail (WL) to the left at 0.2 mile. Skirting the edge of a Norway spruce grove, it reaches a road into the lower village compost site and briefly follows it. As it bears left to enter the woods it becomes narrower. Heading uphill, the Hermits Grave Trail wanders through a stream bed, and after crossing the North South Trail (NS), it again heads uphill. At a T junction at 0.4 mile, an unmarked trail on the left leads 0.2 mile to the Hermits Wetlands Trail (HW). At 0.5 mile, the Sunset Rock Trail (SN) to the right leads to Sunset Rock, while the Hermits Grave Trail goes left. The trail turns right and heads downhill with a rock outcropping towering overhead. At a T intersection, an unmarked woods road leads left to an inactive dump, while the Hermits Grave Trail goes right.

Hermits Grave

The Hermits Grave Trail reaches a junction where the Monument Loop goes in both directions and the Hermits Grave Trail goes left along a pathway lined with logs. The two trails turn right onto a woods road. At 0.8 mile, the Monument Loop heads to the right on a concrete road, a former entrance to the Saw Mill River Parkway. The Hermits Grave Trail continues on the woods road for 200 feet, turns left to leave it, and climbs uphill to end at the Hermits Grave. The woods road goes straight ahead for 0.7 mile, ending at Mountain Road.

North South Trail *Length: 0.6 mile Blaze: NS*

Beginning at the road to the lower composting site, the North South Trail heads uphill. It reaches a former road and turns left. This former road leads downhill to parking at the bend in Cyrus Field Road. On the right at 0.2 mile, the Sunset Rock Trail (SN) veers somewhat straight ahead, and an unmarked woods road heads 0.2 mile uphill to the Monument Loop Trail (ML). Shortly, to the left, an unmarked trail descends to the lower composting site.

The North South Trail jogs right and then left as it crosses the Hermits Grave Trail (HG) to ascend steeply. It passes the Split Rock Trail (SR) to the left, then the Hermits Wetlands Trail (HW) to the right at 0.4 mile. After crossing a bridge, it reaches the top of the rise and parallels a ravine with a steep rock face. The North South Trail ends at a T junction at the road to the upper composting site.

Monument Loop Trail *Length: 0.8 mile Blaze: ML*

Because the Monument Loop Trail is a circle, there are many places to begin walking. Start by heading counterclockwise along the Monument Loop Trail from the junction where the Hermits Grave Trail (HG) and the Monument Loop Trail are co-aligned. Almost immediately, the Monument Loop Trail passes a small split rock on the left and heads steeply uphill to reach a level section. At the top of the rise, it passes an unmarked woods road to the right which leads downhill to meet the North South Trail (NS) in 0.2 mile.

The Monument Loop Trail passes an unmarked trail to the left as it continues downhill. At 0.3 mile, the Monument Loop Trail passes another unmarked trail leading 80 feet out to Cyrus Field Road. At a rock outcropping far to the right, the trail crosses a gas line. It reaches a trail junction at 0.4 mile. Straight ahead is a nest of unmarked ATV tracks. To the left, the rock sidehilling and steps in their original state would have added an element of grandeur to the trail. Traffic noise from the Saw Mill River Parkway in the valley below is audible at this point. The Monument Loop Trail reaches a junction at 0.5 mile. Bearing left, the trail is on a woods road. To the right, a trail leads to a second junction where a side trail heads 100 feet downhill, either to the left toward the Macy Monument or straight to pass rock benches and eventually lead into unmarked ATV tracks.

Bearing left along the woods road, almost immediately the Monument Loop Trail passes steps to a stone bench to the left. Crossing the gas line again, the trail passes other benches and, at 0.7 mile, heads uphill along two at-grade sections before reaching still more benches. Ahead on the right is a massive stone retaining wall which supports an abandoned concrete road. The trail turns left to avoid running into the side of the hill. It continues uphill, reaches a dirt road 50 feet above the end of concrete paving, and joins the Hermits Grave Trail (HG). The combined trails continue uphill steadily on a pathway lined with logs. The Monument Loop Trail closes the loop at 0.8 mile, just as the Hermits Grave Trail leaves to the right.

Waterline Trail *Length: 0.4 mile Blaze: WL*

Heading south from the Ice Pond Trail (IP), the Waterline Trail follows an underground waterline. In 50 feet, it passes to the right an unmarked woods road, which circles 0.2 mile back to the Ice Pond Trail and then passes the first of several fire hydrants. At the next intersection it turns right, where an unmarked trail heads into the upper composting site to go 0.2 mile back to the Ice Pond Trail. At 0.2 mile, the trail crosses a stream with a rock-lined course. The Barney Brook Trail (BB) is to the right and the Split Rock Trail (SR) is to the left. Heading downhill, the Waterline Trail ends at the Hermits Grave Trail (HG).

NEARBY TRAIL: South County Trailway

DRIVING: To reach the southern section of the parks, take Route 9 to Irvington and turn east onto Harriman Road, heading away from the Hudson River. When Harriman Road reaches the Irvington Reservoir, it makes a sharp right turn and becomes Cyrus Field Road. Follow Cyrus Field Road to the park entrance on the left, where there is limited parking. Cyrus Field Road can also be reached from the southbound Saw Mill River Parkway, just south of Great Hunger Memorial at Woodland Lakes Park. There is no access to Cyrus Field Road from the northbound lanes.

To reach the northern section of Irvington Woods, take Route 9 to the Irvington/ Tarrytown line. Turn east onto East Sunnyside Lane and head uphill away from the Hudson River. At 0.6 mile, turn right onto Mountain Road, and head for 0.7 mile to a parking area to the right. Mountain Road can also be reached from an exit on the southbound Saw Mill River Parkway, just after driving under the Thruway. There is no access to Mountain Road from the northbound lanes.

PUBLIC TRANSPORTATION: None available

For contact information, see Appendix, Greenburgh, Irvington.

Eugene and Agnes Meyer Preserve

Armonk • 6.5 miles, 247 acres

Comprised of two parcels of land connected by a long-abandoned section of Oregon Road, the Eugene and Agnes Meyer Preserve offers both gentle and rugged walks. The western portion, located off Sarles Street, has open meadows and woodlands; the eastern portion off Oregon Road has steep ridges and rocky crags. The preserve offers wildflowers, meadows, vernal pools, rock outcroppings, wetlands, a ravine, and birding.

At one time, the preserve was Seven Springs, the weekend retreat estate of Eugene and Agnes Meyer. Eugene Meyer was, at various times, an investment banker, a public servant under seven presidents, and the owner of a communications network which included the *Washington Post*. His wife Agnes was an activist, journalist, author, lecturer, and the first chair of Westchester County's Department of Recreation. Their daughter, Katherine Meyer Graham, eventually owned and ran the *Washington Post*. In 1973, the Meyer Foundation donated the land to The Nature Conservancy.

WESTERN SECTION

The trailhead on Sarles Street is the gateway to the western section of the preserve. The fields are completely mowed every few years. Because paths through the fields are mowed annually, their location can vary. During hot summer months, the fields, full of butterflies and insects, contrast with the woodland trails, where temperature is lower, and little, if any, insect noise is heard. The approximately 1.5 miles of unmarked mowed paths give access to blazed trails in the southern and eastern portions of this part of the preserve. Although the fields present a challenge to those who prefer their trails marked, hikers should take this opportunity to become comfortable using unmarked tracks.

Yellow Trails   *Length: 0.6 mile Blaze: yellow*

There are two yellow trails in this section of the Meyer Preserve, and they are connected. To minimize confusion, based on how they appear on the map they will be referred to as the U-shaped or the J-shaped yellow trail.

The U-shaped yellow trail begins at the far end of the fourth field, 0.5 mile from the parking off Sarles Street. It enters the forest at a stone wall and descends across a steep slope toward a hemlock forest below. At a stone wall with a large boulder, it

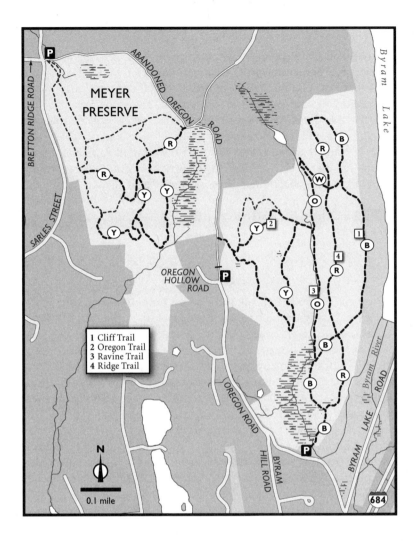

passes the J-shaped yellow trail to the right. Heading straight, the U-shaped yellow trail ends at the red trail at 0.3 mile.

The J-shaped yellow trail is followed more easily from east to west. It begins on the red trail, about 330 feet to the right from where the U-shaped yellow trail ended. Turn left around a huge rock, and at 0.2 mile, briefly follow the edge of a stream. The J-shaped yellow trail ends at a stone wall near a T junction with the U-shaped yellow trail at 0.3 mile.

Red Trail

Length: 0.3 mile Blaze: red

Starting from abandoned Oregon Road, the red trail passes the unmarked mowed paths through fields and enters the woods. At 0.1 mile, it passes the J-shaped yellow trail to the left and a mowed track in the field to the right. After passing the U-shaped yellow trail, it crosses a stone wall to end in a field.

CONNECTING THE SECTIONS

A woods road and the abandoned section of Oregon Road separate the preserve from private lands and connect the two sections. From parking on Sarles Street, head straight ahead. The trail crosses a brook, continues on a rocky woods road, heads steeply uphill, and passes a glacial erratic. The woods road turns sharply right onto the abandoned section of Oregon Road, where a gated road leads into private land. At 0.2 mile, the road skirts a white pine plantation. It passes, at 0.5 mile, the two trails that connect to fields in the western section of the preserve and then the red-blazed trail leading to the western section. Skirting the edge of wetlands to the right, abandoned Oregon Road passes private fields to the left, and, at 0.7 mile, continues with preserve property now on both sides. It passes the junction with the Oregon Trail (yellow) at 0.8 mile, and after going through a gate, ends at 0.9 mile.

EASTERN SECTION

Oregon Road, off Byram Lake Road, is the access point to the eastern section of the Meyer Preserve. Hiking through this portion gives an impression of what the area might have looked like years ago. The rocky crags and elevation gains along the trails are a vivid contrast to the trails in the fields of the western section. Mosses and ferns add color to the many gray rocks. In spring, vernal pools are adjacent to, or sometimes in the trails, making wet feet a real possibility. On hot summer days, the towering trees and exposed rock have a cooling effect. All trails are blazed. The Cliff (blue) and the Ridge (red) trails form a figure eight.

Cliff Trail   *Length: 1.0 mile Blaze: blue*
From the first parking area on Oregon Road, the Cliff Trail passes through a mountain bike barrier to enter a wetland and then a hemlock-hardwood forest. At

a Y junction at 0.1 mile, the Cliff Trail heads left along the edge of a wetland, while the Ridge Trail (red) goes right, through an opening in a large stone wall 50 feet away. The Cliff Trail passes the Ravine Trail (orange) to the left and heads uphill. The Ridge Trail crosses the Cliff Trail at 0.4 mile. Continuing uphill, the Cliff Trail passes a large rock outcropping to the right. Along the ridge, I-684 is both visible and audible. There are views closer to the top edge of the cliff band,

Woolly Adelgid

An aphid-like insect, the woolly adelgid feeds on hemlocks by sucking fluid from the base of the needles. As it feeds, it may also inject toxins into the tree, weakening the tree and accelerating needle drop and branch dieback. Introduced into the northeastern United States in the 1950s, this insect has been devastating hemlocks ever since, and is spreading. Many stands of these graceful trees are already gone, and few of those remaining are unaffected. Natural selection will eventually replace hemlocks with other species, but they will be missed because they are so often dominant in local woodlands and in moist ravines where they provide shade.

but take care. At the bottom of a dip at 0.8 mile, the trail passes a white trail to the left, which leads in 0.1 mile to the Ridge and the Ravine trails. The Cliff Trail turns away from the views of Byram Lake, heads uphill, and leaves the noise from I-684 behind. After turning, the Cliff Trail descends through hemlocks devastated by the woolly adelgid. Dead trees litter the area, their bare dead branches sticking up like spines on a porcupine. The trail reaches the property boundary and turns left to end at the Ridge Trail at 1.0 mile.

Oregon Trail   *Length: 0.9 mile Blaze: yellow*

Not to be confused with abandoned Oregon Road, the Oregon Trail is a large loop with a stub connecting to the Ravine Trail (orange), and another to abandoned Oregon Road. From the Ravine Trail, the Oregon Trail begins by immediately crossing a bridge and heading steeply uphill. In 250 feet, it reaches a junction where yellow blazes lead in both directions. Head counterclockwise and continue ascending. At the top of the hill, a chimney visible through white pines and Norway spruces is all that remains of the Meyer Estate, destroyed by fire in the 1940s.

The Oregon Trail turns onto a woods road and follows a stone-lined path for a short distance. At 0.3 mile, a short stub bears to the right out to the abandoned Oregon Road, where there is parking and the connection to the preserve's western section. Turning left, the Oregon Trail wiggles its way through the woods, heading downhill. At 0.6 mile, it reaches the southernmost point and turns. It passes around a huge rock to the left, makes a sharp right, and descends. It turns right to descend more steeply, closing the loop at 0.9 mile.

Ravine Trail   *Length: 0.5 mile Blaze: orange*

Beginning at a Y junction on the Cliff Trail (blue), the Ravine Trail heads north. It passes a large wetland to the left and a towering ridge to the right. Ascending sometimes steeply, it passes through the narrowest part of the ravine at 0.2 mile, hugging the side of the hill with a stream so close you can touch it. Climbing above the stream, the trail passes, at 0.3 mile, the Oregon Trail (yellow) to the left at a bridge. At 0.5 mile, the Ravine Trail ends at the white trail at the property line. The white trail connects uphill in 0.1 mile to the Ridge (red) and Cliff trails.

Ridge Trail   *Length: 0.8 mile Blaze: red*

From the north end of the preserve, where the Cliff Trail (blue) ends, the Ridge Trail descends into a ravine and a notch, where it crosses the white trail connecting the Cliff Trail with the Ravine Trail (orange). Continuing downhill, it passes a vernal pool at 0.5 mile, then crosses the Cliff Trail. As the trail heads through a ravine, I-684 can be heard, but not seen. The trail turns right to follow the base of a massive rock outcropping and then enters an open area.

Through the trees to the left is a 0.4-mile aqueduct lined with moss-covered stones. The aqueduct reroutes the stream (which empties the wetlands next to the preserve's entrance) so that the water can enter Bryam Lake, Mt. Kisco's water supply, instead of flowing into the outlet from the lake. It is possible to walk beside the aqueduct down to Route 22 near the dam (parking). The Ridge Trail enters the woods. After it crosses a stone wall capped with flat rocks, it ends at the Cliff Trail at 0.8 mile.

Aqueduct on the Ridge Trail

DRIVING: To reach the preserve's western section, take I-684 to NY 172 and turn west toward Mt. Kisco. Make a left onto Sarles Street and drive 2.7 miles. A small parking area for 2 or 3 cars is located across from the intersection of Sarles Street and Bretton Ridge Road.

To reach the eastern section from southbound I-684, take Exit 3 (Route 22). If northbound, use Exit 3N (Route 22). Take Route 22 north to the traffic light at Cox Avenue and turn left. Follow Cox Avenue to where it bears left, and continue straight on Byram Lake Road. At 1.4 miles, turn left onto Oregon Road, where you will find the parking area in 0.2 mile. There is additional parking at the end of the road and access to the Oregon Trail (yellow), which begins just past the fourth telephone pole on the abandoned road, near a boundary sign.

PUBLIC TRANSPORTATION: None available

For contact information, see Appendix, The Nature Conservancy.

Mianus River Gorge Preserve

Bedford Village • 5.0 miles, 719 acres

Tranquility greets you when you enter the Mianus River Gorge Preserve. Photogenic and scenic, it is both relaxing and stimulating. The trail system is laid out to encourage visitors to walk in on one trail and out on another. With numerous crossover trails, the preserve offers hikes of varying distances, and one need not walk the full length of the preserve.

The preserve is open April 1st to November 30th, 8:30 am to 5:00 pm. Entrance is strictly forbidden at all other times. Eating is permitted only at the entrance area, either in a car or on the grassy rim surrounding the parking area.

Founded in 1953, the Mianus Gorge Conservation Committee is dedicated to preserving "the virgin forest and abundant wildlife along the Mianus River in Bedford, New Castle, and Pound Ridge, New York." Mianus River Gorge Preserve was the first preserve affiliated with The Nature Conservancy and, in 1964, became the first natural area to be designated a National Natural Historic Landmark. More than 70 transactions have increased the preserve to its present size.

TRAILS

The trails are well delineated, with the main trails marked in just one direction. The Brink of Gorge Trail is the outgoing trail to the preserve boundary at the S.J. Bargh Reservoir, and the Fringe of Forest Trail is the return path, a round trip distance of 4.5 miles. At times the trails are co-aligned. The first portion of the Bank of the River Trail is wheelchair accessible until it reaches a bench overlooking the Mianus River.

Brink of Gorge Trail   *Length: 2.2 miles Blaze: red*
Beginning at the information kiosk, the Brink of Gorge Trail heads to the left toward a bench on the river at the Streamside Study Area. The trail passes through a series of stone walls and, at 0.2 mile, reaches the Old Field of Succession, reminders of the area's agricultural past (1800-1920). After crossing a stream on a flat stone bridge, the Brink of Gorge Trail joins the Fringe of Forest Trail (blue). To the left, at 0.4 mile, the two trails pass a junction with the 0.2-mile Bank of River Trail (green), which follows the Mianus River and passes the Safford Cascade, an intermittent tributary.

At 0.5 mile, the trails separate; the Brink of Gorge Trail turns to the left and the Fringe of Forest Trail heads uphill to the right. After passing a shortcut to the Bank

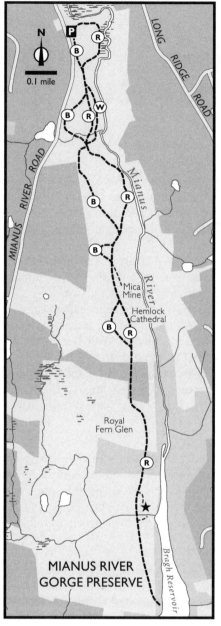

MIANUS RIVER GORGE PRESERVE

of River Trail at 0.6 mile, the red and the blue trails come together briefly, only to split again. The Brink of Gorge Trail descends to pass the narrowest part of the gorge at the Rockwall Breach. It climbs sharply around a rock outcropping above the river to reach Monte Gloria, honoring Gloria Hollister Anable who, with four others, worked to protect the gorge, resulting in the establishment of the preserve in 1953. The red and blue trails come together for the third time at 0.9 mile and then split once again. At 1.0 mile, the Hobby Hill Quarry Trail (mica mine) leaves to the left. The red and blue trails join for the fourth time, only to diverge at 1.1 miles.

With a soft tread underfoot and the gurgle of the river below, the trail passes a hemlock forest with trees 350 years and older. The cathedral-like forest invites hikers to enjoy peace and solitude. Crossing three stone walls in the next 0.3 mile, the two trails join for the final time at 1.3 miles. At 1.8 miles, the co-aligned trails pass a vernal pool. A short side trail leads to a view of the reservoir at 1.9 miles. To the left at 2.0 miles is a short steep trail leading to Havemeyer Falls. Both trails end at the S.J. Bargh Reservoir at 2.2 miles.

Fringe of Forest Trail
Length: 2.1 miles Blaze: blue
Blazed in a way to be used on the return trip from the reservoir, the Fringe of Forest Trail is initially co-aligned with the Brink of Gorge Trail (red). They pass trails to Havemeyer Falls and a view of the reservoir at 0.2 and 0.3 mile, respectively. After skirting a vernal pool at 0.4 mile, the trails head through the James and Alice de Peyster Todd Woodlands, an area donated by preserve founders. At 0.9 mile the trails split, with the Fringe of Forest Trail going left. They rejoin, having crossed stone walls which like others on the property, date back to the first half of the nineteenth century. In quick succession, the trails pass the Hobby Hill Quarry Trail at 1.2 miles, split, and then join again.

After the third split, the Fringe of Forest Trail passes between fields, some of which were grazed by livestock as recently as the 1920s. At 1.7 miles, the trails join briefly and split. They rejoin, and at 1.9 miles, pass the Bank of River Trail (green) to the right. After the last red/blue trail split, the Fringe of Forest Trail ends at the parking area at 2.1 miles.

Hobby Hill Quarry
Length: 0.1 mile Blaze: none
This short side trail leads to Hobby Hill Quarry, the site of a former mica, quartz, and feldspar mine, active in the 1700s. Exposed mica and white and pink quartz are visible at the quarry. Through the years, flat pieces of loose mica have gradually wandered off; half the shimmering material is now gone. Please do not accelerate its disappearance.

Along the Fringe of Forest Trail

DRIVING: Take I-684 to Exit 4 (NY 172) and head east toward Bedford Village. At NY 22 turn left, and then, at the grassy triangle in Bedford Village, take the right fork onto Pound Ridge Road. At the gas station, turn right onto Long Ridge Road. Take the first right onto Millers Mill Road, make the left turn just past the bridge, and proceed to the preserve parking area.

PUBLIC TRANSPORTATION: None available

For contact information, see Appendix, Mianus River Gorge Preserve.

Mountain Lakes Park

North Salem • 9.9 miles, 1,083 acres

Happy campers and plans for a luxury development are part of the history of Mountain Lakes Park, the northernmost park of Westchester County's park system. The park has a rugged landscape within a hardwood forest, and offers a quiet hike with no road noise. Mt. Bailey, the highest point in Westchester County at 982 feet, can be reached from an unmarked trail off the orange/white trail; however, trees have closed in the views.

TRAILS

Mountain Lakes is a favorite walking place for its neighbors. The orange trail is easy on the knees with a gentle grade that makes elevation gains and losses almost imperceptible. Many of the trails at Mountain Lakes Park are blazed with two colors. In general, the two-color blazes connect trails of the same color. Thus the red/green trail connects the red trail and the green trail.

Across the northern part of the park, between Hunt Lane and the ATT cable line, there are unauthorized mountain bike tracks of varying degrees of visibility. A power line cuts through and then parallels the northern edge of the park. Theoretically, the 1.1 miles should be clear enough to walk, but sections may often be overgrown with both multiflora rose and barberry bushes, depending on how recently the utility company has cleared brush. The ATT line running across the park for 1.6 miles is closed to hiking. Birding opportunities abound in these edge environments.

Orange Trail   *Length: 3.2 miles Blaze: orange*
Beginning from the entrance into Mountain Lakes Park, a road with orange blazes makes a loop through the park. Although walking along a road might at first seem disheartening to a hiker, it is easy to follow and allows several people to walk abreast. Because the first three-quarters-mile of the road is paved and well-graded, the orange trail is handicapped accessible. Stonework supports the road and keeps it at a gentle grade for its entire length. Aside from some buildings and trail junctions, there are few landmarks, but a walk along any portion is relaxing. The grades make for easy cross-country skiing when snow cover is sufficient and not too many people have walked on the road.

From the parking area near the entrance gate, the orange trail heads uphill through an open forest. It passes to the left, at 0.1 mile, a green-blazed paved road

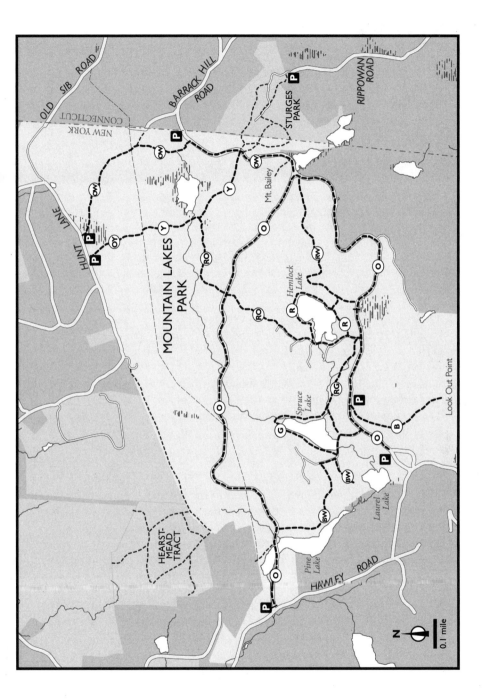

History of Mountain Lakes Park

Records indicate that 25 men from Norwalk Connecticut, settled in an area called Ridgefield, a portion of which is now Mountain Lakes Park. The New York-Connecticut line was moved in 1731, and this land became the Town of North Salem. By 1840, George Bailey of circus fame owned what is now park property. Henry Anderson, a prominent attorney, owned the property from 1906 to 1918. He planned to create a development which would rival Tuxedo Park, located on the west side of the Hudson River. The teahouse he built had glassed-in porches where one could enjoy both food and a view. Although World War I ended the sales promotion, the teahouse continued to operate into the 1930s. A developer bought the property in 1956; it was sold to the county in 1961.

A county-run summer camp at Croton Point Park was moved to Mountain Lakes in 1964. Hemlock Camp for boys and Spruce Camp for girls both functioned until the county closed the facility in 1994. The property now offers a variety of seasonal recreational opportunities. Starting in 2008, Mountain Lakes Park once again hosts happy campers. County-owned Camp Morty offers children in foster care an overnight outdoor experience, often with siblings.

that leads into what was Spruce Camp. Continuing uphill, it reaches the blue trail to Look Out Point, at 0.3 mile to the right. At 0.5 mile, it passes a gate on the paved road (red trail) leading into the former Hemlock Camp, where there is lake boating in season. A gate to block vehicles is at 0.6 mile, and just beyond it the red/white trail leaves to the left into the woods on a narrow path, sometimes hard to follow. An unmarked road leads into Tamarack Camp to the right.

The pavement ends at 0.8 mile and for the rest of the way the surface is crushed stone. After crossing a long stone causeway, the orange trail passes an unmarked and well-graded woods road to the right which leads 0.6 mile uphill to end near the property boundary. The orange trail gently curves left and, as it curves back to the right at 1.0 mile, passes the Larch lean-to. The road curves along the edge of the property and passes the red/white trail to the left at 1.4 miles. This latter trail is easily missed because it is just shy of a major triangle intersection. From the intersection, the orange/white trail leads to the right.

To the left, the orange trail heads slightly downhill to the left. It passes the Balsam lean-to at 1.5 miles and then the two Cedar lean-tos. Continuing downhill, at 1.9 miles the orange trail crosses the red/orange trail. At 2.2 miles, it crosses a stone bridge over a stream. The ATT cable line crosses the orange trail the first time at 2.4 miles. After passing the Roaring Tent campsite to the left, the trail heads downhill and, at 2.8 miles, crosses the ATT line a second time.

At 3.0 miles, a woods road to the left leads to the three Big Pine lean-tos and the blue/white trail. In 100 yards, the two Little Pine lean-tos are to the right and the blue/white trail to the left leads back through a wetland towards the Big Pine lean-tos. To avoid getting wet feet, use the woods road to the Big Pine lean-tos instead. Passing in front of the Little Pine lean-tos, an unmarked woods road leads to the ATT line.

Pine Lake

The orange trail crosses the causeway over Pine Lake. After it passes a woods road to a dam, it heads steadily downhill beside the fast-moving outlet stream. It ends at 3.2 miles near the locked access gate, with room to parallel park two cars. Although one could walk 0.9 mile along Hawley Road back to the main entrance, the narrow road has a poor line of sight.

Blue Trail — *Length: 0.4 mile Blaze: blue*

It is only a quarter of a mile from the entrance gate along the orange trail to the beginning of the blue trail to the right. The wide woods road heads uphill at a gentle grade and passes a high rock outcropping to the left. It ends at Look Out Point, with a sweeping view over Lake Waccabuc and Lake Oscaleta.

Blue/White Trail — *Length: 0.6 mile Blaze: blue/white*

Although the trailhead of the blue/white trail is across from the three Little Pine lean-tos, it crosses a stream and wetlands without any bridges, guaranteeing wet feet. To stay dry shod, start from the unmarked woods road into Big Pine lean-to and follow the blazes from there.

After passing the Big Pine lean-tos at 0.1 mile, the blue/white trail heads uphill and crosses a stone wall. The trail has a short steep climb and enters former Spruce Camp where it heads downhill on a gravel road. Reaching a paved road at 0.4 mile, the blue/white trail turns right. This turn is not blazed in the opposite direction, but a sign indicates a left turn to Buildings #18-26. Near the edge of the lake, the blue/white trail turns right, leaves the paved road, and heads towards building #10. The green trail is straight ahead on the paved road. After following along on a camp road, the trail heads towards a demolished building and ends in the woods.

Green Trail   *Length: 0.9 mile Blaze: green*

From the first gate to the left of the orange trail, a paved road with green blazes leads into the former Spruce Camp. The green trail passes the now empty dining hall and crosses the spillway of the dam. At 0.3 mile, it turns right to head clockwise around Spruce Lake. It follows the shore, sometimes closely and other times either farther away, or above it. At 0.5 mile, it crosses the inlet stream to the lake on a bridge and then turns to briefly parallel the stream. Again the green trail follows the lakeshore. It travels on top of a rock outcropping and, at 0.8 mile, reaches a bridge over a second inlet stream. Green blazes head in both directions at a trail junction. To the right, the trail heads towards the dining hall and closes the loop at 0.9 mile. To the left, green blazes follow the edge of the stream and soon become both red and green, marking the beginning of the red/green trail which connects, in 0.2 mile, with the red trail around Hemlock Lake.

Orange/White Trail   *Length: 1.1 miles Blaze: orange/white*

Beginning at Hunt Lane, across from #222, the orange/white trail is on a woods road as it heads into the woods. The blazes start 100 feet further along the trail, as it heads uphill at-grade and passes unmarked bike paths. At 0.4 mile, the trail crosses the ATT line. Straight ahead are orange and white blazes leading to Barrack Hill Road, which heads to a triangle intersection. A right-hand turn onto Pine Lake Road leads back to the orange/white trail. There is another orange/white blaze to the right.

Turning right, the orange/white trail leaves the woods road to wiggle through woods, in sharp contrast to the woods roads it connects. Those traveling north on the orange/white trail will not see a blaze for the trail's off-road section. After crossing a stream on a bridge at 0.6 mile, the trail heads gradually uphill to reach the grade of a woods road. Turning right, the orange/white trail continues on a wide woods road through the open woods. It passes the yellow trail to the right at 0.9 mile, almost directly opposite two unmarked trails to the left which lead into Sturges Park, a Ridgefield town park with a 0.9-mile network of trails. Beyond a field to the right, the orange/white trail passes the unmarked trail to the top of 982-foot Mt. Bailey. Unfortunately, the vista on top is overgrown. The orange/white trail ends at the triangle intersection at the orange trail at 1.1 miles. The orange-white blazes are not immediately visible from the orange trail at the triangle intersection.

Red Trail   *Length: 0.7 mile Blaze: red*

From the second gate to the left, 0.5 mile along from the beginning of the orange trail, red blazes along a paved road lead into what once was Hemlock Camp. Beginning a counterclockwise loop, the red trail turns right to pass through the parking lot behind the former dining hall. Heading towards the lake, it crosses a small bridge and then reaches a junction with the red/white trail at 0.2 mile. Following the shore, at times closer than at others, the red trail reaches the far end of Hemlock Lake and turns at 0.3 mile. It crosses the end of a stone wall and passes a lean-to at 0.5 mile as it reenters the camp. The red trail reaches a paved road and turns left. The end of the red/orange trail is to the right. After crossing the lake's outlet at 0.6 mile, the red trail closes the loop at the former dining hall.

Geocaching

Hidden treasures have always intrigued people and geocaching is a high-tech way to go on a treasure hunt. Instead of a map and perhaps a compass, a global positioning system (GPS) receiver is used to locate a hidden object. People of all ages can enjoy geocaching, which is also a great outdoor family activity.

In order for this adventure to work, someone has to have first hidden a small object and a log book in a waterproof container. They note the latitude and longitude coordinates of the geocache and then post the coordinates on a website such as www.geocaching.com. To participate, log onto a geocaching website and load the posted coordinates into your GPS. Once you have found the geocache, swap your trinket for another in the container, and sign the log book. Upon returning home, log back onto the website to record your trip. Whether you are placing a geocache or finding one, use existing hiking trails, avoid extensive bushwhacking where possible, and be careful not to trample vegetation when off-trail.

It is estimated that there are well over 800,000 registered geocaches in more than 100 countries and on all seven continents, even Antarctica. In and around Westchester County, there are about 1,000 geocaching sites.

To minimize impact on sensitive areas and protect natural resources, many parks require a permit to leave a geocache. Before establishing a geocache in a park, please obtain permission from the park. For contact information, check the Appendix.

Red/Green Trail   *Length: 0.2 mile Blaze: red/green*

This footpath connects the two trails around the lakes. Beginning at the green trail, the red/green trail heads east. It crosses a stream, then turns to follow it. Passing a series of water pipes, the red/green trail leads uphill to end at the guardrail on the road to the former Hemlock Camp.

Red/Orange Trail   *Length: 0.6 mile Blaze: red/orange*

Heading south from the yellow trail, the red/orange trail crosses two stone walls and then parallels another. It crosses a stream at 0.2 mile, and the orange trail at 0.3 mile. The trail works its way gently uphill. Approaching Hemlock Camp, it joins a gravel road and passes a large water tank to the right. The trail descends alongside the former camp buildings. The red/orange trail ends at the red trail at 0.6 mile.

Red/White Trail   *Length: 0.7 mile Blaze: red/white*

To make things confusing, there are two starting points for the red/white trail. One point is just beyond the second gate on the orange trail, 0.6 mile from the park's entrance; the other is on the red trail, heading counterclockwise just past the dining hall near the lake. These two legs are essentially identical in length.

From the orange trail, the red/white trail heads north and joins the leg coming from the red trail. The trail turns left at the base of a steep slope at 0.1 mile. It shortly makes a sharp right turn to work its way uphill, at first gradually, then more steeply. At 0.4 mile, it passes stones set in a row (for reasons unknown) and an errant picnic table off to the right. It reaches a trail junction and heads left. The unmarked trail to the right leads to the Larch lean-to. The red/white trail heads downhill at 0.5 mile and passes a stone pile. It then heads uphill to end at the orange trail. To the left is the triangle intersection with the orange/white trail.

Yellow Trail *Length: 0.5 mile Blaze: yellow*
From the orange/white trail, the yellow trail heads northwest along a narrow trail which then widens out. The trail becomes more and more gullied as it gradually heads downhill. The yellow trail passes the end of the red/orange trail to the left at 0.3 mile and a vernal pool to the right. After crossing a stream, the yellow trail heads back uphill along a stone wall to the left. It passes a 20-foot diameter pit where a nearby tree supports multiple poison ivy vines. Crossing through large rocks set in a row, the yellow trail turns left to end at the ATT line at 0.5 mile. Across the ATT line, the orange/yellow trail continues for 0.3 mile to reach Hunt Lane (parking).

DRIVING: Take I-684 to Exit 6 (Route 35) and drive east on Route 35. Turn left where Route 121 leaves Route 35, and head north for 4.5 miles. At Hawley Road, turn right and continue 1.5 miles to the park entrance to the left.

PUBLIC TRANSPORTATION: None available

For contact information, see Appendix, Westchester County Parks—Mountain Lakes Park.

Hearst-Mead Tract

North Salem • 1.2 miles, 73 acres, green NSBT tag

Except for a short shared boundary with Mountain Lakes Park, the Hearst-Mead Tract of the North Salem Open Land Foundation is surrounded by private property with posted signs, prominently displayed. It can be accessed through a narrow right-of-way along a woods road off Grant Road (Route 121), or along the power line which parallels the north boundary of Mountain Lakes Park. Inside the property, there are 1.2 miles of North Salem Bridle Trail Association (NSBT) equestrian trails connected to trails on private property.

Muscoot Farm

Somers • 5.7 miles, 777 acres

Unbeknown to many who drive on Route 100 along the Croton Reservoir in Somers and notice the simple sign for Muscoot Farm, there is much more at hand than just a farm. The low hills north and northwest of the farm and the broad point of land over to the reservoir to the south host 5.7 miles of old farm roads and blazed trails.

Muscoot Farm's animals are typical of those that would be found at a gentleman's farm in the early twentieth century. There are a variety of domestic animals: fowl, cows, sheep, horses, donkeys, and goats, many of which are unusual or rare breeds. Children may be disappointed by not being able to touch or feed them. However, the park offers many educational activities throughout the year, especially during summer months.

Muscoot means "something swampy." It was the name the Hopkins family used for their dairy farm, owned through three generations. The farm initially served as a summer estate; in 1924, it became their year-round residence. When New York City acquired some of the Hopkins land for the Croton Reservoir, they moved the Georgian Colonial farmhouse to its present location to preserve it. When the water level in the reservoir is low, stone walls and foundations that were once part of the original property are visible. In 1967, the family sold the farm to Westchester County; it opened as a park eight years later.

TRAILS

The trails at Muscoot Farm follow rolling hills, sometimes in the woods, at other times across former farm fields. Several unmarked trails head towards the Muscoot River. Although there are no viewpoints along the wooded trails and farm roads, several open fields with expansive vistas of the surrounding forest are a short distance from the farm proper. In winter, with sufficient snow cover, those fields are ideal for cross-country skiing.

Yellow Trail *Length: 3.3 miles Blaze: yellow*
To reach the yellow trail, go to the far end of the parking lot and follow a service road past a barn. Pass a wooden gate to reach a T junction with a farm road leading from farm buildings to the right. If the gate is closed, start from the middle of the parking lot, walk between farm buildings, and follow around to the farm road beyond the gate. Turn right.

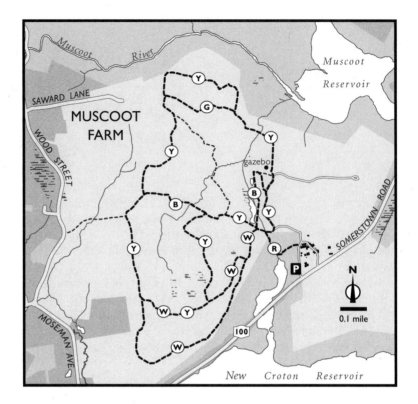

From the junction near the wooden gate, the farm road curves to the west with a grazing field to the north. It reaches a junction where yellow blazes head off in both directions; the yellow loop begins and ends here. At this point the yellow trail is on farm roads; later it becomes a narrow footpath. Going counterclockwise, follow the farm road. In front of a sloping field, the yellow trail passes the blue-blazed farm road. Almost immediately there is an intersection with another farm road in an open field. The one to the left descends to merge with the blue farm road, while the one to the right heads east for 0.8 mile, to a section of the park with no blazed trails.

The yellow trail continues straight ahead and ascends a gentle slope past a gazebo to the left. The trail follows the western edge of a long field and stays close to a meadow with a variety of seasonal wildflowers. At the end of the grassy traverse at 0.6 mile, the trail turns left and crosses a narrow strip of trees separating this field from a parallel one to the west. It follows the northern edge of the second field, crossing a seasonal creek on a wooden bridge before penetrating another hedgerow of trees. The trail continues along the northern edge of a third field for a short distance, becoming a narrow footpath as it enters the forest.

Passing the east end of the green trail at 0.8 mile, the yellow trail follows along a stone wall. The impressive girth of a huge white oak tree pushes against a crumbling section of a stone wall at 0.9 mile. The trail then quickly whisks away from the stone wall and crosses a seasonal stream. A faint side trail heads north to the Muscoot River at 1.1 miles. Sheltered by a narrow grove of eastern hemlocks, the yellow trail reaches a confluence of stone walls defining the edge of the park, and turns south.

The yellow trail junction passes the west end of the green trail at 1.3 miles. Shortly after, it passes a farm road leading down to the center of the park. The yellow trail crosses a stone wall and reaches the west end of the blue trail at 1.8 miles. Here, at the crest of a long broad hill, the forest is noticeably inching forward to reclaim a few fields. The yellow trail follows the eastern edge of dense shrubbery and joins the white trail. A farm road to the right leads nowhere.

The yellow and white trails are co-aligned for a short distance. The yellow trail splits to the left at 2.5 miles, widening as it descends, and looking more like a woods road. Once past the junction with the blue trail at 3.0 miles, the yellow trail is clearly on a woods road. At the bottom of the hill, it reaches another woods road bracketed by stone walls. The trail continues between small fields to the left and to the right. In a corner of a field at 3.2 miles, the blue farm road leaves to the left, and soon after, the white trail begins to the right. A short distance further, the red trail begins off to the right and the yellow trail closes its loop.

Blue Farm Road   *Length: 0.3 mile Blaze: blue*
This short farm road follows along a pond surrounded by an extensive wet area and is a favorite with families. It is an easy, level stroll starting on the yellow-blazed farm road near where the white trail also begins. There is a bench where one can rest to contemplate the pond, surrounding vegetation, and bird life. At the north end, the blue farm road reaches the edge of a biodiversity-protected area, one of the largest open fields in the park. The farm road turns sharply right and climbs through grass to join another yellow-blazed farm road. A short distance to the north is a gazebo, a nice perch from which to gaze at the surrounding fields.

Blue Trail   *Length: 0.3 mile Blaze: blue*
Designed as a shortcut, the blue trail heads off the yellow trail, climbs through a somewhat rugged part of the park, and then goes back to the yellow trail.

Green Trail   *Length: 0.3 mile Blaze: green*
A mostly east-west trail, the green trail begins and ends on the yellow trail. Heading west, it traverses north-facing gentle slopes that descend towards the Muscoot River. The green trail ends at the yellow trail.

Red Trail   *Length: 0.2 mile Blaze: red*
Beginning just before a wooden gate along the service road which is a continuation of the parking lot, the red trail first heads mostly west and then veers north. After crossing the corner of a field, it ends at the yellow-blazed farm road.

White Trail   *Length: 1.6 miles Blaze: white*
The white trail begins off the yellow-blazed farm road west of the farm and heads southwest. When the trail splits at 0.3 mile, take the left fork to go clockwise around the loop. For 0.5 mile, the trail traverses south-facing steep slopes along a narrow and rough track (suitable for experienced cross-country skiers). Sounds

Through the woods

of traffic along Route 100 are audible here. The steepness moderates as the trail reaches its southernmost point. The trail veers north and heads to the crest of a long broad hill, skirting a field being taken over by scrubby vegetation. The white trail joins the yellow trail at 1.0 mile and heads east. The white trail splits from the yellow trail at 1.3 miles and heads downhill to complete the loop.

NEARBY PARK: Lasdon Park, Arboretum & Veterans Memorial

DRIVING: From I-684 take Exit 6 (NY 35) and head west. At Route 100, turn left. Muscoot is 1.5 miles from the intersection. Note: the gate is locked at 4 pm, so plan accordingly.

PUBLIC TRANSPORTATION: None available

For contact information, see Appendix, Westchester County Parks—Muscoot Farm.

Sprain Ridge Park

Yonkers • 9.1 miles, 278 acres

Wedged along a ridge between the Sprain Brook Parkway and the New York State Thruway is Sprain Ridge Park. Although known as a mecca for mountain bikers, there are places of interest to hikers and walkers, as well as birding opportunities along the power line.

Because the park is situated between two major highways, expect road noise. When you cross from the west side of the ridge to the east, the noise shifts from the sounds of heavy trucks to that of fast-moving cars. During summer months, the park resounds with the laughter of happy day campers. Hikers who are Westchester County residents can, for a fee, enjoy a swim at the pool.

In the past, the park had been overrun with ATVs. The abuse ceased in the 1990s, when access to the power line paralleling the Sprain Brook Parkway was cut off. The ATV activity meant wider trails for mountain bikes, but it takes years for signs of the misuse to disappear, if at all. The rutted banked turns remain as evidence of this destructive illegal activity.

To keep from intruding on the mountain bikers' space, hikers should use the park during weekdays and avoid weekends and evenings, especially during the summer. With sufficient snow cover, the varied and sometimes steep terrain provides interesting snowshoeing; some of the gentler portions are good for cross-country skiing.

HISTORY OF SPRAIN RIDGE PARK

There are two theories about the origin of the word "sprain." One claims the word is a corruption of *spraints*, a Native American word for otter dung; many otters were once found in the area. The other is that it was taken from the word "sprain," which means "to sow seeds by hand."

In 1965, Westchester County purchased the property from the Boyce Thompson Institute for Plant Research, which relocated to Ithaca, New York, in 1978. The Institute is a not-for-profit botanical research center that studies plant life and its associated organisms for the benefit of society. Thus there are many unusual plants to be found on the property.

William Boyce Thompson (1869-1930), a financier, lived at Alder Manor, an estate overlooking the Hudson River. Thompson's legacy is also evident at the Boyce Thompson Arboretum in Superior, Arizona.

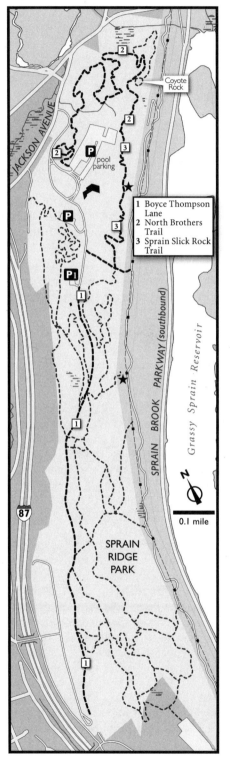

Coyote
Rock

pool
parking

1	Boyce Thompson Lane
2	North Brothers Trail
3	Sprain Slick Rock Trail

SPRAIN BROOK PARKWAY (southbound)

Grassy Sprain Reservoir

N

0.1 mile

87

SPRAIN
RIDGE
PARK

TRAILS

Contrary to county-produced maps, in 2008 the trails in Sprain Ridge Park were, for the most part, not blazed. The trails depicted on the map twist and turn, sometimes they snake down or up the ridge at an angle acceptable to bikers. Hikers will find the almost constant grade and twists a bit tiresome. This is particularly true in sections to the south and east of Boyce Thompson Lane. Given that there are so many renegade tracks, it is difficult to determine the exact trail mileage in the park. With so many unmarked trails, it also could be a problem to figure out exactly where you are. This park is suitable for people who feel comfortable navigating without much direction.

Because trail locations change over time, the 6.1 miles of unmarked trails is an estimate. The 2.2 miles of trails on the west side of the park include Danny Wray Ramble, an easy mountain bike loop. Several woods roads provide access to unmarked trails and the power line pathways. Located east of the picnic parking area, Eric's Over the Log Trail, which traverses steep terrain for 0.9 mile, is suitable for advanced mountain bikers. It is accessible either from Boyce Thompson Lane or the woods road to the power line. The southeast section of the park is a rabbit warren of trails, some more used than others.

Boyce Thompson Lane
Length: 1.1 miles
Beginning beside the entrance to Area #1, Boyce Thompson Lane serves as the main route into the network of trails in the southern portion of the park. It is not blazed, but is such a dominant feature of this half of the park that for most of its length it does not need blazing. Only remnants of pavement remain.

Heading downhill, Boyce Thompson Lane passes bike paths on the right and left. Just beyond a bridge at 0.3 mile, it heads gradually uphill; there is access here to a trail to the left and to another trail to the right. As the trail descends, road noise from the Thruway increases. Beginning at 0.7 mile, there is a succession of unmarked trails heading uphill to the left. The trail narrows but still follows the former road. Continuing to gradually descend, it ends at 1.1 miles.

Sprain Slick Rock Trail *Length: 0.8 mile Blaze: blue/white*
From the woods road proceeding southeast from the access road to the power line, the Sprain Slick Rock Trail switchbacks uphill. It contours along the ridge, ending at the east edge of the pool parking lot.

North Brothers Loop *Length: 1.6 miles Blaze: white*
From the far end of the pool parking lot, a short entrance trail leads to the North Brothers Loop on the left. Level at first, it soon climbs to the ridge to contour along its side. Descending, at 0.2 mile the trail reaches a junction with a trail to Coyote Rock. This unmarked trail to the right is an alternate route of 0.3 mile around Coyote Rock. The trail heads gradually downhill to a stone wall and turns left. The trail through the stone wall is the other end of the trail around Coyote Rock.

North Brothers Loop follows the stone wall, then turns away from it to head uphill. For the next 0.8 mile it winds its way, often doubling back on itself, sometimes so close that the pathway ahead is visible to the right or left. It becomes less convoluted and parallels Jackson Avenue briefly. Working its way downhill, at

Bridge on Boyce Thompson Lane

1.3 miles it reaches a boardwalk near the park entrance road. Again, the turning becomes convoluted as it ascends and descends on its way to the parking lot.

DRIVING: From the Sprain Brook Parkway, take the Jackson Avenue Exit. Turn west and drive 0.5 mile to reach the entrance to the left.

PUBLIC TRANSPORTATION: None available

For contact information, see Appendix, Westchester County Parks—Sprain Ridge Park.

Westchester Wilderness Walk
Zofnass Family Preserve

Pound Ridge • 5.7 miles, 150 acres

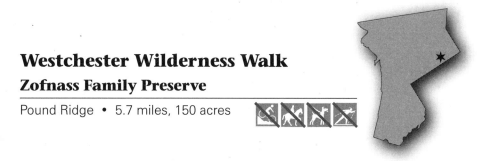

Lover Trees, Grand Stone Staircase, and Layer Cake Rock are just a few places to visit in Westchester Wilderness Walk. With these many enticing names, it is an intriguing place to go for a walk. Be forewarned, if there is something interesting to see, the trail designers have routed the trail to go there even if it means taking a circuitous route. The trails travel up and down steps, across stepping stones, along a stream bed, adjacent to a wetland, and even along the top of a stone wall.

Westchester Land Trust board member Paul Zofnass assembled 150 acres over the course of more than a decade. Zofnass, who conceived the idea, not only donated the initial properties as part of the Zofnass Family Trust, but also convinced his neighbors to donate land or easements. He then designed and financed the park's trail system.

TRAILS

All trails are marked with the same green Westchester Wilderness Walk/Westchester Land Trust tags; however, signs at intersections indicate options and the direction back to the parking area. Logs of various sizes delineate the path, making it easy to follow. The trails are loops and allow hikers to choose a different route on the return trip.

South Loop   *Length: 2.5 miles Blaze: green*
Starting from the parking area on Upper Shad Road, the South Loop passes a kiosk and follows a woods road beside wetlands. After heading along the top of a low stone wall, the trail reaches an intersection at 0.3 mile, where the loop begins. Turn right to go counterclockwise around the loop.

The South Loop heads towards Becky's Brook and then reaches Tom's Cabin at 0.5 mile. After passing the South Loop Short Cut at 0.6 mile, the trail descends and crosses Waterbury Way, a private road at 0.9 mile. On a former road, the South Loop next passes a short side trail leading to Fowler Rock and reenters the woods.

After passing Tulip Tree Heights and heading uphill, the South Loop reaches the Central Roundabout at 1.0 mile and turns left. The trail passes the other end of the Central Roundabout and again turns left, going uphill through Wedge Walk Rock. The trail heads up the aptly named Streambed Steps and reaches Fowler Rock at 1.2 miles. As the South Loop continues along the ridge, there are brief views into the ravine below. After passing Jurassic Rock, the trail descends and reaches, at 1.6 miles, wetlands near the shortcut back to the parking area. The trail passes Lookout Rock and Layer Cake Rock. It continues along the ridge, crossing through stone walls. At 2.1 miles, it makes a U turn and heads downhill past a seasonal cascade. The South Loop is level along the wetlands. Continuing to skirt the wetlands, the South Loop closes the loop at 2.5 miles. It is 0.3 mile to the parking area on Upper Shad Road.

Central Roundabout *Length: 1.0 mile Blaze: green*

Forming a hub, the Central Roundabout connects all three loop trails. It starts from the intersection with the South Loop, heads uphill and, going counterclockwise at 0.2 mile, meets the East Loop. Turning left at the intersection, the trail crosses a wet area on large flat rocks and reaches Razor Ridge Rock. At 0.5 mile, the trail goes the long way around Little Roundabout Rock. It passes the junction with the North Loop and heads south to meet the South Loop at 1.0 mile at Wedge Rock, a great spot for a snack or lunch.

East Loop *Length: 1.4 miles Blaze: green*

From the junction with the Central Roundabout, the East Loop goes through an open area at 0.1 mile and crosses a stone wall. The trail splits at the top of the

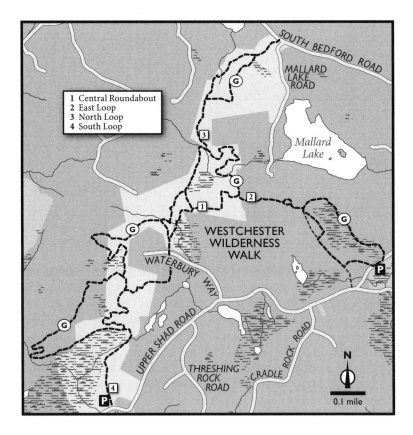

Fox Grape Vine on the South Loop

Grand Staircase. The trail to the right is shorter and steeper than the one to the left, and is best avoided in icy conditions. The East Loop continues downhill and reaches a trail junction at 0.2 mile.

Turn left to walk along the edge of extensive wetland. The East Loop slowly curves and parallels a stone wall. At 0.3 mile, it passes a rock outcropping looming overhead and the wetland on the right. The trail skirts the wetland and eventually parallels a stone wall. It leaves the wetland at 0.5 mile, reaches a paved road, and turns right to follow the road for 250 feet. Turning right again, it leaves the road at 0.6 mile, follows a path lined with logs, and reenters the woods. The trail parallels a stone wall, turns away from the wetland, and reaches a T junction with a woods road at 0.7 mile. (To the left, it is 0.1 mile to Upper Shad Road.)

Turn right and follow the woods road. At 0.8 mile, the East Loop leaves the woods road and heads uphill, reaching seasonal views over the wetlands below. The trail crosses the rise and heads downhill to close the loop at 1.0 mile. The hike from the Central Roundabout and return is 1.0 mile, skipping the trail out to Upper Shad Road. For those who hike from Upper Shad Road around the loop and return to the road, the hike is 1.1 miles.

North Loop   *Length: 0.7 mile Blaze: green*
From the northwest portion of the Central Roundabout, the North Loop heads uphill, crosses a stone wall, and turns right. It reaches the loop portion of the North Loop at 0.2 mile, where there are a quartz quarry and a Civil War-era garbage pit. Continuing to the right, the trail is on easy terrain and reaches the other end of the loop at 0.4 mile. The green sea of Christmas ferns scattered across the Upper Escarpment is especially noticeable in the leaf-off season. Descending, the North

Loop reaches the corner of South Bedford and Mallard Lake roads at 0.5 mile (no parking). On the return trip, turn right at the trail junction to pass the Awesome Oak and arrive at the trail leading back to the Central Roundabout. This fork of the loop is also 0.2 mile. The trip out to the road and back to the Central Roundabout is a round trip of 1.0 mile.

DRIVING: From I-684, take the Route 172 Exit. Follow Route 172 through Bedford and turn right at the gas station at Long Ridge Road. Drive 2.6 miles and turn left onto Upper Shad Road. The parking area is 0.3 mile from the intersection. Although there are access points at South Bedford and Mallard Lake roads, and also at the end of Waterbury Way, parking is available only at Upper Shad Road.

PUBLIC TRANSPORTATION: None available

For contact information, see Appendix, Westchester Land Trust.

Westmoreland Sanctuary

Mt. Kisco • 9.2 miles, 625 acres

V isitors are drawn to Westmoreland Sanctuary for several reasons: a variety of habitats, a well laid-out trail system, birding, and a wide range of nature programs. On the east side of Route 22, 150 acres of the sanctuary have been set aside for wildlife management activities and group study. This area is closed to the public.

In 1957, Edwin Bechtel, Helen Clay Frick, John Kieran, Nicholas Shoumatoff, and Frank E. Mason established Westmoreland Sanctuary, a community resource for conservation and natural history education. From the onset, the public has been offered programs with an emphasis on those of interest to young people. The sanctuary was named for Westmoreland County, near Pittsburgh, Pennsylvania, where Helen Clay Frick spent her childhood. Additional land donations have increased its size.

The building that houses Westmoreland's museum and headquarters was originally built in 1783 and was, at that time, the Third Church of Bedford. It stood on Guard Hill Road at a spot that is now the Bedford Golf and Tennis Club. In 1973, the church was dismantled and reassembled at its present location.

TRAILS

Well-marked trails with signs at intersections make Westmoreland Sanctuary a good choice for the novice hiker wanting to take longer hikes. Because the paths range from wide and smooth, to rocky and narrow, there are trails to suit a variety of skill levels. Trails pass wetlands, rock outcroppings, seasonal streams, and four ponds. The many options offer plenty of exercise; there are ridges to climb and valleys to traverse. Be forewarned, return trips are all uphill.

A Bedford Riding Lanes Association (BRLA) equestrian trail which is reached from a private driveway off Fox Lane (no parking) provides hoof and foot access to the sanctuary. Although not part of the trails maintained by Westmoreland Sanctuary, both BRLA trails are part of the trail system and are included in total trail mileage.

Easy Loop   *Length: 0.6 mile Blaze: red*
The entrance to the trail system is through Easy Loop, which starts from the paved drive leading to the sanctuary museum and headquarters. It is actually a figure eight, which makes the easy part of the loop even easier. If the shortcut is used,

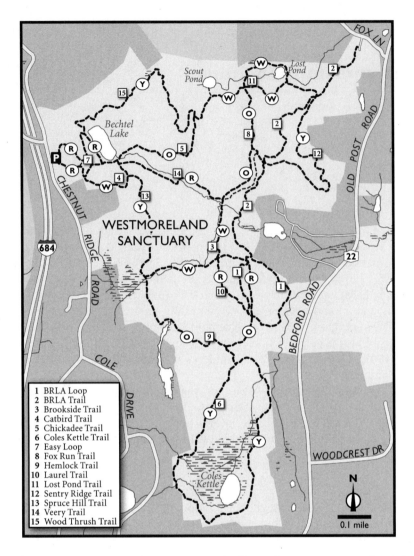

the hike on Easy Loop is only a quarter mile. From the entry gate to the right of sanctuary headquarters, Easy Loop passes a trail leading to an outdoor education station and then heads downhill. At a T junction, a 100-foot shortcut turns left to join the other side of Easy Loop. To the right, Easy Loop passes through a stone wall. At 0.1 mile, it descends steeply to turn left at a trail junction where the Catbird Trail (white) continues straight ahead. Easy Loop parallels the edge of Bechtel Lake, named for one of the sanctuary's founders. It then passes the skating shed and a massive tulip tree before turning away from the lake.

At 0.3 mile, Easy Loop passes the Wood Thrush Trail (yellow) on the right and heads uphill to overlook Lake Bechtel. Turning, it continues uphill to pass a shortcut trail to the left. To the right, at 0.5 mile, the trail passes a community cemetery active from 1824 to 1915. Easy Loop climbs over a rock outcropping and heads toward the sanctuary headquarters to close the loop.

BRLA Loop
Length: 0.6 mile Blaze: BRLA

Intertwined with the Laurel Trail (red) in the heart of Westmoreland Sanctuary, the BRLA Loop is for equestrians as well as for walkers. The following description starts at the intersection of the Hemlock (orange) and Laurel trails and continues clockwise. The Laurel Trail and BRLA Loop join for 80 feet; the former then heads straight ahead while the latter turns right to go uphill along a wide shelf. The trail curves at the base of a ridge and heads downhill. It enters an open area to cross the Laurel Trail, leaves the open area, and turns right onto a woods road. To the left, it passes the BRLA Trail leading out to Fox Lane.

Immediately crossing a stone wall, the trail parallels a fence to the left. At 0.3 mile, it passes below boulders which have tumbled down the hillside. The trail heads along a stream and crosses a seasonal wet area before heading uphill. After passing through another seasonal wet area, the BRLA Loop turns right at 0.5 mile. Ascending, it turns to go through a side ravine and continues its ascent. The BRLA Loop descends to cross a stream and closes the loop at a junction with the Hemlock and Laurel trails.

BRLA Trail to Fox Lane
Length: 1.0 mile Blaze: BRLA

Up, down, and around are the features of the BRLA Trail out to Fox Lane. From the BRLA Loop, the trail parallels a fence to the right as it enters a wetland. A boardwalk is not practical because the trail is used by equestrians. Turning away from the fence, the trail reaches slightly higher ground. Massive tulip trees line the trail in an area devoid of rock outcroppings.

The BRLA Trail reaches the top of the rise at 0.3 mile and descends on a narrow path. It crosses a woods road, contours on the side of the hill, and turns left. In the valley to the left, boulders are perched like oversized hawks searching for prey. The trail turns, continues its ascent and, at 0.4 mile, crosses the Sentry Ridge Trail (yellow) for the first time. Continuing its relentless assault on the hill, the trail skirts outcroppings to the right. The BRLA Trail ascends and descends numerous times, often steeply. There is a sense of isolation in this section with its valleys and ravines.

After crossing the Sentry Ridge Trail a second time at 0.8 mile, the BRLA Trail is on a well-trod pathway that wiggles its way through the woods and heads uphill. As it passes though a grove of young trees, the trail heads downhill, then turns to parallel a driveway. At 1.0 mile, it ends at a break in a stone wall at the driveway where Fox Lane is in view to the left (no parking).

Brookside Trail
Length: 0.4 mile Blaze: white

From the junction of the Hemlock (orange) and Spruce Hill (yellow) trails, the Brookside Trail meanders downhill on a woods road that parallels a brook to the right. It crosses the brook on a raised bed and bridge and continues downhill, traveling through a seasonal wet area. Passing the Laurel Trail (red) at 0.3 mile, the pathway narrows and crosses the stream on a bridge. Shortly past the lowest point in the sanctuary (390 feet), the Brookside Trail ends at the junction of the Veery (red) and Fox Run (orange) trails.

Catbird Trail
Length: 0.3 mile Blaze: white
From Easy Loop (red), the Catbird Trail heads downhill, paralleling a stone wall. It reaches the Spruce Hill Trail (yellow) and the Veery Trail (red), and ends at a T junction with the Chickadee Trail (orange).

Chickadee Trail
Length: 0.4 mile Blaze: orange
From the junction of Easy Loop (red), where it turns to parallel the shoreline of Bechtel Lake, the Chickadee Trail heads downhill along a stone wall. It passes the Catbird Trail (white) at a break in the stone wall, the outlet from Bechtel Lake, and then a glacial erratic. On a woods road, it passes over a rock ledge and bears left, steeply ascending a short rise at 0.3 mile, then descending to a more level path at the base of rock outcroppings. The noise of I-684 is gone. The Chickadee Trail ends

Rock outcropping on the Chickadee Trail

at a trail junction with the Lost Pond (white) and Wood Thrush (yellow) trails at 0.4 mile.

Coles Kettle Trail
Length: 1.4 miles Blaze: yellow
From the Hemlock Trail (orange), the Coles Kettle Trail crosses a stone wall and reaches a T junction. Going counterclockwise, the trail passes wetlands on the left and boulders on the right. The wetlands are part of Coles Kettle, a geologic feature created by a receding glacier leaving behind blocks of ice which, after melting, left a hollow.

After crossing a seasonal stream, the trail heads uphill, passes rock outcroppings on the right, and soon turns downhill to cross seasonal wet areas, streams, and stone walls. It veers left at 0.4 mile, passing more outcroppings. At 0.6 mile, the trail reaches a 400-foot boardwalk which ends at a T junction. The trail turns left to cross a stone wall. Heading uphill, it travels between wetlands on the left and a hill that rises up to the right. The pathway narrows at 0.8 mile, and it is necessary to walk carefully along the steep slope.

The Coles Kettle Trail heads uphill steeply, reaches the top of the rise, and then descends on a woods road. The trail is at the edge of the wetlands, just far enough away for feet to stay dry, but close enough to see and feel the more open space. At 1.0 mile, the trail turns and heads up through rocks along a woods road. Now heading downhill, it passes an unmarked trail into private property. It crosses a seasonal wet area and, at 1.2 miles on a woods road above a stone wall, leaves the kettle behind. It turns left to cross a bridge over a stream and head uphill to an area of stately trees. At 1.4 miles, it closes the loop. Turn right to return to the Hemlock Trail on the opposite side of the stone wall.

Fox Run Trail   *Length: 0.4 mile Blaze: orange*
From the junction with the Lost Pond Trail (white), the Fox Run Trail heads south along a woods road with rock outcroppings to the left. It gradually ascends and, at 0.2 mile, intersects the Sentry Ridge Trail (yellow). The Fox Run Trail enters a steep-sided, but wide valley with rock outcroppings towering overhead. After crossing the shoulder of the hill to leave the valley, the trail heads downhill steeply on a loose gravel pathway to end at the Brookside Trail (white).

Hemlock Trail   *Length: 0.5 mile Blaze: orange*
Starting from the junction with the Brookside (white) and Spruce Hill (yellow) trails, the Hemlock Trail crosses a bridge over a creek and heads uphill on a woods road. Passing a broad ravine to the right, it crosses a seasonal wet area at 0.2 mile and again heads uphill. It continues through a valley with small rocky ridges sticking up like the backs of sleeping dinosaurs. At 0.4 mile, it passes the Coles Kettle Trail (yellow) and gradually descends. Shortly after crossing a stone wall, the Hemlock Trail ends at the Laurel (red) and BRLA trails.

Laurel Trail   *Length: 0.5 mile Blaze: red*
Forming a loop in the heart of the sanctuary, the Laurel Trail serves as a connection to the Brookside (white), Hemlock (orange), and BRLA Loop trails. Going clockwise from the eastern end of the Hemlock Trail, the Laurel Trail heads uphill through a small ravine, with the BRLA Loop Trail leaving to the right. It ascends steeply into a valley where it levels out, passes a massive tulip tree, and resumes its steep ascent. At 0.1 mile, the trail descends and passes large stone slabs that appear as if glued to the hill to the right. It reaches an intersection where, at 0.3 mile, the Brookside Trail is to the left and straight ahead; at this point the Laurel Trail turns right. Continuing downhill into an open area with bluebird boxes, it crosses the BRLA Loop Trail. At the far side of the open area, the Laurel Trail heads uphill passing a rock outcropping on the right. It closes the loop when it meets the Hemlock Trail straight ahead and the BRLA Loop Trail to the left.

Lost Pond Trail   *Length: 0.6 mile Blaze: white*
From the junction with the Wood Thrush (yellow) and Chickadee (orange) trails, the Lost Pond Trail descends gradually to cross a stone wall. It passes a short, unmarked side trail out to Scout Pond, a vernal pool. At 0.2 mile, it reaches a junction with the Fox Run Trail (orange) to the right. The Lost Pond Trail makes a loop around the pond and leaves it, turning left at the junction with the Sentry Ridge Trail (yellow).

On a bridge, the trail crosses the outlet of Lost Pond then parallels its shore. The trail reaches a bench with a view of the pond at 0.4 mile, and veers away from the pond to follow a woods road. After crossing a stone wall, the trail passes a vernal pool on a woods road, and then turns left off the woods road. The Lost Pond Trail crosses the inlet of Lost Pond and heads gently uphill, closing the loop.

Sentry Ridge Trail   *Length: 1.0 mile Blaze: yellow*
Going clockwise from the junction with the Lost Pond Trail (white), the Sentry Ridge Trail heads gradually downhill through a valley. It turns right onto the BRLA Trail, joins it for 10 feet, and leaves to the left. The trail wiggles its way through the woods, sometimes steeply. Over the next 0.4 mile, the Sentry Ridge Trail goes up and down along the ridge. At 0.5 mile, it parallels the edge at a top of a steep drop to the left, and then heads uphill. The trail continues its undulating path and at 0.7 mile, heads steeply downhill, passing below rock outcroppings. At 0.9 mile, it crosses the BRLA Trail. Heading gradually uphill, the Sentry Ridge Trail ends at the Fox Run Trail (orange).

Spruce Hill Trail   *Length: 0.4 mile Blaze: yellow*
From the Catbird Trail (white), the Spruce Hill Trail heads south along a woods road. After crossing a stone wall, it goes uphill gradually into a forest with sparse understory, then downhill to end at the Hemlock (orange) and Brookside (white) trails.

Veery Trail   *Length: 0.4 mile Blaze: red*
From the Fox Run (orange) and Brookside (white) trails, the Veery Trail parallels a stream and a stone wall as it heads uphill. It crosses a series of stone walls, enters a small valley with more stone walls, and turns right onto a woods road at 0.2 mile. Continuing its ascent, the Veery Trail enters a hemlock grove and ends at the Catbird Trail (white).

Wood Thrush Trail   *Length: 0.7 mile Blaze: yellow*
From the junction with Easy Loop (red), the Wood Thrush Trail goes through a stone wall toward two bridges and heads slightly uphill. It crosses a stone wall, then turns to parallel it. The trail begins an assault on the hill along a narrow path overlooking Bechtel Lake. It reaches rock outcroppings on both sides of the pathway. Leveling off, the trail passes vernal pools and heads uphill once again.

It reaches a sign noting the park's high point (730 feet) at 0.4 mile, crosses stone walls, and then descends, sometimes more steeply. After reaching a flat area at 0.6 mile, the trail makes a sharp right turn and again descends steeply. A brief ascent leads to a junction with the Lost Pond (white) and Chickadee (orange) trails.

NEARBY PARK: Butler Memorial Sanctuary

DRIVING: From I-684, take Exit 4 (Mt. Kisco/Bedford Hills) and turn west onto Route 172 toward Mt. Kisco. Take the first left onto Chestnut Ridge Road. Westmoreland Sanctuary is 1.3 miles on the left.

PUBLIC TRANSPORTATION: None available

For contact information, see Appendix, Westmoreland Sanctuary.

PAUL MECK

Rockefeller State Park Preserve

SECTION VI

LARGE PARKS

- Have ten plus miles of trails
- Encompass extensive ecologically diverse areas
- Provide enough trails for multiple visits
- Offer longer and more complex hiking opportunities

Blue Mountain Reservation
Depew Park

Peekskill • 22.6 miles, 1,538 acres

The rolling woodlands with large granite boulders, glacial erratics, and rock outcroppings make Blue Mountain Reservation a great place to hike. Massive rock outcroppings of the 500 million-year-old Cortlandt complex tower above trails. With lichens, ferns, and stately trees, the setting is definitely picturesque. Although at first glance the trails seem to be alike, the many nuances make it possible to see new things with every visit. Primarily a park for mountain bikes, the reservation is large enough so that hikers will usually encounter just a small number of bikers except when races are held. Hikers wishing to minimize encounters should visit the park on weekdays, when there are almost no bikes.

As with many places near the Hudson River, the land now known as Blue Mountain Reservation was originally part of Van Cortlandt Manor, purchased from local Native Americans in 1677. Much later, the Lounsbury family owned the property and operated a sand, gravel, cement, brick, and general contracting business; the gravel pit was located at the present-day beach parking lot. The family constructed New Pond and Lounsbury Pond for making ice in winter; once cut, the ice was stored to be sold in summer. In 1927, the county purchased the property. During Franklin D. Roosevelt's administration, a Civilian Conservation Corps (CCC) camp was established there. The CCC built woods roads, the Trail Lodge, and two comfort stations, now historically significant.

TRAILS

The trails in Blue Mountain meander up hills and down through valleys. Aside from the single-track trails created by mountain bikers, the trails are on wide woods roads built by the CCC during the Depression. They are perfect for hiking two or three abreast.

Blazes and numbered posts change all too frequently because groups decide on their own to mark a trail. The blazes might or might not agree with the park's map or the map in this book. Single-track trails are mentioned, but not described.

Unpaved Montrose Station Road goes 1.4 miles across the park; gated at both ends to prevent vehicular access, it is an alternate access to trails. Parking is not available at local access points except at Depew Park, Montrose Station Road, and the Sportsman's Center (not shown on map).

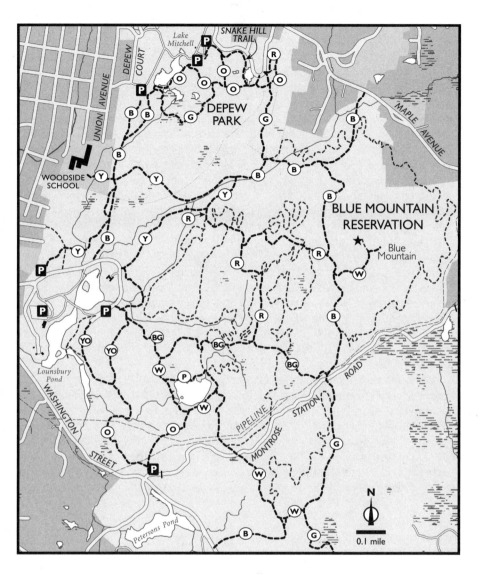

Blue Trail

Length: 2.4 miles Blaze: blue

Just as one would expect, there is a blue trail in Blue Mountain Reservation. It branches out and envelops the park. From the parking lot furthest from the main entrance, the blue trail and the Briarcliff Peekskill Trailway (green) head uphill on a woods road. After passing the yellow trail to the left and the yellow/orange trail to the right, the woods road goes through a hemlock grove devastated by the woolly adelgid. At 0.3 mile, the blue trail turns left. To the right, the white trail heads 1.1 miles to reconnect with the Briarcliff Peekskill Trailway.

The blue trail and the Briarcliff Peekskill Trailway continue uphill and make a turn to the right. The co-aligned trails pass, to the right, a 0.1-mile unmarked trail the purple trail around the lake. After passing a single-track trail to the left, the trails continue to ascend. At 0.8 mile, they reach a terminus of the red trail to the

CIVILIAN CONSERVATION CORPS

In the Great Depression, the United States was suffering from massive unemployment and destruction of natural resources. Legislation establishing the Emergency Conservation Work Act was passed by Congress and signed into law on March 31, 1933 to establish what is commonly known as the Civilian Conservation Corps (CCC); the induction of the first enrollees took place 37 days later. By bringing together two wasted resources, the CCC provided employment to young men. Applicants had to be single males, between 18 and 25, unemployed, from a needy family, not in school, healthy, and capable of doing physical labor. Eventually, veterans were admitted to the program. Sent out into healthful surroundings, this vast army of the unemployed renewed decimated forests and rebuilt infrastructure.

The first CCC camp was established in George Washington National Forest. Peak numbers for the entire corps were reached in August 1935 with 505,000 enrollees in 2,650 camps. Approximately 40 camps were operational in any given year. When projects were completed, camps were closed. Initially, there were 32 camps in New York; but by the time the program ended there had been as many as 208 camps, the largest number in any state. Projects in Westchester were in Ward Pound Ridge Reservation, Blue Mountain Reservation, and Franklin D. Roosevelt State Park (Mohansic State Park at the time) with camps at the first two locations.

Although the program is cited as restoring depleted natural resources, it also provided economic support to the families of enrollees and stimulated the local economy of CCC host communities. Other benefits to corps members were the improvement of their health and physical development, the provision of technical training, and the advancement of their education, including teaching 40,000 to read and write. The program gave these men the self-discipline, self-esteem, and sense of purpose, which would prove critical in World War II. The CCC is considered to be one of the most successful initiatives of the New Deal.

left. After passing a massive wetland and heading downhill, the blue trail and the Briarcliff Peekskill Trailway turn left at 1.1 miles to follow a pipeline.

After the Briarcliff Peekskill Trailway leaves to the right to cross Montrose Station Road, the blue trail follows the pipeline and then leaves it to enter the woods. A tree eating a blaze is to the right. Passing a rock outcropping, the blue trail heads uphill and, at 1.3 miles, passes to the right a 2.8-mile unmarked bike trail which reconnects to the blue trail. The cobbled surface of the woods road has just enough incline to provide a workout, but not enough to exhaust you. The forest changes and becomes predominantly deciduous trees. At 1.5 miles, the blue trail passes a white trail leading a quarter-mile steeply up to a viewpoint near the top of Blue Mountain and then to the viewless top.

Continuing straight as it descends to cross a seasonal stream, the blue trail passes an arm of the red trail at 1.6 miles. The heavily cobbled section ends and the trail passes broken-off boulders, scattered and looking like the pieces of a puzzle. Under massive trees, the blue trail is on a bumpy treadway and then heads down a sweeping turn. At the bottom, a row of maple trees and then extensive barberry bushes line the trail.

At a T junction at 2.0 miles, the blue trail goes left, while a different blue trail goes 0.3 mile through wetlands to the Maple Avenue entrance (no parking). The blue trail passes the other end of the 2.8-mile unmarked bike trail, veers left and, at 2.2 miles, passes the Blue Mountain Summit Trail (green) leading 0.4 mile into Depew Park. The blue trail ends at the junction with both the yellow and yellow disk trails at 2.4 miles.

Blue Disk
Length: 0.3 mile Blaze: blue disk

As a continuation of the blue disk trail from Depew Park, the blue disk trail heads south along a woods road. It passes both ends of a short 0.1-mile yellow trail, an alternative to the woods road. At the next junction, an unmarked trail to the right leads 0.4 mile to the overflow parking area at the entrance to the park. Below and to the left is a stream. At 0.3 mile, the blue disk trail ends at the entrance road across from Loundsbury Pond.

Briarcliff Peekskill Trailway
Length: 2.9 miles Blaze: green

The northern terminus of the Briarcliff Peekskill Trailway is in the parking lot further from the main entrance. It is co-aligned with the blue trail north of former Montrose Station Road. See Briarcliff Peekskill Trailway, page 342.

Orange Trail
Length: 0.8 mile Blaze: orange

From the yellow/orange trail, the orange trail parallels a stone wall and wetlands to the right. At 0.2 mile, the trail crosses the outlet stream of the pond and goes through a stone wall. After reaching a gas pipeline, it crosses a wooden bridge and heads along a rock turnpike to cross wetlands. Turning left and heading uphill along another pipeline, the orange trail then leaves the pipeline and turns right to pass through a gap in a massive stone wall. It reaches a T junction with an unmarked road heading 100 feet to Montrose Station Road with parking at Washington Street. After turning left at the junction, the orange trail crosses the two pipelines again at 0.6 and 0.7 mile, respectively. On a corduroy and gravel treadway, the orange trail ascends, then descends, to reach a pond where it ends on the white trail.

Purple Trail
Length: 0.3 mile Blaze: purple

From the white trail, the purple trail heads towards a pond and wiggles its way around the north shore. It heads steeply uphill to the top of rocks overlooking the pond. Just before a small bridge over the inlet stream to the pond, an unmarked trail leads 0.1 mile to the co-aligned blue trail and the Briarcliff Peekskill Trailway (green). The purple trail turns right, descends, and ends at the white trail at 0.3 mile.

Red Trail
Length: 1.0 mile Blaze: red

Shown on the map as a path shaped like a Y with the jitters, the red trail is entirely along woods roads. It begins at the intersection of the yellow trail in the northern

A CCC-built drainage ditch

part of the park and heads uphill. It passes the first of four unmarked mountain bike trails and, at 0.4 mile, reaches a large rock outcropping and splits. To the right, the red trail heads 0.4 mile to the co-aligned blue trail and Briarcliff Peekskill Trailway. Turn left. Going steeply uphill, the red trail passes a single-track trail to the left and then curves past a sloping face of bedrock. Drainage ditches show the durability of CCC work. The red trail passes a vernal pool and then more single-track trails. It works its way uphill and ends at 0.6 mile at the blue trail.

At the trail junction where the red trail splits, a second section of the red trail heads downhill and crosses the first of several low areas on a raised treadway. It makes a sharp left and then a sharp right. It passes a trail so convoluted that only mountain bikers could love it. After crossing a stream on a raised treadway, the red trail passes another vernal pool at 0.2 mile and heads uphill. It ends at a junction with the blue trail and Briarcliff Peekskill Trailway at 0.4 mile.

White Trail
Length: 1.1 miles Blaze: white

From the blue trail, 0.3 mile from the main parking lot, the white trail goes straight and uphill where the blue trail and Briarcliff Peekskill Trailway turn left. The white trail passes the purple trail to the left, heads through an open area, and crosses the outlet of a pond. After going downhill, it turns and passes to the right the orange trail, which leads to Montrose Station Road in 0.3 mile. The white trail follows the shore of the pond, with a short side trail out to a view, and then heads uphill. At a T intersection at 0.4 mile, it turns right where the purple trail is to the left. The white trail ascends more steeply, crosses two gas pipelines, reaches a rock barrier, and crosses Montrose Station Road at 0.7 mile. Continuing past an expanse of skunk cabbage, the white trail goes uphill and at 0.9 mile passes a mountain bike trail to the left. At a wide intersection it turns left; straight ahead is a blue trail (not connected to the 2.4-mile main blue trail) leading 0.3 mile to Washington Street (no parking). The white trail heads uphill to end at the Briarcliff Peekskill Trailway at 1.1 miles.

Yellow Trail (north from parking lot)   *Length: 0.8 mile Blaze: yellow*

From the blue trail/Briarcliff Peekskill Trailway, the yellow trail crosses a culvert over a seasonal stream and heads uphill. At 0.1 mile, it passes a mountain bike trail connecting to other bike trails which, unlike many mountain bike trails, are great for hiking. Crossing another culvert, the trail heads downhill and passes a trail to the left leading to the Trail Lodge. The woods road goes through a grove of hemlocks and then passes rocks that have tumbled down the hillside. After the trail heads more steeply uphill, it parallels a rushing stream in a ravine to the left. The yellow trail heads steeply uphill. At 0.5 mile, an unmarked trail to the left leads to a bridge and the yellow disk trail. After passing a series of vernal pools, the yellow trail reaches a T junction where the red trail begins to the right. Turning left, the yellow trail passes through an area littered with debris from hemlocks devastated by the woolly adelgid. The trail crosses a stream on a wide bridge and ends at a T junction with the yellow disk and blue trails.

VERNAL POOLS

Depressions with no obvious inflow or outflow stream, vernal pools are a special type of wetland. Generally they are quite small, below the size that would ensure their legal protection as wetlands. Vernal pools typically have water in late winter and early spring, thus the term "vernal." They may be wooded or open, with plant life specifically adapted to the wetland habitat.

The unique feature of vernal pools is that they have no fish, a result of their drying up completely in summer. Thus, they are ideal breeding places for amphibians and insects. After a pond has dried and the young amphibians have matured, they may range for hundreds of feet. Consequently, large protected space is needed for them to thrive. Frogs, toads, and salamanders return the following spring to the pool in which they were born, to mate and reproduce. In early spring, the songs of wood frogs and spring peepers will lead you to a vernal pool.

Yellow Disk Trail   *Length: 0.6 mile Blaze: yellow disk*

Although the yellow disk trail starts in Blue Mountain Reservation, it ends in neighboring Depew Park. From the junction where the blue and yellow trails end, the yellow disk trail heads west along a well-used woods road that parallels a stream. It passes, to the left, a bridge over a stream and enters Depew Park; however, there are no signs. Vernal pools are to the left at 0.3 mile. At 0.5 mile, the yellow disk trail reaches a trail junction. To the left is a blue disk trail with occasional yellow blazes. To the right, a blue trail leads to the network of trails in Depew Park. Straight ahead, the yellow disk trail ends at the Woodside School on Depew Street.

Yellow/Orange Trail   *Length: 0.5 mile Blaze: yellow/orange*

On topography gentler than in any other section of the park, the yellow/orange trail is a short loop on a narrow path connected to both ends of the main parking lot. Starting from the co-aligned blue trail and the Briarcliff Peekskill Trailway (green), the yellow/orange trail passes tall trees with sparse understory. It goes steeply downhill and reaches a trail junction at a quarter-mile. Straight ahead is the orange trail, which leads 0.5 mile to Montrose Station Road. The yellow/orange trail turns right and heads downhill. It parallels the outlet stream from Loundsbury Pond and, at a Y junction, turns right. It heads uphill and ends at 0.5 mile at the edge of the woods at the parking lot.

SINGLE-TRACK BIKE TRAILS

The 10.1 miles of marked and unmarked single-track trails snake in and out of areas circled by woods roads. These trails often change, and might not be exactly where they are shown on the map. They travel through narrow valleys, past rock outcroppings, and through hemlocks decimated by the woolly adelgid. Because these narrow trails frequently have a short sight line, hikers are encouraged to stay off them, especially on busy weekends and late afternoons.

DRIVING: From Route 9, take the Welcher Avenue Exit and turn east away from the river. Follow Welcher Avenue to the park entrance.

PUBLIC TRANSPORTATION: From the Metro-North Hudson Line Peekskill Station, head east on Hudson Avenue, away from the river. It is a 0.7-mile walk to Walnut Street, where there is a sign: To Depew Park. Follow Walnut Street 0.1 mile into the park and then take the unmarked trail from the swimming pool parking lot into Blue Mountain Reservation.

For contact information, see Appendix, Westchester County Parks—Blue Mountain.

Depew Park

Peekskill • 2.9 miles, 192 acres

J ust as quirky as its namesake, politician Chauncey Mitchell Depew, Depew Park provides many recreational opportunities. The park includes a swimming pool, basketball courts, horseshoe pits, baseball fields, Sachoes Nature Center, and Peekskill High School's football field and track. It is an urban park, where neighbors make use of the opportunities to walk and teens to hang out. Witty, skilled orator Chauncey Mitchell Depew (1834-1928), a native of Peekskill, was a lawyer, businessman, and politician. A Republican, he served in the New York State Assembly, as Secretary of State for New York , and in the United States Senate. After his defeat in a bid for a third term in the Senate, he was associated with railroads as counsel and later as president of New York Central Railroad until his death. Depew gave 40 acres of what was long-known as Depew's Woods to the Village of Peekskill in 1901. Two years later, the land became a public park. The park has grown to its current size through gifts and purchases.

Lake Mitchell

TRAILS

The trail system at Depew Park is greatly enhanced by its proximity to the trails at Blue Mountain Reservation. Once away from the frenzied activity of organized sports, the atmosphere within the park is relaxed. An orange trail and a 0.4-mile paved road closed to vehicles form the backbone of the trail network. The closed road also connects to roads leading to the entrance at Montrose Street (no parking). A 0.2-mile nature trail is near the entrance at Ferris Street (no parking).

Orange Trail *Length: 0.8 mile Blaze: orange*

Access to the orange trail is at the rear of the parking lot in front of the horseshoe pits. One section heads west to connect with the blue trail into Blue Mountain Reservation and the other section heads east.

Heading west, the orange trail is along a wood chip path initially following the shore of Lake Mitchell. It leaves the shore, returns, and turns left at a signboard. Re-entering the woods on a path lined with logs, it immediately reaches a Y junction. To the left is a 0.4-mile green trail which connects to the other segment of the orange trail. The orange trail bears right and narrows down just before ending at a blue-blazed gravel road at 0.2 mile.

To head east, the orange trail goes alongside the ruins of a stone building likely to have been restrooms, and then turns to ascend steeply. It descends to a seasonal wet area where the green trail is to the right near a stone wall. Heading uphill, the orange trail passes a 0.1-mile orange-blazed woods road leading left to the closed paved road. Ascending quite steeply, the orange trail reaches the top of the rise and descends. To the left, the Snake Hill Trail heads 0.3 mile to the park maintenance building. The orange trail reaches a large pond, crosses the outlet on a large slab of rock, and turns left to end at 0.3 mile at the closed paved road. An orange trail to the right crosses the Blue Mountain Summit Trail and ends in 0.1 mile at the Ruth Rusch Interpretive Trail (red).

Blue Disk Trail   *Length: 0.5 mile Blaze: blue disk*
On the west side of the park, two blue disk trails start from the parking lot near the swimming pool. The blue trail that runs south into Blue Mountain Reservation starts at the edge of the woods south of the swimming pool parking lot. The trailhead of this arm of the blue trail is across the field at a wooden bridge. Heading south, the trail crosses a stone wall and a massive upended root ball of a downed tree. It goes downhill, passing at 0.1 mile the other blue trail coming from the left. It crosses a yellow trail and, at 0.5 mile, enters Blue Mountain Reservation. The blue trail with occasional yellow paint blazes continues south into Blue Mountain Reservation to end on the entrance road near Loundsbury Pond.

The shorter blue trail begins as a gravel road in the northeast corner of the parking lot and then parallels the eastern edge. It passes a red building to the left and goes uphill as a dirt road. At 0.1 mile, it heads downhill on a path with a steep valley to the left. Veering to the right, it continues steeply downhill to a stream. It crosses a bridge, ascends, and joins, at 0.2 mile, the blue trail mentioned above.

Blue Mountain Summit Trail   *Length: 0.3 mile Blaze: green*
Beginning off the closed paved road, this green trail crosses the orange trail and goes steeply downhill. After crossing a stream, the trail enters a more open area and turns to parallel the stream while heading slightly downhill. The trail passes wetlands to the right and then rock outcroppings. It ends at 0.3 mile at the blue trail in Blue Mountain Reservation. Turn left and follow the blue trail 0.7 mile to the white trail leading to the top of Blue Mountain.

Green Trail   *Length: 0.4 mile Blaze: green*
To reach the green trail, take the orange trail heading west from the parking lot. The green trail begins just past the signboard where the orange trail enters the woods. Turn left off the orange trail and head uphill. Descending into a small valley, at 0.1 mile the green trail crosses a seasonal wet area on a bridge. It passes through three more seasonally wet areas and heads uphill. After crossing a stone wall, it ends at the orange trail.

Snake Hill Trail   *Length: 0.3 mile Blaze: none*
Unmarked Snake Hill Trail begins near the road to the park maintenance building on a wood chip path lined with logs for almost its entire length. Heading along a small stream and just before reaching the closed paved road, it first turns away from the road, then turns back to parallel it. After reaching the orange trail at 0.1 mile, the Snake Hill Trail turns right and immediately leaves to the left. It skirts the base of Snake Hill and ends at the orange trail.

DRIVING: From Route 9, take the South Street/Hudson Avenue Exit and head uphill on Hudson Avenue away from the river and train station. At 0.5 mile, turn right onto Walnut Street at a sign: To Depew Park. The entrance is 0.1 mile straight ahead. Alternate entrances are via two trails from Blue Mountain Reservation and off either Montrose Avenue or Ferris Street (no parking).

PUBLIC TRANSPORTATION: From the Metro-North Hudson Line Peekskill Station, head east on Hudson Avenue, away from the river. It is a 0.7-mile walk to Walnut Street, where there is the sign for the park. Follow Walnut Street 0.1 mile into the park.

For contact information, see Appendix, Peekskill.

Rockefeller State Park Preserve
Greenrock Corporation

Sleepy Hollow • 40.4 miles; 1,385 acres

In the seemingly tranquil landscape at Rockefeller State Park Preserve there is plenty of activity regardless of the season or time of day. It is safe to say that visitors to the park are not couch potatoes. Consider it an action park, as there are few benches and picnicking is not permitted. The well-graded carriageways are ideal for jogging, walking, or riding. Dogs are required to be leashed and, unlike other parks, the law is enforced. Horses and carriages are welcome at the park; riders and drivers must secure a non-transferable permit from the park office. Licensed anglers fish in Swan Lake and the Pocantico River. Birders should note that 180 species of birds have been recorded.

The Greenrock Corporation manages the Rockefeller family property; the public is permitted to walk or ride through the farm and adjacent woodlands. Signs are posted where the roads enter the Greenrock property. However, unlike trails in the park, these trails have no identifying signs. Visitors are asked to be aware of farm vehicles and give them the right-of-way. For walkers wishing more solitude, unmarked roads are less crowded than the named trails in more developed parts of the preserve.

At Rockefeller State Park Preserve and Greenrock Corporation lands, most of the trails are wide gravel carriageways. The 15.7 miles of named trails are on state-owned property; there are an additional 24.7 miles of trails that are unmarked and unnamed. Some of the unmarked trails are part of the park, and others are on Greenrock lands. Trail names are posted at intersections along with arrows pointing toward a return route to the visitors center. However, names on some signs are visible only from one direction.

The trails go through or by a variety of habitats: stream, river, lake, wetland, woodland, and meadow. There are relatively few views, most of which are along farm roads. Trails are clustered into four areas, two of which contain unnamed farm and carriage roads. With several roads crossing the park, there are multiple access points to trails. The park-issued map has more details than the ones included in this book. However, the park-issued map does not show any unmarked trails through Greenrock Corporation property or the land east of Route 448.

Because the trails were originally designed as carriageways, the intersections are often triangles; in two instances, the triangle is large enough so that a trail has three ends instead of two. Spook Rock Trail has one side of the triangle twice as long as and half as steep as the other. Both sides of Witch's Spring Trail connect to the Pocantico River Trail.

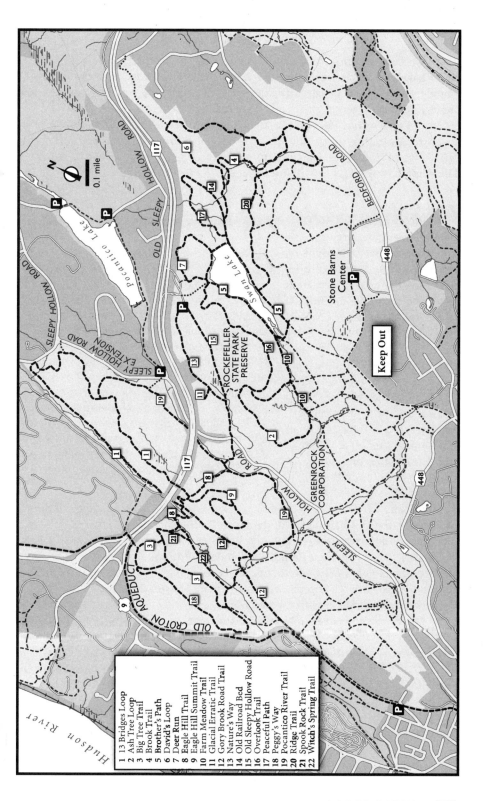

Hudson River

Pocantico Lake

Swan Lake

ROCKEFELLER
STATE PARK
PRESERVE

Stone Barns
Center

Keep Out

GREENROCK
CORPORATION

OLD SLEEPY HOLLOW ROAD

SLEEPY HOLLOW ROAD EXTENSION

SLEEPY HOLLOW ROAD

BEDFORD ROAD

MOTTON ROAD

SLEEPY HOLLOW ROAD

OLD CROTON AQUEDUCT

N

0.1 mile

117
448
9

1 13 Bridges Loop
2 Ash Tree Loop
3 Big Tree Trail
4 Brook Trail
5 **Brother's Path**
6 David's Loop
7 Deer Run
8 Eagle Hill Trail
9 Eagle Hill Summit Trail
10 Farm Meadow Trail
11 Glacial Erratic Trail
12 Gory Brook Road Trail
13 Nature's Way
14 Old Railroad Bed
15 Old Sleepy Hollow Road
16 Overlook Trail
17 Peaceful Path
18 Peggy's Way
19 Pocantico River Trail
20 Ridge Trail
21 Spook Rock Trail
22 Witch's Spring Trail

SWAN LAKE AREA

A short access trail from the visitors center leads to Brother's Path, which circles Swan Lake and serves as the hub for trails in the Swan Lake Area. Swan Lake is popular at any time of year, so expect to see hikers, joggers, dog walkers, and birders. In winter, gentle grades and wide roads attract cross-country skiers.

From David's Loop, an equestrian trail provides a 0.9-mile access route for two local stables on the north side of Route 117. At 0.2 mile, a loop goes off to the left. Rows of linden trees planted in a level area grace what might have been a landscaped overlook, now without a view.

Ash Tree Loop   *Length: 0.8 mile*

From the south end of the Farm Meadow Trail, across from where two roads enter the Greenrock property, the Ash Tree Loop begins to the right. As it heads uphill, the size of trees decreases. Many of the ash trees along the trail have succumbed to ash yellows disease. The trail is somewhat level as it circles the top. To the left at 0.5 mile, a shortcut leads 0.1 mile steeply down to the Old Sleepy Hollow Road Trail. The Ash Tree Loop turns right at the junction with the Overlook Trail. A small quarry is to the left at 0.7 mile, just before the junction with the Farm Meadow Trail.

Ash Yellows

In the northeast, ash yellows disease is causing severe growth reduction, decline, and dieback of white ash trees; green ashes appear to be more tolerant. It is unclear how this mycoplasma-like organism (MLO) enters the trees; insect vectors are one possibility. The MLO inhabits the living vascular tissue just inside the tree's bark. See http://tinyurl.com/5oh5uj for a 1987 *New York Times* article. Since then, the problem has greatly worsened. Many standing dead ash trees can be seen on the Ash Tree Loop.

Brook Trail   *Length: 0.8 mile*

Starting on the Old Railroad Bed, the Brook Trail meanders for most of its length along a brook, crossing it frequently. It passes the junction with David's Loop to the left and a breached dam. At 0.2 mile, the Brook Trail curves away from the brook and levels off, only to ascend more steeply. To the right at 0.4 mile, a side trail crosses two bridges to rejoin the main trail in 200 feet. To the left, an unmarked trail connects with David's Loop.

At 0.5 mile, a short, steep uphill path to the right connects to the Ridge Trail. After crossing another bridge, the Brook Trail passes a drained cistern to the left with a large solitary rock that was never removed. To the left, the trail heads upstream along the brook cascading over rocks. It passes an area where the spillways of small dams are now part of the cascading stream, and at 0.6 mile turns away from the brook and passes the other end of David's Loop to the left. Heading slightly downhill, the Brook Trail reaches a T junction with the Ridge Trail, where it ends at 0.8 mile. To the left on Greenrock property, is an unmarked carriageway which leads under Route 448 to additional unmarked farm roads. Narrow unmarked paths lead up to Route 448 (limited parking).

Brother's Path   *Length: 1.1 miles*

Given that Brother's Path circles Swan Lake, it is not surprising that this trail is extremely popular. It could almost be called crowded on midsummer weekends, considering that there are visitors every 100 feet along the trail. However, the trail's width offers plenty of space with little noise.

From the access trail at the visitors center, head counterclockwise around the lake. Brother's Path varies in how closely it follows the lakeshore. At 0.4 mile, the Farm Meadow Trail goes right. Brother's Path crosses two inlet streams as it rounds the end of the lake. It reaches an intersection with two carriageways into Greenrock property. To the left, a narrow path created by Canada geese leads down to the lake; to the right, another path goes up under the fence to a field for grazing.

At 0.5 mile, Brother's Path passes two access roads to the Greenrock property to the right. It enters a rock cut to overlook the lake. Set on top of the retaining wall, large rocks serve as balustrade and guardrail. At 0.7 mile, drifting downhill almost imperceptibly, the trail reaches lake level with the Ridge Trail to the right.

Brother's Path reaches a triangle junction at 0.9 mile. The Old Railroad Bed is straight ahead. Brother's Path turns left to cross the outlet flow from Swan Lake on stepping stones to reach the other side of the triangle. It passes one end of Deer Run to the right and then, to the left, two stone benches, most likely the only benches in the park. Brother's Path passes the other end of Deer Run and closes the loop at 1.1 miles at the trail to the visitors center.

David's Loop   *Length: 0.9 mile*

Beginning at a junction with the Brook Trail where it is close to Route 448, David's Loop passes through tall trees. At 0.2 mile, it passes an unmarked trail to the left leading 0.1 mile down to the Brook Trail and then to the first of three trails into private property. To the right at 0.6 mile, an equestrian trail leads 0.4 mile downhill to Old Sleepy Hollow Road. Just past the equestrian trail, David's Loop heads downhill. Wherever there are wet areas, the understory is thick and lush with invasive plants. Sometimes there is no transition between areas with dense or sparse understory. At 0.8 mile, the Brook Trail is visible across the brook. At 0.9 mile, David's Loop closes the loop at the Brook Trail.

Deer Run   *Length: 0.4 mile*

Beginning on Brother's Path and heading clockwise 130 feet past the access trail to the visitors center, Deer Run immediately heads uphill. At 0.1 mile, an access trail goes steeply down to the equestrian parking lot to the left. The trail gently wiggles its way downhill and ends at Brother's Path. It is 0.1 mile back to the access trail to the visitors center.

Farm Meadow Trail   *Length: 0.4 mile*

Turn right from a Y junction with the Brother's Path at the southwest end of Swan Lake where the Farm Meadow Trail heads slightly downhill. It passes one end of the Ash Tree Loop at 0.2 mile. Dense understory and wetlands are to the right. The trail passes a farm road into Greenrock property to the left. At 0.4 mile, the Farm Meadow Trail ends. Straight ahead and to the left, the roads lead into Greenrock property. To the right is the beginning of the Ash Tree Loop.

Nature's Way
Length: 0.4 mile

Beginning on the north side of the parking lot near the visitors center, Nature's Way is along a narrow path. It heads southwest, passing a maintenance area almost immediately. At a quarter-mile, the Glacial Erratic Trail leaves to the right and ends in 300 feet at a glacial erratic more than 20 feet high. Nature's Way ends at Old Sleepy Hollow Road Trail at 0.4 mile.

Old Railroad Bed
Length: 0.3 mile

Beginning on Brother's Path near the outlet, the Old Railroad Bed passes one end of Peaceful Path. At 0.1 mile, the trail is on a causeway to keep it at-grade above wetlands. It reaches the end of the causeway, enters a rock cut, and ends at Peaceful Path. Evidence of the railbed continues past the junction with Peaceful Path. When Route 117 was built between 1969 and 1971, the railbed was cut off. The Old Railroad Bed is what remains of the section of the Putnam Division Line which passed through the Rockefeller Estate until 1931, when John D. Rockefeller, Jr. financed the relocation of a section of the railroad.

Old Sleepy Hollow Road Trail
Length: 0.6 mile

Beginning from the parking lot at the end farthest from the visitors center, Old Sleepy Hollow Road Trail first goes through a gate. Heading gradually downhill, at 0.3 mile it passes a 0.1-mile unnamed trail to the Ash Tree Loop to the left and then, 125 feet further, passes Nature's Way to the right. At 0.5 mile, Old Sleepy Hollow Road Trail crosses Sleepy Hollow Road (limited parking) and the 0.1-mile section of Old Sleepy Hollow Road Trail serves as an access road to the Eagle Hill Area. A kiosk displays a park map.

Overlook Trail
Length: 0.7 mile

At the end of the access trail to the visitors center, just before reaching the Brother's Path, is the Overlook Trail. It immediately heads uphill on one of the steeper grades in the park. It circles a grassy area to the left. The grade lessens, but the trail continues uphill. At 0.3 mile, it passes a sugar maple whose trunk is covered with poison ivy. It leaves the meadow and passes a low flat building which is a water tank. Heading downhill through the woods, the Overlook Trail ends at 0.7 mile at the Ash Tree Loop.

Peaceful Path
Length: 0.4 mile

Considering all the road noise from adjacent Route 117, one wonders why this trail was named Peaceful Path. From the north end of the Old Railroad Bed, the Peaceful Path heads downhill. It crosses a bridge at 0.1 mile and turns; here the road noise is barely heard. The trail narrows, and just after leaving the woods, it widens and joins Brother's Path near the dam of Swan Lake.

Ridge Trail
Length: 0.9 mile

Beginning at the junction of the Brook Trail and a farm road that leads under Route 448, the Ridge Trail is one of the few trails in the park with a view. It goes along farm fields and passes two unmarked roads into Greenrock property. It

History of Rockefeller State Park Preserve

In 1893, John D. Rockefeller, Sr. began purchasing property in the Pocantico Hills area. His 40-room mansion overlooking the Hudson River, Kykuit (Dutch for lookout), became the country home of this wealthy and influential family. Both John, Sr. and his son John, Jr. enjoyed driving carriages. During the 1920s and 1930s, they had 55 miles of carriage roads constructed on their property, moving or destroying farm buildings in the process. Although much of the land returned to its former natural state, portions of the estate have been continuously farmed. With the opening of Stone Barns Center for Food and Agriculture in May 2004, the Rockefeller family's commitment to agriculture continues.

The Rockefeller family's initial gift of 750 acres established the park in 1983. The John D. Rockefeller, 3rd Fund provides an endowment for operation and maintenance of the property. Through subsequent gifts the park has grown, extending onto both sides of Route 448 and Old Sleepy Hollow Road. The property east of Route 448 was donated by Laurence Rockefeller, with the most recent addition of 91 acres bequeathed to the state in 2004.

enters the woods at 0.2 mile and heads gently downhill. At 0.4 mile, an unmarked path leads steeply downhill to the Brook Trail, which is visible through the trees. To the left is a small retaining wall, evidence of the cutting and filling that took place to build the carriageways in the park. The Ridge Trail passes one entrance to a maintenance area for Greenrock property at 0.5 mile and then another at 0.6 mile. Making a sweeping curve to the right, it heads downhill to end on Brother's Path at Swan Lake.

EAGLE HILL AREA

More trees and fewer meadows are characteristic of the terrain surrounding the trails in the Eagle Hill Area. There are elevation gains and losses, but most often the trails maintain an even grade. There are two access points to this section of the park. One is off Sleepy Hollow Road, where a 0.1-mile section of the Old Sleepy Hollow Road Trail provides access to the Pocantico River Trail. The second access point is at the end of Gory Brook Road in Sleepy Hollow. At both places, parking is limited.

13 Bridges Loop   *Length: 1.9 miles*
Beginning at the intersection of the Eagle Hill and Eagle Hill Summit trails, 13 Bridges Loop heads north to cross Route 117 on a bridge. Along each side of the bridge there is a separate pedestrian walkway; however, the vegetation growing there indicates that these walkway portions of the bridge are not used. The open terrain has little or no understory and, by 0.3 mile, the noise from Route 117 is no longer audible. The trail passes the northern terminus of the Pocantico River Trail at 0.6 mile and then heads slightly uphill. After passing a rock outcropping to the left, it stays at-grade on a retaining wall. At 0.8 mile, Sleepy Hollow Road is both

13 Bridges Loop

seen and heard. An unmarked trail to the right leads 400 feet out to gate P6 near the intersection of Sleepy Hollow Road and Sleepy Hollow Road Extension (limited parking). At 0.9 mile, the trail turns left with wetlands visible below to the right. An unmarked trail at 1.0 mile goes out 200 feet to Sleepy Hollow Road Extension (parking for one car).

As the 13 Bridges Loop enters a hemlock grove, Gory Brook below is audible. The trail goes down a switchback and begins to live up to its name as it crosses a bridge, the first of thirteen, over a feeder stream into Gory Brook. The brook and the trail are intertwined in a valley with trees towering overhead. At 1.2 miles, the trail passes an unmarked carriageway leading to a gate into private property. It is not until 1.4 miles that the trail crosses the second bridge. With an unobstructed view of the trail ahead, it is easy to spot the upcoming bridges. At about 1.6 miles, the ninth, tenth, and eleventh bridges cross Gory Brook within 100 yards of each other. This area is where Route 117 can again be heard. An unmarked carriageway leads to the Old Croton Aqueduct at 1.7 miles and the 13 Bridges Loop crosses the last bridge. The trail then passes under Route 117 to end at the intersection of Eagle Hill and Gory Brook Road trails at 1.9 miles.

Big Tree Trail   *Length: 0.9 mile*

Beginning at the intersection of Peggy's Way and the access trail from the Old Croton Aqueduct, the Big Tree Trail heads downhill to meet the Witch's Spring Trail at 0.1 mile. It bears left to go uphill along a retaining wall with large rocks looking like a jagged balustrade. It is easy to see how the trail got its name: there are many towering trees lining the trail. The trail gently curves, straightens, and continues uphill. At 0.5 mile, it reaches the beginning of a loop with the Big Tree Trail going in both directions. To the right, the trail ascends to meet the Spook Rock Trail at 0.6 mile and continues uphill to the crest of the ridge. It heads downhill to meet a side trail to the right which connects to the Old Croton

Aqueduct. Continuing downhill, the Big Tree Trail passes the north terminus of Peggy's Way at 0.8 mile. After passing a rock outcropping to the left, the Big Tree Trail closes the loop at 0.9 mile.

Eagle Hill Summit Trail   *Length: 0.6 mile*

From the junction of Eagle Hill Trail and 13 Bridges Loop, the Eagle Hill Summit Trail heads uphill. At 0.2 mile, it reaches a junction with the loop that circles the top of the hill. The left branch reaches the viewless top at 0.3 mile. The trail curves right and descends to close the loop at 0.6 mile.

Eagle Hill Trail   *Length: 0.3 mile*

Leading uphill from the Pocantico River Trail, the Eagle Hill Trail passes 13 Bridges Trail to the right and Eagle Hill Summit Trail to the left at 0.2 mile. It then heads steeply downhill on a switchback to end at the junction of Gory Brook Road Trail and 13 Bridges Loop.

Gory Brook Road Trail   *Length: 0.7 mile*

Sections of Gory Brook Road were abandoned in 1979 and the Gory Brook Road Trail follows some portions. In Sleepy Hollow at the end of Gory Brook Road, a 0.4-mile abandoned portion parallels the Old Croton Aqueduct with crossovers to the Aqueduct and farm roads into the Greenrock property.

The abandoned road enters the Rockefeller State Park Preserve and become the Gory Brook Road Trail at a Y junction where a gravel carriageway goes left and it continues straight along a narrow path. At a quarter-mile, the Gory Brook Road Trail joins the Pocantico River Trail. Together they follow the Pocantico River upstream, turn right at the next junction, and cross it. At the intersection across the river, the trails turn right, leaving abandoned Gory Brook Road. At the next intersection, the Pocantico River Trail goes straight and the Gory Brook Road Trail turns left and enters woods. Between the junction of the Witch's Spring Trail at 0.6 mile and the Eagle Hill Trail, the abandoned roadbed is visible to the left. Gory Brook Road Trail ends at the junction of 13 Bridges Loop and the Eagle Hill Trail at 0.7 mile.

Peggy's Way   *Length: 0.5 mile*

A large rock with Peggy's Way 1994 carved into it greets hikers at the south end of Peggy's Way. Named for Peggy Rockefeller, wife of David Rockefeller, the trail traverses a long ridge with no views. Noticeable almost immediately, the trail is about three feet narrower than and not as straight as other trails in the park. At first there is little or no understory, but by 0.2 mile, it has become dense. Peggy's Way descends to end at the Big Tree Trail at 0.6 mile.

Pocantico River Trail   *Length: 1.9 miles*

Together the Pocantico River and the Pocantico River Trail wander through the park. The trail begins at the junction of the Big Tree and Witch's Spring trails and crosses the Pocantico River on a stone bridge with triple arches. It goes left at a T junction with an unmarked trail heading to the abandoned Gory Brook Road and immediately passes a fire hydrant. Following the river upstream, the trail turns right at a T junction at 0.4 mile. The Witch's Spring Trail is to the left over a stone bridge. The Pocantico River Trail curves away from the river, but returns to it upon reaching abandoned Gory Brook Road at 0.5 mile.

Co-aligned with the Gory Brook Road Trail, the Pocantico River Trail heads upstream following the river, at times closer than at others. It turns left to cross the Pocantico River and then turns right. To the right, an unnamed road goes into a meadow where an unmarked road leads straight into Greenrock property; Gory Brook Road Trail is to the left. The Pocantico River Trail circles the base of Eagle Hill and passes a meadow to the left. At 0.7 mile, it reaches an intersection with a fire hydrant to the left and a barrel-arch stone bridge to the right. Unnamed roads heading straight ahead and to the right lead into Greenrock property. The trail turns left with the river below to the right.

The Pocantico River Trail heads uphill at 1.0 mile, turns away from the river, and returns 0.1 mile later above a series of cascades. At 1.2 miles, it passes Eagle Hill Trail

DANIEL CHAZIN

Triple Arch Bridge

to the left and then Old Sleepy Hollow Road Trail to the right. After going under Route 117 at 1.4 miles, the trail passes an unmarked access trail to the right. It is 400 feet to gate P6 near the junction of Sleepy Hollow Road Extension and Sleepy Hollow Road (limited parking). Continuing at-grade, the Pocantico River Trail ends at the 13 Bridges Loop at 1.9 miles.

Spook Rock Trail   *Length: 0.2 mile*
From Witch's Spring Trail, there are two access points to Spook Rock Trail. Take your pick: either steep and short, or gentle uphill but twice as long. After the two segments join, Spook Rock Trail continues uphill. Spook Rock, which is an easily missed boulder, is on the inside of the turn in the switchback. The trail ends at Big Tree Trail.

Witch's Spring Trail   *Length: 0.5 mile*
From Gory Brook Road Trail, Witch's Spring Trail heads downhill and crosses abandoned Gory Brook Road. It passes one end of Spook Rock Trail at 0.2 mile and then the other. After following Gory Brook for a short distance, it reaches and heads along the Pocantico River. At 0.4 mile, the trail splits. The segment to the right soon reaches the end of the Pocantico River Trail while the segment to the left crosses a bridge and also ends at the Pocantico River Trail.

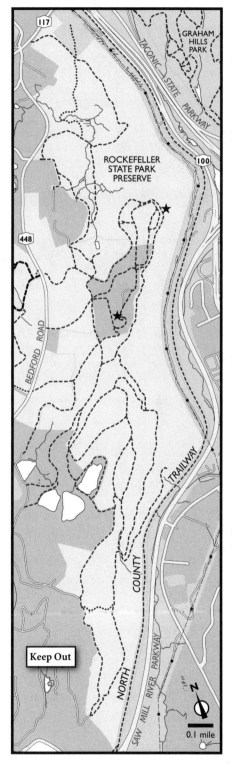

EAST OF ROUTE 448

The title of Thomas Hardy's novel *Far from the Madding Crowd* comes to mind when walking the roads in the area east of Route 448. Aside from serious joggers using the trails, expect to see far fewer people than in other sections of the park. The open farm fields with vistas and woodlands beg to be explored. The view from Buttermilk Hill dates to Revolutionary War times. The crags on the ridge provide habitat for raptors who hunt along the Saw Mill River Parkway and the power line. Evidence of the 2006 tornado is along the road leading down from the ridge which dead ends before reaching the North County Trailway.

Access to this area is from Route 448 (0.7 mile north of Stone Barns) across from the entrance to Stone Barns (no parking). It is also accessible from a large parking lot next to a small one at the North County Trailway on Route 117. A footpath, the longest narrow trail in the park, leads from the southwest corner of the parking lot into the woods.

Unlike trails in the Eagle Hill or Swan Lake areas, these 16.5 miles of trail are unnamed and without signs. Work is underway to develop signage and make the section more user-friendly. The North County Trailway, Route 9A/100, and the Saw Mill River Parkway are below the ridge and form a barrier to the east.

CONNECTING TRAILS & NEARBY PARKS: Old Croton Aqueduct, North County Trailway, Douglas Park, Pocantico Lake Park, Rockwood Hall, Sleepy Hollow Cemetery

DRIVING: There are numerous access points. To reach parking at the visitors center from Route 9, north of Phelps Memorial Hospital in Sleepy Hollow, take Route 117 east. The park entrance is to the right on the road's south side.

Stone Barns Center for Food and Agriculture

Located off Route 448 are Norman-style stone barns built in the 1930s by John D. Rockefeller, Jr., to be part of his vision of a self-sufficient family estate. Thanks to David Rockefeller and his daughter, Peggy Dulany, the renovated

MARIE BARCIA-MARCY

buildings now house Stone Barns Center for Food and Agriculture. The idea for the not-for-profit center began in the early 1990s and the center opened in May, 2004. Stone Barns not only produces food, but teaches and promotes community based sustainable agriculture. See www.stonebarnscenter.org.

Blue Hill (a first class restaurant) and the snack bar serve food grown on the farm. This fare is unlike food served at establishments in other parks and thus higher priced. If the amount on a receipt from the restaurant, snack bar, gift shop, or a class is equal to or greater than the vehicle exit fee, that fee is waived.

Alternately, take Route 9A to Route 117 and head west for 1.6 miles to the park entrance to the left.

To reach parking along Route 448, take Route 9A to Route 117 and head west. Turn left at the traffic light to follow Route 448 for 1.0 mile (limited parking). Continue an additional 0.7 mile to reach the Stone Barns Center. No parking is permitted near the entrance road to Stone Barns Center, but there is parking at Stone Barns with a parking fee to be paid when leaving.

To reach parking on Sleepy Hollow Road, take Route 9A to Route 117 and head west. Turn left at the traffic light to follow Route 448 to the first right turn, Sleepy Hollow Road, which crosses under Route 117. Cross under Route 117 for a second time to find parking along Sleepy Hollow Road, just beyond the overpass.

To reach parking at Gory Brook Road in Sleepy Hollow, follow Route 9 north to a complex intersection with Route 448. Do not turn onto Route 448; instead, continue straight on New Broadway. At 0.2 mile, turn right onto Gory Brook Road, which dead ends at parking near the Old Croton Aqueduct.

To reach parking for the unnamed and unmarked trails east of Route 448, take Route 9A to Route 117 and head west. Turn left into the second parking lot, the larger of the two.

PUBLIC TRANSPORTATION: No direct public transportation is available. However, there is access to Rockefeller State Park Preserve from Gory Brook Road in Sleepy Hollow. From the Metro-North Hudson Line Tarrytown Station, walk north on Depot Place to Main Street, turn right, and head uphill to Route 9 (North Broadway). Turn left, walk north toward Route 448, and follow the Gory Brook Road driving directions given above.

Beeline Bus #13 stops near Rockwood Hall. A walk through Rockwood Hall to the Old Croton Aqueduct provides access to the Eagle Hill area of the park.

For contact information, see Appendix, Rockefeller State Park Preserve.

Pocantico Lake Park

Sleepy Hollow • 1.0 mile, 164 acres

An undeveloped county park, Pocantico Lake Park has year-round views out over a former reservoir. Roads closed to traffic lead north and south from parking at barriers on Pocantico Lake Road.

Heading southwest, the road ends in 0.3 mile at a dilapidated building, once part of the county waterworks. Just before the building, a trail leads out 370 feet to the dam with an open view of the entire lake. A footpath leads around the side of the building. It reaches an access road from Sleepy Hollow Road to the buildings at the base of the dam. It is not safe to enter these buildings, which are becoming more and more decrepit. Much of the access road follows the Pocantico River.

Going northwest, the road is a bit farther from the lake. It turns to cross a causeway and terminates at a barrier at the end of Old Sleepy Hollow Road.

NEARBY PARK: Rockefeller State Park Preserve

DRIVING: From Route 9A, take Route 117 and turn west toward Tarrytown. Turn left at the traffic light at Route 448 (Bedford Road). Take the first right onto Sleepy Hollow Road. Go 0.9 mile to Pocantico Lake Road and turn right. The road dead ends at a barrier where there is parking.

PUBLIC TRANSPORTATION: None available

For contact information, see Appendix, Westchester County Parks.

Saxon Woods Park

Scarsdale • 12.9 miles, 711 acres

If you live in southern Westchester County and want a half-day hike with as little driving as possible, look no further than Saxon Woods Park. The topography of the park is best described as typical Westchester woodland with tall trees, wetlands, rock outcroppings, and little understory. For the most part, the trails have gentle grades with only small elevation gains or losses. Furthermore, most of the trails are on woods roads inviting people to walk and talk.

Designed to be connected, the trails in Saxon Woods Park were developed at about the same time that the Hutchinson River Parkway was built, in 1929. The two sections are linked via the Colonial Greenway along Mamaroneck Road and the Hutchinson River Pathway near Mamaroneck Avenue.

Traffic noise is audible in most of the southern section, but there are many parts of the northern section where it is not. Even with signs posting No Bikes, mountain bikers use the park, especially the southern part. Fortunately, their use has not damaged the woods roads; however, in the park's southern section, lots of trails connecting Loop #1 have been created. The northern section has a swimming pool and ball field off Mamaroneck Avenue and a golf course off Mamaroneck Road. The southern section has a picnic area.

Westchester County purchased what is now Saxon Woods Park in 1925. It was first managed as woodlands, but later, in 1931, the county opened an 18-hole golf course on the site. The area known as Saxton Forest in Colonial times was named for William Saxton, owner of a saw mill on the West Branch of the Mamaroneck River. Eventually, local usage changed the name to Saxon, which was the name adopted for the park.

NORTHERN SECTION

Except for the white trail, the trails in the northern section of Saxon Woods are not blazed. Two trails have signs, but only in one direction. There are 2.2 miles of unmarked trails and woods roads through the woodlands. An unmarked 0.8-mile trail skirts the golf course on the northwest side of the park and there is another 0.8 mile of narrow bike trails (not on the map).

White Trail   *Length: 3.0 miles Blaze: white*
On woods roads for its entire length, the white trail is a loop circling the wooded area in the park. Even though there are multiple access points to the white trail,

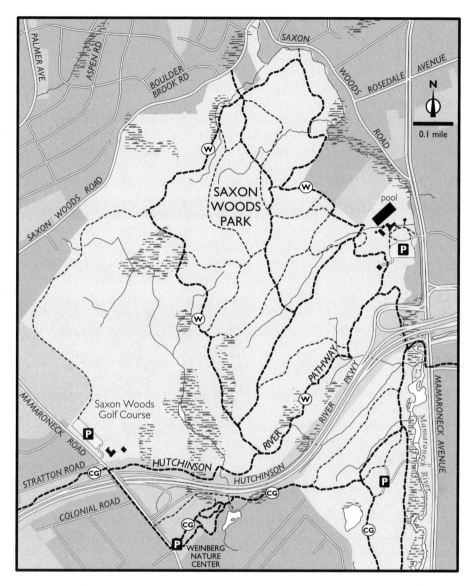

the one where it is easiest to find parking is the swimming pool parking lot off Mamaroneck Avenue. Most trails and woods roads passed by the white trail are to the left and cross the interior of the park.

In the swimming pool parking lot on the side opposite the entrance, a driveway leads to a park residence. Take the white trail as it crosses the driveway on a woods road and go counterclockwise. There are numerous short steep ascents and descents as the trail heads north. It enters the woods and heads uphill through a small ravine. Noise from the Hutch begins to decrease. The trail passes a rat's nest of unmarked woods roads looping back onto the white trail.

At a T junction at 0.2 mile, the white trail turns right to cross a stone bridge. To the left is a 0.6-mile woods road, which, when walked from the other direction, is marked at intersections with signs To Mamaroneck Avenue. The white trail continues at-grade along a short stone retaining wall. It crosses a stream at 0.3 mile at a T junction and turns onto a road built by the Civilian Conservation Corps. To the left, a woods road loops back to join the rat's nest of trails mentioned above. The white trail narrows down at 0.5 mile and descends along an eroded treadway. There is no noise from the Hutchinson River Parkway.

The trail turns right at the bottom of the descent. It then parallels a stone wall where there is a derelict boardwalk on adjacent private property. Houses are visible through the trees. At 0.7 mile, there is a noticeable change in the understory. Invasive vegetation crowds the trail in a section that at one time was cobbled. Several bike paths go off to the left. The trail reaches a Y junction and turns left. To the right, an unmarked trail leads 175 feet to Saxon Woods Road. After passing the other end of the triangle intersection at 1.0 mile, the white trail heads gradually uphill at a steady grade. It crosses the Saxon Woods Trail at 1.1 miles. To the right is an entrance from Saxon Woods Road (no parking).

The white trail passes two unmarked trails to the left (shown as one trail on the map); the first leads back to the Saxon Woods Trail and the other heads to a trail winding through the woods. The white trail passes through a seasonal wetland and goes uphill. At 1.3 miles, the trail climbs more steeply and levels off. It turns left at 1.5 miles, where the trail to the right continues west and south along the edge of the golf course, eventually reaching the clubhouse in 0.8 mile (parking).

After passing restrooms, the trail briefly skirts the edge of the golf course only to leave it at 1.6 miles. The trail goes uphill and passes an unmarked trail to the left at 1.7 miles

Large fungus

and two others in quick succession at 2.0 miles. The whine of high-speed traffic is audible and gradually becomes more pronounced. At 2.2 miles, the golf course is once again visible through trees to the right. After passing the Mamaroneck Avenue Trail to the left, the white trail reaches a T junction with the Hutchinson River Pathway at 2.3 miles and turns left to join it.

As it heads downhill, the white trail is on an eroded woods road, often 12 to 18 inches lower than the surrounding woodland. To the left at 2.7 miles are stone trestles. The trail heads uphill on a switchback and, at 2.9 miles, goes straight when the Hutchinson River Pathway turns right toward the Hutch. Heading downhill on a gravel path to meet the parking lot, the white trail closes the loop at the driveway of a park residence.

Hutchinson River Pathway   *Length: 1.2 miles*

Use the Hutchinson River Pathway to connect the two sections of Saxon Woods Park. It is 0.2 mile from a trail leading into Saxon Woods Park South to where the pathway joins the white trail. The pathway is co-aligned with the white trail for 0.6 mile and then parallels the Hutch before leaving the park at Mamaroneck Road. For a full description, see Hutchinson River Pathway, see page 351.

Mamaroneck Avenue Trail   *Length: 0.6 mile*
Signs pointing to Mamaroneck Avenue suggest that this otherwise unmarked trail has a name. It serves as an alternative to the white trail, and provides a shorter route with less road noise than the Hutchinson River Pathway. Beginning at the junction with the white trail, the Mamaroneck Avenue Trail heads northeast, passing an unmarked bike trail which heads right 0.3 mile to the white trail at the stone trestles. It passes one end of the Saxon Woods Trail at 0.3 mile. At a Y junction at 0.5 mile, the trail bears left, and immediately turns right when another trail merges from the right. It ends on the white trail at 0.6 mile just before a bridge.

Saxon Woods Trail   *Length: 0.7 mile*
Consider the Saxon Woods Trail to be a belt across the middle of the northern section of Saxon Woods Park. Signs pointing to Saxon Woods Road hint that this trail has a name; there are laminated signs with SWT. Most trails leading off the Saxon Woods Trail connect to the white trail; some form loops along its length.

Beginning at an entrance off Saxon Woods Road, the Saxon Woods Trail crosses the white trail and almost immediately passes a trail going to the left, which makes a figure eight with the Saxon Woods Trail. Heading straight ahead, the Saxon Woods Trail twice crosses the trail mentioned earlier. After passing the interconnected unmarked trails, at 0.6 mile the Saxon Woods Trail crosses an unmarked trail connecting to the white trail in both directions. The trail to the right is not as obvious as the one to the left. At 0.7 mile, the Saxon Woods Trail ends at a T junction with the Mamaroneck Avenue Trail.

SOUTHERN SECTION
Massive rock outcroppings and towering trees grace the woods roads. Three ponds, roads, and the western branch of the Mamaroneck River provide natural barriers. In summer months, picnickers enjoy the southern section of Saxon Woods Park. Only the Colonial Greenway is blazed. Mountain bikes are not permitted in the park, but they heavily use the southern part because the terrain is more challenging. There is a mile of short connecting trails. The many bike tracks connecting the long sides of Loop #1 are not included in total miles.

Loop #1   *Length: 3.0 miles*
As the main trail in the southern section of Saxon Woods Park, Loop #1 has side trails leading to it and connecting trails crossing it. Going clockwise from where it intersects the entrance road, Loop #1 is on a wide gravel road. It passes large rocks and a rock outcropping. An unmarked trail enters from the right. At 0.4 mile, the trail reaches a Y junction with an unmarked woods road leading uphill past a utilities building to the other side of Loop #1.

The trail goes left on a stone bridge over a stream with flat rocks placed to define its course. The gravel ends, and the western branch of the Mamaroneck River is visible through trees. Following the river, the trail passes wetlands to the left at 0.8 mile and then goes through two massive rocks. Road noise from Mamaroneck Avenue has diminished. At a trail junction at 0.9 mile, go left. Straight ahead, the trail continues for 0.1 mile to connect with Loop #1.

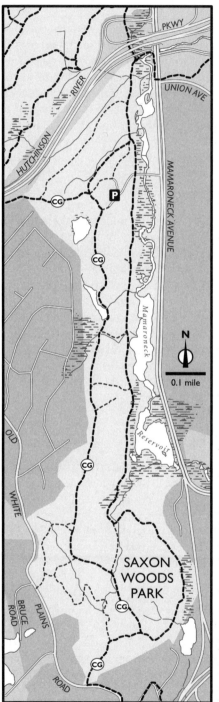

The trail heads uphill, gradually turns, and passes back yards. A vernal pool is to the right at 1.1 miles and another is to the left as the path narrows. Descending, Loop #1 is in woodland with dense understory. It passes a pond to the left at 1.3 miles. The surface of an impressive rock outcropping to the left shows scratches where mountain bikes have come down its face. Just past the rock face, the Colonial Greenway joins Loop #1 for the next 1.2 miles.

After crossing a stone bridge at 1.6 miles, Loop #1 passes to the right an unmarked woods road, the shortcut mentioned above. Loop #1 passes an unmarked trail and a stone building which was once restrooms. The side trail leads 0.2 mile out to Old White Plains Road with parking for two or three cars. At 2.0 mile, the treadway is at-grade on a slightly raised bed. Houses are visible to the left and the whine of I-95 is audible. At 2.2 miles, the trail goes down slab rock. It reaches an unmarked woods road to the right heading downhill to the stream that has been lined with rocks, mentioned earlier.

Heading uphill, Loop #1 follows the edge of a pond to the left. It turns away from the pond at 2.4 miles and again goes along slab rock. It reaches the picnic area at 2.7 miles only to turn away from it. At a Y junction, where the Colonial Greenway leaves to the left, Loop #1 turns right and, at a triangle intersection at 2.9 miles, it turns right again. To the left, it is 0.2 mile

Passing through

to the junction with the Hutchinson River Pathway. Loop #1 reaches the entrance road to close the loop.

Colonial Greenway   *Length: 2.1 miles*
From Old White Plains Road between #1015 and #1011, the Colonial Greenway heads into the woods on a footpath, in some places lined with logs. After reaching Loop #1 at 0.2 mile, it turns left to co-align with Loop #1 for 1.2 miles. Just past the picnic area restrooms, the Colonial Greenway turns left at a Y junction and leaves Loop #1. At the triangle intersection at 1.6 miles, a trail leaves to the right heading 0.4 mile to the Hutchinson River Pathway. On a gravel path paralleling the Hutch, the Colonial Greenway Trail fords a stream and crosses a bridge at 1.8 miles. It turns to the left onto a narrow path leading to Weinberg Nature Center. As it reaches the nature center parking lot, it turns right again, crosses an equestrian trail, goes along Mamaroneck Road and then the northbound entrance and exit ramps for the Hutchinson River Parkway. After crossing over the Hutch, the Colonial Greenway turns left to join the Hutchinson River Pathway at 2.3 miles, just beyond the parkway's southbound entrance ramp. For the next section, see Hutchinson River Pathway (Mamaroneck Road), pages 352-353.

CONNECTING TRAILS: Hutchinson River Pathway, Colonial Greenway

DRIVING: There are multiple entrances to Saxon Woods Park, all accessible from the Hutchinson River Parkway.
　　To reach the trail system in the northern section, take Exit 23N (Mamaroneck

Avenue) and head toward White Plains. Turn right at the end of the exit ramp and drive to the park entrance on the left. It is 0.1 mile from the end of the southbound exit ramp to the park entrance. Another access to the northern section of Saxon Woods Park is through Saxon Woods Golf Course. Take Exit 22 (Mamaroneck Road) and turn right. The golf course is to the right, at the first right turn after the southbound exit ramp.

For the southern section of Saxon Woods Park, take Exit 23S toward Mamaroneck and turn right at the end of the exit ramp. From the southbound exit ramp, it is 0.4 mile to the park entrance on the right, and from the northbound entrance ramp, 0.3 mile.

PUBLIC TRANSPORTATION: Beeline Bus #60 along Mamaroneck Avenue

For contact information, see Appendix, Westchester County Parks—Saxon Woods Park.

Weinberg Nature Center

Scarsdale • 0.6 mile, 11 acres

The Village of Scarsdale's nature center is a memorial to Wilhem Weinberg (1886-1957), financier, art collector, and philanthropist. Located on 11 acres at the site of his estate, the nature center opened in 1958. The 0.6-mile of unmarked trails wander through young forest, meadow, wetlands, and former gardens and along streams. These habitats provide the basis for nature programs. One trail is part of the Colonial Greenway.

DRIVING: From the Hutchinson River Parkway, take Exit 22 (Mamaroneck Road) and turn left. Weinberg Nature Center is to the left, just east of northbound entrance and exit ramps of the parkway.

PUBLIC TRANSPORTATION: Beeline Bus #60 along Mamaroneck Avenue

For contact information, see Appendix, Weinberg Nature Center.

Teatown Lake Reservation

Teatown • 13.3 miles, 834 acres

There is something interesting year-round at Teatown Lake Reservation. Buckets hanging on sugar maple trees announce that spring is on the way. Wildflowers bloom from April through September. Summer's heat is much more bearable with a walk in the cool woods. In fall, views over the lake or from the Back 40 Trail are a showcase of color. When Teatown Lake freezes and there is snow on the ground, cross-country skiing and snowshoeing opportunities abound, allowing you to see Teatown, as it is affectionately called, from a different perspective.

Teatown's habitats include a 33-acre lake, a scenic ravine, streams, hardwood swamps, mixed forests, vernal pools, meadows, and hemlock and laurel groves. This not-for-profit organization provides environmental educational opportunities for both children and adults. The 13.3 miles of trails spread in every direction from Teatown's Nature Center and make it possible to have long or short hikes. Not only do shortcut trails provide ways to shorten a hike, but they also connect trails to create longer hikes. The Cliffdale-Teatown Trail connects the trails at Cliffdale Farm with the trail system around Teatown Lake.

In 1913, Arthur S. Vernay built The Croft, a Tudor-style house sitting high on a hill overlooking Spring Valley Road. The stables, also Tudor-style, were built in 1920 and currently house the Nature Center. Gerard Swope, Sr., president of General Electric, began purchasing properties and reassembling parcels that originally were part of Van Cortlandt Manor, but subsequently had been divided and sold. He dammed Bailey Brook to create Teatown Lake. After his death in 1957, his heirs wished to donate the land. Teatown Lake Reservation was founded in 1963, when the Brooklyn Botanic Garden accepted stewardship of the property. The reservation was incorporated in 1971 and became an independent not-for-profit in 1987. Since the 1990s, Teatown has continued Swope's vision of protecting open space and in recent years, has assumed an additional leadership role of protecting natural resources in the region.

NATURE CENTER

Forming the hub of Teatown Lake Reservation is the Nature Center. It is where visitors naturally gravitate because it is the access point of the original trail network, including the trail around Teatown Lake. The Nature Center has a cider shed, a sugar house, and a small collection of animals. Hawks, eagles, owls, and turkey vultures, all of whom are unable to survive in the wild on their own, are

Teatown Lake Dam

housed outdoors. Inside the Nature Center are reptiles and amphibians. The self-guided 0.2-mile Spencer Nature Trail (red) is located near the Nature Center in the northwest corner of the parking lot and honors Ossining resident Sara Spencer. It is co-aligned with a portion of the Lakeside Trail.

Lakeside Trail   *Length: 1.6 miles Blaze: blue*

It is easy to see why the Lakeside Trail is the most popular trail at Teatown. It goes around Teatown Lake, affording hikers a pleasant walk in all seasons and leading to many other trails. Directions are given counterclockwise, but for variety, walk the trail in the opposite direction.

Access to the Lakeside Trail is from steps at the north side of the parking lot, through a gate behind the Nature Center, or from the front of the Nature Center. From either of the latter two access points, head toward a kiosk and go downhill. At the bottom of the hill, continue straight along the shore of the lake. The Lakeside Trail passes, in quick succession: Erica's Way leading to a bird blind, the trail to the Lakeside parking lot, a boathouse, and the Hilltop Shortcut Trail (black), which leads 0.1 mile up steps to the Hilltop Trail (orange). The Lakeside Trail reaches a Y junction and heads left to follow the lakeshore. The unmarked trail to the right is a wet weather route. At 0.3 mile, that unmarked trail reenters from the right. At a T junction, the Lakeside Trail turns left; the Hilltop Trail is to the right.

Descending to below the dam, the Lakeside Trail passes the Northwest Trail (yellow) to the right. Heading uphill, the Lakeside Trail reaches the end of the dam and turns left. Straight ahead, the Cliffdale-Teatown Trail (white) goes 1.1 miles to Cliffdale Farm. The Lakeside Trail passes a foundation and crosses a wet area on two sections of puncheon. It turns left at 0.6 mile, where the Lakeside Shortcut

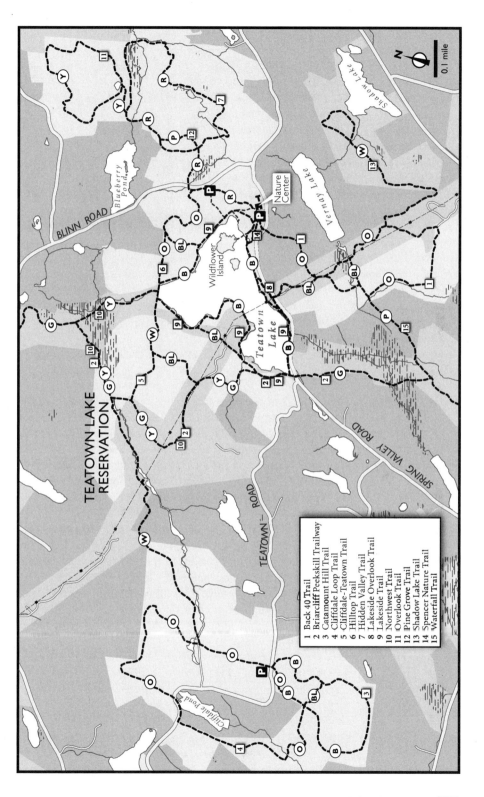

1 Back 40 Trail
2 Briarcliff Peekskill Trailway
3 Catamount Hill Trail
4 Cliffdale Loop Trail
5 Cliffdale–Teatown Trail
6 Hilltop Trail
7 Hidden Valley Trail
8 Lakeside Overlook Trail
9 Lakeside Trail
10 Northwest Trail
11 Overlook Trail
12 Pine Grove Trail
13 Shadow Lake Trail
14 Spencer Nature Trail
15 Waterfall Trail

TEATOWN LAKE
RESERVATION

Trail (black) heads straight, shortcutting 0.2 mile across a peninsula.

After crossing a long section of puncheon, the Lakeside Trail heads out onto a peninsula with open views across Teatown Lake. It passes under power lines at 0.7 mile, goes through a stand of fir trees, then moves away from the edge of the lake. At 0.9 mile, the other end of the Lakeside Shortcut Trail is to the right. After crossing a bridge and passing through a stone wall, the Lakeside Trail reaches a junction with the Northwest Trail and the Briarcliff Peekskill Trailway (green), which come in from the right. Together, the latter and the Lakeside Trail head downhill.

At 1.1 miles, the Briarcliff Peekskill Trailway goes straight to cross Spring Valley Road, while the Lakeside Trail turns left onto a 0.1-mile floating boardwalk on

Teatown Lake (pictured on the front cover). At the end of the boardwalk, the trail crosses a bridge and then a short access road to the lake. It heads uphill over and close to large rocks. At 1.4 miles, the 0.2-mile Lakeside Overlook Trail (pink) leaves to the right. It provides views over the lake and connects with a 0.2-mile black-blazed trail which leads to the Back 40 Trail (orange). The Lakeside Trail descends to lake level, passes the other end of the Lakeside Overlook Trail, and goes onto a wide boardwalk. It passes the gated entrance to Wildflower Island at 1.5 miles and is co-aligned with the Spencer Nature Trail (red). The stairs to the right lead to the parking lot at the Nature Center. The Lakeside Trail goes onto a boardwalk and closes the loop at the access trail which also leads back to the Nature Center.

Back 40 Trail   *Length: 1.3 miles Blaze: orange*

The trailhead for the Back 40 Trail is on the west side of the parking lot at the Nature Center; white signs with trail information are posted on trees. The trail heads uphill, almost immediately reaches a stone wall, turns left around the end, and crosses Spring Valley Road. Heading uphill, the trail passes a private residence and enters the woods. After emerging into an open area under a power line, the Back 40 Trail passes a black-blazed trail to the right which leads 0.2 mile to the Lakeside Overlook Trail (pink). The Back 40 Trail cuts diagonally left and passes an arrow and a directional sign. At 0.3 mile, turn right at another sign indicating the beginning of the loop. Turn counterclockwise to go around the loop, but go clockwise if you wish a shorter route to connect with the Shadow Lake Trail (white) in 0.3 mile.

The trail heads downhill and into the woods. After passing through a stone wall, the Back 40 Trail turns left, crosses a wetland on stepping stones, and reaches a boardwalk. At the end of the boardwalk at 0.5 mile, the trail turns right at a

T junction. To the left, a black-blazed trail leads 0.1 mile to the other side of the loop. At the next junction, the Back 40 Trail turns left. To the right, the Waterfall Trail connects in 0.3 mile to the Briarcliff Peekskill Trailway.

The Back 40 Trail ascends, initially with a short, steep section and then more gradually, all the while going on and off woods roads. It passes a stream in a gully to the right and then wiggles its way steadily uphill. Before reaching the top, the trail turns right just as it passes two large cement and rock pillars to the left. At a T junction with the Con Edison access road at 0.8 mile, the Back 40 Trail turns left and passes a third stone pillar.

After reaching the top of the rise, the Back 40 Trail briefly descends and then goes back up to cross under the power lines at 1.0 mile with a view to the north. It reenters the woods and turns left to descend steeply, passing the end of the Shadow Lake Trail to the right. Turning right, the Back 40 Trail leaves the wide treadway, continues to descend, and crosses under the power lines several times. It heads into the woods and to the right, passes Vernay Lake, more visible in leaf-off season. Descending steeply, it turns right onto a boardwalk at 1.2 miles. Straight ahead is the other end of the shortcut mentioned above. The Back 40 Trail continues onto a causeway, heads uphill, and goes under the power lines to close the loop at 1.3 miles. To return to the Nature Center, turn right.

Briarcliff Peekskill Trailway   *Length 1.4 miles Blaze: green*
A north-south linear corridor, the Briarcliff Peekskill Trailway is co-aligned with the Lakeside Trail for a short distance and with the Northwest Trail for most of its length in Teatown Lake Reservation. Because of the co-alignment, its mileage is not included in the miles of trails at Teatown. For a full description, see Briarcliff Peekskill Trailway, pages 340-346.

Hidden Valley Trail   *Length 1.5 miles Blaze: red*
Starting from behind the Nature Center, the Hidden Valley Trail passes the sugar house and the outdoor bird and animal exhibits. It heads towards Blinn Road and parallels it. The trees to the right were part of a living fence. Flat fence wire fastened to them has been there for so long that the trees have grown around it. After crossing the Lakeside parking lot, the Hidden Valley Trail passes the Hilltop Trail (orange) to the left. The trail turns right to cross Blinn Road at 0.2 mile and enter the woods. It crosses a wetland on a boardwalk with sensitive ferns growing along its edge and enters a field. At 0.3 mile, the trail reaches a junction which is the start of a loop. Straight ahead, the Pine Grove Trail (pink) connects in 0.1 mile with the Hidden Valley Trail to the left.

Turn right. The Hidden Valley Trail reenters the woods on a woods road and passes a sugar maple grove. In spring, buckets on the trees collect sap for maple syrup, to be made in the sugar house. The trail turns left off the woods road and goes uphill, passing through rock outcroppings. After leveling off, the trail passes a vernal pool at 0.7 mile and enters a laurel grove.

Leaving the laurel grove, the trail descends into Hidden Valley, first gradually, then more steeply. At the base of the descent, it begins to parallel a stream. The trail reaches a boardwalk crossing wetlands at 1.0 mile. At the end of the boardwalk, the trail turns left along a woods road. Although sections are built slightly above the wetlands, the trail is often muddy in wet weather. New York, Christmas, and cinnamon ferns line the path to the left, with rocks rising steeply to the right.

At 1.2 miles, the Overlook Trail (yellow) begins to the right. The Hidden Valley Trail continues ahead and soon bears left to cross a stream on a short bridge. After ascending quite steeply, the trail passes through a gap in a stone wall. It levels off and passes the Pine Grove Trail to the left. After turning right to cross another stone wall, the Hidden Valley Trail enters a meadow and then closes the loop at 1.5 miles. From here, it is a 0.3-mile walk back to the Nature Center.

Hilltop Trail   *Length: 0.4 mile Blaze: orange*

The Hilltop Trail provides an alternate route to the dam at Teatown Lake. From the Hidden Valley Trail (red) just beyond the Lakeside parking lot, the Hilltop Trail climbs through an open forest of mixed deciduous trees. At 0.2 mile, the trail parallels a stone wall and passes the Hilltop Shortcut (black), which leads 0.1 mile back to the boathouse. After descending, the Hilltop Trail ends at 0.4 mile at the Lakeside Trail (blue), just before the dam.

Northwest Trail   *Length: 1.2 miles Blaze: yellow*

The Northwest Trail traverses the northwestern portion of the property, passing through a variety of habitats: stream, wetland, edge environment, and forest. All but the first quarter-mile of the Northwest Trail is co-aligned with the Briarcliff Peekskill Trailway (green). The Northwest Trail starts on the Lakeside Trail (blue) just before the dam, 0.3 mile from the Nature Center parking lot. It follows a gravel path along a stream, turns left, and crosses a bridge. Ferns line the path as it parallels the stream. The Northwest Trail turns left away from the stream and goes into Griffin Swamp at 0.2 mile. A long, high bridge crosses wetlands with skunk cabbage, New York fern, and royal fern. At 0.3 mile, the trail turns left to join the Briarcliff Peekskill Trailway coming from straight ahead.

The two trails continue on a treadway along the edge of Griffin Swamp with its vast seasonal array of skunk cabbage. At 0.5 mile, the trails cross a bridge. They turn left at the next intersection as the Cliffdale-Teatown Trail (white) comes in from straight ahead. After crossing a boardwalk, the three trails head uphill to an intersection where the Cliffdale-Teatown Trail splits to the left and the Briarcliff Peekskill Trailway and Northwest Trail head right. The two trails continue their ascent of Teatown Hill through

DOGWOOD ANTHRACNOSE

Native dogwood populations have been decimated by dogwood anthracnose. The fungus causing this disease was probably introduced into the country in the mid-1970s. Its origin is unknown; however, it has yet to be found on any dogwood species outside the United States. The young leaves of infected trees are attacked in spring; the fungus then forms cankers throughout the structure of an entire tree. Affected trees die within 1-3 years; saplings may die in the same year they are infected. Dogwoods are not towering trees dominating forests; they are a shade-tolerant understory species found also in edge environments.

laurel along a woods road. They pass under power lines and ascend even more steeply to the utility service road which parallels the power lines. At the top of the climb, a short detour to the power line tower to the left offers a view with power lines marching off into the distance. Crossing under the power lines a second time and descending, the trails continue along the service road. They pass the Northwest Shortcut Trail leading 0.2 mile to the left to the Cliffdale-Teatown Trail. Along the power lines, multiflora rose bushes provide a habitat where rabbits can hide. In mid-May, dogwood trees bloom along the edge of the woods.

Hikers need to pay attention at 0.8 mile, where the trails cross under the power lines for the third time. The trails continue across the open area, leave the service road, and reenter the woods. If instead, you cross and re-cross the power lines, you will eventually reach the Lakeside Trail. Once in the woods, the two trails cross over the shoulder of a hill, descend, then turn right onto a woods road paralleling a stream. After crossing the stream, they reach a junction with the Lakeside Trail. The Northwest Trail ends and the Briarcliff Peekskill Trailway joins the Lakeside Trail. To the right, it is 0.6 mile back to the Nature Center parking lot via the Lakeside Trail.

Overlook Trail   *Length: 1.0 mile Blaze: yellow*

Like the Hidden Valley Trail, the Overlook Trail is one of the more strenuous trails at Teatown. From the Nature Center, it can be reached via the Hidden Valley Trail (red) at 1.2 miles if going counterclockwise, or at 0.6 mile if going clockwise. Immediately after leaving the Hidden Valley Trail, the Overlook Trail begins a steep ascent up a rock strewn slope. It reaches the start of a loop at the edge of a pond across from a house dating from the Revolutionary War. Turn right to go counterclockwise around the loop. The trail crosses a short bridge, climbs steeply, and passes to the right a side trail leading to a seasonal view over Hidden Valley. The trail continues to climb steeply with occasional dips.

Ascending on rock steps, the Overlook Trail reaches the viewless high point at 0.4 mile. After descending through evergreens, it goes down steps and turns left onto a woods road paralleling a stone wall. Gently ascending the shoulder of a knob, the trail reaches an open meadow with blueberry bushes at 0.6 mile. The trail continues to descend and then levels out as it passes behind homes. It turns left onto a private paved drive at 0.8 mile, turns right, leaves the road at the end of a stone wall, and winds its way downhill. After passing the pond mentioned above, it closes the loop at 1.0 mile.

Shadow Lake Trail   *Length: 0.9 mile Blaze: white*

The Shadow Lake Trail begins on the Back 40 Trail (orange) at 0.3 mile, clockwise from where the Back 40 splits to form a loop. After going uphill on switchbacks, the Shadow Lake Trail follows the edge of the power lines, but is in the woods. It goes through a stone wall and crosses a mat of tree roots which indicate just how shallow the soil is. At 0.2 mile, after passing through a stone wall, it reaches the Shadow Lake property and turns left. The trail is among tall trees with no understory. It goes through a stone wall at 0.5 mile and crosses a bridge over a creek. When the trail splits, turn right to follow the loop counterclockwise. At 0.7

mile, the Shadow Lake Trail reaches the dam of Shadow Lake with wildlife viewing opportunities. It turns left along a woods road and then shortly leaves the woods road to loop back to the bridge at 0.9 mile. The round trip from the Nature Center to Shadow Lake using the most direct route along the Back 40 Trail is 2.0 miles. The longer route is a 3.1-mile round trip.

Waterfall Trail *Length 0.3 mile Blaze: pink*
Beginning at the boardwalk on the Back 40 Trail (orange), the Waterfall Trail follows a woods road. At 0.2 mile, it crosses a wet area on puncheon and passes a small waterfall. It ends at 0.3 mile at the Briarcliff Peekskill Trailway (green).

CLIFFDALE FARM

Cliffdale Farm and its surrounding property was a bequest to Teatown in 1990 from Marion Rosenwald Ascoliti, a former trustee. A portion of the property is the site of Teatown's summer day camp, which focuses on nature and the outdoors.

Cliffdale-Teatown Trail *Length: 1.1 miles Blaze: white*
From the gate at the Cliffdale Farm parking on Teatown Road, follow the Cliffdale Loop Trail (orange) towards the building at the far end of the field. Just past the building, a red post marks the beginning of the Cliffdale-Teatown Trail, which goes right, while the Cliffdale Loop Trail goes straight.

Almost immediately, the Cliffdale-Teatown Trail leaves the woods road and descends on a path flanked by a stone wall to the right. After crossing a small bridge over a stream, the trail passes through extensive wetlands and then heads uphill. At

Along a boardwalk

Wetlands

Often called swamps, marshes, bogs, or fens, wetlands are ecosystems which must contain some or all of three components: water, wetland soils, wetland flora. Wetlands are found on every continent except Antarctica, from tundra to the tropics. The land must be wet often enough to create wetland soils which encourage the growth of specific water-loving plants. Even when the ground is not obviously wet, the presence of these soils and plants indicates that it is a wetland. Various state and local jurisdictions have their own specific requirements, generally based on U.S. Fish and Wildlife Service definitions.

Inland wetlands are commonly found where groundwater reaches the soil surface or where rainfall saturates the soil: on floodplains along rivers and streams, in depressions surrounded by dry land, along the margins of lakes and ponds, and in other low-lying areas. Roots of wetland plant species and the soils surrounding wetlands help clean the water by processing nutrients and filtering out suspended materials including pollutants. In addition, wetlands slow the rate of surface water flow, reduce the erosion force of running water, and absorb potentially damaging flood waters. Typical eastern wetland flora includes cattails, tussock sedges, ferns, reeds (phragmites), and purple loosestrife. Although not actually wetland indicators, frogs, turtles, and red-winged blackbirds are common inhabitants.

The impact of higher density development throughout the county has placed these ecosystems under stress. Fortunately, the public is becoming more aware of their valuable, irreplaceable function in our environment.

0.5 mile, it passes under a power line and crosses two bridges. At a T junction with an obscure woods road, the trail turns left shortly after reaching another wetland. Rock cliffs are to the left. Numerous bridges cross over streams and wet areas in Griffin Swamp. At 0.7 mile, the co-aligned Northwest Trail (yellow) and Briarcliff Peekskill Trailway (green) are straight ahead. All three trails turn right and cross a boardwalk. At a Y junction, they split, with the Cliffdale-Teatown Trail turning left and the two other trails going right.

At 0.9 mile, the Cliffdale-Teatown Trail passes the Northwest Shortcut Trail (black) and follows a stone wall. Turning left and heading uphill, the trail crosses several stone walls before descending. As the trail reaches the crest of the rise, Teatown Lake is visible to the right. The Cliffdale-Teatown Trail ends at the dam straight ahead. It is 0.5 mile back to the Nature Center along the Lakeside Trail.

Catamount Hill Trail
Length: 1.0 mile Blaze: blue

From the Cliffdale Farm parking area on Teatown Road, cross the road, go past a gate, and turn right. The co-aligned Catamount Hill Trail and the Cliffdale Loop Trail (orange) cross the field and enter the woods on a woods road. At 0.1 mile, the 0.1-mile Catamount Hill Shortcut (black) is to the left. As the trails enter the next field, they split; the Cliffdale Loop Trail heads diagonally across the field, while the Catamount Hill Trail goes staight to the edge of the field. After diagonally crossing the next field, it enters the woods, goes uphill, and passes a rock outcropping. The trail descends at 0.7 mile to reach the Catamount Hill Shortcut. It enters a field and at 1.0 mile closes the loop at the gate.

Cliffdale Loop Trail
Length: 1.6 miles Blaze: orange

From the Cliffdale Farm parking lot on Teatown Road, the Cliffdale Loop Trail heads towards the building at the far end of the field, passing it to the left to reach a woods road. The Cliffdale Loop Trail goes past a red post at the end of a stone wall, where the Cliffdale-Teatown Trail (white) bears to the right. The Cliffdale Loop Trail follows a woods road through a mixed forest, reaches a grassy area, and then exits along a barberry-lined path. At 0.3 mile, the trail reaches another grassy area, continues across it, and then turns left to follow a stone wall lined with maple trees. At 0.4 mile, it passes through a stone wall into another field and follows the right-hand edge.

Near the far end of the field, the Cliffdale Loop Trail passes to the right through another stone wall and reenters the woods. It reaches a T junction with a woods road and turns left just beyond a vernal pool. Going downhill, the trail reaches a gate at Teatown Road at 0.7 mile. The trail turns right to follow the road and then turns left at a gate onto a woods road. Turning left again onto another woods road, it climbs and passes a low rock outcropping. The treadway narrows and continues uphill, with a pond in view to the left. After reaching the top, the trail descends steeply, with wide steps and a handrail to aid the descent.

At 1.2 miles, the Cliffdale Loop Trail crosses a bridge over a wetland and joins a woods road. It crosses a stream on two bridges. At an intersection of two woods roads, it turns left and goes steeply uphill. Leveling off at 1.4 miles, the trail reaches an open field. Going diagonally across, it joins the Catamount Hill Trail (blue) at the far end of the field. The two trails reenter the woods along a woods road. As the trails curve to the right, Teatown Road is visible on the other side of a stone wall. Entering a field, the trails curve to the left and end at Teatown Road.

CONNECTING TRAIL & NEARBY PARK: Briarcliff Peekskill Trailway, John E. Hand Park

DRIVING: From the Taconic State Parkway, take the Route 134 Exit and turn west towards Ossining. Just past the southbound entrance ramp, turn right onto Grant Street, immediately passing a small house to the left. (Do NOT make the hard right turn onto Illington Road.) At a stop sign, turn right onto Spring Valley Road. Drive 0.6 mile to a large intersection and continue on Spring Valley Road. The Nature Center is 0.1 mile past the intersection. Parking is just beyond the buildings. Another large parking lot is on Blinn Road, the right-hand turn at the previously mentioned large intersection.

To reach Cliffdale Farm from the Nature Center parking lot, return to Blinn Road and turn left passing Lakeside parking. Continue 1.4 miles to Quaker Ridge Road. Turn left, and in 1.1 miles turn left again onto Teatown Road. Cliffdale Farm parking is 0.9 mile to the left.

PUBLIC TRANSPORTATION: None available

For contact information, see Appendix, Teatown Lake Reservation.

Ward Pound Ridge Reservation

Cross River • 41.9 miles, 4,700 acres

One visit to Ward Pound Ridge Reservation does not even begin to reveal all it has to offer. Visitors can picnic, camp, explore a stream, visit the Trailside Nature Museum and wildflower garden, and of course, depending on the season, walk, hike, snowshoe, or cross-country ski along the 41.9 miles of trails and woods roads. The Trailside Nature Museum features exhibits of birds, reptiles, mammals, insects, minerals, and Native American artifacts. Throughout the year, it offers weekly nature programs. Adjacent to the Trailside Nature Museum is the half-acre Luquer-Marble Memorial Garden, home to over 100 species of wildflowers. Art in the Park, in the reservation's administration building, is a changing exhibit of work by Westchester artists.

Dwarfing by far all other parks in Westchester County, Ward Pound Ridge Reservation is not just a large park. Its 4,700 acres are the core of a 22,000-acre biodiversity area that extends on all sides of the reservation. In 2001, it was designated a biodiversity reserve. Programs reflect this status, and environmental considerations take precedence over recreational use.

TRAILS

The named blazed trails are loops, making it easy for hikers to follow one color blaze for an entire hike. Aside from the Deer Hollow and Fox Hill trails, no trails cross Reservation Road. The trail descriptions are divided to reflect that segmentation. A sign at Michigan Road directing visitors to "hiking" is slightly misleading, because trails are accessible from all parking lots. Although the trails do not gain or lose much elevation, changes in elevation are noticeable. Lower elevations were once farmed and have more stone walls and wetland; slab rock, laurel, and rock outcroppings are indicative of slightly higher elevations

Trail descriptions reference the county-issued map available at the reservation entrance and kiosks. This color map is more detailed than the book's map and has trail junction numbers; however, only the map in this book includes Lewisboro Town Park trails.

In October 2006, Ward Pound Ridge Reservation began the enormous task of reblazing its trails. Trails leading into sensitive areas were closed and redundant trails eliminated. Volunteers from the New York-New Jersey Trail Conference systematically removed old blazes and nailed up metal tags. Trail junctions were

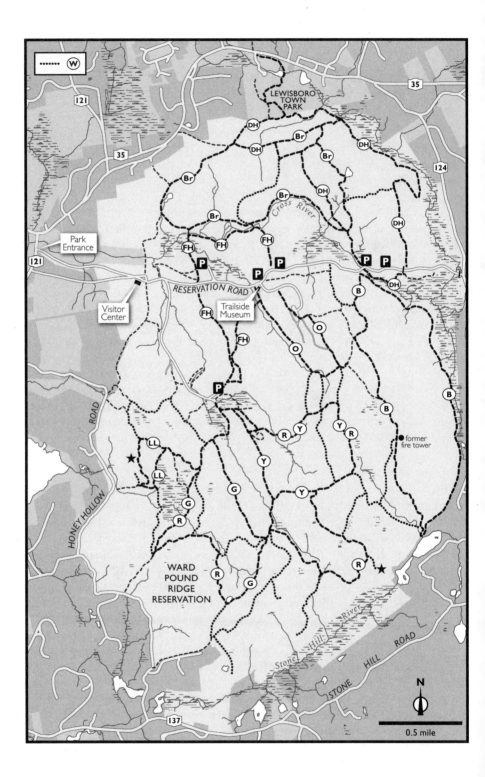

History of Ward Pound Ridge Reservation

In 1925, the county purchased a 796-acre tract of land, eventually combining it with fields and wood lots of more than 32 farms to create Pound Ridge Reservation. Over the years, additional land purchases increased the park's area to 4,700 acres. In 1926, there were more than 40 dwellings within park boundaries, mostly modest two-story frame buildings. Through neglect, fire, and the ravages of nature, they fell into disrepair. Because preservation of older buildings was not an accepted practice at that time, the county destroyed rather than repaired them. The eight remaining buildings have become the park office and residences for park employees.

Pound Ridge Reservation, as it was known prior to 1938, was the base for a unit of the Civilian Conservation Corps (CCC). Remains of their camp are along a white trail which is off the unmarked trail leading east from junction 23. Their work is evident throughout the park: the Trailside Museum, stone bridges, graded treadways, lean-tos, and stonework to direct water off woods roads. They also planted thousands of young trees, including Norway spruce, red pine, and white pine. These plantations are found throughout the park, easily recognized by the similarly sized trees marching in rows.

The park landscape is always changing. Pioneer vegetation had been allowed to reclaim farmland in some places, but in other areas of the park, efforts are made to keep the former farm fields open. They are mowed annually to prevent forest from encroaching and, at the same time, provide meadow habitat and edge environment for wildlife. Frequently mowed paths lead visitors through the grass. Farm fields left on their own often become overrun with invasive plants, but when compared with other parks, Ward Pound Ridge Reservation has relatively few invasives. In 1950, a big blow felled a quarter of the white pines in a section north of Reservation Road. A tornado touched down near the Cross River in 1992, rendering a trail impassable. A micro-burst in May 2007 felled white pines along the south side of the entrance road. That area is being reforested and is protected from deer by a high fence.

assigned numbers. Many previously unmarked trails were blazed white. Other unmarked trails were blazed and strung together to create two loops which cross Reservation Road. Coupled with the Westchester County Department of Planning map (available at locations throughout the reservation), the improved trail system vastly enhances the hiking experience in Ward Pound Ridge. For their efforts, the park and volunteers received an award from Westchester magazine: Best of Westchester 2008 Editor Pick for the Most Improved Hiking and Riding Trails.

Almost all trails are suitable for cross-country skiing. The trails are not groomed and hikers are asked to stay out of the ski tracks.

The roads bordering the reservation are narrow, twisty, and without shoulders. No parking is allowed along any of them and local police actively ticket offenders.

Boutonville Oak

NORTH OF RESERVATION ROAD

All picnic area parking lots along Reservation Road provide access to trails in the northern section of the reservation. Trails are suitable for cross-country skiing with short, steep sections as well as longer hills. The white trails connect the Brown Trail and the Deer Hollow Trail and make it possible to create interesting loops. Open meadows parallel Reservation Road east of the reservation entrance, providing an opportunity to walk in a field environment. The park mows 0.5 mile of paths which connect the Meadow Picnic Area past a stream and interconnecting ponds to the maintenance barns.

A portion of Reservation Road is closed to vehicular traffic, but is open for hikers, cyclists, and equestrians. Features along the 0.6-mile road include a large sugar maple, the Boutonville Oak (accessible from a short side trail), and a scenic spot by the bridge over the Waccabuc River. Reservation Road is handicapped accessible.

Brown Trail   *Length: 3.8 miles Blaze: brown on white*
Accessible from trailheads in all picnic area parking lots along Reservation Road, the Brown Trail is a loop. To reach it from the Meadow parking area, follow the Fox Hill Trail (FH) north for 0.1 mile. Continue straight where the Fox Hill Trail turns right. The Brown Trail is just over the bridge at junction 1. Turn right to follow

the Brown Trail counterclockwise. After entering a white pine plantation with needles cushioning the path, the Brown Trail parallels the Cross River. The trail crosses feeder streams as it goes gently up and down. At 0.3 mile, it crosses the corner of a stone wall and parallels it to the left. At 0.4 mile, the Brown Trail reaches junction 2, where, to the left, a white trail heads 0.6 mile uphill to connect to the Deer Hollow Trail at junction 4. To the right, a bridge leads to the Fox Hill Trail, which runs along the opposite side of the Cross River.

The Brown Trail goes uphill, follows the river, and turns away at 0.5 mile. Multiple short trails provide access to the water. At 0.7 mile, the trail has several routes through a seasonal wet

History of the Park's Name

The original name of Westchester's largest park was Pound Ridge Reservation. It was so named because there are many long ridges within the reservation where Native Americans were said to conduct hunting drives, forcing deer up against a long high ridge, then impounding them.

When the reservation and Trailside Nature Museum were formally dedicated in 1938, the name was changed to honor William L. Ward (1856-1933). A Republican politician, he worked to create an overall plan for recreation in Westchester and laid the groundwork for Westchester's extraordinary park system.

area. To the right, it passes a ford of the river, too deep and wide to cross on foot because of the lack of stepping stones. The trail passes rock outcroppings uphill and to the left. At 0.9 mile, the treadway widens as it goes through a seasonal wet area. It reaches a 165-foot boardwalk and then two short sections of boardwalk at 1.1 miles. The Deer Hollow Trail enters from the left at 1.2 miles to briefly join the Brown Trail. At junction 3, the Brown Trail turns left to head uphill, while the Deer Hollow Trail turns right to reach the Kimberly Bridge Picnic Area in 0.2 mile.

Heading uphill quite steeply, the Brown Trail crosses a stone wall and reaches the top of a rise near a small rock outcropping. At 1.4 miles at junction 7, a white trail to the right leads 0.3 mile to junction 8 and the Deer Hollow Trail. The Brown Trail contours uphill, continues through the open forest, then curves left as it ascends more steeply. At the top, the Brown Trail crosses a stone wall at 1.7 miles. Heading downhill, it crosses additional stone walls. At junction 41, a 0.1-mile white trail to the left leads to the Deer Hollow Trail at junction 42. The Brown Trail turns right, continues downhill, and at 2.0 miles reaches junction 6, where it turns left. To the right, a 0.1-mile white trail leads to the Deer Hollow Trail at junction 40.

At 2.3 miles at junction 43, the Deer Hollow Trail comes in from the left, joining the Brown Trail. After heading downhill, the co-aligned trails follow a causeway through wetlands and then climb steadily, passing acres of barberry on both sides of the trail. At 2.5 miles, the Brown Trail turns left at junction 5, while the Deer Hollow Trail turns right. The Brown Trail descends and, at junction 44, passes to the right a broad woods road leading 0.3 mile to Route 35 (no parking).

On a slightly raised level treadway, the Brown Trail passes extensive barberry bushes to the left at 3.2 miles and then heads uphill. At 3.4 miles at junction 45, an unmarked woods road to the right goes 0.2 mile to the edge of the property; adjacent landowners use the unmarked trail for equestrian access. The Brown Trail reaches junction 46 at 3.6 miles and turns left. To the right, a woods road heads out into meadows with mowed paths leading 0.5 mile past the maintenance barns to the reservation entrance. The Brown Trail descends on a woods road and crosses a stone wall. It enters a mixed evergreen grove and an area with dense undergrowth. After crossing another stone wall, it closes the loop at junction 1 at 3.8 miles.

Deer Hollow Trail
Length: 4.0 miles Blaze: DH

Beginning in the northwest corner of the parking lot for the Kimberly Bridge Picnic Area, the Deer Hollow Trail follows a woods road paralleling the Cross River. It enters the woods on a narrow path which soon becomes a woods road. At 0.2 mile, it reaches a Y intersection with the Brown Trail at junction 3. The Deer Hollow Trail turns left, joins the Brown Trail, goes uphill, and almost immediately turns right to leave it.

The Deer Hollow Trail continues uphill, with the treadway becoming more rugged as it proceeds through a forest with low understory. At 0.5 mile, the trail levels off. The forest opens up at 0.8 mile and the trail reaches junction 42, where it turns left. To the right, a white trail leads 0.1 mile to the Brown Trail. At junction 4, the Deer Hollow Trail turns right. To the left, a white trail leads 0.6 mile downhill to the Brown Trail.

Reaching junction 43 at 1.1 miles, the Deer Hollow trail turns left and joins the Brown Trail again. After heading downhill, the co-aligned trails follow a causeway through wetlands and climb steadily, passing acres of barberry on both sides of the trail. At 1.3 miles at junction 5, the Brown Trail turns left, while the Deer Hollow Trail turns right to head into Deer Hollow.

At 1.6 miles, the Deer Hollow Trail passes a blue trail to the left leading into the Lewisboro Nature Preserve. Under the power line, the trail ascends, descends,

Along the Deer Hollow Trail

and passes a second blue trail into the preserve. From the high point along the trail at 1.8 miles, the Deer Hollow Trail descends steeply and crosses an intermittent stream near a horse fence. Leveling off, it reaches junction 40 at 2.1 miles. The trail to the right leads 0.1 mile to the Brown Trail at junction 6.

From Junction 40, the Deer Hollow Trail descends on a woods road through New York, sensitive, and cinnamon ferns. It turns away from a stream, passes the first of many outcroppings to the right, and traverses several seasonal wet areas. At 2.5 miles, it crosses a stone wall and reaches the top of a rise. After descending steeply, it levels out and passes a rock outcropping. Going uphill at 2.7 miles, it passes several more rock outcroppings. It heads left onto a narrow path to avoid an eroded section of the woods road and then crosses that woods road to ascend steeply, avoiding another eroded section. The trail returns to the woods road and levels out.

The Deer Hollow Trail reaches junction 8 at 3.0 miles, where a 0.3-mile white trail to the right heads to the Brown Trail at junction 7. Passing through dense understory of scrub oak and blueberry, the Deer Hollow Trail goes downhill, then uphill at 3.4 miles, and descends steeply. It reaches Reservation Road at 3.6 miles and crosses the road diagonally to the right to reenter the woods at a maple tree. Now on a narrow path, the Deer Hollow Trail turns to parallel the road, just in sight of it. It crosses stone walls and reaches the Cross River at 3.8 miles. Turning right, the trail follows the stream and leaves it to head steeply uphill. It passes a lone picnic table, descends, and at 4.0 miles crosses Reservation Road to return to parking at the Kimberly Bridge Picnic Area.

SOUTH OF RESERVATION ROAD

Trailheads for trails south of Reservation Road are off Michigan Road, on Pell Hill, at Kimberly Bridge, and near Trailside Nature Museum. The many unnamed white-blazed trails connect the major trails and make it easy to shorten or lengthen hikes. Other white trails lead to features in the park.

Red Trail   *Length: 5.6 miles Blaze: red*
The primary trail in the southwestern portion of the reservation is the Red Trail, accessible from the Michigan Road parking area. Many trails lead off it, making it possible to have other loop hikes and explore the reservation in more depth. The Red Trail is also a cross-country ski trail and has a recommended direction of travel (counterclockwise). It is co-aligned with the Green Trail for the first 2.4 miles and with the Yellow Trail for the last 1.6 miles.

The Red Trail begins at the kiosk near the circle at the Michigan Road parking area and is co-aligned with the Green and Yellow trails. At junction 70, the Red Yellow Trail heads left, while the Red and Green trails go right. The two trails are on a built-up gravel road which, at 0.2 mile, crosses a stream, with wet areas on both sides of the trail. The Red-Green Trail heads uphill to junction 53, where to the left the Green Trail closes its loop. At 0.3 mile at junction 54, the Red-Green Trail passes, to the right, a white trail heading toward lean-to 8. To the right at junction 31, the Leatherman's Loop (LL) leads to Leatherman's Cave. At junction

25, the Red-Green Trail passes a white trail leading 0.4 mile south to junction 32. The Red-Green Trail is on a raised bed as it passes wetlands in Honey Hollow and, at 0.8 mile, crosses a stream flowing through a large culvert into Honey Hollow. Going gradually uphill, it reaches junction 30 at 1.1 miles and makes a sharp left turn. Ahead is a woods road leading downhill a short distance to a 0.4-mile woods road around Honey Hollow to junction 28 and the Leatherman's Loop (LL), and continuing 0.3 mile to Honey Hollow Road (no parking).

On a raised treadway created by cut-and-fill, the Red-Green Trail goes gradually uphill. It curves left, levels off, and reaches junction 32, where a white trail on the left goes 0.4 mile back to junction 25. It gradually approaches a stream and then veers away from it at 1.4 miles. After crossing the stream, the Red-Green Trail begins to climb significantly. At 1.6 miles, at junction 34, it passes a white trail to the left leading 0.4 mile to junction 35. The Red-Green Trail passes a rock outcropping to the right and maintains a steady grade on a cut-and-fill treadway. It passes through laurel to reach, at 1.8 miles, a hollow with a very large puddle, at times 80 feet long, which is possible to skirt.

The Red-Green Trail continues to climb and, at 1.9 miles, reaches junction 38. The woods road to the right leads to junction 39 and continues to Honey Hollow Road parallel to the power line. The Red-Green Trail bears left at junction 38 and climbs to the top of a rise, with a rock field on both sides of the trail at 2.0 miles. It goes through more laurel as it heads gradually downhill and crosses a stream at 2.2 miles. Passing a seasonal wet area to the right at 2.3 miles, the trail heads uphill. It reaches junction 35 at 2.4 miles, where the Red and Green trails separate; the Green Trail heads left to return to Michigan Road, while the Red Trail continues straight ahead.

In a short distance the Red Trail reaches junction 36, where a white trail leads straight ahead 0.2 mile to junction 22, and the Bear Rock Trail begins sharply to the right. Bearing right, the Red Trail goes uphill along a woods road through hay scented, royal, New York, and Christmas ferns. At junction 47 at 2.9 miles, the Castle Rock Trail leads 0.5 mile downhill through a scenic valley to end at Castle Rock, a large outcropping.

CIVILIAN CONSERVATION CORPS

Most CCC work was done without the aid of power tools. Nationwide, they:
- stocked more than one billion fish
- planted more than three billion trees
- established 8,192 parks
- treated more than 21 million acres for tree disease and pest control
- built 9,805 small reservoirs
- constructed 3,400 fire towers
- established 4,622 fish-rearing ponds
- built 651,087 miles of roadway
- constructed 28,087 miles of trails
- spent 6.5 million days fighting forest fires

Raven Rocks

Turning uphill, the Red Trail passes through laurel. It reaches junction 48 at 3.3 miles, where a white trail on the right goes 0.1 mile to Raven Rocks, a cliff with a view overlooking a valley, (one of two sweeping views in the park). After descending, the Red Trail continues through more laurel before again heading uphill. At 3.5 miles, it reaches junction 21, where a 0.3-mile white trail to the right leads to Indian Rock Shelter. The Red Trail goes downhill on a rocky tread only to flatten and descend again. At 4.0 miles, it reaches junction 33, where the Yellow Trail joins from the left. The Red Trail turns right and is co-aligned with the Yellow Trail for the remaining 1.6 miles to Michigan Road.

After passing lean-to 6 with an inviting grassy front lawn, the Red-Yellow Trail reaches junction 20. The white trail to the left leads 0.5 mile to junction 50 and provides an alternate route to the Red-Yellow Trail. At 4.2 miles, the Red-Yellow Trail reaches junction 19, where to the right the Indian Rock Shelter Trail (white) heads 0.6 mile to end at the Laurel Trail (blue) at junction 17. The Red-Yellow Trail continues through laurel and passes a rock outcropping to the left at 4.4 miles. Heading downhill on an eroded section of woods road and crossing wetlands, the trail turns and continues downhill. At 4.5 miles, squared-off boulders litter the area. The trail reaches junction 12 and turns left. Straight ahead is a white trail leading 0.2 mile to the Orange Trail at junction 13.

At 4.8 miles, the Red-Yellow Trail crosses a white trail at junction 50. To the left, it is 0.5 mile to junction 20, and to the right it is 0.2 mile to junction 51 on the Orange Trail. The Red-Yellow Trail reaches junction 11 at 4.9 miles, where another white trail heads 0.2 mile to the Orange Trail at junction 10. After passing through a grassy area and then heading uphill, the Red-Yellow Trail turns right where an unmarked woods road continues ahead, leading through the site of a former CCC camp toward junction 23. The Red-Yellow Trail goes gradually uphill; at the top of the rise at 5.4 miles, it is on sandy soil. It heads into and leaves a meadow and, at 5.6 miles, reaches junction 70, closing the loop.

Bear Rock Trail   *Length: 1.2 miles Blaze: white*

From junction 38, the Bear Rock Trail heads along a woods road to reach junction 39 at 0.2 mile. To the right, a 0.4-mile unmarked woods road heads downhill to Honey Hollow Road (no parking). Turning left, the Bear Rock Trail parallels the power line, almost immediately reaches the northern end of the Spy Rock Trail, and passes a power line maintenance road. Heading uphill, it goes by Bear Rock, which has an outline of a bear's head on its surface. After heading up a short

section of slab rock, the trail parallels the power line and then crosses under it. At junction 37 at 0.8 mile, a white trail to the right goes 0.2 mile to Dancing Rock, a large open flat rock with no view. Dancing Rock was so named because farm workers celebrated the end of the harvest by dancing on it.

Heading uphill on slab rock, the Bear Rock Trail passes through laurel and, at 1.0 mile, descends to end at the Red Trail. It is 225 feet uphill to the Red-Green split at junction 35 and 150 feet downhill to junction 36.

Bear Rock

Castle Rock Trail   *Length: 0.5 mile Blaze: white*

Beginning at junction 47 on the Red Trail, the Castle Rock Trail heads along a woods road and descends into a broad valley. It crosses a stream and passes through laurel. There is a feeling of remoteness as the trail continues downhill. After crossing a stream for the third time, it ascends to end at a power line below towering Castle Rock.

Fox Hill Trail   *Length: 2.2 miles Blaze: FH*

From junction 9 on the Orange Trail, the Fox Hill Trail crosses a breached dam and immediately heads uphill to cross a stone wall at 0.1 mile and turn left. It briefly enters a field, follows a stone wall, and turns left to reenter the forest. The trail ascends and crosses several stone walls; at 0.3 mile, it heads slightly downhill to descend steps as it crosses another stone wall. After crossing two more stone walls at 0.6 mile, it reaches a large intersection and turns right. At the next intersection, a white trail heads left to the upper Michigan Road parking area near lean-to 5. The Fox Hill Trail turns right onto a woods road, heads uphill, and at 0.9 mile, descends. At 1.2 miles, it goes by an open field to the left and a pine plantation to the right. It crosses Reservation Road at 1.3 miles.

After entering a field on a mowed path, the Fox Hill Trail follows the western edge of the Meadow Picnic Area parking lot. Passing between two parallel stone walls, the trail enters the woods and crosses a stream on two short bridges. Just before reaching the Cross River, it turns right to follow the shore on a wide woods road, at times closer than at others. On a high bank, the trail continues to follow the river, and then bypasses the Meadow Picnic Area. After crossing the corner of a stone wall, the trail parallels it. The trail passes a ford to the left at 1.9 miles and reaches a major junction where an unmarked trail leads left across a bridge over the river to the Brown Trail at junction 2. Turning right, the Fox Hill Trail heads uphill, passing a stone restroom built by the CCC. The woods road to the right leads 0.1 mile to lean-to 7. The Fox Hill Trail ends at the Bergfield Picnic Area at 2.2 miles.

Green Trail   *Length: 3.1 miles Blaze: green*

For the first 2.4 miles, the Green Trail is co-aligned with the Red Trail (for a description, refer to the entry for the Red Trail). The Green Trail is also a cross-country ski trail, but with a caveat. After it diverges from the Red Trail at junction 35, there is a portion which is, in skier's terms, Most Difficult. The Green Trail is described counterclockwise although hikers can walk the trail in either direction.

At junction 35, the Green Trail splits from the Red Trail and turns left. The trail goes through laurel and then a wooded section with no understory. At 2.7 miles, it reaches a height of land and heads downhill. It drops more steeply at 3.0 miles and closes the loop with the Red Trail at 3.1 miles.

Honey Hollow Trail   *Length: 0.4 mile Blaze: white*

Starting south from the Red-Green Trail at junction 30, this wide woods road almost immediately reaches a junction and turns sharply right to head north. Beginning at 0.1 mile and continuing for most of its length, the trail is along a raised treadway. It reaches the west side of Honey Hollow at 0.3 mile and crosses the outlet stream on a stone bridge to end at junction 28 with the Leatherman's Loop. To the left, it is 0.2 mile to Leatherman's Cave; to the right, it is 0.8 mile uphill to the Red-Green Trail.

Indian Rock Shelter Trail   *Length: 0.6 mile Blaze: white*

Beginning at junction 17 at the southernmost point on the Laurel Trail (blue), this white trail crosses a wet area on puncheon and heads slightly uphill. It passes through a wet area on higher ground with a stream to the right. As it ascends, the trail becomes steeper and rockier. It crosses a stream, and at junction 49, a 0.5-mile white trail heads uphill to junction 16 near the site of the fire tower. At junction 18 at 0.5 mile, a 0.3-mile white trail heads left to junction 21 on the Red Trail; a short side trail goes to the right to the Indian Rock Shelter. The trail passes a vernal pool to the left, crosses a bridge, and goes through a rocky area to avoid a wet area to the right. It passes a large outcropping and crosses another bridge. After rejoining the woods road, it ascends steeply to end at junction 19 on the Red-Yellow Trail.

Laurel Trail   *Length: 3.8 miles Blaze: blue*

The trailhead for the Laurel Trail, a loop in the southeast section of the park, is in a tiny picnic area southwest of Kimberly Bridge. Going clockwise around the loop, the first half of the Laurel Trail is along a CCC-built woods road. Its gentle ups and downs make it ideal for a leisurely stroll or cross-country skiing. In sharp contrast, the middle section which reaches the high point in the reservation is steep with some rock scrambles. The last part of the loop is a woods road coming down off the ridge.

Banks of ferns line the woods road, which at 0.1 mile, crosses the first of many small dips designed to channel run-off from the steep slopes to prevent its flowing onto the trail. At 0.7 mile, rock outcroppings loom high on the hillside. The woods road passes a balanced rock to the right at 0.9 mile and then parallels a stream and wetlands to the left beginning at 1.0 mile. To the right is a large talus field. At 1.5 miles, a woods road leads to the left to houses, and the Laurel Trail continues uphill leaving the wetlands behind. The built-up roadway is another example of the high quality of CCC work. The trail passes a rock field and a stream in wetlands to the left, and a talus field to the right. At 1.9 miles, the Laurel Trail leaves the woods road and turns right. To the left is a woods road into private property at Gilmore Pond; straight ahead, the woods road ends in 20 feet at a gate.

The character of the Laurel Trail changes here. Heading uphill steadily, it passes through a laurel grove and reaches junction 17 at 2.0 miles where a white trail to the left leads 0.6 mile to junction 19 on the Red-Yellow Trail. Curving gently around rock outcroppings, the trail passes a seasonal stream and goes through a root-filled seasonal wet area. After following a rocky creek bed, it ascends quite steeply. At 2.1 miles, it heads downhill and curves slightly to the left. The beauty of Ward Pound Ridge Reservation is apparent with tall ferns carpeting the forest floor and large rock outcroppings towering above. The trail resumes its steep ascent and enters a laurel grove at 2.3 miles. It goes through a seasonal wet area and crosses another wet area littered with uprooted trees and dead or dying hemlocks, in sharp contrast to the area just 0.2 mile back.

The Laurel Trail continues through a rock field with a high rock outcropping to the left and climbs a steep rock face almost straight up the fall line. Scrub oak and blueberry bushes are on the level top. To the left at junction 16, the Laurel Trail passes a white trail leading 0.5 mile downhill to junction 49. Now on a woods road, at 2.6 miles it reaches the former site of a fire tower, the highest point in the reservation (elevation 860 feet). The open area has a bench, a non-functioning pump, and the ruins of a stone cabin formerly used by the forest fire observer. The trail heads downhill, sometimes over slab rock and sometimes on gravel.

At junction 15 at 2.9 miles, the Laurel Trail heads right. To the left, a white trail leads 0.3 mile downhill to junctions 52 and 13 and the lean-tos and picnic area on Pell Hill. The Laurel Trail passes a vernal pool and goes downhill to reach junction 14 at 3.3 miles. At this four-way intersection, a 0.5-mile white trail heads straight and descends along a woods road to reach the Pell Hill Picnic Area in 0.5 mile. The white trail to the left goes 0.2 mile downhill to junctions 52 and 13. The Laurel Trail turns right onto a narrow treadway. At 3.4 miles, the trail goes through a wash gully, a dense laurel grove, and then another wash gully. It levels out and passes junction 56 where a white trail leads 0.7 mile back to the Trailside Nature Museum. After descending a short steep pitch and then going onto a woods road, Laurel Trail closes the loop at the picnic area.

Leatherman's Loop   *Length: 1.3 miles Blaze: LL*

A popular hiking destination, Leatherman's Cave, is on a side trail off Leatherman's Loop, which begins from junction 31 on the Red-Green Trail at a sign for Leatherman's Cave. After crossing a raised treadway, the Leatherman's Loop heads uphill. At 0.2 mile, it passes to the left a 0.3-mile woods road which leads past a glacial erratic and ends at the Red-Green Trail.

The loop begins at junction 26. To reach Leatherman's Cave via the shorter route, turn left. After descending steeply on a narrow footpath, the trail levels off and widens. It passes Honey Hollow Swamp to the left, goes up a rise, and descends to a convergence of stone walls. At 0.5 mile, it reaches junction 28 and turns right. To the left, a white trail goes 0.4 mile through Honey Hollow to intersect with a woods road just south of junction 30. Passing a foundation to the right, the trail parallels a stone wall and heads downhill. At junction 29, a 0.2-mile unmarked trail goes straight to Honey Hollow Road. Leatherman's Loop turns right. Leatherman's Cave is about 250 feet to the left and steeply uphill.

Continuing on Leatherman's Loop, turn right at the sign. The trail ascends a narrow treadway to an overlook. Leatherman's Loop passes under a large overhang at 0.7 mile, turns left away from a stone wall, and continues to climb steeply.

LEATHERMAN

No written material about Ward Pound Ridge Reservation would be complete without including the Leatherman. He first appeared in the area in 1863. Because he did not speak, little was known about him, adding to his mystique. Clad in a 60-pound suit made entirely of leather, he walked a 365-mile circuit through parts of Westchester and Fairfield counties. The Leatherman completed his circuit every 34 days on a route which did not vary, sometimes on roads, at other times bushwhacking cross-country.

The Leatherman regularly visited certain families, many of whom kept dishes for his use. He begged for food, but would not stop at a household which had once made him feel unwelcome. No reports exist of his doing work of any kind. However, he did establish small shelters which he kept supplied with firewood, boughs for a bed, and cooking utensils. If anyone disturbed his things, he refused to return to the place. Leatherman's Cave on reservation property is one of his many stopping places.

In 1889, the Leatherman died of cancer in his cave near Ossining. After his death, his identity was uncovered. Born in France, Jules Bourglay was the son of a woodcarver. He worked for a leather merchant and fell in love with his employer's daughter. Various reports have him ruining the business in an attempt to win her hand or being refused as a potential suitor. Whatever the reason, he left France for the United States, beginning his silent walk over the next 35 years.

The trail reaches an overlook to the left and then turns off the woods road to reach a second overlook with a view over the Cross River Reservoir (one of two unobstructed sweeping views in the park). After rejoining the woods road, the trail turns right and then makes two 90-degree turns in quick succession. At the bottom of a steep section at 0.8 mile, the trail curves left and at 1.0 mile, levels out. At junction 27, Leatherman's Loop turns right. A white trail heads left to reach junction 55 in 0.9 mile. The Leatherman's Loop follows a built-to-grade woods road, another of the many examples of CCC work. In the surrounding forest there is not understory. The trail closes the loop at 1.2 miles at junction 26. Straight ahead, it is 0.2 mile back to the Red-Green Trail.

Mill Pond Trail   *Length: 0.3 mile Blaze: white*
North of the Michigan Road parking area, the Mill Pond Trail leaves Michigan Road, crosses a bridge over the outlet of a dammed pond, and heads into the woods. Going downhill, it crosses a stream and then a bridge before arriving at the site where a saw mill once operated. A sign explains why the stream was dammed a distance away from the mill: more power was created and thus there could be more powerful saws as well as better control. The trail turns away from the mill site and heads uphill in sight of the stonework of the former mill race. The trail returns to Michigan Road at 0.3 mile.

Orange Trail   *Length: 1.6 miles Blaze: orange*
Beginning to the west of the Trailside Nature Museum at a farm gate, the Orange Trail is a loop that goes up to the Pell Hill parking area and then back down towards Reservation Road. Heading uphill on a woods road, the Orange Trail passes the trail to the Wildflower Garden, fenced to keep out deer. A path from the Trailside Museum merges from the left just before a boardwalk. At 0.1 mile, the Orange Trail passes an outdoor classroom to the right and the Fox Hill Trail (FH) at junction 9. The Orange Trail continues uphill at a constant grade, crosses a stream, and parallels another stream to the left. It enters a broad valley and heads onto a causeway over a wet area. At 0.6 mile, the trail passes a stream gauge to the right and crosses a bridge to reach junction 10. Straight ahead, a white trail goes 0.2 mile to junction 11 on the Red-Yellow Trail. The Orange Trail turns left and heads uphill.

At a Y junction at junction 51, the white trail to the right leads 0.2 mile to junction 50, also on the Red-Yellow Trail. The Orange Trail goes left, crosses a bridge, and passes stone walls of a former lean-to. Continuing uphill, it

A resident of the reservation

reaches lean-to 29 to the right and then junction 13. The Orange Trail bears left along the access road to the lean-tos; at 1.0 mile, it bears left again, continuing along the access road. To the right a white trail leads 0.4 mile uphill to the Laurel Trail (blue). The Orange Trail reaches a major junction of gravel roads and a kiosk at 1.2 miles.

From the kiosk, the trail heads towards the parking lot near the playground. It bears left toward lean-to 15, and at the front of the lean-to heads across open rock surface steeply downhill. At the bottom of the steep pitch, the trail goes left and enters a pine forest. Take care, because the other paths in this area can be confusing. The Orange Trail turns onto a woods road, turns right at a T junction with another woods road, and goes through a stone wall. At 1.5 mile, the trail passes through a white pine plantation, crosses a field, and ends at the paved road to Pell Hill at 1.6 miles. To return to the trailhead, walk downhill and turn left onto Reservation Road.

Spy Rock Trail *Length: 0.4 mile Blaze: white*
Beginning just past junction 39 on the Bear Rock Trail (white), the Spy Rock Trail goes through a stone wall and then along a path lined with logs. At a Y junction, the Spy Rock Trail goes left; a Bedford Riding Lanes Association (BRLA) woods road heads right only to loop back onto the Spy Rock Trail. At 0.4 mile, the trails reach Spy Rock, which once had a commanding view. Now trees obscure a view of houses. The BRLA trail continues for another 0.9 mile, descending through a scenic area to reach Route 137 near Honey Hollow Road (no parking).

Trailside Museum (Wheeler Trail) *Length: 0.7 mile Blaze: white*
From the parking lot for the Trailside Nature Museum, the Wheeler Trail heads across a field on a mowed path. It enters the woods at 0.1 mile and crosses two streams on bridges. After a third bridge, the trail turns right at 0.4 mile and heads uphill to end at junction 56 on the Laurel Trail.

Yellow Trail *Length: 2.6 miles Blaze: yellow*
Like the Green Trail, the Yellow Trail is co-aligned with the Red Trail for most of its length and can be used to make a shorter loop. As a cross-country ski trail, the Yellow Trail has a recommended direction of travel (counterclockwise). It is co-aligned with the Red Trail for the last 1.6 miles. The Yellow Trail begins at the kiosk near the circle at the Michigan Road parking area. At first, it is co-aligned with the Red-Green Trail. At junction 70, the Yellow Trail heads left, while the Red-Green Trail goes right. At 0.1 mile, at junction 24, the Yellow Trail begins its loop Then, at junction 24, an unmarked trail to the left leads to ruins of a CCC camp and continues to a junction with the Red-Yellow Trail in 0.2 mile.

Continuing uphill steadily, the Yellow Trail passes a sugar maple perched on a rock to the left. At 0.5 mile, it goes through a section of the forest where the trees are smaller and closer together. Passing a vernal pool to the left, the trail parallels a broken-down stone wall and reaches junction 22 at 0.7 mile. Straight ahead, an unmarked woods road leads 0.2 mile to the Red Trail at junction 36. Heading left at junction 22, the Yellow Trail goes slightly downhill and crosses several stone

A hike in the fall

walls before heading uphill again. It passes an unmarked woods road and reaches junction 33 at 1.0 mile where the Red Trail joins from the right. For the next 1.6 miles, the Yellow Trail is co-aligned with the Red Trail. (For a description of the return route to the Michigan Road parking area, see the entry for the Red Trail).

White Trail (Pell Hill Picnic Area to junction 14)

Length: 0.4 mile Blaze: white

For those camping in lean-tos 23-29, on Pell Hill, this white trail provides the shortest access to the former fire tower. It begins on the Orange Trail near lean-to 29 and passes a sign on a tree: To Fire Tower. Heading uphill, it first goes along the edge of a field, then enters the woods at a rock barrier at 0.1 mile, and continues uphill along a woods road through open forest. The white trail ends at the Laurel Trail (blue) at junction 14. The fire tower site on Pell Hill is 0.7 mile to the right.

White Trail (junction 16 to junction 49)   *Length: 0.5 mile Blaze: white*

From junction 16 near the site of the fire tower, the white trail descends through laurel on a narrow footpath. At 0.1 mile, it goes straight down the fall line and passes rocks which have tumbled from rock outcroppings. The trail goes through a ravine at 0.3 mile and drops steadily. It crosses a confluence of streams and ends at junction 49.

White Trail (junction 20 to junction 51)   *Length: 0.7 mile Blaze: white*

On a narrow track, this white trail heads north from junction 20. At 0.3 mile, it descends steeply and turns to parallel a stone wall. After crossing the Red-Yellow Trail at junction 50 at 0.5 mile, the white trail drifts downhill. It crosses a stone wall to end at junction 51 on the Orange Trail.

White Trail (junction 25 to junction 32) *Length: 0.4 mile Blaze: white*
Cutting off a V-shaped section of the Red-Green Trail, the white trail begins at junction 25 on the Red-Green Trail and heads south. It goes up steps and through laurel before descending. Shortly after crossing a bridge over a stream, it ends at the Red-Green Trail.

White Trail (junction 35 to junction 34) *Length: 0.4 mile Blaze: white*
Beginning near junction 35, where the Red and Green trails join, this narrow trail begins by heading south. It parallels a stream to the left and then curves right to leave the stream at 0.1 mile. Curving left, the trail crosses two mossy areas and a rise before heading downhill. It reaches a bridge at 0.4 mile, turns right onto a woods road, and ends at the Red-Green Trail.

White Trail (junction 54 to junction 27) *Length: 0.9 mile Blaze: white*
From the Red Trail at junction 54, this white trail leads uphill toward lean-to 8. At 0.2 mile, it passes on the right a 0.2-mile unmarked trail leading to the Michigan Road parking area. When the white trail reaches junction 55, it turns left. To the right, it is 0.1 mile to lean-to 4. The white trail follows a woods road through an area with no understory and, at 0.7 mile, turns left to cross a bridge; straight ahead, a 0.1-mile unmarked trail leads to Old Schoolhouse Road. The white trail turns left again onto a woods road where, to the right, a 0.2-mile unmarked trail leads to Honey Hollow Road (no parking). After heading uphill, the white trail ends on the Leatherman's Loop at junction 27. Ahead, the Leatherman's Loop returns to the Red Trail; to the right, it leads to Leatherman's Shelter.

UNMARKED TRAILS

There are three unmarked trails at Ward Pound Ridge Reservation which are of interest to hikers. Other unmarked trails lead out to Honey Hollow Road (no parking) or are along the meadows parallel to Reservation Road.

Boone Trail *Length: 1.2 miles*
Named in memory of Clinton Boone, a descendant of Daniel Boone and a 27-year resident of the area, this trail has numbered posts but is not otherwise blazed. A booklet describing the features of interest at the numbered posts is available at the reservation office, at a box near the kiosk at Michigan Road, and at the Trailside Nature Museum. The Boone Trail begins at the kiosk at the Michigan Road parking area and at first is co-aligned with the Red-Green Trail. At 0.3 mile at junction 54, the Boone Trail turns right and follows a white trail. Heading uphill, it passes lean-to 8 to the left at 0.4 mile and then heads downhill. To the right at 0.5 mile, a 0.1-mile unmarked trail to the right leads back to the parking area on Michigan Road. At 0.7 mile, the Boone Trail turns right at junction 55. Heading downhill

Property deeds for large tracts of land in the early part of the eighteenth century often included an allowance for roads. This meant that five acres were to be set aside for every 100 acres of land. Old maps show a network of woods roads; some of these were originally designed as paths for oxen to transport logs by wagon or cart from wood lots. County and CCC attempts at improving them for use as fire roads were limited. In many places, the roads continue to be rugged and inhospitable to vehicles, particularly at higher elevations. In addition, steep slopes and rocky terrain discourage east-west travel. This network of woods roads has become the basis for the trail system in Ward Pound Ridge Reservation.

gradually, the Boone Trail passes lean-to 4. Just where the pavement begins, it turns right into the woods and reaches Michigan Road at 0.9 mile. Turning right, it follows Michigan Road to the parking area circle.

Junction 39 to Honey Hollow Road   *Length: 0.4 mile*
From junction 39 heading downhill, this woods road is lined with dogwood trees, a habitat attractive to birds adapted to living in edge environments. The woods road goes between stone walls, which parallel the power line. At 0.3 mile, it turns away from the power line and drops below the grade of the stone wall supporting Spring House Road. It ends at Honey Hollow Road (no parking).

Old Schoolhouse Road to Honey Hollow Road   *Length: 0.7 mile*
From near the entrance booth, Schoolhouse Road heads south, uphill past a gate, and passes a cemetery to the left. After going by an open field, at 0.2 mile it reaches a sunken road leading left 0.1 mile out to Michigan Road. Continuing uphill along the property boundary, it goes over the top of a rise and parallels a stone wall. It passes a Christmas tree plantation at 0.4 mile and a horse field at 0.5 mile. A gravel driveway to the right leads into private property. Continuing along the gravel road, the trail reaches a second gate. Just beyond the gate, a trail heads left to connect with a 0.4-mile white trail to the Boone Trail. Schoolhouse Road ends at Honey Hollow Road (no parking).

CONNECTING PARK & TRAILS: Lewisboro Nature Preserve, Lewisboro Horsemen's Association trails, Bedford Riding Lanes Association trails

DRIVING: From I-684, take Exit 6 (Route 35) and turn east. Go 3.8 miles and turn right onto Route 121. It is 0.1 mile to the reservation entrance. An entrance fee is charged during the week in season and on weekends year-round. Westchester County residents can register for a card which reduces the fee.

PUBLIC TRANSPORTATION: None available

For contact information, see Appendix, Westchester County Parks—Ward Pound Ridge Reservation.

Lewisboro Town Park & Lewisboro Nature Preserve

Cross River • 0.9 mile, 68 acres

A small white sign along busy Route 35 indicates the entrance to Lewisboro Town Park. But it is also the entrance to Lewisboro Nature Preserve, wedged between the town park and Ward Pound Ridge Reservation. There is no visible boundary between the two town entities.

In Lewisboro Town Park, there are marked and unmarked trails. The unmarked trails are uphill from the upper parking lot behind the ball field; they were ski trails when the park had a ski tow. The blue trails connect to Ward Pound Ridge Reservation and thus increase walking opportunities. One section of the blue trail is also an equestrian trail, part of the Lewisboro Horsemen's Association (LHA) trail system. Red LHA tags are at major intersections.

Blue Trail   *Length: 0.3 mile Blaze: blue*
From the south side of the upper parking lot behind the baseball diamond, the blue trail goes uphill on a former ski trail. It reaches a Y junction and heads left only to have the right branch join at 0.1 mile. An unmarked trail goes steeply uphill and the blue trail goes left. It passes the blue-red trail on the left. At 0.2 mile, the blue trail goes right, while the blue-red trail continues straight. Crossing under the power line, the blue trail ends at the Deer Hollow Trail (DH) in Ward Pound Ridge Reservation. To the right, it is 0.3 mile along the Deer Hollow Trail to the Brown Trail at intersection 5. To the left, it is 0.1 mile to the blue-red trail.

Blue-Red Trail   *Length: 0.6 mile Blaze: blue-red*
From Deer Hollow Trail (DH) in Ward Pound Ridge Reservation, the blue-red trail heads under power lines and reenters the woods. At 0.1 mile, it reaches a T junction at a woods road and turns left. To the right, it is 150 feet to a camping area (permit only) with tent platforms and picnic tables. After leaving the woods road at 0.2 mile, the blue-red trail heads downhill. The trail goes behind tennis courts and circles around to the service road. It turns right at 0.4 mile and crosses a bridge by a pond where an unmarked trail heads around the pond to the left. The red-blue trail passes an outdoor craft center housed in a lean-to and turns left, paralleling Route 35. It turns toward the road and then turns left to parallel it once more, finally ending at the road at 0.6 mile. The LHA trail into Old Field Preserve is across the road from the entrance to town facilities.

CONNECTING PARKS: Ward Pound Ridge Reservation, Old Field Preserve

DRIVING: From I-684, take Exit 6 (Route 35) and turn east onto Route 35. Drive 5.7 miles to the park entrance.

PUBLIC TRANSPORTATION: None available

For contact information, see Appendix, Lewisboro.

North County Trailway

SECTION VII

LINEAR CORRIDORS

- ◆ Offer one-way walks with return via public transportation
- ◆ Provide a wide range of distances to walk
- ◆ Are corridors for wildlife
- ◆ Highlight the ecological, economic, and social diversity of the county

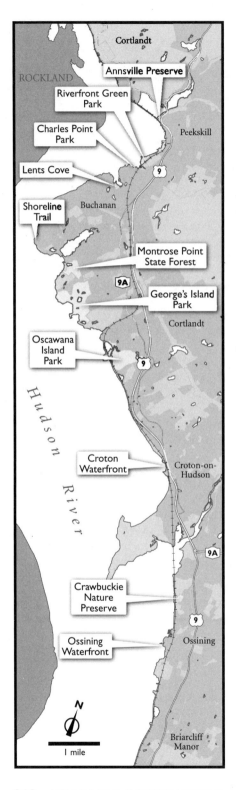

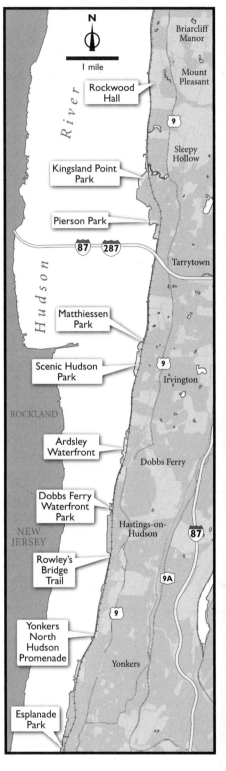

Along the River

Cortlandt to Yonkers • 13 miles

Like small beads spread along a necklace, the tiny parks and preserves along the Hudson River provide many places for short walks. Although each might not be considered a hiking destination in itself, they all are, nevertheless, areas to walk and enjoy views of the river and access to it. Grouped together as one section, an apt description of the parks is the title of the song *Down by the River Side*.

Parks with more than one mile of trail are cross-referenced and listed in their respective sections. However, when several small parks are adjacent and it is not obvious where jurisdictions start and end, they are described as a unit.

In 1989, the Hudson River Access Forum published *Between the Railroad and the River*, a study which described sites, evaluated potential uses, and made recommendations. By 2009, the river access situation in Westchester County has definitely improved. The Village of Irvington, for example, has enhanced its waterfront by transforming a portion of an industrial area into a park and adaptively reusing old buildings.

Westchester County, for its portion of the Hudson River Valley Greenway Trail, published a plan, *Hudson RiverWalk,* in 2003. To review it online, go to www.westchestergov.com/planning and search for RiverWalk. Much of the route is in the planning phase and subject to change. Where the route already exists, it is described with mileage included.

The Metro-North Hudson Line for most of its length is close to the river in Westchester. Using the train is a convenient way to avoid needing two cars for a shuttle. Parking at train stations is free on weekends and holidays except at the Croton-Harmon Station.

Camp Smith Trail
See Day Trippers, page 205

Annsville Creek Paddle Sports Center to Annsville Preserve

Peekskill • 0.9 mile, 2.7 and 9.7 acres

Cooperation between two municipalities and two state agencies has resulted in a trail that connects two parks: Annsville Creek Paddlesport Center and Annsville Preserve. Now a part of Hudson Highlands State Park, the Paddlesport Center was a New York State Department of Transportation equipment yard. A 0.2-mile gravel path circles the property. After heading out onto busy Route 6/202, walkers reach

Gate to Annsville Preserve

a cantilevered pedestrian walkway along Annsville Bridge at 0.4 mile. At the end of the bridge, a sidewalk heads uphill to the right leading to a path which, at 0.6 mile, heads downhill into Annsville Preserve, a City of Peekskill park. There is a paved path at the preserve and a dirt path along the creek. Continue south along the road parallel to the tracks, protected by a chainlink fence, to reach a gate at 0.9 mile and several parking spots. The gate is locked at night and unlocked at about 7:30 am. The Peekskill Station and Riverfront Green are a 0.6-mile walk along Pemart Avenue, whose name changes first to Water Street and then to South Water Street.

DRIVING: To reach the Paddlesport Center from Route 9, go to the Annsville Circle and take the Route 6/202 Exit for Bear Mountain Bridge and Camp Smith. The entrance to the Paddlesport Center is almost immediately to the left.

To reach Annsville Preserve directly from Route 9, take the Route 6/202 Exit and turn right onto Main Street heading downhill toward the river. Turn right onto Pemart Avenue, which goes through a commercial area. Parking is at the end of the road.

PUBLIC TRANSPORTATION: Metro-North Hudson Line Peekskill Station. Walk along South Water Street, which becomes Water Street, and then is Pemart Avenue. Continue through the commercial area to end at a gate. The distance from train station to trailhead is 0.6 mile.

For contact information, see Appendix, Peekskill.

Peekskill Riverfront Green Park

Peekskill • 0.7 mile, 23.9 acres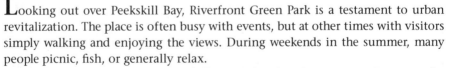

Looking out over Peekskill Bay, Riverfront Green Park is a testament to urban revitalization. The place is often busy with events, but at other times with visitors simply walking and enjoying the views. During weekends in the summer, many people picnic, fish, or generally relax.

Although there are no paths, following the shoreline is easy. Begin at the northern part of the park near two bridges connecting to an undeveloped Scenic Hudson property. Walk toward the river, turn left, and follow the shore. Take the sidewalk leading from a cement pad at the edge of the river. When the sidewalk meets another sidewalk, turn right and head toward a kiosk with information about the Hudson River Estuary. Continue toward the boat launch at 0.3 mile. Go through the boat launch access road toward the station, turn right, and head south on the road paralleling the tracks.

Passing the high chainlink fence of Peekskill Yacht Club, the road continues, curving right at 0.5 mile, and then bearing left onto Bushey Way. Just beyond a stop sign, turn left onto a gravel road, a parking area for boat mooring permit holders. At a turnaround, a path leads through a rock barrier to end at 0.7 mile. Unfortunately, the cove and the railroad tracks cut off access to Louisa Street.

DRIVING: From Route 9, take the Hudson Street Exit and head downhill to the river following signs to the railroad station. Cross the railroad tracks to enter the park.

PUBLIC TRANSPORTATION: Metro-North Hudson Line Peekskill Station

For contact information, see Appendix, Peekskill.

Charles Point Park

Peekskill • 0.2 mile, 3.8 acres

A paved path extends from the entrance of Charles Point Park to Fleichmann's Pier. Access along the pier gives walkers views upriver to Peekskill Bay and beyond to the Hudson Highlands.

DRIVING: From Route 9, take the Louisa Street Exit and head toward the river. At John Welch Boulevard, go straight into the park.

PUBLIC TRANSPORTATION: None available

For contact information, see Appendix, Peekskill.

Lents Cove

Buchanan • 0.3 mile, 9.3 acres

A boat launch and ball fields are the prominent features of Lents Cove. The Tropiano Trail honors Joseph Tropiano, a village trustee. It begins on the north side of the ball field along a wide wood chip path lined with Japanese wineberry bushes. It heads slightly uphill into the woods with views over Lents Cove toward a waste cogeneration plant. When the wood chips end, there is a fisherman's path leading an additional 0.1 mile to an outcropping, which overlooks the Hudson River across to Jones Point at the base of Dunderberg Mountain.

To the right of the entrance, a 0.9-mile walk along Broadway leads to Verplanck. The first 0.2 mile has a sidewalk on the east side, but for the last 0.7 mile, the road has no shoulder.

DRIVING: From Route 9, take the Louisa Street Exit and head toward the river. At John Welch Boulevard, turn left and go 0.5 mile. The entrance to Lents Cove is to the right, just past the traffic island.

PUBLIC TRANSPORTATION: None available

For contact information, see Appendix, Buchanan.

Shoreline Trail to Montrose Point State Forest

Verplanck • 2.6 miles

Beginning at the Buchanan/Verplanck line, the green-blazed Shoreline Trail heads south on Broadway in Verplanck. It reaches Hardie Street at 1.7 miles. Steamboat Dock (3.6 acres) is 0.1 mile to the right. It is 0.5 mile from the dock along Hardie Street/Riverview Avenue to the sidewalk on Kings Ferry Road across from the marina. Montrose Point State Forest is 0.4 mile further along Kings Ferry Road, which in some places has no sidewalk.

DRIVING: From Route 9, take the Louisa Street Exit and head toward the river. At John Welch Boulevard, turn left and continue 1.6 miles to where Broadway begins in Verplanck.

PUBLIC TRANSPORTATION: None available

For contact information, see Appendix, Cortlandt.

Montrose Point State Forest
See Pocket Parks, page 38

George's Island Park
See Afternoon Jaunts, page 124

Oscawana Island Park
See Morning Strolls, oage 86

Croton Waterfront to Ossining

Croton-on-Hudson • 3.8 miles, 25.1 acres

A recipe for success: Take two small linear parks along the Hudson River, add public access behind condominiums, add a road walk with access to a train station, and a safe bike/pedestrian route along a busy road connecting to another linear park. The end result is a convenient, accessible place to exercise and spend time outdoors. Make it part of RiverWalk and inform the public.

Stretching along the Hudson River, a paved path runs through Croton Landing

Park, Senesqua Park, Half Moon Bay, and Discovery Cove. Thanks to the developers of Half Moon Bay and Discovery Cove, to the Village of Croton, and to Metro-North, the portion through condominiums is now a pedestrian commuter route. It also provides public access to two parks through private property. The boundaries between the four parcels are real in terms of ownership and maintenance. However, to the user, it is a continuous path with views over the Hudson River and access to its shoreline.

As part of repairs to Route 9 near the Croton River, the New York State Department of Transportation built a separate pedestrian and cyclist path along the road. CrOssining, as it is called, is a combination of the names of the two communities it joins: Croton and Ossining. A barrier separates the high-speed traffic from pedestrians and cyclists.

From Croton Landing Park, a paved path heads north and wiggles along the edge of the river just back from the riprap. Because it dead ends at 0.3 mile, the route must be retraced. At the south end of the parking lot, the pathway parallels a road with the railroad on the opposite side. At 0.4 mile, it passes the entrance to the Croton Yacht Club and, at 0.5 mile, enters Senesqua Park (Croton residents only). At 0.7 mile, the trail passes a low tunnel (dated 1912) under the road and then heads uphill on a ramp. It crosses the entrance road and parallels the tracks at 0.9 mile. After passing under a bridge at 1.0 mile, the trail parallels the Metro-North Croton-Harmon Yards.

Between the rail yards and a fence, the trail passes through a gate behind the Discovery Cove condominiums, where gates in the fence allow residents access to the bikeway. The route behind Discovery Cove and along the emergency access road is also a pedestrian commuter route to the Croton-Harmon Station. The trail crosses the emergency entrance gate to Discovery Cove at 1.5 miles. The trail heads up along the back of a landfill, passing riprap drainage on both sides. At 1.9 miles, it reaches Croton Point Avenue. To the right is Croton Point Park. (See Day Trippers, page 213.)

View from CrOssining Bridge

From the end of the access road, turn left and walk facing traffic along Croton Point Avenue. Cross the road to the sidewalk and, at 2.1 miles, reach the bridge over the railroad tracks. Pass the entrance road to the Croton-Harmon Station at 2.3 miles and continue to the entrance ramp to southbound Route 9. Turn right onto the path alongside the entrance ramp where a bike path begins at 2.4 miles. Benches, interpretive signs, and a viewing platform are along the route. Once across the Croton River, the path passes a rock cut to the right. Numerous igneous inclusions undulate through the Fordham gneiss base, one of the oldest rocks in New York State. The bike path ends at 3.3 miles. It is 0.5 mile along the sidewalk to the Old Croton Aqueduct.

DRIVING: From Route 9, take the Route 9A/129 Exit. Turn west toward the river and then turn left toward Half Moon Bay. At a stop sign, turn right and take the ramp down to the parks. There is parking at the north end of Croton Landing Park, but none at the south end.

PUBLIC TRANSPORTATION: Metro-North Hudson Line Croton-Harmon Station

For contact information, see Appendix, Croton.

Crawbuckie Nature Preserve

Ossining • 0.3 mile, 12.1 acres

Situated on the upland side of Metro-North tracks, Crawbuckie Nature Preserve overlooks tidal marshes. The Village of Ossining purchased the property in 1970 from the federal government under an open space program. The land had been intended as an interchange of the proposed Hudson River Expressway (I-487), but in 1961 the plan was scrapped and I-684 in the eastern part of the county was built instead. (See www.nycroads.com/roads/croton.)

Almost immediately at the entrance, the trail reaches a Y junction. At the sign, follow Loop 1 to the right and head downhill to another Y junction at 0.1 mile. To the right, the trail steeply descends 200 feet to the edge of a tidal marsh and seasonal wash gully. To the left, the trail continues downhill to a trail junction. Straight ahead in another gully, the trail becomes impassable. Turning left, the trail continues uphill along a narrow ridge and closes the loop near the preserve entrance. The Old Croton Aqueduct is uphill, 0.5 mile from the entrance.

DRIVING: From Route 9 north of Ossining, turn west onto Beach Road. Northbound, the left turn is a block past Cedar Lane. Southbound, the turn is 0.5 mile south of Eagle Bay Condominiums. A gas station is on the corner of Beach Road. Follow Beach Road to parking in the cul-de-sac.

PUBLIC TRANSPORTATION: Metro-North Hudson Line Ossining Station; Beeline Bus #14 on Route 9. A 0.5-mile walk along Beach Road leads to the preserve.

For contact information, see Appendix, Ossining.

Ossining Waterfront

Ossining • 0.4 mile, 5.3 acres

Short walks are possible along Ossining's waterfront. Harbor Square is just beyond the Ossining Metro-North Station and is connected via a sidewalk to Engel Park, north of Sing Sing Correctional Facility. Engel Park has a short walking trail with signs telling about the prison.

The Joseph G. Caputo Community Center near the intersection of Broadway and North Highland Avenue houses the Ossining Heritage Area Visitor Center. This small museum provides information about Sing Sing and the Old Croton Aqueduct. The exhibits include a furnished cell and another cell that visitors may enter.

DRIVING: From Route 9, take Main Street and head downhill toward the river, following signs for the Ossining Station. Cross the bridge at the station and head south to the end of the parking lot.

PUBLIC TRANSPORTATION: Metro-North Hudson Line Ossining Station

For contact information, see Appendix, Ossining.

Rockwood Hall
See Afternoon Jaunts, page 167

Kingsland Point Park

Sleepy Hollow • 0.5 mile, 18.7 acres

Located in Sleepy Hollow, Kingsland Point Park was one of the first county parks in Westchester. The property was once home to Ambrose C. Kingsland (1804-1878), a little known New York City mayor (1851-1853). His summer estate became Philipse Manor Country Club and was to include an amusement park, which was never built. The county purchased the property in 1924.

The beach was popular at that time. With increased public awareness of pollution in the Hudson River, the beach was closed in 1976; swimming is still not permitted. Part of the 1930s-style stone, tile, and steel bathhouse is currently used as a maintenance building. South of the park is the site of the former General Motors plant, closed in 1996. The property is being redeveloped with a path connecting to the park. Aside from paved paths leading to views of the Tappan Zee and the bridge, there are no trails at Kingsland Point Park. From the parking lot, it is a 0.5-mile round trip walk along the retaining wall to the gate blocking the path to Tarrytown Lighthouse. Built in 1883, the lighthouse was taken out of service in 1961, decommissioned in 1965, and listed on the National Register of Historic Places in 1979.

DRIVING: From Route 9 in Tarrytown, head north into Sleepy Hollow. Just beyond the entrance to Philipsburg Manor, turn left onto Pierson Street, which becomes Bellwood. Turn left onto Palmer Avenue, following signs to the park. Cross over the railroad tracks and turn left. Southbound on Route 9, 1.3 miles from the westbound junction with Route 117, turn right onto Palmer Avenue. Follow signs to the park.

PUBLIC TRANSPORTATION: Metro-North Hudson Line Philipse Manor Station; Beeline Bus #13 along Route 9 near Sleepy Hollow Cemetery. It is about a 0.3-mile walk to the park entrance from either the train station or the bus stop.

For contact information, see Appendix, Westchester County Parks.

Pierson Park

Tarrytown • 0.3 mile, 6.1 acres

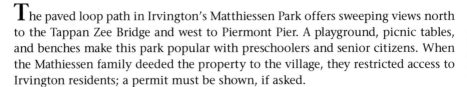

The benches along the retaining wall in Tarrytown's Pierson Park encourage everyone to enjoy views west across the Hudson River to Nyack. Aside from a short gravel section, the path is paved and handicapped accessible.

DRIVING: From Route 9, take Main Street toward the river. At the traffic light at the bottom of the street, drive up the ramp. Once at the top turn left, cross the bridge over the tracks, and turn left down the ramp on the other side. Follow signs to Pierson Park.

PUBLIC TRANSPORTATION: Metro-North Hudson Line Tarrytown Station

For contact information, see Appendix, Tarrytown.

Matthiessen Park

Irvington • 0.3 mile, 7 acres

The paved loop path in Irvington's Matthiessen Park offers sweeping views north to the Tappan Zee Bridge and west to Piermont Pier. A playground, picnic tables, and benches make this park popular with preschoolers and senior citizens. When the Mathiessen family deeded the property to the village, they restricted access to Irvington residents; a permit must be shown, if asked.

DRIVING: From Route 9, take Main Street downhill to the river. Turn right onto North Astor Street and then left to cross over the tracks. The park is to the right.

PUBLIC TRANSPORTATION: Metro-North Hudson Line Irvington Station; Beeline Bus #1W on Route 9 to Main Street and follow the driving directions above.

For contact information, see Appendix, Irvington.

Scenic Hudson Park

Irvington • 0.6 mile, 17.5 acres

Situated directly on the Hudson River, Scenic Hudson Park is part of a larger adaptive reuse and waterfront revitalization project in Irvington. The land on which it sits was originally part of the Dearman Farm. In 1849, with the arrival of the railroads along the Hudson River, small industries flourished. Lumberyards occupied the property beginning in 1853. From 1890 to 1940, parts of the river were filled in to accommodate the need for additional land. Scenic Hudson Land Trust saved this land from proposed residential development. Through a partnership of Scenic Hudson Land Trust, the Village of Irvington, Westchester County, and New York State, 12 acres of contaminated land were restored and the park was created. The short loop trail is handicapped accessible with benches for enjoying views of the Palisades, Hudson River, Manhattan skyline, and Tappan Zee Bridge.

DRIVING: From Route 9, take Main Street downhill to the river. Turn right onto North Astor Street and then left to cross the tracks. Turn left to reach the park.

PUBLIC TRANSPORTATION: Metro-North Hudson Line Irvington Station; Beeline Bus #1W on Route 9 to Main Street and follow the driving directions above.

For contact information, see Appendix, Irvington.

Tappan Zee Bridge from Scenic Hudson Park

Ardsley Waterfront

Ardsley-on-Hudson • 0.7 mile, 8.6 acres

An unmarked route leads from the Metro-North Hudson Line Ardsley-on-Hudson Station to riverfront access at the end of Landing Drive at The Landing condominiums. From the station, head south and uphill. A paved path to the right leads to Mercy College. Cross the basketball courts and parking lot and walk toward the athletic field. Follow the track to the southeast corner and turn left to go through the parking lot behind Mercy College buildings. Turn right at the emergency access gate at 0.3 mile and head downhill, bearing right at all intersections. At the end of Club House Drive, turn right onto the bridge over the railroad tracks. At the bottom of the steps on the river side is access to the river, where a seawall extends south along a phragmites marsh. From the seawall, there are views north to the Tappan Zee Bridge, south to the George Washington Bridge, and west to the Palisades.

DRIVING: From Route 9, follow signs to the Ardsley-on-Hudson Station and take West Ardsley Avenue toward the river. On weekends and holidays, parking is permitted without a permit. Parking for six hours or less is possible uphill from the station, in a lot near tennis courts.

PUBLIC TRANSPORTATION: Metro-North Hudson Line Ardsley Station

For contact information, see Appendix, Dobbs Ferry.

Dobbs Ferry Waterfront Park

Dobbs Ferry • 0.3 mile, 13.8 acres

From the north end of the park, it is possible to walk along the waterfront with views across to the Palisades. One portion has benches and is paved. Another path circles Willow Point and is either gravel or situated on a seawall. A restaurant at the south end of the park has views south along the river to the George Washington Bridge and Manhattan skyline and north to the Tappan Zee Bridge.

DRIVING: From Route 9, take Walnut Street toward the river and the Dobbs Ferry Station. Turn left onto High Street and cross the tracks. Turn right into the park. Free parking at the station is available on holidays and weekends. On weekdays with a permit, parking for recreational purposes is permitted for up to four hours.

PUBLIC TRANSPORTATION: Metro-North Hudson Line Dobbs Ferry Station

For contact information, see Appendix, Dobbs Ferry.

The Palisades

Rowley's Bridge Trail

Hastings-on-Hudson • 0.5 mile

Tucked between railroad tracks and a busy road in Hastings, Rowley's Bridge Trail and the Hubbard Trail Extension make use of an area overgrown with invasive vegetation that in turn has been overrun with other invasive species. Named for gentlemen farmers who, in 1846, settled in the Pinecrest area of Hastings, Rowley's Bridge allows Warburton Avenue to cross over Rowley's Brook. The 100-foot stone-arch masonry bridge was designed in 1892 by Samuel Cooper.

Beginning at the parking area, the Rowley's Bridge Trail heads south, passing a garden of the Plateau-Hastings Beautification Committee and then a sweeping view across the Hudson River to the Palisades. The wood chip trail reaches a bench at a second viewpoint. The trail splits at a Y junction to go left across Rowley's Brook and continue uphill, reaching Rowley's Bridge at 0.3 mile. To the right is the Hubbard Trail Extension, at 0.1 mile going uphill steeply on steps and then becoming considerably steeper. The hill has deep side cuts to accommodate the trail. Rope handrails are on both sides of the trail. At 0.2 mile, the trail reaches Warburton Avenue (no parking). To reach the Old Croton Aqueduct, head up the stone steps or take the Graham School service road.

DRIVING: From Route 9, follow the signs to the Hastings Station. Head south for 0.8 mile along Southside Avenue through an industrial area, which has an MTA police station. A parking area for four cars is just beyond the closed Zinsser Bridge.

PUBLIC TRANSPORTATION: Metro-North Hudson Line Hastings Station; Beeline Bus #1 along Warburton Avenue

For contact information, see Appendix, Hastings.

Yonkers North Hudson Promenade

Yonkers • 0.4 mile

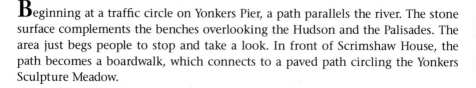

Beginning at Hudson Fulton Park with a statue dedicated to Henry Hudson and Robert Fulton, the Yonkers North Hudson Promenade heads south along Warburton Avenue to Otis Park. There are sweeping views across to the Palisades and two places to sit and enjoy them. Steps lead from Hudson Fulton Park down to the Metro-North Hudson Line Greystone Station.

DRIVING: From Route 9, just north of Untermyer Park, take Odell Avenue down to Warburton Avenue. Turn left. Hudson Fulton Park is directly across the street.

PUBLIC TRANSPORTATION: Metro-North Hudson Line Greystone Station; Beeline Bus #1 along Warburton Avenue

For contact information, see Appendix, Yonkers.

Esplanade Park

Yonkers • 0.3 mile, 2.5 acres

Beginning at a traffic circle on Yonkers Pier, a path parallels the river. The stone surface complements the benches overlooking the Hudson and the Palisades. The area just begs people to stop and take a look. In front of Scrimshaw House, the path becomes a boardwalk, which connects to a paved path circling the Yonkers Sculpture Meadow.

DRIVING: From Route 9, take Main Street and head west toward the river. Go through the underpass at the Metro-North Hudson Line Yonkers Station and turn south at the traffic circle. On-street parking is metered.

PUBLIC TRANSPORTATION: Metro-North Hudson Line Yonkers Station; Beeline Buses #6, 9, 25, 32, and 91 stop at the station.

For contact information, see Appendix, Yonkers.

Along the Sound

Pelham Manor to Rye • 7.4 miles

Along the ragged shoreline of Long Island Sound, numerous parks beckon walkers. Although crowds fill the beaches in summer, when the hoards disappear, it is time to watch the tide ebb and flow and hear the waves lap the shore. Parks with restrictions as to who may use them are noted; however, some restrictions are only seasonal. Marshlands Conservancy and Edith G. Read Sanctuary are chapters in Morning Strolls.

Pelham Manor Shore Park

Pelham Manor • 0.4 mile, 11 acres

Very close to, and almost in the Bronx, Pelham Manor Shore Park overlooks Long Island Sound. Its vast expanse of grass has a 0.4-mile path around its edge. Shore Road southbound has a bike lane, which becomes a bike path to Pelham Bay Park in the Bronx. The park is for Pelham Manor residents and a pass is required if asked.

DRIVING: From I-95, take Exit 15 and head south on Route 1. Turn left onto Pelhamdale Avenue (the first major crossroad) and follow it to Shore Road. Turn right onto Shore Road and then left into the park, just past the entrance to the New York Athletic Club.

PUBLIC TRANSPORTATION: Beeline Bus #45 along Shore Road

For contact information, see Appendix, Pelham Manor.

Glen Island Park

New Rochelle • 1.7 miles, 105 acres

Highly developed county-owned Glen Island Park attracts multitudes to its beach and picnic areas, but during off-season months, walkers, cyclists, and in-line skaters come for fresh air and sunshine. A walk around the perimeter of the park, primarily on the seawall, is 1.7 miles. Part of the route is handicapped accessible. In season, a Westchester County Parks Pass is required. There is an extra charge for beach use.

The park is on the site of a former amusement park operated by John H. Starin from 1881 to 1906 on a cluster of five islands, each of which had a theme. The castles, reminiscent of Germany's Rhineland, were constructed in the late

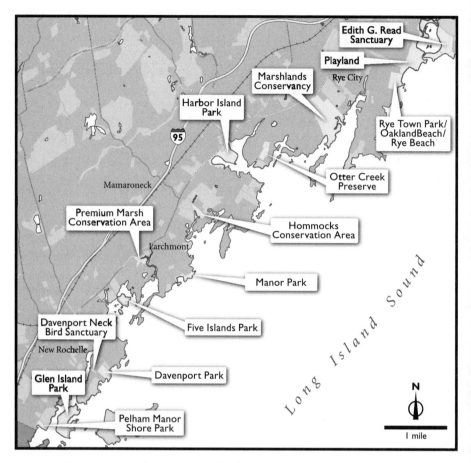

nineteenth century and were part of a beer garden and restaurant. Eventually, enough fill was brought in to connect the islands. A drawbridge between Glen Island Park and New Rochelle was built in 1929 after the park had been open for two years.

DRIVING: From I-95, take Exit 15 and turn north onto Route 1 (Boston Post Road). Turn right onto Weyman Avenue and follow it into the park.

PUBLIC TRANSPORTATION: Beeline Bus #45 along Pelham Road

For contact information, see Appendix, Westchester County Parks—Glen Island Park.

Davenport Park

New Rochelle • 0.5 mile, 20 acres

The sweeping view of Long Island Sound from Davenport Park is a good incentive to walk out to the shore. However, the sea wall protecting the grassy area from erosion prevents easy access to the water.

DRIVING: Take I-95 to Exit 15 and turn north onto Route 1 (Boston Post Road). Go 0.2 mile, turn right onto Weyman Avenue, and continue 0.7 mile. Turn left onto Pelham Road. Continue for 1.0 mile and turn right at Church Street, which becomes Davenport Avenue. Follow Davenport Avenue, turning right at a traffic light. It is 0.3 mile to the park on the left. A New Rochelle OMNICARD is required in-season.

PUBLIC TRANSPORTATION: Beeline Bus #45 along Pelham Road

For contact information, see Appendix, New Rochelle.

Davenport Neck Bird Sanctuary

New Rochelle • 0.2 mile, 2.4 acres

Located across the street from and south of the entrance to Davenport Park, Davenport Neck Bird Sanctuary offers a different view. A short trail through the woods loops around the property with a view out over New Rochelle Creek. Bring binoculars to better see some of the more than 50 bird species observed there.

DRIVING: Parking is available at Davenport Park. From the entrance to Davenport Park, walk diagonally across the street.

PUBLIC TRANSPORTATION: Beeline Bus #45 along Pelham Road

For contact information, see Appendix, New Rochelle.

Five Islands Park

New Rochelle • 0.6 mile, 18 acres

Connected by fill to the mainland, Oakwood Island is the largest island of Five Islands Park. Bridges connect Oakwood Island to Big and Little Harrison islands. The park has many amenities, but the paths along the shore will interest walkers the most. Several short paths go right down to the shoreline. There are benches for enjoying the scenery after a walk.

DRIVING: Take I-95 to Exit 15 and turn north onto Route 1 (Boston Post Road). It is approximately two miles to the corner of Lefevres Lane. Look for Salesian High School on the northeast corner, a better landmark than the small park sign. Follow Lefevres Lane past the sewage treatment plant to where the road ends in the park. A New Rochelle OMNICARD is required year-round.

PUBLIC TRANSPORTATION: Beeline Bus #60 along Boston Post Road

For contact information, see Appendix, New Rochelle.

Premium Marsh Conservation Area

Larchmont • 0.1 mile, 13 acres

Squeezed among houses, Premium Marsh Conservation Area has a trail to the edge of the marsh. It is possible to walk safely along the nearby narrow, twisty roads because vehicles move slowly. Parking close to the trail is difficult.

DRIVING: Take I-95 to Exit 15 and turn north onto Route 1 (Boston Post Road). It is approximately 2.4 miles farther to Dillon Road in Larchmont. Turn right onto Dillon Road and continue 0.2 mile to an unpaved road to the left, just before Pheasant Run.

PUBLIC TRANSPORTATION: None available

For contact information, see Appendix, Mamaroneck (Town).

Manor Park

Larchmont • 0.5 mile, 16 acres

Surrounded by stately Victorian houses originally built as summer homes and estates for the wealthy elite of New York City, Manor Park has views over Long Island Sound. In 1892, residents established Larchmont Manor Park Society to maintain, preserve, and protect the park, which is open to the public. A narrow paved path meanders along and above the shoreline. Benches and two gazebos encourage people to sit, read, or just enjoy views. Portions of the path are handicapped accessible.

Sunday in the park

DRIVING: From Route 1 (Boston Post Road) in Larchmont, head towards Long Island Sound on either Beach or Larchmont avenues; both roads deadend at the park. Parking is available on some streets, but not on weekends or legal holidays.

PUBLIC TRANSPORTATION: None available

For contact information, see Appendix, Larchmont Manor Society.

Hommocks Conservation Area

Mamaroneck • 0.3 mile, 7.6 acres

A tiny trail system goes through meadows, woodlands, and salt marsh at Hommocks Conservation Area. Sailors sighting the hillocks along the marshy shore named the area Hommocks. Salt grasses were harvested and used to thatch roofs, feed livestock, and fill mattresses. The trail starts at a fence at Hommocks Middle School's ball field. From the parking lot, a side trail leads to a bird observation deck with a view over the marsh and to the sewage overflow building in Flint Park. There are opportunities to walk to the shore, but wet feet are quite likely.

Because of his wife's ardent interest in conservation, Ralph Burger, a neighbor to the town-owned property and president of the Atlantic and Pacific Tea Company, deeded 3.6 acres and enlarged the conservation area.

DRIVING: From the junction of Route 1 (Boston Post Road) and Route 125 (Weaver Street) in Mamaroneck, head towards Hommocks Middle School on Hommocks Road. The parking lot is on the right side of Hommocks Road across from #510.

PUBLIC TRANSPORTATION: None available

For contact information, see Appendix, Mamaroneck (Town).

Harbor Island Park

Mamaroneck • 1.1 miles, 44.5 acres

Jutting out into Mamaroneck Harbor, Harbor Island Park offers a choice to walk either on an expanse of grass or on a seawall. A paved path goes along one section of the harbor and a well-trod path with swinging benches is along another. There is no access through the beach during the summer.

DRIVING: From northbound I-95, take Exit 18A and turn right onto Fenimore Road. Go 0.6 mile to Route 1 (Boston Post Road) and turn left. The park entrance is on the right. There is a parking fee when the beach is open.

From southbound I-95, take Exit 18A (Mamaroneck Avenue) and turn right onto Mamaroneck Avenue heading toward Long Island Sound and Route 1 (Boston Post Road). Harbor Island Park is at the intersection of Mamaroneck Avenue and Boston Post Road.

PUBLIC TRANSPORTATION: Metro-North New Haven Line Mamaroneck Station. Walk along Mamaroneck Avenue through the business district. Beeline Bus #60 on Palmer Avenue

For contact information, see Appendix, Mamaroneck (Town).

Otter Creek Preserve

Mamaroneck • 0.6 mile, 27 acres

Bring your binoculars to Otter Creek Preserve. This urban jewel has wildlife watching opportunities along its short loop trail through a tidal creek, marsh, and upland woodlands. More than 100 species of birds, as well as abundant terrestrial and marine life, make this area their home.

DRIVING: From northbound I-95, take Exit 18A (Fenimore Road). Turn right and head 0.6 mile to Route 1 (Boston Post Road). Turn left, go 1.1 miles, and turn right onto Taylor Lane. *Follow the road for 0.4 mile until the Private Entrance sign. Park on the right hand side of the road and walk approximately 300 feet to the preserve entrance.

Boardwalk in Otter Creek Preserve

From southbound I-95, take Exit 18A (Mamaroneck Avenue) and head toward the Mamaroneck Station. Continue past the station to Route 1(Boston Post Road). Turn left to head north on Route 1 for 0.8 mile and turn right onto Taylor Lane. Follow the directions from * above.

PUBLIC TRANSPORTATION: None available

For contact information, see Appendix, The Nature Conservancy.

Marshlands Conservancy
See Morning Strolls, page 74

Rye Town Park/Oakland Beach/Rye Beach

Rye • 0.3 mile, 36 acres

A walk through Rye Beach, Rye Town Park, and Oakland Beach is short, but when combined with a walk along the boardwalk at Playland, it is good exercise. The walks here are best done in off-season or early in the morning during summer months. Binoculars are a must during bird migration.

DRIVING: From the New England Thruway (I-95), take Exit 19 (Playland Parkway). Follow the parkway to Forest Road, just before the traffic circle at Playland, and turn right. Rye Town Park is to the left with the two beaches between it and the shoreline. Parking at Playland is available for a fee. No parking is permitted on neighboring streets from May 1 to October 1.

PUBLIC TRANSPORTATION: Three seasonal Beeline Buses stop at the bus terminal: #75-Rye Railroad Station; #91-New Rochelle, Mt. Vernon, Yonkers; #92-White Plains Express; #76-Portchester, Rye runs on a commuter schedule.

For contact information, see Appendix, Rye.

Playland

Rye • 0.7 mile, 121 acres

When the crowds leave Playland at the end of the season, the boardwalk is nearly empty and you can see the water lapping the beach. Serenity envelopes the area and welcomes those who love to walk close to the shore or along the boardwalk. With the change of seasons, neighbors once again visit their special place, enjoying the outdoors amid the Art Deco architecture. Playland is the only government-owned and operated amusement park in the country. It became a National Historic Landmark in 1987. From the end of the boardwalk, walk south to Rye Beach, Rye Town Park, and Oakland Beach. A paved path parallels the Playland Parkway and is part of the East Coast Greenway.

Along the boardwalk

DRIVING: From I-95 take Exit 19 (Playland Parkway). Follow the parkway directly into the park and around the traffic circle. A parking fee is charged from May through October.

PUBLIC TRANSPORTATION: Three seasonal Beeline Buses stop at the bus terminal: #75-Rye Railroad Station; #91-New Rochelle, Mt. Vernon, Yonkers; #92-White Plains Express; #76-Portchester, Rye runs on a commuter schedule.

For contact information, see Appendix, Westchester County Parks—Playland.

Edith G. Read Sanctuary
See Morning Strolls, see page 94

Briarcliff Peekskill Trailway

Ossining to Peekskill • 13.1 miles, 206 acres

The Briarcliff Peekskill Trailway wends its way through forest and wetland, under power lines, and past back yards, on a route that was purchased in 1929 to become a parkway connecting Briarcliff Manor with Peekskill. Only the section of the proposed parkway between Briarcliff and the Armory on Route 9A in Ossining was built. The remainder of the route became a footpath officially designated a trailway in 1977. County publications indicate that the trailway ends at Watch Hill Road, but on the ground, it is blazed and actually extends as far as the main parking lot in Blue Mountain Reservation.

THE TRAILWAY

Hikers are encouraged to stay on the trail at all times because the Briarcliff Peekskill Trailway is always close to private property. Even as it goes through deep woods, the trail borders homes when it crosses paved roads. Because the trailway is a linear footpath, hikers must retrace their steps, leave a car where they will end their hike, or rely on public transportation. The trailway either connects or is near five parks; thus, circuit hikes are possible. Trail descriptions are arranged in segments dictated primarily by major road crossings or access to parking.

Ryder Road to Spring Valley Road   *Length: 2.8 miles*
From the south trailhead on Ryder Road near Sunset Drive, the Briarcliff Peekskill Trailway is relatively straight as it heads north, mainly along woods roads. Unfortunately, for the first half-mile, it is never far from the road noise of Route 9A. This trail section is lightly used and often overgrown.

A stream runs to the west of the trail between the trailway and Route 9A. At 0.5 mile, the trail crosses the stream, goes through a stone wall, and heads away from Route 9A. At 1.1 miles, the trail crosses Grace Lane and passes a kennel with its resident chorus of barking dogs. After heading slightly uphill, the trail runs parallel to a stone wall to reach Route 134 at 1.8 miles. It now crosses a succession of streams and, at 2.0 miles, goes by a massive moss-covered rock face to the left. The trail follows a well-built woods road, leaves it at 2.3 miles, and then rejoins it. Passing through wetlands on a bridge, the trail crosses the outlet of a stream and reaches Spring Valley Road at 2.8 miles.

Waterfall

Spring Valley Road to Croton Gorge Park

Length: 2.7 miles

Beginning at Spring Valley Road, the Briarcliff Peekskill Trailway enters Teatown Lake Reservation and joins the Lakeside Trail (blue). A boardwalk to the right heads along Teatown Lake and back to parking at the Nature Center. At 0.3 mile, the trailway leaves the Lakeside Trail and joins the Northwest Trail (yellow) as it begins a short climb toward the power line. The trail crosses under power lines twice and, at 0.7 mile, heads steeply downhill.

The two trails run north along a generally straight woods road through laurel and hemlock. The Cliffdale-Teatown Trail (white) joins from the right and leaves to the left. The Briarcliff Peekskill Trailway now follows the western edge of Griffin Swamp, off and on boardwalks. At the north end of the swamp, the Northwest Trail turns right and the trailway continues straight. At 1.0 mile, the Briarcliff Peekskill Trailway jogs left along a stone wall to leave Teatown Reservation.

At Blinn Road, the trailway reaches the west side of a culvert at 1.4 miles. Parking and access to the trails at John E. Hand Park are across the road just east of the culvert. The trailway turns slightly left as it continues north. After crossing Blinn Road, it goes through a stone wall, and follows a brook. It reaches a Y junction at 1.6 miles and turns right. At the next trail junction, it turns left and, at 2.0 miles, enters a wetland. When it reaches the intersection of Quaker Ridge and Croton Dam roads, the trailway heads straight across and follows Croton Dam

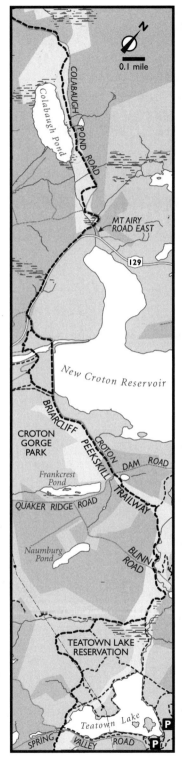

Road. A side trip onto the dam offers sweeping views from both sides. In the past, the trail utilized the road (sometimes also closed to pedestrians and bicycles) over the dam. Instead, just before reaching the dam at 2.5 miles, the trail turns left onto a gravel road, makes a right, and descends to a flat area below Croton Dam.

Croton Gorge Park to Watch Hill Road
Length: 4.7 miles

From the picnic area at the base of Croton Dam, the Briarcliff Peekskill Trailway crosses the Croton River on a bridge for traffic entering the park from Route 129. Looking upward, one sees the water tumbling down from the steps of the granite spillway of the dam, and then flowing through an impressive gorge leading to the Hudson River. In 50 feet, the paved road crosses a small stream. The trailway turns right at this point, heading steeply uphill and onto a woods road. At a large beech tree with braided roots, it turns right continuing to ascend steeply. It reaches the guardrail, where it turns left at 2.0 miles and follows paved Croton Dam Road. After crossing Route 129, it turns right. Use caution walking along this busy road.

At 0.7 mile, the trailway reaches Mt. Airy Road East, follows it to a junction with Colabaugh Pond Road at 1.2 miles, and reenters the woods. Parking is available along the road. The trailway parallels the road and, at 1.5 miles, enters wetlands adjacent to Colabaugh Pond. The trailway crosses the inlet of the pond at 1.9 miles and is once again on a woods road. It turns left at 2.1 miles and follows Colabaugh Pond Road. At 2.5 miles, it turns right to leave the road and enters the woods on a woods road between stone walls (no parking).

After crossing a stream, the trailway heads uphill. At the top, on days when the Sportsman Center is open, you will hear gun shots. At this point, the shooting range is more than two miles away. At 3.0 miles, the park buildings of Charles Cook Park can be seen to the left and in summer, the laughter of children enjoying a swim can be heard. The trailway crosses Furnace Dock Road at 3.4 miles and heads along a woods road. It reaches a 0.1-mile footbridge over wetland at 3.7 miles. The trailway turns right at 4.0 miles and works

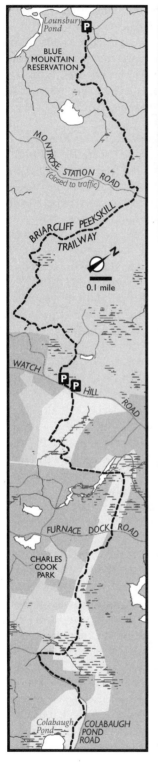

In Blue Mountain Reservation

its way uphill to a large parking area on Watch Hill Road.

Watch Hill Road Through Blue Mountain Reservation   *Length: 2.9 miles*

From the parking area on Watch Hill Road, the trailway crosses the road and heads along the entrance road to the Sportsman Center. It crosses the parking lot to the northwest corner where, at 0.4 mile, the trail enters the woods and ascends steeply along a wide woods road. It passes to the left, at 0.8 mile, the trail to Mt. Spitzenberg, with a short, steep climb to the top and views of the Hudson Valley. After crossing wetlands on a built-up treadway, it passes the end of the white trail at 1.3 miles and turns right. At 1.8 miles the trail crosses Montrose Station Road, reaches the gas pipeline, and turns left heading uphill. It reenters the woods and heads gradually downhill on a woods road. At the junction with the blue and red trails at 2.1 miles, the trail turns left. At 2.4 miles, it turns right, continues to follow the blue trail, and turns right again, co-aligned with the white trail as together they head downhill. After going through a grove of devastated hemlocks, the Briarcliff Peekskill Trailway passes an orange/yellow trail at 2.8 miles and then the yellow trail as it ends at Blue Mountain Reservation's parking lot #3 (main parking lot).

CONNECTING PARKS & TRAIL: Teatown Lake Reservation, John E. Hand Park, Old Croton Aqueduct State Historic

Park, Croton Gorge Park, Blue Mountain Reservation

DRIVING: There are many access points to the trailway, including ones established by adjacent private residences. Not all road crossings have parking. Use a Westchester County map to reach various parking areas. Parking is available at the following locations, with the number of parking places indicated in parentheses only if there are fewer than 12 spots: Spring Valley Road (4); Teatown Lake Reservation (use the Lakeside, Northwest, or Cliffdale-Teatown trail to reach the trailway); John E. Hand Park just east of the Blinn Road crossing (4); New Croton Dam at the southeast end on Croton Dam Road; Croton Dam Park (seasonal fee); Watch Hill Road; Blue Mountain Reservation (seasonal fee).

PUBLIC TRANSPORTATION: Metro-North Hudson Line Ossining Station (taxi to Rider Road); Croton-Harmon Station (taxi to Croton Gorge Park); Peekskill (taxi to entrance of Blue Mountain Reservation)

For contact information see Appendix, Westchester County Parks.

Bronx River Reservation

Valhalla to Mount Vernon • 12.3 miles, 807 acres

Completed in 1925, the Bronx River Reservation was the first Westchester County Park, laying the groundwork for an impressive park system that continues to grow. When people think of the Bronx River Parkway, they do not realize that this commuter route is part of a park. The Bronx River Pathway is the non-motorized portion of the park. Entwined with the railroad, river, and parkway, it is never far from any of the three. The pathway is heavily used by nearby residents for exercise, a chance to be with family and friends, or just to be outdoors in an otherwise distinctly urban area. The paved portions are handicapped accessible.

THE PATHWAY

There are three distinct paved segments of the Bronx River Pathway. They can be savored in small or large bites, given the proximity of the Metro-North Harlem Line stations every few miles. The three segments are described, as well as the on-road route linking the two sections north and south of Scarsdale. Interchanges of the Cross County Parkway isolate the third section of the pathway.

The 1967 safety improvements to the parkway in Scarsdale resulted in the removal of a 2-mile section. Adjacent local streets now serve as a 1.6-mile link to the portions along the parkway and are included in the total mileage. Because little parking is available, public transportation is recommended.

BICYCLE SUNDAY

Every Sunday from 10 am to 2 pm in May, June, and September, the Bronx River Parkway is closed to motorized traffic. Although motorist groups originally were critical of this event when it began in 1974, it has become a popular tradition with cyclists and in-line skaters. In 2008, the program was expanded to include walkers, joggers, and strollers. Rain cancels the event.

Valhalla to Scarsdale (Greenacres Avenue) *Length: 5.3 miles*
This section of the Bronx River Pathway is a wide asphalt path at its start but later narrows in places to four or five feet. After White Plains, there are short, steep bluffs, sudden turns, and unpaved sections suitable for cyclists who do not mind riding on dirt trails. Inexperienced cyclists may find significant challenges because of poor surface conditions, a twisting route, and sharp climbs and descents.

To reach the beginning of this section from the Valhalla Station on the Metro-

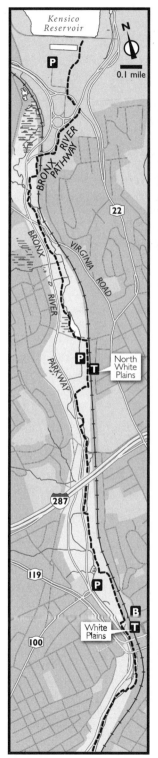

Along the Bronx River Pathway

North Harlem Line, walk south to the old station, currently a restaurant. Cross over the Taconic State Parkway at the traffic light, turn right onto Broadway, the village's main street, and continue until you reach a church. Just beyond the church parking lot, take the faint path heading off to the left through the woods to the Kenisco Dam Plaza.

The trail begins on the east side of the Kenisco Dam Plaza, near the steps to the top of the dam. The pathway initially turns left and runs parallel to the access road to Route 22. It then heads uphill, goes under an overpass, and immediately turns right. After passing ball fields, it uses the first of many viaducts over the railroad tracks. A plaque in the stonework of the viaduct gives details of the park's construction.

The pathway crosses Virginia Road at 1.0 mile and then Holmes Road, which leads to the Metro-North rail yards. Paralleling the Bronx River, the path crosses Fisher Lane at 1.6 miles. Turn left and head toward the railroad underpass, passing the parking lot entrance to Metro-North Harlem Line North White Plains Station. Just past the parking lot entrance, turn right onto the pavement running between the parking lot guardrail and the railroad embankment. Pass a walkway up to the station and a second access to the platforms. Turn right to cross the road leading to additional parking at 2.0 miles. The paved path goes through park-like meadows while paralleling the parkway and then

History of the Bronx River Reservation

The parkway portion of the Bronx River Reservation is the first parkway in the United States; it introduced the concept of exit and entrance ramps as well as the use of designed landscaping to border a road. The parkway was established so that unsanitary conditions along the Bronx River could be cleaned up. Not only was there a cleaner river, but also a pleasant place for transportation and recreation. Over the years, the original winding route has been straightened in places to accommodate heavy commuter traffic. The Bronx River Reservation is an example of balancing conservation with other needs of the population.

Westchester County still owns and operates the Bronx River Reservation. The Department of Public Works maintains the parkway and vehicle bridges; the Parks Department maintains the rest. It is the only parkway in Westchester not owned and managed by the East Hudson Parkway Authority. See www. westchestergov.com/wcarchives/ and search to learn more history of the Bronx River Parkway.

heads into the woods. It crosses the Bronx River, more like a stream at this point, crosses Old Tarrytown Road at 2.3 miles, and passes under I-287 bridges. After going along an exit road from the parking lot of the Westchester County Center, it enters the parking lot. Follow the paved road running along the base of the railroad embankment to the left, which passes a 1910 pedestrian tunnel leading to the White Plains Station and bus depot at 3.2 miles.

The pathway turns right opposite the tunnel and continues south along the Bronx River. It passes under three bridges, the last of which has a path entering from the left, and then merges with a second path to the left coming from Main Street along the exit ramp. At 3.6 miles, the pathway crosses a bridge over the river. From here to Greenacres Road in Scarsdale, the pathway, river, railroad tracks, and parkway twist like strands of spaghetti, sometimes really closely, at other times out of sight of each other.

At 4.1 miles, looming overhead, the massive arches of the Woodlands Viaduct carry the parkway across the valley, the river, the pathway, and the railroad. About 100 feet beyond the viaduct, the pathway makes a sharp left to cross the river on a footbridge. It immediately goes under the railroad and turns right to wedge between the parkway and the river. At 4.6 miles, the pathway passes through an extremely low arch of a bridge under the parkway, then heads uphill through the woods onto a bluff above the river. Along this stretch, numerous small paths connect to Walworth Avenue.

The path, now gravel and often narrow, ascends and descends frequently as it goes through the most natural setting of all the sections. It finally comes down to the edge of the Bronx River with numerous benches and an occasional wood duck house. After passing a small dam at 5.1 miles, the river curves back under the highway as the pathway turns away from it. Following a narrow path along a fence behind the private County Tennis Club of Westchester, the pathway passes a small pond constructed for the Haubold Gunpowder Mill in the 1840s.

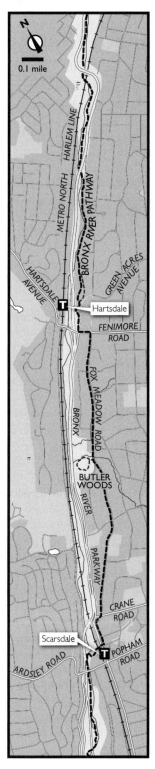

0.1 mile

When the pathway reaches Greenacres Avenue at 5.3 miles, walkers should cross Greenacres Avenue onto Fountain Terrace. To avoid the steps on Fountain Terrace, cyclists may prefer to turn right onto Greenacres Avenue, go past the Hartsdale Station, and then up a short hill to connect with Fenimore Avenue. There is no parking available here or on nearby streets. To reach the Hartsdale Station, where there is parking, turn right onto Greenacres Avenue and cross the bridge over the parkway. Metered parking is restricted to permit holders, except on Sundays.

Scarsdale (Greenacres Avenue to Scarsdale Station) *Length: 1.6 miles*

A walk through residential areas along quiet streets connects the two off-road sections. With numerous shops near the train station, there are plenty of places to stop. Directly across the street from the end of the pathway at Greenacres Avenue is Fountain Terrace (a private road). Walk up the road passing the remains of a formal garden, once part of the Bronx River Reservation. Take the steps up to Fenimore Road and turn left. Use the pedestrian crosswalks to cross over and then go south on Fox Meadow Road. While walking along this residential street, notice the variety of architecture. At 0.8 mile, pass Butler Woods, once part of a 500-acre tract known as Fox Meadow Estate. Emily Butler donated 25 acres to the Parkway Commission in 1913, and later added 7.5 acres.

Continue south on Fox Meadow Road to reach Crane Road at 1.6 miles; cross it and turn right heading towards the parkway. Watch for turning cars because this intersection is near an exit/entrance ramp. Turn left onto East Parkway, go through the parking area, and head toward the Scarsdale Station.

Scarsdale Station to Bronxville *Length: 4.5 miles*

The paved pathway from the Scarsdale Station into Bronxville is mostly flat, wide, and anything but straight. From Harney Road, the path crosses the Bronx River numerous times and is frequently sandwiched between railroad and parkway. Residents of many adjacent apartment buildings use this section to walk or just sit on benches reading and enjoying fresh air. There are many road crossings that for the most part, are exit and entrance ramps of the parkway. Use

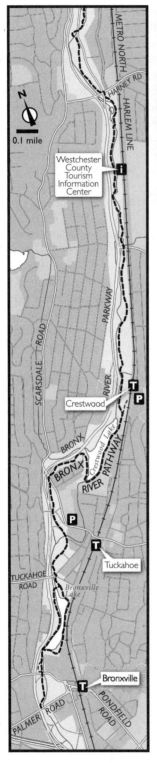

Crossing under the parkway

caution and do not assume that traffic will stop if you are in the crosswalk.

At the Scarsdale Station, cross to the southbound side of the tracks. The path to the right is paved almost to the steps up the Crane Road Viaduct and a dirt path continues and ends at 0.3 mile at a break in the guardrail on Aqueduct Road. The southbound pathway gracefully curves down to a bridge over the Bronx River and enters Garth Woods, paralleling the northbound parkway. At 0.4 mile, the pathway turns left to cross the river on a rustic bentwood bridge. It wiggles through large trees and at 0.5 mile, as the pathway heads under the parkway, is just inches from the water in the Bronx River. It is necessary to duck because the girders are only about five feet above the path. The pathway crosses a long bridge onto an island in the river, then leaves the island on another bridge and crosses the northbound parkway at Harney Road.

At Harney Road at 0.9 mile, the pathway heads across a large open area, passes a pond to the right, and then re-crosses the river. A former gas station, now a Westchester County Tourist—Information Center, is at 1.2 miles. Restrooms are available when the center is open on Sundays during good weather months.

The pathway crosses the river again and, at 1.5 miles, crosses Leewood Drive. Staying within view of the parkway, the pathway, at 2.1 miles, turns right onto a service road leading to the central facilities of the Westchester County Department of Parks, Recreation and Conservation. Following the service road, the pathway crosses Thompson Avenue, the access road to the Crestwood Station. Continuing to meander along the river, the pathway reaches Crestwood Lake. Passing ball fields at Malcolm Wilson Park to the left, at 2.7 miles it reaches the dam at the south end of the lake. Here it turns around the end of the lake to head towards the parkway. The pathway crosses Exit 16 and reaches a cul-de-sac. At 3.1 miles, it crosses Scarsdale Road. Use caution during the next 0.5 mile because the pathway crosses three roads including Tuckahoe Road, a main thoroughfare. The pathway splits at 3.7 miles and circles Bronxville Lake. The two parts meet and split again just before crossing Pondfield Road. The pathway ends at 4.5 miles at Palmer Avenue behind Lawrence Hospital. To reach the Metro-North Station Harlem Line Bronxville Station, turn left (east). There are numerous eateries and shops to while away time waiting for the next train.

Mount Vernon (Oak Street Path) *Length: 0.6 mile*

Separated by many miles from the longer off-road sections, the Oak Street Path is tucked between the parkway, the Bronx River, and the Metro-North tracks. The pathway entrance is easily missed because it is right beside the northbound entrance ramp of the Bronx River Parkway.

The pathway heads north for 0.1 mile and turns away from the parkway to cross the river. It immediately turns again to head north between the river and the railroad. Short informal paths lead to the river, with fishing and birding spots on its shore. The wood duck boxes are part of a restoration project along the river. At 0.4 mile, the pathway splits. Its left branch is overgrown and becomes impassible at 0.1 mile from the split. The right branch of the pathway ends in a large open area just before the exit ramp of the Cross County Parkway and near the access road to Metro-North tracks.

CONNECTING PARK: The 97-acre Kenisco Dam Plaza is the northern terminus of the pathway. Think of the broad expanse at the foot of the dam as an oversize track in the shadow of a massive structure. On nice days, the area is filled with joggers, children learning to ride bicycles, in-line skaters, and walkers.

DRIVING: For the Valhalla to Hartsdale section, take the Bronx River Parkway to its end at Kenisco Dam Plaza. There is parking at the Kenisco Dam Plaza, the Metro-North Harlem Line North White Plains Station (free on weekends), Cross County Center, and the Transportation Center in White Plains. The southern end of the first section is off Greenacres Avenue in Hartsdale. It is not recommended that you try to park in Scarsdale; parking there is by permit only, except on Sundays. For the section in Mount Vernon, take the Bronx River Parkway to Oak Street

PUBLIC TRANSPORTATION: Metro-North Harlem Line stations at Valhalla, North White Plains, White Plains, Hartsdale, Scarsdale, Bronxville, and Mount Vernon West

For contact information, see Appendix, Westchester County Parks.

Hutchinson River Pathway

White Plains to Mount Vernon • 12.9 miles, 717 acres

Many commuters speeding their way south toward the Bronx on the Hutchinson River Parkway do not realize that a trail parallels the parkway. In 1924, the Westchester County Parks Commission recommended construction of a parkway in southern Westchester, which would also be a park and a means to protect water sources. Construction began the same year and, in December 1927, a two-mile section in Pelham was complete. By October 1928, the 11-mile section between Route 1 in Pelham and Westchester Avenue in White Plains serving mostly local traffic was finished. Complying with design standards of the era, the parkway's four nine-foot-wide travel lanes were designed for speeds up to 40 mph; it did not have shoulders, median separators, or acceleration-deceleration lanes. The $12 million cost of building the 11 miles of parkway included establishing a bridle path along the right-of-way and a riding academy where the public could rent horses.

Over the years, sections of the Hutch, as it is fondly called, have been upgraded, but not without opposition from neighbors. As a result of such improvements, the parkway has been made safer. However, in the process, some trails and pathways were moved or even eliminated. The last 3.2 miles of the pathway are along streets; in some county publications, this 3.2-mile route is considered part of the pathway, in other publications, it is not.

THE PATHWAY

Most of the Hutchinson River Pathway is never far from the steady whine of high-speed traffic. It is unfortunate that there is so much highway noise, because there are short sections where the trail is a pleasant place to walk and houses are not visible. Bring either an iPod or earplugs to walk along this trail designed for equestrians. The description of the pathway is divided into sections according to where parking is available. Nearby residents, of course, have access to the trail at numerous road crossings or directly from their property.

The Hutchinson River Pathway is only occasionally blazed. When co-aligned with the Colonial Greenway on county property, the pathway has a painted blue blaze with a star.

North of Route 127 (North Street)   *Length: 0.6 mile*
The northernmost section of the Hutchinson River Pathway is a trail to nowhere. Adjacent to the northbound parkway entrance ramp, this wide, grassy strip heads

Maple Moor
Golf Course

0.1 mile

north from Route 127. Paralleling the Hutch, it is within sight and sound of the parkway for its entire length. To the right, heading north, it parallels a chainlink fence marking a DOT right-of-way.

Route 127 (North Street) through Saxon Woods Golf Course *Length: 3.0 miles*

From the parking lot at Maple Moor Golf Course, head east on Route 127 (North Street) and pass all entrance and exit ramps. Cross Route 127 and look for an opening in the woods near a manhole cover. The trail turns onto a woods road and then turns left to parallel the Hutch. Wooden guardrails separating the trail from the parkway keep horses from straying into traffic or going down steep banks beside the woods.

Heading downhill, the trail passes several houses to the left at 0.6 mile. It alternates between being within sight of the parkway and separated from it by a buffer. At 1.0 mile, the trail turns to cross the East Branch of the Mamaroneck River and then passes along the base of a high stone retaining wall supporting the parkway. It passes a breached dam and later turns to parallel the northbound entrance ramp. The pathway crosses the East Branch of the Mamaroneck River at 1.4 miles and turns away from the entrance ramp. Once across the entrance road to the Kentucky Riding Stable at 1.6 miles, the trail heads across Mamaroneck Avenue (no parking).

On the south side of Mamaroneck Avenue, the trail turns and heads northwest, now protected from the heavy traffic by a guardrail. Turning left, away from Mamaroneck Avenue at 1.8 miles, it crosses two bridges over the West Branch of the Mamaroneck River. It reaches a junction with an unmarked trail to the left, which leads 0.2 mile into Saxon Woods Park South. Bearing right, the trail goes under the Hutch and heads upstream along the West Branch of the Mamaroneck River. After passing through a tunnel under the southbound entrance ramp, it goes toward a soccer field, but turns left before reaching it. The trail then heads uphill, away from the soccer field, and enters the woods at 2.0 miles at an easily missed trail junction. Both trails end up in the same spot, but the one to the right is slightly shorter.

Turning away from the parkway, the Hutchinson River Pathway reaches a Y junction with a white trail at 2.0 miles and turns left to join it. Although noise from the parkway is present, it lessens considerably in the next

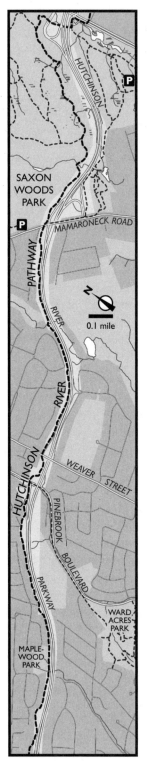

half-mile. The wide eroded trail passes two unmarked trails to the right in quick succession. After passing an unmarked trail to the left, it switchbacks downhill, passes stone trestles to the right, then heads uphill. The treadway is often eroded, and in places is 12-18 inches lower than the forest floor. At 2.6 miles, the white trail turns right and the pathway continues straight. Once again the noise level rises, and cars on the parkway are visible through trees. The trail crosses a bridge heading toward the golf course. Turning left, it comes close to the parkway at 2.8 miles. It parallels the southbound exit ramp and reaches Mamaroneck Road at 3.0 miles. To continue on the next section, cross Mamaroneck Road at the break in the stone wall. Parking is available at the golf course.

Saxon Woods Golf Course to Webster Avenue
Length: 5.6 miles

From the parking lot at Saxon Woods Golf Course, head toward the entrance and walk along the stone wall at the east side of the entrance road. After going through the break in a stone wall east of the golf course entrance, cross Mamaroneck Road. The entrance to the pathway is between Stratton Road and the southbound entrance ramp to the Hutch. The Colonial Greenway joins the Hutchinson River Pathway here; they are co-aligned for the next 3.2 miles.

The trail is on a grassy strip with cars whizzing past so closely it is a bit disconcerting. Over the next half-mile, the trail alternates between having buffers and being right next to the traffic. The trail crosses a stream, parallels the southbound exit ramp, and crosses Weaver Street at 1.0 mile. It heads downhill to reach Pinebrook Boulevard. To the left, a section of the Colonial Greenway goes 0.6 mile along Pinebrook Boulevard to Ward Acres Park.

The pathway crosses Pinebrook Boulevard and then parallels the southbound entrance to the Hutch. Over the next mile, it again alternates between being close to the Hutch and having a buffer. At 1.9 miles there is access from Maplewood Park off Gaby Lane. The trail parallels the southbound exit ramp and turns left at 2.5 miles to cross Wilmot Road and follow the sidewalk. It reenters the woods near a fire hydrant.

The path heads downhill to the base of the dam of Lake Innisfree and crosses the spillway. (The lake was created by damming the Hutchinson River.) The

Lake Innisfree Dam

pathway crosses the bridge over exit and entrance ramps and then switchbacks steeply down to head alongside the Hutchinson River under Mill Road. Emerging on the south side of Mill Road, the pathway crosses an exit ramp first and then an entrance ramp. At 3.0 miles, the trail enters Twin Lakes Park on a grassy strip, where the trees are heavily draped with vines. Equestrians are the primary users of Twin Lakes Park; hikers are asked to yield to them on trails. In the park, trails are constrained by the parkway, reservoirs, and California Road. Unmarked paths to the right lead to the River Ridge Equestrian Center.

At a large grassy triangle intersection, the Hutchinson River Pathway turns left, heading toward the parkway. At the next intersection, at 3.2 miles, the Colonial Greenway leaves to the right. The pathway turns left at a T junction at 3.4 miles to cross a bridge, and then turns again, wedged between the river and the parkway. The trail passes a breached dam at 3.6 miles, enters a heavily overgrown area, and turns onto a woods road. Leaving the woods at 3.9 miles, the pathway is between the shore of Reservoir #3 and the Hutch. At the end of the reservoir, the pathway turns right to cross the dam.

At a T junction, the trail turns left to join the Colonial Greenway; they are co-aligned for the next 1.3 miles. After crossing a bridge over an entrance ramp, the path heads down a ramp which switchbacks to cross a bridge below the dam. Having passed under the Hutch at 4.1 miles, with the Hutchinson River in a concrete channel to the left, the pathway enters an area blanketed with invasive plants. It reaches Reservoir #2 and then parallels it. To the right at 4.5 miles, a 0.2-mile trail goes through a flood control area to reach a dam. The pathway passes

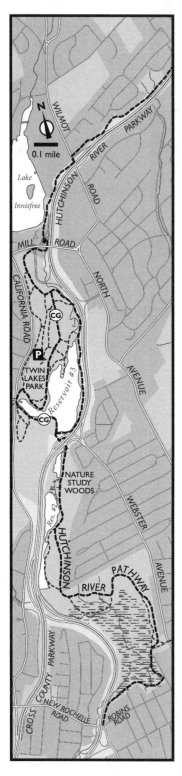

an unmarked trail to the left to Bon Air Avenue. Entering Nature Study Woods, the pathway is along a railbed. To the right at 2.0 miles, a lone trestle of the former New York, Westchester & Boston Railway looms overhead. Just beyond the trestle at a Y junction, an unmarked trail to the right heads 0.2 mile out into the flood plain of the Hutchinson River. The Hutchinson River Pathway passes a large stone outcropping to the left at 5.0 miles and turns left at a point where the path, coming from the dam, rejoins. A narrow unmarked path enters from the right. Now more frequently blazed blue, the pathway crosses a bridge at 5.2 miles. At a wide intersection, it turns right. The Colonial Greenway goes through the intersection on the wide path and heads toward Webster Avenue. The Hutchinson River Pathway follows a narrow path and turns right when it meets another trail coming from Webster Avenue opposite Flandreau Avenue.

Webster Avenue to New Rochelle Road
Length: 0.5 mile
To reach this short section, follow the wide unmarked entrance trail at the corner of Webster and Flandreau avenues. Head across the wide intersection, go slightly downhill, and then turn left at the next trail junction. An Eagle Scout project refurbished this section through a wetland. Wood chips make the surface more comfortable to walk on. Culverts allow water to drain from one side of the wetland to the other. At 0.3 mile, the trail passes a massive beech tree. It leaves the woods and heads onto a grassy strip behind apartment buildings to end at the corner of Robins and New Rochelle roads (no parking).

New Rochelle Road to St. Paul's Episcopal Church
Length: 3.2 miles
Radically different from sections north of New Rochelle Road, the Hutchinson River Pathway through this section does not run along the parkway. Instead, it follows city streets through residential, small retail, urban sprawl, and industrial areas.

At the end of Robins Road, turn right onto New

ANNE HUTCHINSON

The Hutchinson River is named for Anne Hutchinson, who, in an age when being outspoken was dangerous, especially for women, spoke out for women's rights, separation of church and state, and free markets. Born in England in 1591, Anne Marbury grew up during the reign of Queen Elizabeth I, an era in which women were given more status and freedom of education than they had been previously allowed. In 1612, Anne married William Hutchinson, who eventually became an affluent businessman. While living in Alford, she met and accepted the teachings of John Cotton, a Puritan minister.

When James I ascended the throne, women's rights were severely cut. Dissident preachers such as John Cotton either stopped preaching or were encouraged to leave England. In 1633, Cotton left England for the Massachusetts Bay Colony; a year later the Hutchinson family followed. Settling in the New World, William Hutchinson prospered as a cloth merchant. Through her nursing and midwifery skills, Anne came into contact with many women whom she tried to enlighten with her religious views. Not surprisingly, her unusual views on the separation of church and state quickly brought her to the attention of both these authorities, which at the time were thoroughly entwined. Eventually she was asked to leave Massachusetts. Anne moved to somewhat more liberal Rhode Island, but her views were not welcome there either. Following the death of her husband in 1642, Anne moved to New Netherland (New York). Shortly after arriving, she and her family, except for her youngest daughter, were massacred in Pelham Neck.

Rochelle Road, following the sidewalk under the Hutchinson River Parkway. Cross New Rochelle Road at 0.1 mile and follow Hutchinson Boulevard past houses with small landscaped lawns. Initially there are no sidewalks. The Hutchinson River is between the parkway and the street. Cross East Lincoln Avenue at 1.0 mile to Bradford Park Road. Take care to stay to the right side of the street to avoid having to cross the parkway's exit and entrance ramps. Willson's Woods Park, with about 0.5 mile of paved paths, is to the right.

Follow Bradford Park Avenue and go under the stone viaduct of the Metro-North New Haven Line. At 1.5 miles, turn left onto Beechwood Avenue, which has houses set close together. At the end of Beechwood Avenue, the path crosses a pedestrian bridge over the parkway to Sparks Avenue. Walk along Sparks Avenue and turn right at Wolf's Lane at 1.9 miles. Wolf's Lane is along the retail section of Pelham with its collection of shops and eateries and is, for a short distance, across the street from a strip of green space. At 2.1 miles, when Wolf's Lane ends at Colonial Avenue, turn right and pass under the parkway, entering Mount Vernon. The route becomes more commercial, with large box stores on both sides of the wide street. Just after passing Memorial Field to the right at 2.4 miles, turn left onto Columbus Avenue (Route 22). Continue through a neighborhood which gradually becomes more heavily industrialized to end at St. Paul's Episcopal Church (a National Historic Site).

CONNECTING PARKS: Saxon Woods Park, Weinberg Nature Center, Twin Lakes Park, Nature Study Woods, Willson's Woods

DRIVING: All sections of the pathway are accessible from the Hutchinson River Parkway. To reach Maple Moor Golf Course, take Exit 25 (North Street/Route 127). The entrance to the Hutchinson River Pathway is on North Street, east of the northbound exit/entrance ramps.

To reach Saxon Woods Golf Course, take Exit 22 (Mamaroneck Road) and turn right. The golf course is the first right turn after the southbound exit ramp.

To reach Nature Study Woods from the northbound Hutchinson River Parkway, take Exit 16, which becomes southbound Webster Avenue. Continue 0.8 mile to the park entrance across from 823 Webster Avenue. From the southbound Hutchinson River Parkway, take Exit 18E (Mill Road East) toward New Rochelle. At 0.3 mile, make a slight right onto North Avenue. Follow North Avenue 1.1 miles to turn right onto Rosehill Avenue. Go 0.2 mile and turn left onto Webster Avenue. It is 0.4 mile to the park entrance to the right, across from 823 Webster Avenue.

PUBLIC TRANSPORTATION: Saxon Woods Park: Beeline Bus #60; Nature Study Woods: Beeline Bus #45 along Webster Avenue or Beeline Bus #53 on New Rochelle Road

For contact information, see Appendix, Westchester County Parks.

Leatherstocking Trail

New Rochelle to Mamaroneck • 2.6 miles, 67.5 acres

To the north and west of I-95, a short strip of green known as the Leatherstocking Trail cuts across the Town of Mamaroneck. Abutting it is Sheldrake River Trails Conservation Area. At one time, these two pieces were a county bridle trail and, in 1926, were slated to become a parkway from Port Chester to the Bronx. Once the New England Thruway was built in the 1950s, this land was no longer needed. Thinking ahead, local and county groups worked together to preserve the land for passive recreation.

The Leatherstocking Trail is part of the outer loop of the Colonial Greenway and eventually connects to Saxon Woods Park. The cross piece of the Colonial Greenway goes from the Leatherstocking Trail to the Hutchinson River Pathway north of Ward Acres Park.

LEATHERSTOCKING TRAIL

Blazed white, the 2.6-mile Leatherstocking Trail follows a narrow strip from Pinebrook Boulevard in New Rochelle to Old White Plains Road in Mamaroneck. As part of the Colonial Greenway, it has many access points, most without parking. The distinguishing features along the Leatherstocking Trail are road crossings and side trails. This pleasant meandering path has houses on one side or the other. In spring before leaves appear, abundant wildflowers are found along the path. Yellow marsh marigolds carpet moist areas in mid-April.

From Pinebrook Boulevard (no parking), the Leatherstocking Trail goes uphill on a wide path. It passes houses, sometimes closer than at others, along the 200-foot corridor. At 0.4 mile, to the right, it goes by a blue-blazed side trail, which heads 0.1 mile to end at a driveway off Devonshire Road. After crossing a stone bridge at 0.5 mile, the Leatherstocking Trail passes a large vernal pool. It next goes by a yellow trail to the right that continues 0.1 mile to end across from 87 Beechtree Drive and then an unmarked trail, also to the right.

At 0.7 mile, there is a huge burl near the base of a tree to the left, where the Colonial Greenway heads to a wooden bridge and boardwalk ending at Bonnie Way. It is 0.3 mile along Bonnie Way to Weaver Street and the parking area at Sheldrake Environmental Center. Just beyond the trail to Bonnie Way, the Leatherstocking Trail heads uphill and splits. An unmarked trail leads to Knollwood Drive. The pieces join, and at 1.0 mile, reach a side trail leading right to South Drive and leading left to a shared driveway off Sacket Circle.

Just after crossing Weaver Street at 1.1 miles, the Leatherstocking Trail heads

Leatherstocking Trail

onto a 300-foot boardwalk and then onto another shorter one. After crossing Highland Road at 1.3 miles, the trail parallels Stratford Road. A short side trail on the right provides access to Woody Lane. At 1.6 miles, the first of the unmarked trails at Sheldrake River Trails Conservation Area leaves to the right. Access and limited parking are on Rockland Avenue on the far side of the Sheldrake River Trails. At Post D, the Leatherstocking Trail turns left and goes over a bridge and onto a 400-foot boardwalk. It passes Post J just before the boardwalk ends. At 1.7 miles, the trail crosses Winged Foot Drive (parking).

After passing a large vernal pool, the Leatherstocking Trail crosses Avon and Fenimore roads in quick succession. It reaches the top of a rise at 2.2 miles and crosses Country Road at 2.3 miles. The trail passes by the Town of Mamaroneck's tree nursery and turns right. It heads downhill and at 2.5 miles, reaches a boardwalk. The Leatherstocking Trail ends on Old White Plains Road at 2.6 miles, but the Colonial Greenway continues across the street on a path that is used far less frequently.

DRIVING: The many entrances to the Leatherstocking Trail include eight road crossings, side trails out to nearby streets, and many other paths established by adjacent private homeowners. Use a map of Westchester County to reach the various road crossings. Parking is limited as the Leatherstocking Trail passes through residential areas for most of its length. Parking areas are located at Sheldrake Reservoir and Winged Foot Drive. There are many places to park a car or two on streets near the trail.

PUBLIC TRANSPORTATION: None available

For contact information, see Appendix, Mamaroneck (Town).

Sheldrake River Trails Conservation Area

Larchmont • 1.0 mile, 23 acres

As depicted on a map, the Sheldrake River Trails Conservation Area is a bulge along the Leatherstocking Trail. Instead, consider it a jewel on a necklace. Its one-mile trail system of six short trails winds through woodlands, along a stream, and through a wetland. Lettered posts are located at intersections. Contact the Town of Mamaroneck Conservation Office (914-381-7845) for a self-guiding booklet to trails in the Conservation Area. The Town of Mamaroneck manages the area for conservation of native plants and animals.

DRIVING: From the southbound Hutchinson River Parkway, take Exit 20 (Weaver Street/Route 125) and turn left onto Route 125. *Go 1.8 miles and turn left onto Rockland Avenue. It is 0.3 mile to the park entrance, two blocks past Highland Avenue. If northbound, take Exit 21 and turn right onto Hutchinson Avenue. At Route 125, turn left and follow the directions from*. Parking on Rockland Avenue is limited to two or three cars.

PUBLIC TRANSPORTATION: None available

For contact information, see Appendix, Mamaroneck (Town).

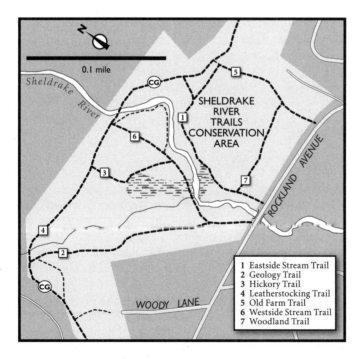

1 Eastside Stream Trail
2 Geology Trail
3 Hickory Trail
4 Leatherstocking Trail
5 Old Farm Trail
6 Westside Stream Trail
7 Woodland Trail

North County Trailway

Baldwin Place to Eastview • 21 miles, 88 acres

While many people are fortunate enough to live near the North County Trailway, there is a resident whose home is right on the trailway. To find out who it is, travel the section of the old Putnam Division of the New York Central Railroad south of Millwood and north of Chappaqua Road. If you decide instead to travel a longer route, you will find a cross-section of Westchester as it passes back yards, parks, and businesses; sometimes it parallels high-speed roads and at other times is well away from them. Along its course, it wends its way through a variety of habitat: wetland, rock cuts, woodlands, and edge environments. Near road crossings and at the former sites of stations, the county has placed interpretive signs with information about the history of the railroad and the surrounding habitats.

Along the 21-mile route are remnants of the railroad, mostly mileage markers and telephone poles. Only three stations still stand: Yorktown Heights, Millwood, and Briarcliff. The former Briarcliff Station is the Briarcliff Manor Public Library; the other two are not open to the public. Two concrete pads are all that is left of the Kitchawan Station. The roundtable was in Yorktown Heights, located just south of Underhill Avenue in an open area to the west. Just north of Eastview at the trail leading to the park-and-ride is a section of old track with switches. The Yorktown Museum has a display of the Putnam Division between Kitchawan and Amawalk. For more information, see www.yorktownmuseum.org.

The trailway is handicapped accessible. Highly recommended destinations are the wetlands south of Yorktown and the bridge over the New Croton Reservoir.

THE TRAILWAY

This converted railbed is a popular place to walk, jog, ride, or in-line skate. Each time of day attracts different users. Joggers use the rail trail in early mornings and evenings. Cyclists can be found at almost any time. On weekends, families with strollers and small kids on bikes enjoy the outdoors together. Even in winter, the route is used. The ambiance includes green tunnels with tree limbs arching over the shaded trail, open sky with high bushes on each side, and wetlands with its wildlife.

The North County Trailway is a linear footpath. Thus, unless hikers plan to retrace their steps, they will have to either leave a car where they will end their hike or rely on public transportation. The trail descriptions are in sections divided primarily by major road crossings or amenities.

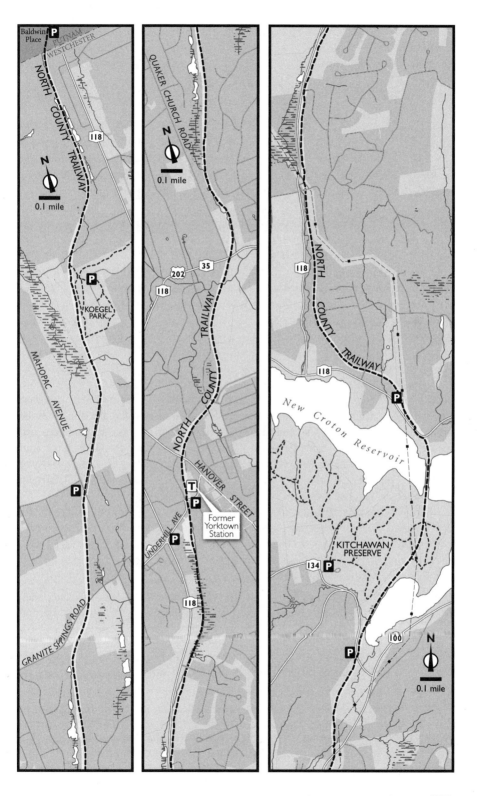

From the north end in Baldwin Place, the trailway continues into Putnam County as the Putnam Trailway. Beyond Eastview at the south end, it is known as the South County Trailway.

Baldwin Place to Yorktown Heights   *Length: 5.6 miles*

From Route 118 in Baldwin Place, the trail heads south, passing homes and then Koegel Park at 1.0 mile. Running parallel to a power line, the trail is on an embankment at times lined with a split rail fence. It crosses Mahopac Avenue at 2.4 miles and then the entrance and parking lot to Jilco (a window company). The trail crosses Granite Springs Road at 2.9 miles. It leaves the power line when it crosses Route 202/18/35 at 4.5 miles and then passes back yards again.

In Yorktown Heights, at 5.5 miles to the right of the trailway's intersection with Hanover Street, are numerous restaurants and services. There is a bike shop on Commerce Street near Downing Drive, a minute from the trailway. Railroad Park has the original Yorktown Station, with benches and old-style lighting. Shopping centers, including a grocery store, are across the street. At 5.6 miles, the trailway crosses Underhill Avenue (parking).

Yorktown Heights to Millwood   *Length: 6.7 miles*

The 4.5-mile section between Underhill Avenue and Route 134, with its stretch of wetlands and a former railroad bridge, is probably the most scenic part of the trailway. In Yorktown, 0.2 mile south of the crossing at Underhill Avenue, the trail passes through an extensive wetland often bustling with wildlife activity. Rabbits scurry into the underbrush and red-winged blackbirds perch on phragmite reeds. Depending on the season, turtles bask atop submerged logs and plop into the water when startled. South of the wetlands, the trailway passes through huge culverts under roads at 0.9, 1.4, and 1.9 miles. While traveling south, the slight but steady downgrade beginning at the second culvert means cyclists can coast for a long distance. The trailway parallels Route 118, but well out of sight and sound. It turns to parallel the reservoir and crosses Birdsall Drive at-grade at 2.9 miles.

After passing a parking lot next to the trailway, the trailway crosses Route 118 at 3.3 miles. Take care because there is a poor line of sight to the left. The trailway passes over the New Croton Reservoir on a restored railroad bridge, a popular destination with sweeping views out over the water. After going through a densely wooded section, the trailway passes under power lines. At 3.9 miles, there are trails into Kitchawan Preserve, where bikes are not permitted. Passing the site of the former Kitchawan Station, the trail goes through a massive culvert under Route 134 at 4.5 miles, where there is roadside parking uphill to the right. Continuing through woodlands, it crosses Route 100 on a former railroad bridge. Beyond the back yards of houses, the trailway crosses Route 120 at 6.4 miles and passes Millwood Station, standing forlorn just north of a trailway parking lot. Across Route 133 is a small shopping center at the junction with Route 100.

Millwood to Route 117   *Length: 5.5 miles*

Being alert is the best way to travel along this section of the North County Trailway. From where it crosses Route 100 to Route 9A, the trailway alternates between being along the road, behind a guardrail, or along a path through wetlands and woods. Whenever it leaves the road, there is the inherent danger of crossing a busy highway, which makes this part of the section more suitable as a commuter route than for weekend family outings. It also shows that the demand for commuter routes has resulted in a redundancy of roads in the area.

From the parking lot in Millwood, the trail curves as it parallels Route 133 and enters wetlands. It reaches Route 100 at the traffic light by the northbound entrance to the Taconic State Parkway at 0.3 mile. Trailway users heading south are on the shoulder of the southbound lanes of Route 100, and when heading north, are next to the northbound lanes. The trailway is on the shoulder until North State Street where it enters a parking area. From this point, it is behind a barrier along the east

Home Sweet Home

side of Route 100. At 1.9 miles, the trailway leaves Route 100 to head through the woods. Passing wetlands, the trailway crosses Chappaqua Road at 2.4 miles. Take care when crossing Route 100 and the exit ramp for Route 9A at 3.1 miles, because drivers in merging lanes are not always aware of pedestrians and cyclists.

Leaving Route 100, the trailway reenters the off-road portion at 3.3 miles and reaches the former Briarcliff Station. Built in 1909, it was a gift from Walter Law, a Village founder. Since 1959, the station has been the Briarcliff Manor Public Library. A significant expansion of the library is a two-story building reflecting the station's English gable design. At 3.5 miles, the trailway is behind a barrier as it goes under Pleasantville Road. It continues to parallel routes 9A and 100, never far from ambient noise. At 5.5 miles, an access path heads up to Route 117 and the trailway goes through a large culvert under Route 117. It passes another access path to a parking lot.

Route 117 to Eastview   *Length: 3.2 miles*
Unlike the other sections, this section has no road crossings. From the parking area on Route 117, the trailway initially parallels a power line and routes 9A and 100. At 0.9 mile, it passes behind the parkway police station. At times in the woods, it follows the Saw Mill River Parkway and the power line. At 2.2 miles, the trailway passes through an area devastated by a tornado that tore through the area in August 2006. Trees bent like toothpicks attest to the power of such storms. Approaching

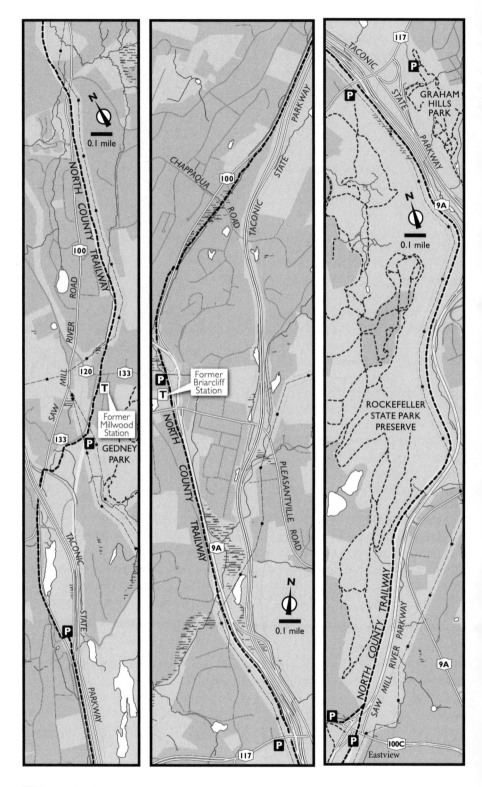

Former Millwood Station

GEDNEY PARK

Former Briarcliff Station

ROCKEFELLER STATE PARK PRESERVE

GRAHAM HILLS PARK

NORTH COUNTY TRAILWAY

SAW MILL RIVER ROAD

TACONIC STATE PARKWAY

CHAPPAQUA ROAD

PLEASANTVILLE ROAD

SAW MILL RIVER PARKWAY

Eastview

N
0.1 mile

Eastview, the trailway reaches a Y junction. Immediately to the right are remains of railroad track. The South County Trailway is to the left across the bridge over the Saw Mill River Parkway. The right fork heads to Saw Mill River Road/Neperan Road and a commuter parking lot just to the west. Parking for the trailways is next to the northbound exit ramp of the Saw Mill River Parkway. The exit ramp is two-way, but only as far as the parking lot entrance.

CONNECTING TRAILS & NEARBY PARKS: Putnam Trailway, South County Trailway, Tarrytown Lakes Park, Koegel Park, Turkey Mountain Nature Preserve, Kitchawan Preserve, Gedney Park, Law Memorial Park, Rockefeller State Park Preserve

DRIVING: There are many access points to the trailway, including some established by adjacent residents. Use a map of Westchester County to reach parking areas. The number of parking places is indicated in parenthesis only when are less than 12. Parking is available at: Baldwin Place (10); Jilco (only on weekends); Route 202/18/35 (7); Underhill Avenue in Yorktown; Route 118; Route 134; Millwood; Chappaqua Road (3); Law Park in Briarcliff Manor; Route 117; and the Eastview commuter lot.

PUBLIC TRANSPORTATION: Beeline Bus #16 to the Somers Town (shopping) Center in Baldwin Place, Beeline Bus #12 to Yorktown Heights, and Beeline Bus #15 to Millwood

For contact information, see Appendix, Westchester County Parks.

Old Croton Aqueduct State Historic Park

Cortlandt to the Bronx • 26.2 miles, 207.8 acres

Affectionately called the Aqueduct, the 26.2-mile Old Croton Aqueduct State Historic Park is heavily used by its neighbors and friends. Joggers, cyclists, dog walkers, nannies, and others of all ages use it to exercise. It is also the route for some as they walk to work or to the train station and for children as they bicycle or walk to school. The entire 41-mile length of the Aqueduct, not just the state park, was designated a National Historic Landmark in 1992.

The Aqueduct is an enclosed masonry structure running through ridges and valleys and over rivers and streams. About every mile along its course, the Aqueduct path passes stone towers, ventilators which allowed air to circulate over the water. Less frequently on the route are larger stone structures known as waste weirs. Each contains a metal gate, which could be lowered to either regulate the flow of water or divert the excess water into a nearby stream, permitting maintenance to take place downstream.

The cost of building the Aqueduct does not reveal the toll on families displaced when their land and homes were seized either for the reservoir or for the corridor in which the Aqueduct was built. Like many early major construction projects of this sort, it was built primarily by immigrant labor; in this case, it was mostly Irish workers, paid between 75 cents and a dollar per 10-hour workday.

THE AQUEDUCT

Wending its way through and between towns, villages, and cities, the Aqueduct traverses woodlands, meadows, and estates. Based on principles used since Roman times, the gravity-fed Aqueduct drops only 13 inches per mile as it travels from the Croton Dam toward New York City. To maintain that gradient as it crossed stream beds and other lowlands, it had to be carried across on earthen embankments. The brick tunnel itself is only a few feet beneath the trail. However, hikers will encounter significant elevation changes near the John F. Welch Development Center of the General Electric Corporation, at Piping Rock Road, and in Rockefeller State Park Preserve.

Each section has its own appeal and flavor, which makes the Aqueduct a favorite place to walk for so many people. In some places its presence is quite obvious, with a raised bed and a level surface. The walking route diverges from the Aqueduct itself at several points for various reasons: a sale of property, a road crossing considered unsafe, or a section actually being removed. Although the description

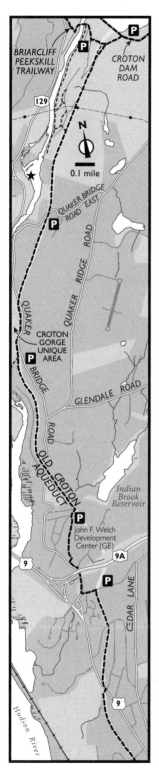

that follows provides a detailed guide to the walking route, it is recommended that walkers also consult the map published by the Friends of the Old Croton Aqueduct. The walking route seldom has signs, although some road crossings do have signposts.

The Aqueduct route generally has a dirt or grass surface with occasional obstacles such as tree roots, street curbs, stairways, and puddles. In most sections, the trail is at least four feet wide and sometimes has a narrow well-worn path down the center. There are areas as wide as 12 feet, while others literally pass through a back yard because its present or previous owner had encroached on the Aqueduct's 60-foot right-of-way.

For convenience, the description of the Aqueduct is divided into sections with public transportation available either nearby or at one end. The Metro-North Hudson Line directly parallels the Aqueduct for most of the way and is a practical way to access it. Suggested places to park are listed with the driving directions. Parking may also be available at some road crossings or on adjacent streets.

New Croton Dam to Ossining

Length: 4.9 miles

The first 2.8 miles of the Aqueduct pass through the most natural setting of its entire length. Trees tower overhead and few houses are visible. There are two access points at the New Croton Dam. Croton Gorge Park off Route 129 has ample parking, great views, and restrooms. To reach the Aqueduct, walk uphill on a wide path and turn right at the top of a hill onto a wide flat path. Alternately, access to the Aqueduct is at a parking area at the southeast end of the dam on Croton Dam Road. Regardless of which access point is used, follow the Aqueduct downhill along a wide path. At 0.2 mile, bear left at the sign for the Old Croton Aqueduct where it begins an almost imperceptible descent towards New York City. At 0.4 mile, it passes the first of 23 ventilators, this one not numbered. The Aqueduct continues through woods with the Croton River far below, passes through a rock cut, and at 1.0 mile, crosses Quaker Bridge Road East. Another unnumbered ventilator shaft is at 1.4 miles. After crossing Quaker Bridge Road, the Aqueduct goes through the DEC Croton Gorge

Unique Area at 1.8 miles, where a 0.2-mile side trail leads down into the gorge. At 2.4 miles, it passes a third unnumbered ventilator and crosses Quaker Bridge Road again.

The walking route turns right off the Aqueduct and crosses Fowler Avenue at 2.8 miles. It follows the perimeter of a fence at GE's John F. Welch Development Center, with a significant ascent and descent. At 3.1 miles, turn right onto the GE entrance road, turn left onto Old Albany Post Road, and cross under Route 9A. Make the next left onto Ogden Road, proceed steeply uphill, and turn right to rejoin

VFW Hall in Crotonville

the Aqueduct at 3.4 miles. An unnumbered ventilator shaft stands at 3.5 miles. Just past this ventilator, the Aqueduct tunnels through a hill and the trail goes up a very steep climb, not easy for bicyclists. After crossing Piping Rock Road, the Aqueduct heads down a steep bank. It crosses Route 9 (Highland Avenue) at 3.8 miles, turns left, and enters the Mearl Corporation property, where it crosses the lawn and a paved driveway at 4.0 miles. At 4.3 miles, the Aqueduct crosses Beach Road. Crawbuckie Nature Preserve is at the end of the road to the right.

At 4.5 miles, the Aqueduct passes a stone structure, crosses Snowden Avenue diagonally, and then Van Wyck and North Malcolm streets. The paved pathway turns right to descend two sets of steps. After crossing Ann Street, the Aqueduct reaches a weir. An imposing stone structure carries the Aqueduct over the Sing Sing Kill valley, a serious natural obstacle. At the center is a great arch with an 88-foot span. This construction project was a significant engineering achievement in 1837. Passing through this arch is another arched bridge carrying Broadway over the stream and giving rise to the name "double arch" for this crossing.

South of the bridge, a trail to the left leads to the Joseph G. Caputo Community Center, housing the Ossining Heritage Area Visitor Center, a museum providing information about the Old Croton Aqueduct and Sing Sing Correctional Facility. The trail to the right leads to a platform with a partial view of the double arch.

For further information about tours inside the weir and Aqueduct tunnel, call Friends of the Old Croton Aqueduct, 914-693-4117, or Old Croton Aqueduct State Historic Park, 914-693-5259.

Ossining to Sleepy Hollow (Gory Brook Road) *Length: 6.8 miles*

There are several sections of road walking in the section from Ossining to Gory Brook Road, but there are also connections to parks and long stretches of wooded areas. From the Joseph G. Caputo Community Center on Broadway, head up to the Aqueduct and turn left. Cross to the south side of Main Street, where the trail continues between buildings. The Metro-North Ossining Station is downhill

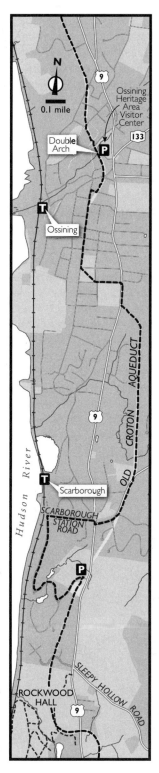

to the right. At Maple Place at 0.1 mile, the walking route turns right to leave the Aqueduct. Turn left onto Spring Street and cross Waller and Broad avenues. At 0.5 mile, ventilator #8 sits in the schoolyard to the left. The Aqueduct crosses Everett Avenue and follows a paved path cutting diagonally across Nelson Sitting Park to reach the corner of Edward Street and Washington Avenue. Turn left onto Washington Avenue and follow it to Route 9 (South Highland Avenue). At 0.9 mile, cross Route 9 and turn right onto the sidewalk. Just beyond the entrance to the parking lot of the apartments, turn left onto a narrow path into trees leading to another parking lot. At the far side of the lot, return to the Aqueduct route.

The Aqueduct enters the woods, curving to the right. It continues past more apartments, sometimes along a high embankment; oddly, no paths lead from the buildings. This section does not have the worn path typical of many sections further south along the route. After passing ventilator #9 at 1.6 miles, the Aqueduct crosses Sparta Brook on an embankment. Leaving this wooded section, it diagonally crosses Scarborough Road at 1.8 miles. At Long Hill Road West, the walking route leaves the Aqueduct. Turn right onto Long Hill Road West, continue a hundred yards, and at 2.2 miles turn left onto Scarborough Road. Cross Route 9 (Albany Post Road), turn right, then immediately left, to follow Scarborough Station Road. Do not attempt to rejoin the Aqueduct by walking along Route 9, which has no shoulders, very short sight distances, and much truck and high-speed traffic. At the T junction with River Road at 2.5 miles, go left. To the right is the Metro-North Hudson Line Scarborough Station. Take River Road uphill to the junction with Creighton Lane and turn left. Where Creighton Lane ends at River Road, continue uphill to the left.

At 3.3 miles, just before River Road reaches Route 9, turn right into a parking lot and then immediately jog right to return to the Aqueduct. Now on a grassy path at 3.4 miles, the Aqueduct passes ventilator #10. After crossing a driveway, bear right for 50 feet and cross a grassy area. Going up an embankment, the path crosses Country Club Drive at 3.7 miles and reenters the woods. From here to Gory Brook Road, horses are permitted. To the right at a wide intersection is the trail to Rockwood Hall with a No Bikes sign. The

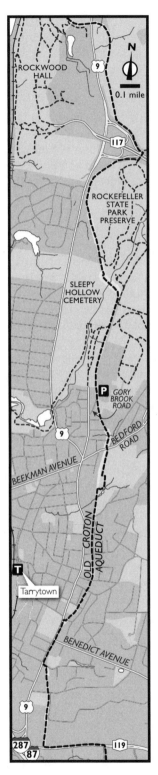

Aqueduct continues left and, at 4.1 miles, reaches the Archville Bridge, built in 1998 to create a safe crossing of Route 9. The original bridge was removed in the 1920s to accommodate increased traffic on Route 9. Plaques commemorate construction of the bridge, the Aqueduct, and the original stone arch bridge, which gave rise to the name "Archville."

The Aqueduct continues slightly uphill and turns right onto a wide gravel road to pass ventilator #11 at 4.3 miles. It turns left, leaving the Aqueduct route and bypassing exit and entrance ramps of Route 117. After heading uphill along a chainlink fence, it turns right to cross Route 117. Straight ahead is a trail leading to the 13 Bridges Trail in Rockefeller State Park Preserve. At 5.1 miles on the south side of the bridge over Route 117, the trail turns right. A short connecting trail leads straight ahead to the Big Tree Trail also in Rockefeller State Park Preserve.

The trail parallels a fence, passes through a rock formation at 5.3 miles, and then returns to the Aqueduct. It reaches an intersection with a No Bikes sign and a gate to the right. Continuing straight, the Aqueduct heads past Sleepy Hollow Cemetery to the right and reaches a weir at 6.1 miles. Curving left, the Aqueduct crosses a valley on a 90-foot-high embankment with the Pocantico River far below. On the east side of the trail before crossing the Aqueduct embankment, is a path which descends to the

Weir

Pocantico River and affords a view of the river as it passes through the embankment. The trail curves right to pass more of Sleepy Hollow Cemetery and parallels the closed portion of Gory Brook Road to the left. At 6.5 miles, an unmarked trail to the right leads to the cemetery and Douglas Park. The Aqueduct reaches a metal gate marked with OCA at 6.8 miles. Limited parking is available at Gory Brook Road to the left.

Sleepy Hollow (Gory Brook Road) to Dobbs Ferry (Walnut Street)
Length: 6.0 miles

Adjacent to the Aqueduct in this section are stately homes with well-kept lawns and gardens, as well as historic sites in several Hudson River villages. Unfortunately, there are two road walks, one of which is along busy roads.

From the gate at Gory Brook Road, the trail diagonally crosses that road and Ridge Road to pass houses and ventilator #12. It passes more houses and continues up onto an embankment. At 0.3 mile, it crosses Bedford Road and enters the parking lot of Sleepy Hollow High School. At the far end of the parking lot, head left around the school building. At 0.6 mile, go back up onto the Aqueduct as the trail continues south on a high embankment and crosses over Andre Brook. The Aqueduct squeezes past back yards as it heads in quick succession between Cobb Lane, McKeel Avenue, and Hamilton Place. These streets provide easy access to Route 9 in Tarrytown, where there is on-street metered and non-metered parking.

The Aqueduct passes ventilator #13 and crosses Neperan Road at 1.1 miles. Follow Neperan Road and Main Street downhill to the Metro-North Hudson Line Tarrytown Station. Passing through an opening in a hedge, it literally travels through back yards (which have made use of the right-of-way) and reaches East Elizabeth Street. It continues between buildings until reaching East Franklin Street, where it is necessary to leave the Aqueduct at 1.3 miles. Turn right, and upon reaching Route 9 (South Broadway), turn left. Follow Route 9 to Leroy Avenue and turn left at 1.5 miles. Turn right into a parking lot behind a medical arts center and rejoin the Aqueduct as it continues on a high embankment behind the building.

Leaving the woods, the Aqueduct crosses Prospect Avenue at 1.7 miles and a parking lot at Martling Avenue. Passing behind a number of buildings, it reaches ventilator #14 at 2.0 miles just before Route 119. The walking route once again diverges from the Aqueduct route and there are two routes for returning to it. The first one is more direct, but is along busy Route 9. The second is longer, but more scenic.

For the first route, turn right and follow Route 119. When you reach Route 9, cross it, turn left, and head south. After crossing over the New York State Thruway (Thruway), go past entrances to a hotel and to Kraft Foods, and continue ahead until reaching an opening in a fence.

For the more scenic route, turn left onto Route 119 (White Plains Road), continue to the second traffic light, and turn right onto Meadow Street. Bear left at the fork and continue under the Thruway. Turn right onto Sheldon Street (the first street after the Thruway) and continue to just beyond Chestnut Street, where the Aqueduct route crosses. Turn left and rejoin the Aqueduct route, which follows an embankment. After crossing the street leading into Gracemere, turn right onto

a gravel path, departing from the Aqueduct route. Follow the gravel path through a small parking area to Route 9, where you cross at the traffic light and turn left.

At 2.6 miles, turn right to return to the Aqueduct and enter the Lyndhurst property, home of Jay Gould, a nineteenth-century railroad magnate. A fee is required to explore any part of the grounds other than the Aqueduct. Just before crossing the paved access road, stop, turn, and look around. The white skeleton of the country's first steel-framed conservatory appears against a background of trees. Trees and shrubs accenting the sweeping lawn are part of an outstanding example of nineteenth-century landscape design.

The Aqueduct passes ventilator #15 at 3.0 miles. The high stone walls to the left are part of Belvedere, a private estate once known as Zeeview, the residence of Sun Myung Moon, head of the Unification Church. In 2004, a conservation easement on land west of the Aqueduct was created as part of a deal with New York State, Westchester County, and the Town of Greenburgh. The Aqueduct crosses Sunnyside Lane at 3.4 miles, entering the Village of Irvington. Down the hill is Washington Irving's home, Sunnyside, an historic site.

The Aqueduct passes large and elaborate houses. On the south side of Fargo Road to the left is an elaborate Italianate garden, part of Villa Lenaro, the former home of Madame C.J. Walker, a self-made millionaire. The Aqueduct parallels Aqueduct Lane at 3.9 miles, enters the parking lot of the Irvington Middle School, and crosses Main Street. Downhill to the right is the Metro-North Hudson Line Irvington Station.

Across Main Street, the Aqueduct enters a permit parking lot. After passing ventilator #16 at 4.0 miles, the Aqueduct crosses Barney Brook (formerly Jewells Brook) on a very high embankment. Cyclists should walk their bikes because traction on the gravel is poor. Ball fields of Memorial Park are to the left at 4.3 miles. Approaching Dows Lane, houses are once again adjacent to the trail. At 4.5 miles, the Aqueduct crosses Clinton Avenue and passes, to the right, the Octagon House, built in 1860. It enters the grounds of Nevis, the stately columned mansion built in 1835 by Alexander Hamilton's son. Currently it houses Columbia University's primary center for experimental physics.

The Aqueduct crosses Ardsley Road, which leads to the Metro-North Hudson Line Ardsley-on-Hudson Station. It

History of the Aqueduct

As early as 1797, New York City officials recognized that the city had a water problem, with respect to both quantity and quality. As the city grew, so did its demand for water. A cholera epidemic in 1832 and a disastrous fire five years later made the situation critical. The net result was that the public became more aware of the city's water needs. After several sites were considered, the Croton River was determined to be the only one with sufficient quality and quantity to meet those needs.

Work started on the Old Croton Aqueduct in 1837 and was completed five years later. It was one of the greatest engineering projects of its time; the total cost, including land acquisition, was $12,500,000. A reservoir is needed to supply a source of water for an aqueduct, and a man-made reservoir requires a dam. The dam built for the Old Croton Aqueduct is currently underwater. It is three miles upstream from the New Croton Dam, constructed to enlarge the first reservoir's capacity. When water level is low, the original dam can be seen.

The Old Croton Aqueduct was built to carry a maximum capacity of 72 million gallons per day. As the city's water demands exploded, engineers gradually increased the flow, but the stress on the structure proved too great. The population of the city and its need for water continued to increase. The New Croton Aqueduct with three times the capacity was later constructed (1885-93) and, eventually, it too became inadequate.

The Old Croton Aqueduct stopped serving New York City in 1955. It continued delivering water to some suburban communities until 1965, when the head gates were finally closed. At the urging of the New York-New Jersey Trail Conference and other outdoor groups, in 1968 New York State purchased from New York City's Bureau of Water Supply the portion of the Aqueduct in Westchester County. Also in 1968, the northernmost section of the Aqueduct was reopened to bring water to Ossining.

passes stately houses with well-groomed yards and gardens. Reaching ventilator #17 at 5.0 miles, on a narrow dirt track through grass, the Aqueduct crosses Hudson Road and enters the grounds of Mercy College and the Village of Dobbs Ferry. After cutting across the back of Our Lady of Victory Academy, it crosses an access road to condominiums and the Sisters of Mercy Convent. For a short while, it is easy to forget that the Aqueduct is in a busy village. No houses are nearby and it is so quiet crossing over Wicker's Creek on the high embankment that flowing water can be heard. Passing a side trail up to Dobbs Ferry High School, the Aqueduct curves right to cross over South Wicker's Creek. To the left at 5.6 miles, a trail descends to the creek. Ahead the Aqueduct goes under Cedar Street, but here it is necessary to turn right, go up steps to a kiosk, turn left, and then right to cross Cedar Street in Dobbs Ferry.

The Aqueduct passes through a permit parking lot, crosses Oak Street, and heads through the municipal parking lot for Dobbs Ferry Village Hall. The dirt path crosses Elm Street and Chestnut Street. Apartment buildings to the left are in view just before the Aqueduct reaches the state park headquarters on Walnut Street, at 6.0 miles. A kiosk with an interpretive exhibit is outside the office. The Metro-North Hudson Line Dobbs Ferry Station is to the right, down Walnut Street, which crosses Main Street and becomes Palisades Street. The station is to the left at Station Plaza.

Dobbs Ferry (Walnut Street) to Yonkers (Lamartine Avenue) *Length: 5.1 miles*

Views of the Palisades across the Hudson River, access to other parks, and long expanses with no road crossings are features of this section. The Aqueduct passes the Keeper's House on the south side of Walnut Street. This brick structure dates from 1857, was occupied until 1955, and is the only extant structure built for Aqueduct caretakers. Restoration of the house is ongoing so that it will become a visitor and education center.

Crossing Broadway (Route 9) at Hatch Terrace, the Aqueduct passes back yards of adjacent homes. It crosses Colonial Street and diagonally crosses Hillside Road at 0.3 mile on an embankment above Route 9. After paralleling Parkway Drive to the left, the Aqueduct crosses Flower Avenue at 0.6 mile and enters the Village of Hastings-on-Hudson. Soon after crossing Minturn Street, the Aqueduct passes stone cottages to the left, which were originally Dutch farm buildings and later became a stagecoach stop on the Albany Post Road. To the right is Zinsser Park with ball fields and community gardens.

After crossing Edgars Lane, Villard Avenue, and Baker Lane, the Aqueduct reaches Five Corners, a busy convergence of Chauncey Lane, Farragut Avenue, Main Street, Old Broadway, and Route 9. Hillside Woods is to the left up Chauncey Lane. To reach the Metro-North Hudson Line Hastings Station from Five Corners, walk down Main Street, cross Warburton Avenue, and continue straight on a driveway into a parking lot. Descend a flight of stairs and the station is almost in front of you.

Diagonally across Five Corners, the Aqueduct reenters the woods next to Grace Episcopal Church. It is on a high embankment until reaching Washington Avenue. Beyond Washington Avenue, the Aqueduct passes Draper Park, the home of scientist-photographer John Draper and five generations of his family. It is a National Historic Landmark.

After paralleling Aqueduct Lane at 1.6 miles, the Aqueduct passes, to the left, a former quarry, which in the nineteenth century supplied dolomitic marble to the east coast. It served as a park in the early twentieth century and much later as the village's yard waste dump, a use halted partially at the urging of the Friends of the Old Croton Aqueduct. It is hoped that the quarry will once again be a park. The Aqueduct reaches a view of the Hudson River and the Palisades, one of many views in the next 2.4 miles. After passing ventilator #18 at 1.9 miles, the Aqueduct briefly follows Pinecrest Drive and reenters the woods. Passing views across the river, it crosses a stream on an embankment. At 2.3 miles, it crosses a narrow road leading uphill to the Graham School and downhill to Warburton Avenue, where there are stops for Beeline Bus #6.

There is an unobstructed view of the river at 2.6 miles. At the end of a row of townhouses, the Aqueduct enters Yonkers. A yellow-blazed path leads up to the Lenoir Preserve. Before reaching Odell Avenue at 2.9 miles, the trail passes a stone building, which once served as a stable for one of the mansions lining the heights. It is a quarter-mile walk downhill along Odell Avenue to reach steps down to the Metro-North Hudson Line Greystone Station.

After passing ventilator #19 and extensive overgrown vegetation along the trail's sides, the Aqueduct reaches stone pillars to the left. A carved lion and headless unicorn guard the overgrown gates, where a former carriage road leads uphill to Untermyer Park. Reaching a rock cut and then a weir at 3.5 miles, the Aqueduct is again on a high embankment. After paralleling Aqueduct Place, it crosses Arthur Place and passes ventilator #20 at 3.9 miles. Here again are views of the Hudson River and the Palisades.

The character of the adjacent area begins to change; houses are closer and there are more apartment buildings. Some sections of the Aqueduct in Yonkers have suffered from dumping or encroachment. When the Aqueduct reaches Shonnard Terrace, it goes through front yards. At 4.5 miles, the Aqueduct crosses Phillipse Road, leading downhill to Trevor Park and the Hudson River Museum. Beginning at the crossing of Phillipse Road, incidents of litter and garbage increase. At 4.7 miles, the Aqueduct crosses Glenwood Avenue. It is a quarter-mile walk downhill to the Metro-North Hudson Line Glenwood Station. The Aqueduct crosses Wicker Street near an empty lot, passes ventilator #21, and reaches Lamartine Avenue at 5.1 miles. To reach the Metro-North Hudson Line Yonkers Station, head west on Lamartine Avenue, turn left (south) onto Warburton Avenue, and turn right (west) onto Main Street.

Gate to Untermyer Park

Yonkers (Lamartine Avenue) to the Bronx   *Length: 3.9 miles*
The fifth section of the Aqueduct is along bustling city streets, wedged behind buildings, or through Tibbetts Brook Park. In Yonkers, large granite posts inscribed with OCA mark the entrances where the walking route is actually atop the Aqueduct. The Aqueduct turns east and ceases to parallel the Hudson River.

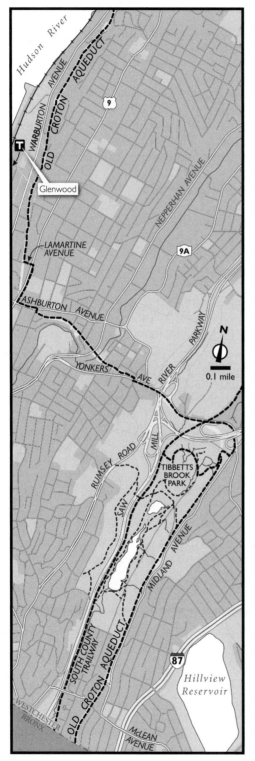

At Lamartine Avenue, the walking route diverges from the Aqueduct, heads uphill away from the Hudson River, and turns right onto North Broadway (Route 9). In a quarter-mile, turn left onto Ashburton Avenue at a traffic light, where the Aqueduct is to the left, but on private property. Continue uphill, turn right onto Palisade Avenue at 0.5 mile, and immediately make a left onto the Aqueduct with its granite post. Beeline Bus #2 stops here.

Leaving behind the bustle of Yonkers, the path heads downhill. It levels out on a high embankment, passes close to apartment buildings, and, at 0.8 mile, crosses Summit Street. The Aqueduct crosses Nepperhan Avenue on a stone-arch bridge dating from 1842, with views from both sides. It crosses Walnut Street and continues behind buildings. After crossing Seymour Street, the walking route follows a macadam path that leads up to Yonkers Avenue and passes ventilator #22. At 1.0 mile, it reaches Yonkers Avenue at Prescott Street, where the walking route diverges once again from the Aqueduct. Cross Yonkers Avenue and walk along the sidewalk on the south side. There are two possible routes from here, one is shorter and crosses the entrance and exit ramps of parkways. The other follows a winding route through Tibbetts Brook Park.

For the shorter route, continue on the sidewalk going under the Cross County Parkway. At Midland Avenue, just beyond the entrance ramps to the parkway, turn right onto a paved path leading into Tibbetts Brook Park, past a New York City waterworks building. Turn left, enter the woods, and almost immediately, leave the paved path to return to the Aqueduct at 1.9 miles as it heads south along the east side of Tibbetts Brook Park. On a well-trod dirt path, the Aqueduct passes a weir and then ventilator #23.

For the route winding through Tibbetts Brook Park, walk along Yonkers Avenue to the former railroad bridge and ascend the stairs to the South County Trailway. Head south, pass the back wall of a motel, go over the Cross County Parkway on a bridge, and turn left down a paved path into Tibbetts Brook Park. Using paths and park roads, cross the park and head uphill to the Aqueduct. Because the route across the park is not well-defined, it is likely that you will rejoin the Aqueduct south of ventilator #23.

Ventilator #23

The Aqueduct joins a paved path. At 2.4 miles it goes under the park entrance road and the surface becomes dirt again. The entrance road leads to many amenities in Tibbetts Brook Park, including a pool, restrooms, playground, and sports fields. An unmarked trail to the right leads down to ball fields in the park. After leaving the south end of the park, the Aqueduct passes back yards, most with gates in their fences and stairways leading up to the Aqueduct. At 3.3 miles, the Aqueduct passes another ventilator and then crosses McLean Avenue. Beeline Bus #4 stops to the left. After crossing Lawton Street, the state park segment of the Aqueduct ends at 3.9 miles. The Aqueduct continues into the Bronx, entering Van Cortlandt Park, a New York City park.

CONNECTING TRAIL & PARKS: Briarcliff Peekskill Trailway, Rockwood Hall, Rockefeller State Park Preserve, Sleepy Hollow Cemetery, Hillside Woods, Lenoir Preserve, Untermyer Park, Tibbetts Brook Park, Van Cortlandt Park

To learn more about the Aqueduct:
   Visit: Ossining Heritage Area Visitor Center on Broadway in Ossining.
   Read: *Water for Gotham: A History*; Koeppel, Gerard T.; Princeton University
      Press, 2001.
   The Old Croton Aqueduct: Rural Resources Meet Urban Needs; Hudson River
      Museum of Westchester, 1992.
   Request: a full-color trail map and guide from Friends of the Old Croton
      Aqueduct, 15 Walnut Street, Dobbs Ferry, NY 10522. Include a check for
      $5.75.

DRIVING: The Old Croton Aqueduct has multiple access points including 90 road crossings. Use the Aqueduct map or a Westchester County map to reach various road crossings. Where the Aqueduct runs through residential areas, parking is limited. Parking areas are at Croton Dam (Cortlandt), Croton Gorge Park (Cortlandt), Joseph P. Caputo Community Center (Ossining), River Road (Scarborough), Gory Brook (Sleepy Hollow), Prospect Avenue (Tarrytown), and municipal lots which require a permit on weekdays. There are many places to park a car on streets near the Aqueduct.

PUBLIC TRANSPORTATION: Metro-North Hudson Line Croton-Harmon, Ossining, Scarborough, Tarrytown, Irvington, Ardsley-on-Hudson, Dobbs Ferry, Hastings, Greystone, Glenwood, and Yonkers stations are within walking distance of the Aqueduct. Although Beeline Buses run along Route 9, they often have limited service. The 1C, 1T and 1W buses along Warburton Avenue terminate at the 242nd Street/Broadway #1 train station at Van Cortlandt Park in the Bronx.

For contact information, see Appendix, Old Croton Aqueduct.

South County Trailway

Eastview to the Bronx • 13.9 miles, 48.2 acres

Along much of its length, the South County Trailway is wedged between the Saw Mill River Parkway and the New York State Thruway, both with their expected sounds and sights. In addition, the trailway crosses the Saw Mill River multiple times. One can look at distribution centers, check out the backs of restaurants and shops, see school bus parking lots, and view the undersides of overpasses and interchanges of parkways. In spite of these trappings of civilization, there are opportunities to find birds in power line corridors, wetlands, woodlands, and even neighbors' gardens. Frequently, the transition from industry to woodland and vice versa is abrupt.

The Putnam Division of the New York Central ran for 54 miles between the Bronx and Brewster in Putnam County from 1881 to 1958, when passenger service ceased. The line continued to be used for occasional freight until 1982. Westchester County owns the 36.2 miles of right-of-way in the county and, after acquiring it in 1992, proceeded to remove track and ties and grade it smooth.

One station on the Putnam Division was Woodlands Lake, also the name of the pond on the Saw Mill River and the name used for this section of V. Everit Macy Park, a county park divided by the Saw Mill River Parkway. This section of Macy Park includes the Great Hunger Memorial Park with a statue dedicated to nineteenth-century Irish potato famine immigrants to America.

THE TRAILWAY

Occasional remnants of track, ties, whistle signs, foundations, and old telephone poles are found along the South County Trailway. At former station sites, interpretive signs provide information on the history of the railroad with respect to that station and the bygone community.

The South County Trailway with 11.8 paved miles is a work in progress. It is possible to walk an additional 2.1 miles, but conditions are similar to an unmaintained woodland trail. The trailway passes through residential, highly industrial, commercial, as well as wooded areas. Unfortunately, industry has intruded on the right-of-way in places, resulting in breaks in the route.

Because the South County Trailway is a linear corridor, hikers have the option to walk out and back on the same route, leave a car where they will end their hike, or rely on public transportation. The trail descriptions are in sections, determined either by major road crossings or the availability of parking.

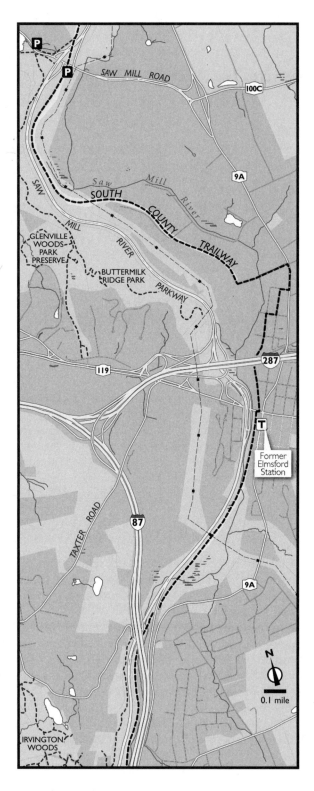

INVASIVE SPECIES

Except for a few highly manicured parks, most of the parks described in this book typically have problems with opportunistic invasive plants. Commonly known as invasives, they have aggressive growing habits and few natural competitors. They tend to dominate the flora of an area and may crowd out native, rare, or beneficial plants. Technically, an invasive is from a foreign country, but popular use of the term includes fast-growing, adaptive native plants such as poison ivy and greenbriar. Some invasives (Japanese barberry is one example) were deliberately imported because they were useful, familiar, or attractive. Others arrived by piggybacking on other commerce. In both cases, their natural control mechanisms were left behind.

Common invasives in Westchester parks include Japanese barberry, multiflora rose, Asian bittersweet, and native grape vine. Any of these aggressive plants can create problems along trails by encroaching on footpaths, sometimes making them impassable. Oriental bittersweet and native grape vines can completely encompass a tree and bring it down. Other invasives, such as garlic mustard, Japanese stiltgrass, and mile-a-minute vine, can quickly overrun an area and threaten native plants. Wetlands are threatened by invasives which are at home in that particular ecosystem. Such plants include phragmite reeds, purple loosestrife, and a variety of pond weeds. The Invasive Plant Council of New York State has a more complete list. See www.ipcnys.org/.

Eastview to Warehouse Lane *Length: 1.8 miles*

The North County and South County trailways connect at Eastview, forming a continuous path. Access to the two trailways is near the intersection of the Saw Mill River Parkway and Saw Mill Road/Neperan Road. From the northbound exit ramp of the Saw Mill River Parkway, turn into the parking lot providing access to the trailway. The exit ramp is two-way only as far as the parking lot entrance. Parking is also available at the commuter lot on Neperan Road just west of the parkway. From the commuter lot, turn left to follow the road and then left again to go up the path along the southbound parkway exit/entrance ramp.

From the North County Trailway, the South County Trailway heads south and crosses over the Saw Mill River Parkway on a bridge. It passes the parking lot off the northbound exit ramp of the parkway. To the right, the noise of the parkway is audible, while to the left, the songs of birds living along the power line can be heard. The sounds of the parkway gradually diminish and, after the trailway crosses under the power line at 0.9 mile, parkway noise is gone. Continuing downhill, the trail crosses Fairview Park Drive and then suddenly is at the back of a Coca Cola distribution center. It passes numerous warehouses and reaches Warehouse Lane. There is a gap between here and NY 119 in Elmsford. The detour along Warehouse Lane heading south to NY 119 along Route 9A is on heavily traveled roads with few sidewalks. It is not a safe route, especially for families with children and cyclists not comfortable in heavy truck traffic.

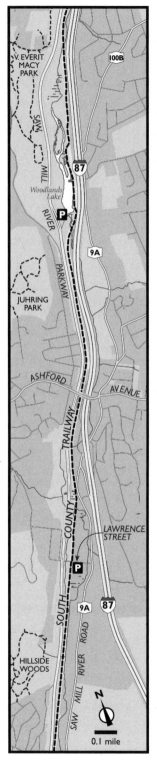

Woodlands Lake

Elmsford (NY 119) to Woodlands Lake
Length: 2.6 miles

Just south of NY 119 and immediately west of Route 9A, the South County Trailway squeezes along its narrow right-of-way and passes shops, restaurants, distribution centers, and light industry. The only remaining station of the South County Trailway now functions as a restaurant; it is located off NY 9A in Elmsford, adjacent to the trailway.

At 0.2 mile, the South County Trailway suddenly leaves commercial and industrial areas and enters the woods. Aside from a short stretch in the open near the Thruway exit ramp leading to the Saw Mill River Parkway, the trail is almost always in woods or near wetland. It parallels the Saw Mill River Parkway, staying just inside the woods, out of sight of cars zooming along. It passes under power lines at 0.6 mile and the Saw Mill River Parkway and New York State Thruway interchanges at 1.1 miles. Entering wetlands on the right, the trailway reaches Woodlands Lake at 2.6 miles, with parking and picnic tables available across the dam that forms Woodlands Lake.

Woodlands Lake to Barney Street
Length: 3.6 miles

The expression "caught between a rock and a hard place" is an apt description of this section of the South County Trailway. Thankfully, trains still ran on the Putnam Division when the Saw Mill Parkway was built, so this narrow corridor between river and parkway was preserved. From Woodlands Lake south, the noise from the two high-speed roads is never far away; however, the trailway has thick vegetation on both sides, which helps to screen out some traffic noise in leaf-on season. Just beyond where the trail passes under the Ashford Avenue bridge at 0.9 mile, the surroundings suddenly become industrial. To reach amenities in Ardsley, turn left at the entrance at Elm Street, just past the Ardsley Bus Company yards. At this point, the New York State Thruway diverges and the noise decreases. The trailway passes a factory and reaches Lawrence Street at 1.6 miles.

Here, the South County Trailway leaves the industrial area. The vegetation is indicative of heavily disturbed soil and trees are so densely festooned with vines that it is difficult to discern exactly how many trees are underneath. The trailway parallels the Saw Mill River to the left and the parkway to the right. At 2.6 miles, at the site of the Mt. Hope Station, a few ties are to the left; a steel girder stands forlorn and naked in the midst of heavy undergrowth. At 3.1 miles, the trailway crosses Farragut Avenue with a parking lot on the left, and then passes many back yards. It crosses Tompkins Avenue at 3.4 miles, parallels Railroad Avenue, and reaches Barney Street.

Barney Street to Touissant Avenue
Length: 1.4 miles
The South County Trailway heads along the edge of a parking lot. Through the chainlink fences lining the trail, there are glimpses of a wide variety of light industry. The trailway goes under the Odell Viaduct at 0.7 mile and passes the former site of the Grey Oaks Station. After crossing a massive bridge over Route 9A,

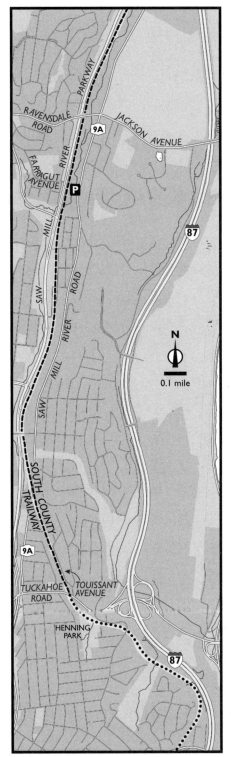

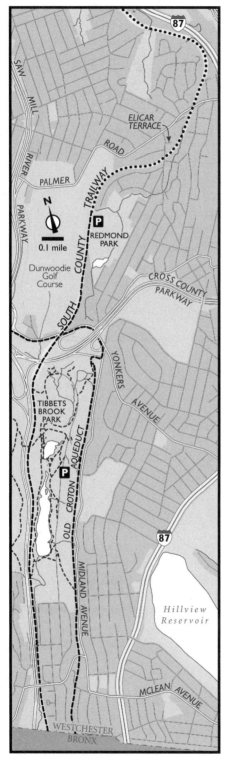

the trailway enters a more residential section with access for neighbors at the ends of dead end streets. A building immediately adjacent to the trail has evidence of a former freight siding. At 1.4 miles, the trailway reaches Touissant Avenue, the former site of the Nepperhan Station with an interpretive sign.

Ahead the trailway is unfinished, although clearly neighbors do walk straight ahead under Tuckahoe Road. The right-of-way passes through a parking lot and behind a strip mall to enter Henning Park on a wood chip path lined with split rail fencing. The tread becomes muddy and impassible 0.4 mile south of Touissant Avenue.

Elicar Terrace to Redmond Park
Length: 1.3 miles
This unpaved section of the South County Trailway is like a path through the woods. At the site of the Bryn Mawr Station on Elicar Terrace, the trail is accessible to the north for approximately 0.4 mile until it becomes rutted and extremely muddy. This section passes below houses and close to the New York State Thruway. South of Elicar Terrace, the trailway passes close to houses and crosses Mile Square Road at 0.2 mile near Little John Place. Right up against the back yards along Homewood Avenue, it descends, but is uphill from the houses. At 0.6 mile, it is downhill from the Dunwoodie Golf Course. Descending, it crosses a gully at 0.8 mile. At 1.3 miles, the trailway reaches the end of this section at a junction with a trail heading downhill to a parking lot in Redmond Park.

Redmond Park to the Bronx
Length: 2.4 miles
For two-thirds of its length, this southernmost section of the South County Trailway is wedged between

Tibbetts Brook Park and the Saw Mill River Parkway. From the parking lot farthest from Redmond Park's entrance, an access trail to the trailway heads uphill.

Once on the trailway, almost immediately the Catskill Aqueduct is visible downhill to the left and the Dunwoodie Golf Course is seen uphill to the right. The trailway goes alongside a fence where a gate and an adjacent parking area indicate that, before the trailway was paved, there were encroachments on the right-of-way. The trailway passes the former site of the Dunwoodie Station, with steps down to Yonkers Avenue, at 0.3 mile. The back wall of a motel is most likely on the railroad's right-of-way.

After passing over the Cross County Parkway at 0.6 mile, the trailway enters Tibbetts Brook Park. At 0.8 mile, a 0.1-mile paved path to the left enters the park. Paralleling the Saw Mill River Parkway, the trailway is never far from the sight and sound of cars. At 1.0 mile, it passes under a pedestrian bridge over the Saw Mill River Parkway; the bridge leads to 1.2 miles of unmarked paths in open space on the west side of the parkway.

At 1.6 miles, a paved path to the left leads into Tibbetts Brook Park. The trailway crosses a bridge over Tibbetts Brook and then at 2.0 miles passes a paved path to Harrison Avenue. The former site of the Lincoln Station is at 2.1 miles, adjacent to the McLean Avenue viaduct. It reaches the county line at 2.4 miles where the pavement ends as the pathway enters Van Cortlandt Park, a New York City park.

CONNECTING TRAIL & NEARBY PARKS: North County Trailway, Buttermilk Ridge, V. Everit Macy Park, Redmond Park, and Tibbetts Brook Park

DRIVING: Because of proximity to the Saw Mill Parkway, the New York State Thruway, and the Saw Mill River, there are far fewer access points to the South County Trailway than along a comparable length of the North County Trailway. Parking is available in Eastview (two lots), Warehouse Lane, Great Hunger Memorial Park (Woodland Lakes), Farragut Avenue, Barney Street, Redmond Park, and Tibbetts Brook Park.

Access to Woodland Lakes/Great Hunger Memorial Park is only from the northbound lanes of the Saw Mill River Parkway. To reach the park if southbound on the Saw Mill River Parkway, exit at Ashford Avenue, cross over the parkway, and reenter it to head north. It is only possible to exit the park northbound on the parkway. To go south, head north and leave the parkway at westbound Route 119; go under the parkway and take the southbound entrance ramp.

PUBLIC TRANSPORTATION: Beeline Buses: #1C, #11, #14, #17, near Elmsford; #5 along Route 9A; #91 on Yonkers Avenue

For contact information, see Appendix, Westchester County Parks.

Yorktown Trailway

Shrub Oak to Crompond • 3.4 miles

Paralleling the Taconic State Parkway near the Putnam/Westchester County line, the Yorktown Trailway utilizes a former equestrian trail and a sewer line. During public hearings concerning the Taconic Parkway reconstruction, comments were made about having a pedestrian bridge to connect the sides of the parkway. As a result, the bridge was built.

In 1927, construction of the Taconic State Parkway in Westchester County began. Considered an extension of the Bronx Parkway, it was expected to head west at Route 202 and become the Bear Mountain Extension. The parkway heading north was to link with a planned parkway through Putnam County. This parkway was to include an equestrian trail connecting what is now Mohansic Golf Course with Fahnestock State Park. Over the years, various road improvements in the area destroyed the Bridle Trail, as it was then known. The Yorktown Trailway and a walkable sewer line have restored much of that route in Westchester County.

THE TRAILWAY

Beginning at a stone wall marking the Putnam/Westchester County line, the Yorktown Trailway heads south into the woods, but never far from the Taconic State Parkway. At 0.5 mile, it crosses Route 6 and follows the southbound entrance ramp. At times the path is inches from high-speed traffic. It crosses Route 132 at 0.9 mile, again follows an entrance ramp, and at one point is high above it. A chainlink fence separates back yards from the trailway. At the end of the cul-de-sac on Buckhorn Street, the fence ends. A riprap ford over the drainage ditch provides access to the trail. At 1.3 miles, the trailway crosses wetlands on an extensive boardwalk, and

Boardwalk

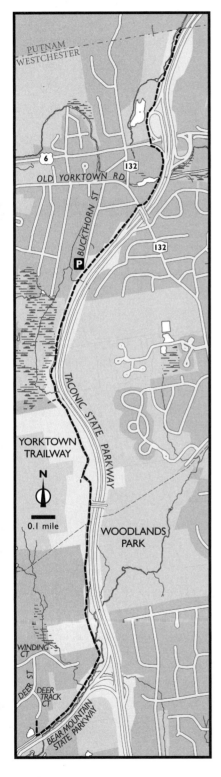

then on a second boardwalk at 1.6 miles.

At 2.1 miles, the Yorktown Trailway turns away from the Taconic. After passing a manhole cover, the trailway follows a sewer line. The footbridge over the Taconic at 2.3 miles has an interpretive kiosk at each end displaying historic photos of the Taconic State Parkway. On the east side of the Taconic, unmarked paths lead into Woodlands Park, a park with ball fields. South of the bridge on the west side of the Taconic, an unimproved path continues along the sewer line through the woods. It goes through many wet areas before paralleling Hunter Brook and the Bear Mountain State Parkway. At 3.4 miles, the trailway leaves the woods and reaches a right-of-way to Deer Track Court (no parking). The sewer line continues on to reach Stony Street and Route 202.

DRIVING: From the Taconic State Parkway, take the Route 6 Exit and head west to Shrub Oak. Turn left onto Route 132; immediately turn left again onto a short dead end road in front of a gas station.

PUBLIC TRANSPORTATION: At the north end, Beeline Bus #16 on Old Main Street in Shrub Oak; at the south end, Beeline Bus #12 on Route 202 at the Staples Shopping Center.

For contact information, see Appendix, Yorktown.

Colonial Greenway, Larchmont Reservoir

SECTION VIII

TRAIL SYSTEMS

- Link communities, parks, and open space
- Offer a wide range of distances to walk or hike
- Are corridors for wildlife

TRAIL SYSTEMS

Entire County • 286.9 miles

In addition to the many parks with trails in Westchester County, there are trails which extend beyond park boundaries to connect and form networks. Also called trail systems, they allow for extended hikes and, like the linear corridors, they allow wildlife to move safely from park to park.

Trail systems are not a new concept in Westchester County. By 1934, the Dirt Trails Association (DTA) had established equestrian trails in the area south of the Croton Reservoir. With permission, hikers were allowed to use the trails. In the late 1960s, the trail system still existed, but the organization is now defunct, as best as can be determined. Bedford Riding Lanes Association (BRLA) has been in existence since the 1930s. Extensive equestrian trail networks do more than just provide riding trails. They bring together citizens who wish to preserve the rural nature of their community and thus protect open space through purchases and conservation easements. Some equestrian trails are for members only.

Bedford Riding Lanes Association

Bedford • 160 miles

What was known in the 1930s as the Private Lanes Association has become the present-day Bedford Riding Lanes Association (BRLA). When the Saw Mill River Parkway was built in the 1950s, riding lanes west of the parkway were severed from the heart of the Bedford trails network and fell into disuse. In other cases, the land was sold to developers. As large pieces of property have changed hands in recent years, the BRLA network has been able to grow. New owners either sell or donate easements to permit riding on their property. These riding trails have become an integral part of Bedford, making it possible for equestrians to ride between residences.

In addition to those within the parks listed below, BRLA trails are also along dirt roads in Bedford and in Beaver Dam Sanctuary, Merestead, St. Matthews Church Woodlands, and Westmoreland Sanctuary.

Guard Hill Preserve

Bedford Village • 1.7 miles, 62 acres

Wetlands next to the entrance to Guard Hill Preserve might make you think you will have wet feet on your hike, but dense vegetation prevents your reaching the standing water in the interior of the preserve. The trail skirts the edge of the property and is marked with BRLA signs.

In 2000, Brian and Amy Pennington of Shannon Stables purchased 62 acres to prevent its being developed. They then donated the land to the Westchester Land Trust, thus permanently protecting it.

From Guard Hill Road, the trail skirts a field in Sunnyfield Farm to the right and a large wetland to the left. At 0.4 mile, it leaves the fields and passes a side trail looping to the right for 0.3 mile. At 0.5 mile, this side trail rejoins the main trail. After crossing wetlands on an embankment, the main trail passes a house at 0.8 mile. Turning left at 1.1 miles, it is along a farm road beside pastures, steeplechase course, riding ring, and barns. The main trail ends at Guard Hill Road at 1.4 miles. A portion through Shannon Stables is open only to BRLA members. Anyone without a BRLA membership tag should honor that request.

DRIVING: From I-684, take Exit 4 (Route 172) and drive 1.2 miles east. Turn left onto Clark Road and then right at Guard Hill Road. Park on the south side of the road, next to the sign at the entrance.

PUBLIC TRANSPORTATION: None available

For contact information, see Appendix, Westchester Land Trust.

John Jay Homestead State Historic Site

Katonah • 1.2 miles, 63.6 acres

For hikers who are Revolutionary War history buffs, a visit to the John Jay Homestead is doubly rewarding. A distinguished public servant for 27 years, Jay served in more capacities than any other of our founding fathers. He was the first chief justice of the United States Supreme Court and the second governor of New York. Jay's unassuming house is set back from Route 22. The grounds are open to walkers and equestrians year-round, but there is a charge to visit the house, built in 1799 and the associated farm buildings. Jay retired here in 1801 and five generations of his family lived in the house until 1953. Its rooms are shown as they were in the 1820s. The house and grounds are open from mid-April to the end of October.

John Jay Homestead

A 0.5-mile trail circles the house, several farm buildings, and the formal grounds and garden. Interpretive signs point out features and show what changes have occurred. The Beech Allée leads to a grove of copper and silver beeches, with benches for quiet contemplation. Pedestrians and equestrians are asked to stay on the trail along the edge of the property and not shortcut across the vast front lawn. BRLA negotiated with the state to allow horses on the property, an activity not often permitted at an historic site. Equestrians are restricted to the marked bridle paths. The BRLA trails at John Jay Homestead connect with BRLA trails across Route 22 for a small loop hike. Another BRLA trail (0.5 mile) leaves from the back of the property to connect with additional BRLA trails at the Harvey School.

DRIVING: From I-684, take Exit 6 (Katonah) and go east on NY 35. Turn right onto Route 22 and head south for 1.5 miles. The entrance is to the left, with parking at the end of a long entrance drive.

PUBLIC TRANSPORTATION: None available

For contact information, see Appendix, John Jay Homestead.

Palmer H. Lewis Wildlife Sanctuary

Cross River • 0.2 mile, 24 acres

Easily missed along Route 121, Palmer H. Lewis Wildlife Sanctuary is a small open field with adjacent woodland and edge environments at the rear. Its mowed paths vary with the season or the year. Adjacent BRLA trails extend hiking opportunities beyond the 0.2-mile sanctuary trail owned by the Bedford Audubon Society.

DRIVING: From I-684 take Exit 6 (Route 35). On Route 35, head 3.9 miles east to Route 121 in Cross River. Turn right and go 2.2 miles to the sanctuary, a field to the right 0.7 mile north of NY 137. The sanctuary sign is in the middle of the field, not clearly in view from Route 121.

PUBLIC TRANSPORTATION: None available

For contact information, see Appendix, Bedford Audubon.

Piney Woods Preserve

Bedford Village • 1.8 miles, 61.5 acres

Access to Piney Woods Preserve is via marked equestrian trails of the BRLA. These well-worn trails and other unmarked ones wander through wetlands and mixed evergreen and deciduous forests. Equestrian jumps of varying difficulty and design are scattered along the trails with one impressive array in an open area. In 1974, Mr. and Mrs. Hobart Lewis donated 24.4 acres to The Nature Conservancy. The following year, an additional 34.6 acres were donated by three sisters, Jane Canfield, Katherine Caulkins, and Marian Coward. In 2001, Tanya and James Lowe along with Kim and Doug Speegle donated conservation easements to add to the preserve.

DRIVING: From I-684, take Exit 6 (Route 35) and head east for 0.3 mile to turn right onto Route 22. At 4 miles, turn right onto Clinton Road and park beside the guardrails at the stream crossing. The preserve entrance is via a BRLA trail.

PUBLIC TRANSPORTATION: None available

For contact information, see Appendix, The Nature Conservancy.

Colonial Greenway

Scarsdale, Eastchester, New Rochelle, Mamaroneck • 15.1 miles

Encompassing an area rich in Colonial history, the Colonial Greenway is a trail system connecting seven parks in lower Westchester: Saxon Woods Park, Hutchinson River Pathway, Twin Lakes Park/Nature Study Woods, Leatherstocking Trail, Larchmont Reservoir, Ward Acres Park, and Weinberg Nature Center. The Colonial Greenway is described within each of these parks it connects. The road walks between parks are described in this section.

The Colonial Greenway includes a 12.3-mile outer loop and a 2.8-mile connection across the center of the loop. This "cross piece" makes it possible to have two shorter loops: the 9.4-mile west loop goes through Twin Lakes/Nature Study Woods; the 8.5-mile east loop goes through the southern section of Saxon Woods. Westchester County's map of the Colonial Greenway indicates designated places to park. In some instances, there are nearby streets with parking for one or two cars. Sometimes it is necessary to take another trail to reach the Colonial Greenway.

OUTER LOOP

Beginning near the clubhouse at the golf course in Saxon Woods, the 12.3-mile outer loop of the Colonial Greenway is described in a counterclockwise direction.

Saxon Woods (Mamaroneck Road) to Mill Road   *Length: 4.2 miles*
The Colonial Greenway is co-aligned with the Hutchinson River Pathway as it parallels the Hutchinson River Parkway (the Hutch). At 1.2 miles at Pinebrook Boulevard, turn left to follow the section to Ward Acres Park, Larchmont Reservoir, and the Leatherstocking Trail. There is no parking at either Pinebrook Boulevard or Mill Road. (For a full description and map, see Hutchinson River Pathway, pages 352-353.)

Mill Road through Twin Lakes/Nature Study Woods   *Length: 2.6 miles*
From Mill Road (no parking), the Colonial Greenway is co-aligned with the Hutchinson River Pathway for 0.3 mile as they enter Twin Lakes Park. When they split, the Hutchinson River Pathway goes left to parallel the Hutch and the Colonial Greenway turns right toward Reservoir #3. They join at the dam of Reservoir #3 and

HISTORICAL FIGURES OF THE COLONIAL GREENWAY

Forming much of the southern section of the Colonial Greenway, the Leatherstocking Trail derives its name from James Fenimore Cooper's anthology, *The Leatherstocking Tales*. A popular and prolific writer in the early nineteenth century, James Fenimore Cooper (1789-1851) lived in Scarsdale. His best known work, *Last of the Mohicans*, is part of *The Leatherstocking Tales*. A collection of stories set in Revolutionary War-era Westchester County, *The Spy*, was published in 1821.

A river, parkway, and bridle pathway honor Anne Hutchinson (1591-1643). Outspoken, she was an early champion for religious freedom at a time when women's rights were also suppressed. For more information about Anne Hutchinson, see Hutchinson River Pathway in Linear Corridors, page 355.

An advocate for social change, Thomas Paine (1737-1809) is famous for his pamphlet *Common Sense*, widely recognized as a major catalyst of the American Revolution. His farm was in the area of New Rochelle now known as Paine Heights. Paine Cottage and Museum are located a block from the Colonial Greenway.

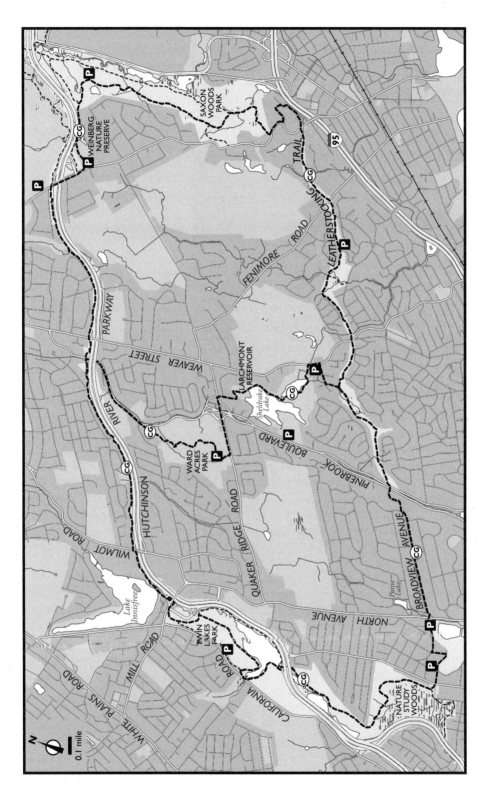

Colonial Greenway

are co-aligned for the next 1.3 miles. The trails split 100 feet before reaching the entrance to Nature Study Woods on Webster Avenue. (For a full description and map, see Twin Lakes/Nature Study Woods, pages 183-184.)

Nature Study Woods to Pinebrook Boulevard
Length: 1.4 miles
A lengthy road walk connects Nature Study Woods to the Leatherstocking Trail. Along the route, one has the opportunity to look at the architectural variety of private homes and their gardens.

From the entrance to Nature Study Woods, cross Webster Avenue to follow Flandreau Avenue. At the intersection with Argyle Avenue, turn left, walk one block to Calton Road, and turn right. Follow Calton Road to the junction with one-way Glenfruin Avenue and turn right, descending behind New Rochelle High School. Turn right onto Braemar Avenue and cross North Avenue to reach Broadview Avenue. Thomas Paine's house is to the left, one block north. Follow Broadview Avenue for 0.7 mile to end at Lyncroft Road. Turn left and walk one block. Just after #316, turn right and walk down the grassy strip along the sewer easement to Hillside Crescent. Follow Hillside Crescent downhill, cross Pinebrook Boulevard, and reach the Leatherstocking Trail. (For a full description and map, see Leatherstocking Trail, pages 357-358.)

Pinebrook Boulevard to Saxon Woods South   *Length: 3.1 miles*
The 2.6-mile Leatherstocking Trail goes from Pinebrook Boulevard to Old White Plains Road. (For a map and full description, see Leatherstocking Trail, pages 357-358.) At the end of the Leatherstocking Trail, continue 0.2 mile through the woods to Rock Ridge Road and turn left to reach Deerfield Road. When Deerfield Road reaches Old White Plains Road, turn right. Old White Plains Road is narrow with a short sight distance. To walk facing traffic, it is necessary to cross the street and then cross the street again to enter Saxon Woods Park South near #1015.

Saxon Woods South to Saxon Woods Golf Course   *Length: 2.3 miles*
The Colonial Greenway is co-aligned with Loop #1 in Saxon Woods Park South. It

leaves the park, parallels the Hutchinson River Parkway, and enters the Weinberg Nature Center. Upon reaching Mamaroneck Road, it turns right, follows the sidewalk, and closes the loop at the golf course. (For a full description and a more detailed map, see Saxon Woods, page 285.)

CROSS SECTION

Two shorter loops are possible with the Colonial Greenway because a section of the Greenway connects the Leatherstocking Trail to the Hutchinson River Pathway. This 2.8-mile section goes through Larchmont Reservoir and Ward Acres Park.

Leatherstocking Trail to Larchmont Reservoir   *Length: 0.3 mile*
On the Leatherstocking Trail, at 0.7 mile from Pinebrook Boulevard, a wooden bridge and boardwalk lead to Bonnie Way, which turns right at an intersection with Addee Court and Park Hill Lane. At Weaver Street, turn left to reach the parking lot for the Larchmont Reservoir.

Larchmont Reservoir   *Length: 0.7 mile*
The Colonial Greenway is co-aligned with the Leddy Trail (blue) until they reach the dam. Together, they follow the Cliff Emanuelson Trail (green) to Dennis Drive. (For a full description and map, see Larchmont Reservoir, page 37.)

Larchmont Reservoir to Ward Acres Park   *Length: 0.6 mile*
At the end of Dennis Drive, cross Quaker Ridge Road. Follow it along the sidewalk to the Ward Acres Park entrance on Broadfield Road, across from William B. Ward Elementary School.

Ward Acres Park   *Length: 0.6 mile*
For a full description and map, see Ward Acres, pages 188-189.

Ward Acres Park to Hutchinson River Pathway   *Length: 0.6 mile*
From the end of the red trail in Ward Acres at Pinebrook Boulevard, the Colonial Greenway follows Pinebrook Boulevard for 0.6 mile to reach the Hutchinson River Pathway.

DRIVING: There are numerous access points for the Colonial Greenway. Parking is located at the parks through which it goes, and occasionally on nearby streets. Specific driving directions and parking availability are listed with each park

PUBLIC TRANSPORTATION: Access by public transportation is also listed in the descriptions of individual parks.

For contact information, see Appendix, Mamaroneck (Town).

WALT DANIELS

Playland Parkway

East Coast Greenway

Portchester to Pelham Manor

Often described as an urban alternative to the Appalachian Trail, the East Coast Greenway (ECG) is a multi-use long distance pathway connecting cities from Calais, Maine, to Key West, Florida. Begun in 1991, it is a multi-modal transportation route for cyclists, hikers, and other non-motorized users. It is envisioned that 80% of the ECG will be off-road; bicycle lanes or designated routes will fill the gaps.

Since 2003, the Westchester County Department of Planning has been working with the East Coast Greenway Alliance to identify a route through the county. The lack of an uninterrupted right-of-way impacts the ability to construct a continuous path in the near future. The New York State Committee of the East Coast Greenway Alliance has taken a two-pronged approach to solving the problem. While trying to secure an off-road route, the two groups will be working together to create Bike Route 1, part of New York State's bicycle route system. Bike Route 1 will generally parallel Route 1 (Boston Post Road) and connect to off-street routes in Connecticut and New Jersey. The only part not on roads is the path paralleling Playland Parkway. For information about the East Coast Greenway, see www. greenway.org. For the Westchester portion of the project, see www.westchestergov. com/planning/Design/trailway.html.

Hudson River Valley Greenway Trail

Entire County • 52.7 miles

Begun in the late 1980s, the Hudson River Valley Greenway is more than just a trail project. It is a legislative initiative which encourages county and local governments to engage in regional planning. One project is the Hudson River Valley Greenway Trail (Greenway). A trail as diverse as the valley, the Greenway crosses urban, suburban, and rural areas to connect the valley's historic, cultural, and recreational resources. Built by and for local communities, this trail system includes riverside walking trails, connecting trails, countryside corridors, a water trail, a bike route, and a car route. A draft trail plan was written in 2004; see www.hudsongreenway.state.ny.us and search for Trail Plan.

Not all Greenway designated trails are along the river. Local municipalities, as well as not-for-profits, may submit a request to the Hudson River Valley Greenway to have trails designated. As of 2008, in Westchester County there were 52.7 miles of designated trails of interest to hikers. The Camp Smith Trail, Cortlandt's Shoreline Trail, George's Island, CrOssining Bridge, Horsemen's Trail, Old Croton Aqueduct, Rowley's Bridge, and Teatown Lake Reservation trails are described

Lake Whoopee

elsewhere in this book. RiverWalk is Westchester County's contribution to the project and portions of it are described in Linear Corridors.

For contact information, see Appendix, Hudson River Valley Greenway.

Lewisboro Horsemen's Association

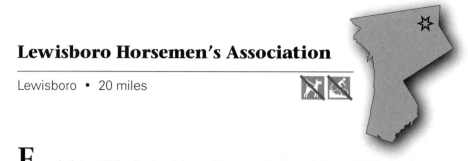

Lewisboro • 20 miles

Founded in 1990, the Lewisboro Horsemen's Association (LHA) develops and maintains bridle trails as well as hosting social and educational events that bring together local equestrians. LHA maintains approximately 20 miles of trails on public and private property in Lewisboro. Franklin Fels, Rose, and Old Field preserves have trails which are part of the LHA network. Other LHA trails connect with bridle trails in Bedford and North Salem.

Opportunities exist to extend the trail system towards Vista by using old carriage roads and bridle trails in Levy Preserve and by connecting to trails in Onatru Preserve. The trails on private property are open only to rider members of LHA; membership tags must be displayed. No dogs are allowed on LHA trails.

North Salem Bridle Trail Association

North Salem • 100 miles

Three organizations in North Salem have close ties and together have made a 100-mile equestrian trail system possible. North Salem Open Land Foundation (NSOLF) preserves open space. Landowners allow North Salem Bridle Trail Association (NSBTA) trails to traverse their property, and Goldens Bridge Hounds (GBH) members contribute to that trail system.

Since its incorporation in 1974, NSOLF has protected more than 900 acres through purchase and conservation easements, providing recreational opportunities and a refuge for wildlife. All properties no longer on tax rolls are open to the public, except where they contain sensitive habitats. The NSOLF tracts which have trails offer a variety of hiking opportunities. These include Baxter, Marx, and Hirsh-Mead. The following three small properties are open to the public.

Bulkley Tract

North Salem • 1.3 miles, 37 acres

Composed primarily of wetland, 30 acres of the Bulkley Tract have trails maintained by the NSBTA. The southern seven-acre portion contains a short section of constructed berm (all that remains of a trolley line proposed in 1900). Another section of the trolley line is on private property visible from Finch Road when traveling west towards Vail Lane. The Bulkley Tract was a gift from the Bulkley heirs to the NSOLF.

DRIVING: From I-684, take the Croton Falls/Hardscrabble Road Exit and head east. When Hardscrabble Road ends at a Y junction at June Road, turn left. Make the first right onto Bloomer Road and then left when Bloomer Road ends on Route 121. Turn at the first right onto Dingle Ridge Road, and then right onto Finch Road. After crossing Vail Lane, it is 0.4 mile to the tract, just past #104 (limited parking).

PUBLIC TRANSPORTATION: None available

For contact information, see Appendix, North Salem Open Land Foundation.

Durand Tract and Nature Trail

Salem Center • 0.5 mile, 10 acres

From the right side of the Ruth Keeler Memorial Library in Salem Center head toward the woods. A sign indicates the beginning of a nature trail with numbered posts. After passing through a wetland and crossing a stream on a bridge, the trail reaches the North Loop at a T intersection. Cedar Lane goes across the loop, making a shorter loop hike possible. The trail intersects with three equestrian trails on private property.

DRIVING: From northbound I-684, take Exit 7 (Route 116) and turn right at the end of the exit ramp. Follow Route 116 as it turns left onto Route 22 (north) and then right to leave Route 22. From where Route 116 leaves Route 22, head east 3.4 miles to North Salem Town Hall. Turn left and head toward the library at the rear of the property.

From southbound I-684, take Exit 8 (Hardscrabble Road) and follow Route 22 south. At the intersection with Route 116 where Route 22 goes off to the right, follow Route 116 and the directions above.

PUBLIC TRANSPORTATION: None available

For contact information, see Appendix, North Salem Open Land Foundation.

Keeler Tract

Salem Center • 1.2 miles, 38 acres

Off Keeler Lane and just past the Titicus River, a hill on the Keeler Tract looms ahead. A mowed path goes around that hill. Go counterclockwise along the edge of the field and follow the equestrian jumps. On the far side of the hill at 0.5 mile, a path descends to cross a stream and enter private property. Although green blazes and NSBTA tags are occasionally visible, this property is closed to the public. Instead, continue to the left around the edge of the field over the hill to parallel Keeler Lane and close the loop at 1.1 miles. A 0.1-mile trail bisects the loop.

DRIVING: From northbound I-684 take Exit 7. Turn right at the end of the exit ramp, then left onto Route 22. Turn right to follow Route 116 (Titicus Road) for 4.6 miles. After Route 121 joins from the right, it is 0.7 mile to a triangle intersection (limited parking). Walk across Route 116 and pass the large brown building (a former union hall built in 1848) to reach Keeler Lane. The tract entrance is to the right just beyond the bridge by a stone wall.

From southbound I-684, take Exit 8 and follow Route 22 south to the intersection with Route 116. Follow Route 116 and the directions above.

PUBLIC TRANSPORTATION: None available

For contact information, see Appendix, North Salem Open Land Foundation.

Along the Bridle Trail at Mohansic Golf Course

SECTION X

OTHER PLACES TO WALK

- ◆ Provide ideas for quick, easy-to-manage, and nearby, walks
- ◆ Help establish a fitness routine
- ◆ Increase comfort level of walking outdoors
- ◆ Are found throughout the county

Other Places to Walk

Parks and preserves are traditionally recognized as places to walk, but in Westchester County there are many other options to consider. Walking is an inexpensive means of exercise, and the availability of various nearby locations makes the task less burdensome, especially if it is what the doctor ordered. Use the following list to help you discover other walkable places close to home.

Cemeteries: Paved roads in large cemeteries meander past rustic resting places. Mt. Hope, Sharon, and Kenisco cemeteries are just three of the many large cemeteries in the county. Because of its history and bucolic setting, Sleepy Hollow Cemetery has its own write-up, see pages 29-30.

Enclosed malls: Think of a mall walk as a welcome haven when the weather is just too miserable to even consider being outside. Some malls have walking clubs that meet before stores open.

College campuses: Colleges in Westchester County range in size and suitability for extended walks. They also vary in how willing they are to allow the public on campus. Manhattanville College is on a former estate, Ophir Farm. It was once the home of Whitelaw Reid, publisher of the *New York Herald Tribune* and ambassador to England. Its public relations department has a brochure with the history of the estate and a map of the campus. At SUNY Purchase, the road around the academic buildings has shoulders wide enough for walking, running, or cycling for most of its three miles.

Dirt roads: In the northeastern portion of Westchester County, there are many dirt roads with little traffic. The rustic lanes north and east of Bedford can be shared with slower-moving traffic, equestrians, and leashed dogs. Reservoir Road, near Route 22 and the Cross River Reservoir, is an example.

Golf courses: Although not good places for a walk during golf season, county-owned golf courses are open for cross-country skiing and snowshoeing in winter. Mohansic Golf Course in Yorktown has a section of a former equestrian trail that paralleled the Taconic State Parkway. A portion of this trail passes a barn, now in disrepair, and connects with other unmarked trails on the property. There is a trail system in Saxon Woods, including the Hutchinson River Pathway and the Colonial Greenway. Access to private golf courses is extremely limited.

Long stretches of sidewalk: A sidewalk with few street crossings is neither a bike path nor a walk in town, but it does allow walking with minimal interruptions. Two examples are the path along Route 117 from Katonah to Bedford Hills Memorial Park and the path along Playland Parkway.

Measured loops: Walking on school tracks provides a measure of the distance walked. People who are beginning a fitness plan or recovering from an injury find tracks useful because they can easily stop when they become tired. Although not a track, a three quarters-mile path circles Huguenot Lake at New Rochelle High School. The paved path around the reservoir in Ossining's Wishnie Park is a third-of-a-mile.

Along Reservoir Road

Preserved open space: New York State, New York City's Department of Environmental Preservation, Westchester County, local land trusts, and not-for-profits have protected many acres of land. Some parcels are not as yet developed with trails; others are left undisturbed because of the terrain or a species needing protection. A few are 100% wetland. Bushwhacking through any of the open spaces without trail systems is a way to get exercise and observe wildlife. Angle Fly Preserve in Somers, Taxter Ridge in Greenburgh, and Trump State Park in Yorktown are large undeveloped tracts with the potential for trail systems.

Tiny neighborhood parks: Tucked behind houses or along streams or wetlands, these smallest of mini-parks can also be simply access between streets. Red Maple Swamp in Scarsdale is between two sections of Valley Road and has a 0.1-mile trail. Carpenter Pond, once part of the Larchmont Reservoir system, is on Daisy Farm Drive, just off Weaver Street in the Heathcote section of Scarsdale. Butler Woods in Scarsdale is on land from the Fox Meadow Estate, donated in 1913 by Emily O. Butler for the Bronx River Reservation.

Town ball fields, tennis courts, and swimming pools: Some of the countless small parks in Westchester have ball fields, tennis courts, or swimming pools. Frequently overlooked as places to walk, they often have trails, grassy areas, or paved paths. Valhalla's Stonegate Park has trails looping through adjacent wood land. A quarter-mile bike path circles the lake in Pleasantville's Nannahagen Park.

Utility rights-of-way: Utility companies have purchased easements on private and public land, however, access varies. The well-worn paths along sewer, gas, phone, and power lines attest that posted No Trespassing signs are mostly ignored. Because they offer edge environments, utility rights-of-way are great places to watch wildlife. Examples include the Catskill Aqueduct and an ATT line across the northern part of the county.

Appendix:
CONTACT INFORMATION

*Visit www.westchester.nynjtc.org for any recent changes
and public transportation-based hikes.*

MTA Schedules • www.mta.info/mta/schedules.htm

Beeline Bus schedules and routes • www.beelinebus.com

Bedford Audubon Society • 914-232-1999; www.bedfordaudubon.org

Bedford Riding Lanes Association • 914-234 2752; www.bedfordweb.net/brla/

Bedford, Town of – Recreation and Parks Dept. • 914-666-7004;
www.bedfordny.info/html/recreation.html

Buchanan, Village of – Recreation Dept. • 914-737-1033

Cortlandt, Town of - Recreation Division • 914-734-1050;
www.townofcortlandt.com

Croton, Village of – Recreation & Parks • 914 271-3006;
www.crotononhudson-ny.gov

Dobbs Ferry, Village of – Dept. of Parks and Recreation • 914-693-5505;
www.design-site.net/dobbsferry

Eastchester, Town of – Recreation Dept. • 914-771-3311;
www.eastchester.org/departments

East Coast Greenway • 401-789-4625; www.greenway.org;
for NY: www.greenway.org/ny.php

Franklin D. Roosevelt State Park (FDR) • 914-245-4434; www.nysparks.com/parks

Greenburgh Nature Center • 914-723-3470; www.greenburghnaturecenter.org

Greenburgh, Town of – Dept. of Parks and Recreation • 914-693-8985;
www.greenburghny.com

Greenwich Riding and Trails Association • 203-661-3062; thegrta.org

Harrison, Town of – Recreation Dept. • 914-670-3035;
www.town.harrison.ny.us/recreation.aspx

Hastings-on-Hudson, Village of – Parks and Recreation Dept. • 914-478-2380;
www.hastingsgov.org/Trailways

Hilltop Hanover Farm and Environmental Center • 914-962-2368;
hilltophanoverfarm.org

Hudson Highlands State Park • 845-225-7207; www.nysparks.com/parks

Hudson River Valley Greenway • 518-473-3835; www.hudsongreenway.state.ny.us/

Irvington, Village of – Parks and Recreation • 914-591-7736; www.irvingtonny.gov/

John Jay Homestead State Historic Site • 914-232-5651; nysparks.state.ny.us/sites

John Jay Homestead, Friends of the • 914-232-8119; www.johnjayhomestead.org/

Larchmont, Village of – Recreation Dept • 914-834-6230; www.villageoflarchmont.org

Lewisboro, Town of – Parks and Recreation Dept. • 914-232-6162;
www.lewisborogov.com

Lewisboro Horsemen's Association • www.lhatrails.org

Lewisboro Land Trust • www.westchesterlandtrust.org/lewisboro

Lytle Arboretum • Croton Arboretum and Sanctuary, Inc.;
www.crotonarboretum.org

Mamaroneck, Town of – Conservation Dept. • 914-381-7845;
www.townofmamaroneck.org/conservation_dept

Mamaroneck, Village of – Parks Dept. • 914-777-7754;
www.village.mamaroneck.ny.us/

Marsh Memorial Sanctuary • 914-241-2808; www.marshsanctuary.googlepages.com

Merestead • 914-666-4258;
www.westchestergov.com/PARKS/NatureCenters05/Merestead.htm

Mianus River Gorge Preserve, Inc. • 914-234-3455; www.mianus.org

Mt. Kisco, Village of – Recreation Dept. • 914-666-3059;
www.mountkisco.org/departments/recreation

Mount Pleasant, Town of – Recreation & Parks Dept. • 914-742-2310;
www.mtpleasantny.com

Mount Vernon, City of – Dept. of Recreation • 914-665-2420; cmvny.com

The Nature Conservancy • 914-244 3271;
www.nature.org/wherewework/northamerica/states

New Castle, Town of – Recreation Dept. • 914-238-3909;
www.town.new-castle.ny.us/parks.html

New York-New Jersey Trail Conference • 201-512-9348; www.nynjtc.org

New Rochelle, City of – Parks and Recreation Dept. • 914 654-2087;
www.newrochelleny.com/parks.asp

New York State, Department of Environmental Conservation • 845-831-8780 ext 309;
www.dec.ny.gov/lands/34976.html

North Salem Open Land Foundation • 914-669-5860; www.nsolf.org/preservesmap.
html

North Castle, Town of – Recreation and Parks Dept. • 914-273-3325;
www.northcastleny.com/recreation.htm

Old Croton Aqueduct State Historic Park • 914-693 5259;
nysparks.state.ny.us/parks

Old Croton Aqueduct, Friends of • 914-693-4117; www.aqueduct.org

Ossining, Village of – Recreation and Parks Dept. • 914-941-3189;
www.townofossining.com/depts/parksrec.htm

Peekskill, City of – Parks and Recreation • 914-734-4228; www.ci.peekskill.ny.us

Pelham Manor, Village of • 914-738-8820; www.pelhammanor.org

PepsiCo, World Headquarters •
www.en.wikipedia.org/wiki/Donald_M._Kendall_Sculpture_Gardens

Pound Ridge Land Conservancy • 914-372-1290; www.prlc.net

Pound Ridge, Town of – Recreation Dept. • 914-764-3987;
www.townofpoundridge.com/parks.cfm

Rockefeller State Park Preserve • 914-631-1470; www.nysparks.state.ny.us/parks

Rockefeller State Park Preserve, Friends of the • 914-762-0209;
www.friendsrock.org

Rye Brook, Village of – Recreation Dept. • 914-939-3235; www.ryebrook.org

Rye, Town of • 914-939-3075; www.townofryeny.com

Rye Nature Center • 914-967-5150; www.ryenaturecenter.org

Saw Mill River Audubon Society • 914-666-6503; www.sawmillriveraudubon.org

Saint Matthew's Church – Woodlands Commission • 914-234-9636;
www.acswebnetworks.com/stmatthewsbedford/

Sheldrake Environmental Center, Inc. • 914-834-1443; www.sheldrakecenter.org

Sleepy Hollow Cemetery • 914-631-0081; www.sleepyhollowcemetery.org

Sleepy Hollow, Village of – Recreation and Parks Dept; 914-366-5109;
www.sleepyhollowny.gov

Somers, Town of – Parks and Recreation Dept. • 914-232-8441; www.somersny.com

Tarrytown, Village of – Recreation Dept. • 914-631-8389; www.tarrytowngov.com

Teatown Lake Reservation • 914-762-2912; www.teatown.org

Weinberg Nature Center • 914-722-1289; www.scarsdale.com/recreation/weinberg.asp

Westchester County Parks
If an individual park is not listed, it does not have a park office; contact the main office in Mt Kisco for information. Use the search feature on the county's website

www.co.westchester.ny.us/parks to find a particular park.

Westchester County Dept. of Parks, Recreation & Conservation · 25 Moore Avenue, Mt. Kisco, NY 10549; 914-864-7000
  Blue Mountain Reservation · 914-862-5275
  Cranberry Lake Preserve · 914-428-1005
  Croton Gorge Park · 914-827-9568
  Croton Point Park · 914-862-5290
  George's Island Park · 914-737-7530
  Glen Island Park · 914-813-6720
  Lasdon Park, Arboretum & Veterans Memorial · 914-864-7263
  Lenoir Preserve · 914-968-5851
  Marshlands Conservancy · 914-835-4466
  Mountain Lakes Park · 914-864-7311
  Muscoot Farm · 914-864-7282
  Playland · 914-813-7000 (pre-recorded)
  Edith G. Read Sanctuary · 914-967-8720
  Ridge Road Park · 914-946-8133
  Saxon Woods Park · 914-995-4480
  Sprain Ridge Park · 914-231-3450 (summer only)
  Tibbetts Brook Park · 914-231-2865
  Ward Pound Ridge Reservation · 914-864-7317

Westchester Land Trust · 914-241-6346; www.westchesterlandtrust.org

Westmoreland Sanctuary · 914-666-8448; www.westmorelandsanctuary.org

White Plains, City of – Recreation and Parks Dept. · 914-422-1336; www.ci.white-plains.ny.us

Yonkers, City of – Parks, Recreation, and Conservation Dept. · 914-377-6450; www.cityofyonkers.com

Yorktown, Town of – Parks & Recreation Dept. · 914-245-4650; www.yorktownny.org

ADDITIONAL RESOURCES

For a more comprehensive list of materials used see
www.Westchester.nynjtc.org/additionalresources

Printed Matter

Cooper, Linda G. *A Walker's Guide to the Bronx River Parkway Reservation.* White Plains, NY: Westchester County Department of Parks, Recreation & Conservation, 2000.

Cooper, Linda G. *A Walker's Guide to the Hutchinson River Parkway Trail.* White Plains, NY: Westchester County Department of Parks, Recreation & Conservation, n.d.

Daimant, Lincoln. *Images of America: Teatown Lake Reservation.* Charleston, SC: Arcadia, 2002.

Hudson River Access Study. White Plains, NY: Westchester County Department of Planning, 2001.

Hudson River Trailway Plan: Hudson RiverWalk—A Greenway Trail. White Plains, NY: Westchester County Department of Planning, 2003.

Hudson River Valley Greenway Trail Vision Plan (draft). Albany, NY: Hudson River Valley Greenway, 2007.

Newsletter. *Friends of the Old Croton Aqueduct.* Dobbs Ferry, NY: Friends of the Old Croton Aqueduct, [various dates].

Newsletter. *Westchester Land Trust.* Bedford Hills, NY: Westchester Land Trust, [various dates].

Preserve Guide: Lower Hudson Region Eastern New York Chapter. Mount Kisco, NY: Eastern New York Chapter of The Nature Conservancy, 2000.

Van Diver, Bradford B. *Roadside Geology of New York.* Missoula MT: Mountain Press Publishing Co., 1985.

Walking Wild Lewisboro: A Complete Guide to Lewisboro's Trail System. Lewisboro, NY: Lewisboro Land Trust, 2007.

Weingold, Marilyn E. *People and the Parks: A History of Parks and Recreation in Westchester County.* White Plains, NY: Westchester County Department of Parks, Recreation & Conservation, n.d.

Williams, Gray. *Picturing Our Past: National Register Sites in Westchester County.* Elmsford, NY: Westchester County Historical Society, 2003.

Yorktown Walk Book: A Trail Guide to Yorktown's Quiet Ways. Yorktown Heights, NY: Yorktown Land Trust, 2005.

Maps

Hike and Bike the Westchester Way. White Plains, NY: Westchester County Department of Tourism, 2005.

Old Croton Trailway State Park. Dobbs Ferry, NY: Friends of the Old Croton Aqueduct, 1998 and 2008.

Websites

Anderson, Steve. *Croton Expressway, Historic Overview.* <http://www.nycroads.com/roads/croton>.

Civilian Conservation Corps. *Civilian Conservation Corps Legacy.* <http://www.cccalumni.org/>.

Cooney, Patrick. *NY-NJ-CT Botany Online.* <http://www.nynjctbotany.org/>.

Groundspeak, Inc. *Geocaching.* <www.geocaching.com>.

Subway. *New York, Westchester & Boston Railway.* <www.nycsubway.org/nyc/nywb/>.

Westchester County, NY. Westchester County Archives. <www.westchestergov.com/wcarchives/>.

Westchester Land Trust. <www.westchesterlandtrust.org/>.

INDEX

Page numbers in **bold** refer to the primary park description.

*W*e invite you to join

the organization of hikers, environmentalists, and volunteers whose skilled efforts have produced this edition of *Walkable Westchester*.

The **New York-New Jersey Trail Conference**, founded in 1920, is a federation of member clubs and individuals dedicated to providing recreational hiking opportunities in the New York-New Jersey region, and to representing the interests and concerns of the hiking community. The Trail Conference is a volunteer-directed public service organization committed to:

- Developing, building, and maintaining hiking trails.
- Protecting hiking trail lands through support and advocacy.
- Educating the public in the responsible use of trails and the natural environment.

Join now and as a member:

- You will receive the *Trail Walker*, a bi-monthly source of news, information, and events concerning area trails and hiking. The *Trail Walker* lists many hikes in the New York-New Jersey metropolitan area, led by some of our more than 100 member hiking clubs.
- You are entitled to purchase our authoritative maps and books at significant discounts. These highly accurate, up-to-date trail maps, printed on durable Tyvek, and our informative guidebooks enable you to hike with assurance throughout the region.
- You are also entitled to discounts of 10% (and sometimes more!) at most local outdoor stores and at many mountain inns and lodges.
- Most importantly, you will become part of a community of volunteer activists with similar passions and ideas.

Your membership helps give us the clout to protect and maintain more trails. As a member of the **New York-New Jersey Trail Conference**, you will be helping to ensure that public access to nature will continue to expand.

NEW YORK-NEW JERSEY TRAIL CONFERENCE
156 Ramapo Valley Road ✦ Mahwah, NJ 07430 ✦ (201) 512-9348
www.nynjtc.org ✦ info@nynjtc.org

Other Hiking Books Available From the Trail Conference!

Authoritative Hiking Maps and Books by the Volunteers Who Maintain the Trails

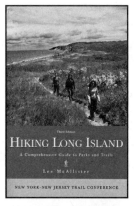

HIKING LONG ISLAND

Third Edition (2008), Lee McAllister

An updated comprehensive guide to parks and trails from eastern Nassau County to the tips of the Twin Forks, with information on geology, flora, and fauna. Whether you are a resident or a visitor, become acquainted with the beauty of Long Island's woods, fields, pine barrens, and beaches. Each hike includes a schematic map, and when public transportation is available, it is listed.

sc. 408 p. 5 3/8 x 8 1/8, B&W photos and maps

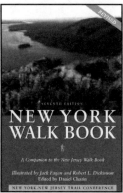

NEW YORK WALK BOOK

Seventh Edition, Revised (2005), Edited by Dan Chazin

The hikers' "bible" since 1923, it is still the same indispensable regional reference book. Full trail descriptions with maps, sections on geology, history, hiking tips, and much more. The magnificent sketches include many new ones by Jack Fagan. This last printing has updated trail descriptions and completely revised chapters for Black Rock Forest, Storm King, and Sterling Forest.

sc. 484 p. 5 3/8 x 8 1/8, B&W illustrations, full color maps

HIKING THE JERSEY HIGHLANDS

First Edition (2007), George Petty

A new illustrated guide to 35 hikes in the Highlands of New Jersey. There are introductory chapters on the Highlands' history and preservation, its geology, plants, and wildlife, with a special 16-page insert of color photos of wildflowers seen along the trails. The hikes are graded from starter hikes for beginners, to challenges for experienced hikers, with a trail map for each.

sc. 420 p. 5 3/8 x 8 1/8, B&W photos and full color wildflower section

Visit www.nynjtc.org—more information and newest products!